UNIVERSITY CASEBOOK SERIES®

2020 SUPPLEMENT TO

CONSTITUTIONAL LAW

CASES AND MATERIALS

FIFTEENTH EDITION

JONATHAN D. VARAT
Professor of Law Emeritus and Former Dean
University of California, Los Angeles

VIKRAM D. AMAR
Dean and Iwan Foundation Professor of Law
University of Illinois College of Law

D1567282

FOUNDATION
PRESS

University Casebook Series is a trademark registered in the U.S. Patent and Trademark Office.

© 2017–2019 LEG, Inc. d/b/a West Academic
© 2020 LEG, Inc. d/b/a West Academic
    444 Cedar Street, Suite 700
    St. Paul, MN 55101
    1-877-888-1330

Printed in the United States of America

ISBN: 978-1-68467-984-3

PREFACE

Constitutional law this past year, both off and on the Court, was dominated by questions of presidential behavior, elections, powers, and privileges. Off the Court, the main events were the Impeachment of Donald J. Trump and the subsequent Senate trial, over which Chief Justice Roberts presided, as the Constitution provides. The House of Representatives, controlled by Democrats, adopted two Articles of Impeachment charging President Trump with abuse of power and obstruction of Congress, respectively. The Senate, controlled by Republicans, voted to acquit him on both charges, with only one Republican Senator, Mitt Romney of Utah, voting for conviction. One argument made by some Republican Senators was that, given the timing of the trial in early 2020, voters rather than elected officials should decide whether President Trump should remain in office.

On the Court, several of the most high-profile and high-stakes cases also focused on the people's role in choosing Presidents and the extent to which elected officials (both in Congress and in the States) can investigate and check possible presidential abuses of power. In a pair of cases involving the independence of electors in the so-called Electoral College, the Justices upheld state laws that punished and allowed replacement of electors who did not follow their earlier pledge to support the presidential candidate favored by their state's electorate. And in another pair of cases, the Court (in one) upheld (albeit with some limitations) a subpoena issued by a New York District Attorney to obtain personal business and tax records of the President in connection with legitimate criminal investigations, and (in the other) remanded to the lower courts the question whether Congress had acted with sufficiently distinctive care and necessity in seeking information in the President's personal records that might be relevant to possible improvements in various regulatory statutes Congress has enacted or might adopt.

Despite considerable partisan division and rancor among the nation's people and elected officials, in none of those cases were the Justices divided along the party lines of the Presidents who appointed them. In both Electoral College cases the Justices were unanimous as to result (although Justice Sotomayor did not participate in one of them). And in both document-subpoena cases, there were seven Justices supporting the outcomes, including a majority of Justices appointed by Presidents of both parties. (One major exception to these notable configurations (and a significant separation of powers ruling), however, was the 5–4 decision in *Seila Law LLC v. Consumer Financial Protection Bureau,* which invalidated the single-director removal-for-cause-only feature of the CFPB as an unconstitutional intrusion on the President's removal power.)

There were still other examples of important constitutional—and statutory—cases this past term of a similar character. They include Chief Justice Roberts joining with the four Justices appointed by Democratic Presidents in concluding that the Administrative Procedure Act (APA) disallowed President Trump's attempt to dismantle (in the way it was done) President Obama's Deferred Action for Childhood Arrivals program (DACA), and in striking down a Louisiana regulation of abortion clinics (although the latter case does raise important questions about the future direction of abortion-law doctrine.) Two other non-constitutional cases of great import followed the same pattern. Justice Gorsuch, joined by Chief Justice Roberts and those same four Justices, authored a major ruling under Title VII interpreting the statute's employment discrimination protections to include individuals who are targeted because of their sexual orientation or gender identity. In addition, he wrote the majority opinion, joined only by those four Justices, in a major ruling upholding significant tribal rights within large swaths of territory in Oklahoma. Not all major cases saw Justices appointed by Presidents of both parties in the majority, to be sure, but neither did partisan affiliations necessarily carry the day in divided decisions.

Yet another noteworthy aspect of the Term was the large number of cases dealing with freedom of religion and the meaning of religious equality, under the Free Exercise Clause and also under the Religious Freedom Restoration Act (RFRA). The explication of RFRA, along with other landmark statutes such as the APA and Title VII, continues a trend (e.g., the census case from the previous Term) in which the Court reinforces the importance of constitutional norms of procedural regularity, sincere explanations and fair treatment through statutory as well as constitutional vehicles.

Finally, it is worth noting the effect of the COVID-19 pandemic on the Court's work this year: In the middle of March, the Court cancelled oral arguments for April, and shortly thereafter decided to hear—and to allow the general public to hear in real time—telephonic arguments in some of those cases in May (a month usually free of arguments). And although COVID-19-related legal cases have not made it to the Court in large numbers yet (though they could as early as next Term), there were emergency applications brought on by the COVID-19 pandemic that the Court needed to resolve, including one (treated in this Supplement) involving claims by religious organizations challenging state public-health restrictions on large-scale gatherings.

In sum, this year's Supplement adds a great deal of constitutional law material, even though the Court decided fewer cases this past year than has been the norm of late. As always, we have tried to include enough material for instructors and students to shape discussions as they see fit, but not so much as to be overwhelming.

TABLE OF CONTENTS

Casebook Page			Supplement Page

PREFACE.. III

TABLE OF CASES XI

PART 1. THE CONSTITUTION AND THE COURTS: THE JUDICIAL FUNCTION IN CONSTITUTIONAL CASES

Chapter 2. Judicial Review... 3
    2.   Congressional Control of Judicial Review by the Federal
        Courts.. 3
41   Patchak v. Zinke.. 3

Chapter 3. The Jurisdiction of Federal Courts in Constitutional
    Cases 5
    1.   Supreme Court Review of State Court Decisions.......................... 5
        A. History and Structure 5
48   Supreme Court Appellate Power to Review Decisions by
             Non-Article III Courts Other than State Courts.................... 5
             Ortiz v. United States 5
    3.   Cases and Controversies and Justiciability 7
        B. Standing... 7
            1. "Conventional" Standing.. 7
66   Town of Chester v. Laroe Estates, Inc. 7
               Gill v. Whitford 7
               Thole v. U.S. Bank... 8
            3. Taxpayer and Citizen Standing... 8
75   Virginia House of Delegates v. Bethune-Hill.................. 8
        C. Mootness 9
83   United States v. Sanchez-Gomez 9
        E. Political Questions 10
95   Rucho v. Common Cause 10

PART 2. ALLOCATION OF GOVERNMENTAL POWERS: THE NATION AND THE STATES; THE PRESIDENT, THE CONGRESS, AND THE COURTS

Chapter 4. The Scope of National Power 13
    2.   Sources of National Power: Early Developments.......................... 13
        A. The Marshall Court's View 13
125   State Power to Administer Presidential Elections............... 13
    3.   The Scope of National Power Today 14
        F. Other Federal Powers 14
            3. Regulation of Aliens 14
217   Trump v. Hawaii... 14

Chapter 5. State Sovereignty and Federal Regulation 15
    1.   State Immunity from Federal Regulation 15
241   Murphy v. National Collegiate Athletic Association..................... 15
    2.   Enforcement of Federal Rights in Suits Against State Officers:
          The Eleventh Amendment 20
246   Congressional Power to Abrogate Eleventh Amendment
          Immunity and Subject States to Suit in Federal Court................ 20
247   State Sovereign Immunity in State Court Suits 20

Chapter 6. The Scope of State Power 21
    1.   Introduction 21
       B. Taxation 21
252   South Dakota v. Wayfair.. 21
    2.   Discrimination Against Interstate Commerce 34
257   Tennessee Wine and Spirits Retailers Assn. v. Thomas............ 34
    6.   Preemption of State Legislation by Federal Legislation—the
          Impact of the Supremacy Clause.. 34
321   Virginia Uranium, Inc. v. Warren.. 34

Chapter 7. Separation of Powers.. 39
    1.   The President's Power to Determine National Policy.................. 39
       B. International Relations 39
348   Trump v. Hawaii.. 39
       C. War and National Defense.. 39
361   Department of Homeland Security v. Thuraissigiam 39
       D. The Line Item Veto... 40
362   Delegation of Legislative Power to the Executive 40
    2.   Congressional Interference with Presidential Prerogatives........ 41
       B. Appointment, Discharge, and Supervision of "Officers of
            the United States" 41
387   Seila Law, LLC v. Consumer Financial Protection
            Bureau.. 41
            Note on Who Counts as an "Officer of the United States"
               Subject to the Appointments Clause 55
            Lucia v. Securities and Exchange Commission 55
    3.   Presidential Immunities 58
402   Trump v. Vance 58
          Trump v. Mazars USA, LLP 74
403   Note on the Impeachments of Presidents William Clinton and
          Donald Trump.. 84

**PART 3. GOVERNMENT AND THE INDIVIDUAL: THE
PROTECTION OF LIBERTY AND PROPERTY UNDER THE
DUE PROCESS AND EQUAL PROTECTION CLAUSES**

**Chapter 8. The Bill of Rights, the Civil War Amendments and
    Their Inter-Relationship**... 89
    3.   Application of the Bill of Rights to the States 89
441   Incorporation and the Jury Trial Cases....................................... 89
461   Timbs v. Indiana... 89

Chapter 9. The Due Process, Contract, and Just Compensation Clauses and the Review of the Reasonableness of Legislation.. **93**
- 1.   Economic Regulatory Legislation.................................... 93
  - B.   The Contract Clause—What Does It Add to the Due Process Limitation?.. 93
498   Sveen v. Melin 93
  - C.   The Just Compensation Clause of the Fifth Amendment— What Does It Add to Due Process?..................... 94
    - 1.   Restrictions on Property Use........................ 94
515   Murr v. Wisconsin 94
    - 3.   Remedies for Takings.................................. 101
533   Knick v. Township of Scott 101
- 2.   Protection of Personal Liberties..................................... 103
  - B.   Family and Marital Relationships 103
572   Pavan v. Smith 103
  - C.   Personal Autonomy 105
608   National Institute of Family and Life Advocates v. Becerra 105
627   June Medical Services L.L.C. v. Russo 105
636   Pavan v. Smith 117

Chapter 10. The Equal Protection Clause and the Review of the Reasonableness of Legislation **119**
- 3.   Suspect Classifications 119
  - A.   Classifications Disadvantaging Racial Minorities.............. 119
691   Trump v. Hawaii 119
  - C.   Classifications Based on Gender.......................... 119
755   Sessions v. Morales-Santana.............................. 119
  - G.   What Other Classifications Will Provoke Heightened Scrutiny?.. 124
    - 2.   Classifications Disadvantaging the Retarded, Homosexuals, the Elderly, the Poor, etc. 124
889   Pavan v. Smith 124
- 4.   Protection of Personal Liberties..................................... 124
  - B.   Voting and Elections 124
    - 2.   Legislative Districting.................................... 124
927   Bethune-Hill v. Virginia State Board of Elections...... 124
          Cooper v. Harris 126
928   Rucho v. Common Cause............................ 132

Chapter 12. Application of the Post-Civil War Amendments to Private Conduct: Congressional Power to Enforce the Amendments **153**
- 2.   Application of the Constitution to Private Conduct.................... 153
  - A.   Private Performance of "Government" Functions.............. 153
1079   Manhattan Community Access Corporation v. Halleck 153

PART 4. CONSTITUTIONAL PROTECTION OF EXPRESSION AND CONSCIENCE

Chapter 13. Governmental Control of the Content of Expression **163**
    3.   Speech Conflicting with Other Community Values: Government Control of the Content of Speech 163
        C.   Control of "Fighting Words" and Offensive Speech 163
1336   Matal v. Tam 163
            Iancu v. Brunetti 175
        D.   Regulation of Commercial Speech 182
1355   National Institute of Family and Life Advocates v. Becerra 182
1376   Barr v. American Association of Political Consultants 196
            Matal v. Tam 200

Chapter 14. Restrictions on Time, Place, or Manner of Expression **201**
    2.   The Non-Traditional Forum: Speech Activities in Public Property Other than Parks and Streets 201
1422   Minnesota Voters Alliance v. Mansky 201
    3.   Speech on Private Premises 203
1447   Packingham v. North Carolina 203
    5.   Government Subsidies to Speech 207
1498   Matal v. Tam 207
1507   Agency for International Development v. Alliance for Open Society International, Inc. 207

Chapter 15. Protection of Penumbral First Amendment Rights **211**
    2.   Compelled Affirmation of Belief 211
1525   National Institute of Family and Life Advocates v. Becerra 211
    3.   Freedom of Association 211
        D.   Compulsory Membership and Funding for Association Speech 211
1539   Janus v. American Federation of State, County and Municipal Employees, Council 31 211

Chapter 17. Religion and the Constitution **233**
    1.   The Establishment Clause 233
        A.   Introduction 233
1697   Trump v. Hawaii 233
        B.   Government Religious Exercises, Ceremonies, Displays, and Practices 250
            2.   Religious Speech and Displays on Public Property 250
1738   American Legion v. American Humanist Assn 250
    2.   The Free Exercise of Religion 265
1804   Our Lady of Guadalupe School v. Morrissey-Berru 265
        Masterpiece Cakeshop, Ltd. v. Colorado Civil Rights Commission 268

1804   Espinoza v. Montana Department of Revenue............................ 279
        South Bay United Pentecostal Church v. Newsom...................... 297
1813   Little Sisters of the Poor Saints Peter and Paul Home v.
        Pennsylvania 298

TABLE OF CASES

The principal cases are in bold type.

Abood v. Detroit Bd. of Ed., 171, 211
Agency for International
   Development v. Alliance for Open
   Society International, Inc., 207
Agins v. City of Tiburon, 98
Alabama Legislative Black Caucus v.
   Alabama, 126
Allegheny, County of v. American
   Civil Liberties Union, Greater
   Pittsburgh Chapter, 254, 260
Allen v. Cooper, 20
Alvarez, United States v., 185
American Legion v. American
   Humanist Assn., 250
American Library Assn., Inc., United
   States v., 169
American Mfrs. Mut. Ins. Co. v.
   Sullivan, 156, 222
Apodaca v. Oregon, 89
Arizona v. Gant, 224
Arizona v. Rumsey, 229
Ashcroft v. Free Speech Coalition,
   205
Austin v. United States, 90
Bachellar v. Maryland, 171
Baker v. Carr, 134
Barr v. American Association of
   Political Consultants, 196
Beck v. Communications Workers of
   Am., 222
Bendix Autolite Corp. v. Midwesco
   Enterprises, Inc., 109
Bethune-Hill v. Virginia State Board
   of Elections, 124
Blum v. Yaretsky, 155
Board of Airport Comm'rs of Los
   Angeles v. Jews for Jesus, Inc., 205
Boumediene v. Bush, 40
Branti v. Finkel, 218
Buckley v. Valeo, 56
Burch v. Louisiana, 89
Burger King Corp. v. Rudzewicz, 26
Burns v. Richardson, 137
Burr, United States v., 68, 75
Burson v. Freeman, 201
Bush v. Vera, 136
Caban v. Mohammed, 121
California Democratic Party v. Jones,
   147
Cammarano v. United States, 169
Cantwell v. Connecticut, 171
Central Hardware Co. v. NLRB, 157
Central Hudson Gas & Elec. Corp. v.
   Public Serv. Comm'n of N. Y., 172
Cheney v. United States Dist. Court
   for D. C., 68, 73, 82

Chester, Town of v. Laroe Estates,
   Inc., 7
Chiafalo v. Washington, 13
Church of Lukumi Babalu Aye, Inc.
   v. Hialeah, 151, 272, 278, 282
Citizens United v. Federal Election
   Comm'n, 189
Clinton v. Jones, 61, 68, 73, 75
Coates v. Cincinnati, 171
Coe, United States v., 6
Cohen v. California, 181
Colorado Department of State v.
   Baca, 13
Columbia Broadcasting System, Inc.
   v. Democratic National Committee,
   158
Communications Workers v. Beck,
   222
Complete Auto Transit, Inc. v. Brady,
   24
Connick v. Myers, 219
Cooley v. Board of Wardens of Port of
   Philadelphia ex rel. Soc. for Relief
   of Distressed Pilots, 23
Cooper v. Harris, 126
Cox v. Louisiana, 171
D. H. Holmes Co. v. McNamara, 24
Davenport v. Washington Ed. Assn.,
   170
De Jonge v. Oregon, 171
Denver Area Ed.
   Telecommunications Consortium,
   Inc. v. FCC, 185
Department of Agriculture v.
   Moreno, 239
Department of Homeland Security v.
   Thuraissigiam, 39
Direct Marketing Assn. v. Brohl, 25
Eastland v. United States
   Servicemen's Fund, 79
Edmond v. United States, 47
Edwards v. South Carolina, 171
El Paso v. Simmons, 93
Ellis v. Railway Clerks, 215
Elrod v. Burns, 218
Employment Div., Dept. of Human
   Resources of Ore. v. Smith, 269
Energy Reserves Group, Inc. v.
   Kansas Power & Light Co., 93
Engel v. Vitale, 244
Espinoza v. Montana Department
   of Revenue, 279
Everson v. Board of Ed. of Ewing,
   281, 290
Fiallo v. Bell, 238, 247

Financial Oversight Board for Puerto Rico v. Aurelius Investment, LLC, 57

Flagg Bros., Inc. v. Brooks, 155

Franchise Tax Board v. Hyatt, 20

Free Enterprise Fund v. Public Company Accounting Oversight Bd., 41

Freytag v. Commissioner, 56

Friedrichs v. California Teachers Assn., 215, 225

Gaffney v. Cummings, 136

Garcetti v. Ceballos, 220

Garrison v. Louisiana, 214

Germaine, United States v., 56

Gibbons v. Ogden, 23

Gill v. Whitford, 7, 133

Gonzales v. Carhart, 112

Granholm v. Heald, 24

Greece, Town of v. Galloway, 242, 245, 254

Gundy v. United States, 40

Hague v. Committee for Industrial Organization, 157

Halliburton Co. v. Erica P. John Fund, Inc., 32

Harper & Row, Publishers, Inc. v. Nation Enterprises, 214

Harris v. Quinn, 213, 225

Heckler v. Mathews, 123

Heffron v. International Soc. for Krishna Consciousness, Inc., 202

Holder v. Humanitarian Law Project, 186

Honig v. Doe, 10

Hosanna-Tabor Evangelical Lutheran Church and School v. Equal Employment Opportunity Commission, 265

Hudgens v. NLRB, 157

Hughes v. Oklahoma, 23

Humphrey's Executor v. United States, 41, 53

Hunt v. Cromartie, 136

Hurley v. Irish-American Gay, Lesbian and Bisexual Group of Boston, Inc., 186, 207, 270

Hustler Magazine, Inc. v. Falwell, 171

Iancu v. Brunetti, 175

Ibanez v. Florida Dept. of Business and Professional Regulation, Bd. of Accountancy, 188

INS v. Chadha, 45

Jackson v. Metropolitan Edison Co., 153, 158, 222

Janus v. American Federation of State, County and Municipal Employees, Council 31, 211

Johanns v. Livestock Marketing Assn., 168

June Medical Services L.L.C. v. Russo, 105

Keyishian v. Board of Regents of Univ. of State of N. Y., 218

Kimble v. Marvel Entertainment, LLC, 32, 229

Knick v. Township of Scott, 101

Knox v. Service Employees, 213, 225

Kolinske v. Lubbers, 222

Korematsu v. United States, 240, 249

Larson v. Valente, 236

League of United Latin American Citizens v. Perry, 136

Lemon v. Kurtzman, 253, 260

Linscott v. Millers Falls Co., 222

Little Sisters of the Poor Saints Peter and Paul Home v. Pennsylvania, 298

Lloyd Corp. v. Tanner, 157

Locke v. Davey, 280, 283, 290, 292

Lucia v. Securities and Exchange Commission, 55

Lugar v. Edmondson Oil Co., 155

Lynch v. Donnelly, 263

Lyng v. Northwest Indian Cemetery Protective Assn., 281, 290, 295

Machinists v. Street, 222

Manhattan Community Access Corporation v. Halleck, 153

Marrs v. Motorola, Inc., 109

Marsh v. Alabama, 156

Marsh v. Chambers, 256, 259

Martin v. Hunter's Lessee, 6

Masterpiece Cakeshop, Ltd. v. Colorado Civil Rights Commission, 247, 268

Matal v. Tam, 163, 200, 207

Mathews v. Diaz, 238

Mazurek v. Armstrong, 112

McCreary County v. American Civil Liberties Union of Ky., 244, 254

McCulloch v. Maryland, 54, 62, 71

McDaniel v. Paty, 282

McGrain v. Daugherty, 78

Miami Herald Publishing Co. v. Tornillo, 214

Milavetz, Gallop & Milavetz, P. A. v. United States, 185, 191

Miller v. Johnson, 136, 151

Minnesota Voters Alliance v. Mansky, 201

Mississippi Univ. for Women v. Hogan, 123

Mobile v. Bolden, 138

Moose Lodge No. 107 v. Irvis, 158

Morales v. Trans World Airlines, Inc., 18

Morrison v. Olson, 41

Murphy v. National Collegiate Athletic Association, 15, 70

Murr v. Wisconsin, 94

Myers v. United States, 41, 45

National Bellas Hess, Inc. v.
Department of Revenue of Ill., 21
National Collegiate Athletic Assn. v.
Tarkanian, 156
National Endowment for Arts v.
Finley, 169
**National Institute of Family and
Life Advocates v. Becerra, 105,
182, 211, 232**
Nevada v. Hall, 20
New York v. United States, 15
Newman v. Piggy Park Enterprises,
Inc., 270
Nixon v. Condon, 156
Nixon v. Fitzgerald, 62, 68, 73
Nixon, United States v., 61, 68, 75
North Carolina v. Covington, 131
Ohralik v. Ohio State Bar Assn., 185
Oklahoma Tax Comm'n v. Jefferson
Lines, Inc., 25
Old Glory Condom Corp., In re, 168
Ortiz v. United States, 5
Our Lady of Guadalupe School v.
Morrissey-Berru, 265
Pacific Gas & Elec. Co. v. Public Util.
Comm'n of Cal., 214
Pacific Gas & Elec. Co. v. State
Energy Resources Conservation
and Development Comm'n, 35
Pacific States Telephone & Telegraph
Co. v. Oregon, 143
Packingham v. North Carolina, 203
Patchak v. Zinke, 3
Patterson v. McLean Credit Union,
32
Pavan v. Smith, 103, 117, 124
Perkins, United States v., 41
PHH Corp. v. CFPB, 44
Philadelphia v. New Jersey, 26
Pickering v. Board of Ed. of Township
High School Dist. 205, Will Cty.,
218, 219
Pike v. Bruce Church, Inc., 24, 30
Planned Parenthood of Southeastern
Pa. v. Casey, 185, 190, 191
Playboy Entertainment Group, Inc.,
United States v., 188
Pleasant Grove v. Summum, 168
Police Dept. of Chicago v. Mosley, 157
Polk County v. Dodson, 156
Primus, In re, 186
Printz v. United States, 15
Prudential Ins. Co. v. Benjamin, 33
Quill Corp. v. North Dakota, 21, 231
Quinn v. United States, 79
R. Enterprises, Inc., United States v.,
65
Railroad Retirement Bd. v. Fritz, 239
Railway Emp. Dept. v. Hanson, 222
Ramos v. Louisiana, 89
Reed v. Town of Gilbert, 190, 197

Regan v. Taxation With
Representation of Wash., 169
Reno v. American Civil Liberties
Union, 203
Reno v. Condon, 18
Riley v. National Federation of Blind
of N. C., Inc., 184, 214
Roberts v. United States Jaycees, 214
Romer v. Evans, 241
Rosenberger v. Rector and Visitors of
Univ. of Va., 280
Rucho v. Common Cause, 10, 132
Rumely, United States v., 80
Rust v. Sullivan, 169
Rutan v. Republican Party of Ill., 218
Salazar v. Buono, 262
San Francisco Arts & Athletics, Inc.
v. United States Olympic Comm.,
156
Sanchez-Gomez, United States v., 9
Santa Fe Independent School Dist. v.
Doe, 244
Schneider v. State (Town of
Irvington), 171
Schwimmer, United States v., 172
Sealed Case, In re, 68
**Seila Law, LLC v. Consumer
Financial Protection Bureau,
41**
Senate Select Committee on
Presidential Campaign Activities
v. Nixon, 68, 78
Sessions v. Morales-Santana, 119
Shaw v. Hunt, 136
Shaw v. Reno, 135
Shelton v. Tucker, 218
Silkwood v. Kerr-McGee Corp., 35
Smith v. Allwright, 156
Sorrell v. IMS Health Inc., 186, 197,
224, 232
South Bay United Pentecostal
Church v. Newsom, 297
South Dakota v. Wayfair, 21, 224
Southeastern Promotions, Ltd. v.
Conrad, 157
Southern Pacific Co. v. Arizona ex
rel. Sullivan, 23, 33
Stevens, United States v., 182
Street v. New York, 171
Sveen v. Melin, 93
Swann v. Charlotte-Mecklenburg Bd.
of Ed., 131
Teachers v. Hudson, 212
Tennessee Wine and Spirits Retailers
Assn. v. Thomas, 34
Terminiello v. Chicago, 171
Terry v. Adams, 156
Texaco, Inc. v. Short, 93
Texas v. Johnson, 171
Thole v. U.S. Bank, 8
Thornhill v. Alabama, 214
Timbs v. Indiana, 89

Tinker v. Des Moines Independent Community School Dist., 171

Trinity Lutheran Church of Columbia, Inc. v. Comer, 280, 289, 292

Trump v. Hawaii, 14, 39, 119, **233**, 254

Trump v. IRAP, 234

Trump v. Mazars USA, LLP, 74

Trump v. Vance, 58

Trustees of Dartmouth College v. Woodward, 158

Turner v. Rogers, 10

United Foods, Inc., United States v., 214

Van Orden v. Perry, 251, 253, 258, 259, 262

Vieth v. Jubelirer, 134

Virag v. Hynes, 65

Virginia House of Delegates v. Bethune-Hill, 8

Virginia Uranium, Inc. v. Warren, 34

Walker v. Texas Div., Sons of Confederate Veterans, Inc., 168

Ward v. Rock Against Racism, 203

Washington v. Davis, 151

Watkins v. United States, 78

Wesberry v. Sanders, 135

West Lynn Creamery, Inc. v. Healy, 27

West v. Atkins, 156

West Virginia Bd. of Ed. v. Barnette, 214

Whalen v. Roe, 192

White v. Communications Workers of Am., AFL-CIO, Local 1300, 222

Wieman v. Updegraff, 218

Wiener v. United States, 46

Williamson County Regional Planning Comm'n v. Hamilton Bank of Johnson City, 101

Willson v. Black Bird Creek Marsh Co., 23

Windsor, United States v., 44

Wooley v. Maynard, 190, 192, 214

Wright v. Rockefeller, 136

Young, Ex parte, 65

Younger v. Harris, 58

Youngstown Sheet & Tube Co. v. Sawyer, 75

Ysursa v. Pocatello Ed. Assn., 170

Zauderer v. Office of Disciplinary Counsel of Supreme Court of Ohio, 185, 191

Zelman v. Simmons-Harris, 281

Ziglar v. Abbasi, 239

Zivotofsky v. Clinton, 139

UNIVERSITY CASEBOOK SERIES®

2020 SUPPLEMENT TO

CONSTITUTIONAL LAW

CASES AND MATERIALS

FIFTEENTH EDITION

PART 1

THE CONSTITUTION AND THE COURTS: THE JUDICIAL FUNCTION IN CONSTITUTIONAL CASES

CHAPTER 2

JUDICIAL REVIEW

2. CONGRESSIONAL CONTROL OF JUDICIAL REVIEW BY THE FEDERAL COURTS

Page 41. Add after Note (3) and change the numbering of what are currently Notes (4)–(8):

(4)   Patchak v. Zinke, 585 U.S. ___, 138 S.Ct. 897 (2018), involved a federal statute dealing with a particular piece of land (known as the Bradley Property) on which an Indian tribe wished to build a casino. The statute, passed while litigation was pending in the District Court, reaffirmed the land as "trust land" under the Indian Reorganization Act and, in section 2(b), provided that "an action . . . relating to [that] land shall not be filed or maintained in a Federal court and shall be promptly dismissed." In assessing § 2(b), the Supreme Court could not generate a majority opinion. But in announcing the judgment of the Court and speaking for himself and three others, Justice Thomas observed: "Section 2(b) strips federal jurisdiction over suits relating to the Bradley Property. The statute uses jurisdictional language. It states that an 'action' relating to the Bradley Property 'shall not be filed or maintained in a Federal court.' It imposes jurisdictional consequences: Actions relating to the Bradley Property 'shall be promptly dismissed.' [It] has no exceptions. And it applies '[n]otwithstanding any other provision of law,' including the general grant of federal-question jurisdiction, 28 U. S. C. § 1331. Although § 2(b) does not use the word 'jurisdiction,' this Court does not require jurisdictional statutes to 'incant magic words.' . . . Statutes that strip jurisdiction 'chang[e] the law' for the purpose of Article III, . . . [and] reflect the so-called Madisonian Compromise, which resolved the Framers' disagreement about creating lower federal courts by leaving that decision to Congress. . . . Thus, when Congress strips federal courts of jurisdiction, it exercises a valid legislative power no less than when it lays taxes, coins money, declares war, or invokes any other power that the Constitution grants it." He went on to say that "this Court has held that Congress generally does not violate Article III when it strips federal jurisdiction over a class of cases. . . . Patchak compares § 2(b) to the statute this Court held unconstitutional in *Klein.* . . . This Court has since explained that 'the statute in *Klein* infringed the judicial power, not because it left too little for courts to do, but because it attempted to direct the result without altering the legal standards governing the effect of a pardon—standards Congress was powerless to prescribe.' . . . Congress had no authority to declare that pardons are not evidence of loyalty, so it could not achieve the same result by stripping jurisdiction whenever claimants cited pardons as evidence of loyalty. Nor could Congress confer jurisdiction to a federal court but then strip jurisdiction from that same court once the court concluded that a pardoned claimant should prevail under the statute. Patchak's attempts to compare § 2(b) to the statute in *Klein* are unpersuasive. Section 2(b) does not attempt to exercise a power that the Constitution vests in another branch. And unlike the selective jurisdiction-stripping statute in *Klein*, § 2(b) strips jurisdiction over every suit relating to the Bradley Property. Indeed, *Klein* itself explained that statutes that do 'nothing

more' than strip jurisdiction over 'a particular class of cases' are constitutional. That is precisely what § 2(b) does."

CHAPTER 3

THE JURISDICTION OF FEDERAL COURTS IN CONSTITUTIONAL CASES

1. SUPREME COURT REVIEW OF STATE COURT DECISIONS

A. HISTORY AND STRUCTURE

Page 48. Add before Section B:

Supreme Court Appellate Power to Review Decisions by Non-Article III Courts Other than State Courts

In Ortiz v. United States, 585 U.S. ___, 138 S.Ct. 2165 (2018), the Court addressed its power to review decisions by the Court of Appeals for the Armed Forces (CAAF), which sits atop the court martial system. Although neither the petitioner (an Airman First Class convicted by a court-martial of possessing and distributing child pornography) nor the United States questioned the Court's jurisdiction, an amicus argued that Marbury v. Madison and Article III foreclosed the Court's appellate review. The Court rejected that argument 7–2 (Justice Alito, joined by Justice Gorsuch, dissenting), with Justice Kagan writing for the majority. She explained:

"We begin with a question of our own jurisdiction to review the CAAF's decisions. Congress has explicitly authorized us to undertake such review in 28 U. S. C. § 1259. Both the Federal Government and Ortiz view that grant of jurisdiction as constitutionally proper. But an *amicus curiae* . . . argues that it goes beyond what Article III allows. That position is a new one to this Court: We have previously reviewed nine CAAF decisions without anyone objecting that we lacked the power to do so. Still, we think the argument is serious, and deserving of sustained consideration. That analysis leads us to conclude that the judicial character and constitutional pedigree of the court-martial system enable this Court, in exercising appellate jurisdiction, to review the decisions of the court sitting at its apex.

". . . [Amicus relies on Chief Justice's Marshall's language in *Marbury*.] '[T]he essential criterion of appellate jurisdiction,' the Chief Justice explained, is 'that it revises and corrects the proceedings in a cause already instituted, and does not create that cause.' . . . Marbury's petition, Chief Justice Marshall held, commenced the cause—or, to use the more modern word, the case; hence, it was not a matter for appellate jurisdiction. [Amicus] contends that the same is true of Ortiz's petition.

"On any ordinary understanding of the great Chief Justice's words, that is a surprising claim. Ortiz's petition asks us to 'revise and correct' the latest decision in a 'cause' that began in and progressed through military justice 'proceedings.' . . . Or, as the Government puts the point, this case fits within Chief Justice Marshall's standard because 'it comes to th[is] Court on review of the Court of Appeals for the Armed Forces' decision, which reviewed a criminal proceeding that originated in [a] court[ ]-martial.' . . . So this Court would hardly be the first to render a decision in the case. Unless Chief Justice Marshall's test implicitly exempts cases instituted in a military court—as contrasted, for example, with an ordinary federal court—the case is now appellate.

"The military justice system's essential character—in a word, judicial— provides no reason to make that distinction. Each level of military court decides criminal 'cases' as that term is generally understood, and does so in strict accordance with a body of federal law (of course including the Constitution). The procedural protections afforded to a service member are 'virtually the same' as those given in a civilian criminal proceeding, whether state or federal. And the judgments a military tribunal renders, as this Court long ago observed, 'rest on the same basis, and are surrounded by the same considerations[, as] give conclusiveness to the judgments of other legal tribunals.' . . .

"The jurisdiction and structure of the court-martial system likewise resemble those of other courts whose decisions we review. . . .

"And just as important, the constitutional foundation of courts-martial—as judicial bodies responsible for 'the trial and punishment' of service members—is not in the least insecure. . . .

. . .

". . . [T]his Court's appellate jurisdiction, as Justice Story made clear ages ago, covers more than the decisions of Article III courts. In Martin v. Hunter's Lessee, 1 Wheat. 304 (1816), we considered whether our appellate jurisdiction extends to the proceedings of state courts, in addition to those of the Article III federal judiciary. We said yes, as long as the case involves subject matter suitable for our review. For our 'appellate power,' Story wrote, 'is not limited by the terms of [Article III] to any particular courts.' . . . The decisions we review might come from Article III courts, but they need not.

"The same lesson emerges from two contexts yet more closely resembling this one—each involving a non-Article III judicial system created by Congress. First, in United States v. Coe, 155 U. S. 76 (1894), this Court upheld the exercise of appellate jurisdiction over decisions of federal territorial courts, despite their lack of Article III status. . . .

"Second, we have routinely, and uncontroversially, exercised appellate jurisdiction over cases adjudicated in the non-Article III District of Columbia courts. . . ."

. . .

3. CASES AND CONTROVERSIES AND JUSTICIABILITY

B. STANDING

1. "CONVENTIONAL" STANDING

Page 66. Add the following before Section 2:

Town of Chester v. Laroe Estates, Inc., ___ U.S. ___, 137 S.Ct. 1645 (2017). The Court held, in a case where a real estate development company sought to intervene under Federal Rule of Civil Procedure 24(a)(2) in a takings lawsuit brought by a land developer against a town over an unsuccessful housing subdivision, that a litigant seeking to intervene as a matter of right under Rule 24(a)(2) must meet the requirements of Article III standing—that is, an injury-in-fact that is traceable to defendant's conduct and redressable by a favorable judicial ruling—if the intervenor wishes to pursue relief not requested by the plaintiff. The Court noted that at least one plaintiff must have standing to seek each form of relief sought in the Complaint, and that principle applies also to intervenors of right; for each aspect of relief sought, there must be a litigant with standing, whether that litigant joins the lawsuit as a plaintiff, a co-plaintiff, or an intervenor of right. Thus, when an intervenor seeks relief beyond that requested by any plaintiff in the case—including a separate money judgment for the intervenor—the intervenor must satisfy Article III.

Gill v. Whitford, 585 U.S. ___, 138 S.Ct. 1916 (2018). A group of Democratic voters in Wisconsin sued to challenge partisan gerrymandering vote dilution resulting from the "packing" and "cracking" of Democratic voters into particular state legislative districts by a Republican-controlled legislature. ("Packing" describes concentrating a party's voters in certain districts to deprive that party of the possibility of votes in other parts of the state, whereas "cracking" refers to the related practice of spreading a party's voters strategically throughout different districts so that they will fall just short of being able to elect their party's candidate in each of those districts.) In a unanimous opinion, the Court declined to reach the merits or decide even whether partisan gerrymandering claims like this are justiciable, "because the plaintiffs in this case have not shown standing under the theory upon which they based their claims for relief." The plaintiffs' alleged vote dilution claim was district specific, but none of them sought to prove at trial that they lived in a particular "cracked" or "packed" district, and so they failed to demonstrate the requisite Article III "injury in fact." And as to their claim of "legal injury" in the form of "statewide harm to their interest 'in their collective representation in the legislature,' and in influencing the legislature's overall 'composition and policymaking,'" the Court said that "our cases to date have not found that this presents an individual and personal injury of the kind required for Article III standing." Rather, a "citizen's interest in the overall composition of the legislature is embodied in his right to vote for his representative." Because the case "concern[ed] an unsettled kind of claim this Court has not agreed upon, the contours and justiciability of which are unresolved[,] . . . and in light of . . . allegations that [four plaintiffs] live in districts where Democrats like them have been packed or cracked," the Court (with Justice Thomas, joined by Justice Gorsuch, disagreeing only on this point) declined to follow its usual practice of directing dismissal, instead remanding "so that the plaintiffs may have an opportunity to prove concrete and particularized injuries using evidence . . . that would tend to demonstrate a burden on their individual votes."

Thole v. U.S. Bank, 590 U.S. ___, 140 S.Ct. 1615 (2020). Two retired participants in a bank's defined-benefit retirement plan sued to challenge mismanagement of the plan. Because under the defined-benefit regime plaintiffs were guaranteed a fixed payment each month regardless of the plan's value or its fiduciaries' good or bad investment decisions, and because both plaintiffs "have been paid all of their monthly pension benefits so far and are legally and contractually entitled to those payments for the rest of their lives," they lacked injury-in-fact to bring the challenge. As to the possibility that "plan participants in a defined-benefit plan [would] have standing to sue if the mismanagement of the plan was so egregious that it substantially increased the risk that the plan and the employer would fail and be unable to pay the participants' future pension benefits," such a claim could not be made by the plaintiffs in this case: although "[i]t is true that the plaintiffs' complaint alleged that the plan was underfunded for a period of time, . . . a bare allegation of plan underfunding does not itself demonstrate a substantially increased risk that the plan and the employer would both fail."

3.   TAXPAYER AND CITIZEN STANDING

Page 75. Add after Arizona State Legislature v. Arizona Independent Redistricting Commission:

Virginia House of Delegates v. Bethune-Hill, 587 U.S. ___, 139 S.Ct. 1945 (2019). After Virginia redrew state legislative (General Assembly) districts following the 2010 census, voters in 12 affected districts sued two state agencies and four election officials alleging that the redrawn districts were racially gerrymandered in violation of the Fourteenth Amendment's Equal Protection Clause. The Virginia House of Delegates (the lower branch of the General Assembly) and its Speaker (collectively, the House) intervened as defendants. They participated in the bench trial, in the appeal to the Supreme Court the first time around, and then (after remand by the Court) at a second bench trial, where a three-judge district court held that 11 of the districts were unconstitutionally drawn, enjoined Virginia from conducting elections for those districts before adoption of a new plan, and gave the General Assembly several months to adopt that plan. Virginia's Attorney General then announced that the State would not pursue an appeal to the Court, but the House did file an appeal.

The Court ruled 5–4 that the House lacked standing to pursue the appeal and to invoke the power of the Court, either to represent the State's interests or in its own right. Justice Ginsburg, joined by Justices Thomas, Sotomayor, Kagan and Gorsuch, wrote for the majority. She reasoned that although the State of Virginia itself had standing to press an appeal from the district court, the State had not designated the House to represent its interests. Under Virginia law, "[a]uthority and responsibility for representing the State's interests in civil litigation . . . rest exclusively with the State's Attorney General." Virginia, observed the Court, "had it so chosen, could have authorized the House to litigate on the State's behalf, either generally or in a defined class of cases. . . . Some States have done just that. Indiana, for example, empowers '[t]he House of Representatives and Senate of the Indiana General Assembly . . . to employ attorneys other than the Attorney General to defend any law enacted creating legislative or congressional districts for the State of Indiana.' . . . But the choice belongs to Virginia, and the House's argument that it has authority to represent the State's interests is foreclosed by the State's contrary decision."

Justice Ginsburg responded to the fact that a Virginia state court had permitted the House to intervene to defend legislation—which the House relied on in support of its claim to represent the State—by observing that being able to participate as a defendant/appellee is not the same as being permitted in federal court to be a plaintiff/appellant. Although she didn't elaborate on why it *should* matter for Article III purposes whether one represents a State as a plaintiff or a defendant, she made clear that it *does* matter: "The House's participation in [the state court case it cites] thus occurred in the same defensive posture as did the House's participation in earlier phases of this case, when the House did not need to establish standing."

Justice Ginsburg then turned to the question of whether the House had standing in its own right, rather than as a representative of the State. The House argued it suffered injury from the lower court's invalidation of the districting measure because the House is "the legislative body that actually drew the redistricting plan," and because "any remedial order will transfer redistricting authority from it to the District Court." The Court rejected this argument, however, noting that the Virginia "constitutional provision the House cites allocates redistricting authority to the General Assembly, of which the House constitutes only a part." That only part of the Virginia legislature was appealing distinguished this case, wrote Justice Ginsburg, from Arizona State Legislature v. Arizona Independent Redistricting Commission. The Court also found Coleman v. Miller inapposite: "Unlike *Coleman*, this case does not concern the results of a legislative chamber's poll or the validity of any counted or uncounted vote."

Justice Alito's dissent, joined by Chief Justice Roberts and Justices Breyer and Kavanaugh, argued that the House had suffered an injury sufficient to confer standing in the present dispute because the district court's ruling would alter the makeup of the House membership itself, and the House as an institution has "a cognizable interest in the identity of its members."

C. MOOTNESS

Page 83. Add at the end of the Section:

In United States v. Sanchez-Gomez, 584 U.S. ___, 138 S.Ct. 1532 (2018), respondents were four criminal defendants who challenged a policy adopted by the United States District Court for the Southern District of California that permitted the use of handcuffs connected to a waist chain, with legs shackled, on most in-custody defendants (including the respondents) who are produced in court for nonjury proceedings by the United States Marshals Service. The district court rejected the challenge, and respondents appealed to the Ninth Circuit. Before the Ninth Circuit could rule on the merits, respondents' underlying criminal cases ended. The Ninth Circuit nonetheless reached the merits, and found the handcuff/shackles policy was unconstitutional. When the United States sought review in the Supreme Court, the Justices ruled 9–0 that the claims were moot, rejecting respondents' arguments that the claims of two of them, Sanchez-Gomez and Patricio-Guzman, fell within the "capable of repetition, yet evading review" exception to mootness. Respondents argued that the exception applied because these two respondents will again violate the law, be arrested, and be subjected to the pretrial full restraint policy. The Court adhered to what it called its consistent position that Article III's case-or-controversy requirement is not satisfied by the possibility that a party "will be prosecuted for violating valid criminal laws." The Court distinguished two civil cases, Honig v. Doe, 484 U. S. 305 (1988), and Turner v. Rogers, 564 U. S. 431 (2011), in which the Court concluded that the expectation that a litigant would repeat the misconduct that gave rise to his claims rendered those claims capable of repetition—holding that the litigants in those cases were unable, for reasons beyond their control, to prevent themselves from transgressing and avoiding recurrence of the challenged conduct. By contrast, the Court observed, Sanchez-Gomez and Patricio-Guzman, are "able—and indeed required by law"—to refrain from further criminal conduct.

E. POLITICAL QUESTIONS

Page 95. Add to the end of Note (2):

Fifteen years after *Vieth*, a divided but emphatic 5–4 Court, drawing on the intervening experience of attempts by lower courts and commentators to fashion a workable standard, held that claims challenging partisan gerrymandering under the federal Constitution are political questions that are not justiciable in federal court. Rucho v. Common Cause, 588 U.S. ___, 139 S.Ct. 2484 (2019) (treated in full at p. 132). The Court did not decide whether excessively partisan gerrymandering in fact offends the Constitution, only that institutions other than federal courts—Congress and the states—were the ones who might address any such problems.

PART 2

ALLOCATION OF GOVERNMENTAL POWERS: THE NATION AND THE STATES; THE PRESIDENT, THE CONGRESS, AND THE COURTS

CHAPTER 4

THE SCOPE OF NATIONAL POWER

2. SOURCES OF NATIONAL POWER: EARLY DEVELOPMENTS

A. THE MARSHALL COURT'S VIEW

Page 125. Add the following at the end of Note, *State Power to Administer Presidential Elections*:

In Chiafalo v. Washington, 591 U.S. ___, 140 S.Ct. 2316 (2020), the Court unanimously upheld a Washington State statute imposing a penalty (a fine up to $1,000) on all presidential electors who fail to live up to their pledge to cast their Electoral College ballots for the presidential candidate who won the popular vote among the state's electorate. Rejecting the notion that the Constitution grants presidential electors independence to cast their votes as they see fit, the Court began by reiterating its prior observation that Article II, which empowers each state to "appoint" electors "in such Manner as the Legislature thereof may direct," " 'convey[s to states] the broadest power of determination' over who becomes an elector." The Court went on to say that "the power to appoint an elector (in any manner) includes the power to condition his appointment—that is, to say what the elector must do for the appointment to take effect." Beyond this argument based on the meaning of "appoint," the Court reasoned that, even if the Framers "expected" electors to enjoy independence, "nothing in the Constitution expressly prohibits States from taking away presidential electors' voting discretion as Washington does." Because, "[w]hether by choice or accident, the Framers did not reduce their thoughts about electors' discretion to the printed page," the Constitution "left much to the future." The Court also relied on the fact that for almost all of the nation's history state legislatures, voters in popular elections and even presidential electors themselves have acted as if the electors' job is to ratify and implement the wishes of the people who select them. Justice Kagan wrote the majority opinion, joined by Chief Justice Roberts and Justices Ginsburg, Breyer, Alito, Sotomayor, Gorsuch and Kavanaugh. Justice Thomas, joined in part by Justice Gorsuch, wrote an opinion concurring in the judgment. The same day, the Court in Colorado Department of State v. Baca, 591 U.S. ___, 140 S.Ct. 2316 (2020), reversed the Tenth Circuit Court of Appeals' invalidation of a Colorado law that provided for replacement of presidential electors who fail to vote in line with the wishes of the state electorate—"for the reasons stated in *Chiafalo*." The ruling by the Court in *Baca* was *per curiam*, with Justice Thomas concurring in the judgment "for the reasons stated in his separate opinion in *Chiafalo*." Justice Sotomayor did not participate in *Baca*.

3. THE SCOPE OF NATIONAL POWER TODAY

F. OTHER FEDERAL POWERS

3. REGULATION OF ALIENS

Page 217. Add after Kleindienst v. Mandel:

Trump v. Hawaii

585 U.S. ___, 138 S.Ct. 2392, 201 L.Ed.2d 775 (2018).

[The report of this case appears infra, at p. 233.]

CHAPTER 5

STATE SOVEREIGNTY AND FEDERAL REGULATION

1. STATE IMMUNITY FROM FEDERAL REGULATION

Page 241. Add after Reno v. Condon:

Murphy v. National Collegiate Athletic Association, 585 U.S. ___, 138 S.Ct. 1461 (2018). The federal Professional and Amateur Sports Protection Act (PASPA) makes it "unlawful" for a State or any of its subdivisions "to sponsor, operate, advertise, promote, license, or authorize by law or compact . . . a lottery, sweepstakes, or other betting, gambling, or wagering scheme based . . . on" competitive sporting events. § 3702(1). In a separate provision relevant to but not directly at issue in the case, Congress has made it "unlawful" for "a person to sponsor, operate, advertise, or promote" those same gambling schemes—provided the person has done any of these things "pursuant to the law or compact of a governmental entity." . . . PASPA does not criminalize sports gambling under federal law but does allow the Attorney General, as well as professional and amateur sports organizations, to bring civil actions to enjoin violations.

When PASPA was passed, some jurisdictions allowed some types of sports gambling, and these activities were grandfathered so as to be unaffected by PASPA. Another provision allowed New Jersey to legalize sports gambling in Atlantic City if New Jersey chose to do so within a year of PASPA's enactment. New Jersey did not invoke that option, but many years later, in 2012 and again in 2014, it did seek to decriminalize some sports gambling that was prohibited at the time of PASPA's passage. The 2014 New Jersey Act, the one in controversy in the case, "declares that it is not to be interpreted as causing the State to authorize, license, sponsor, operate, advertise, or promote sports gambling. Instead, it is framed as a repealer. Specifically, it repeals the provisions of state law prohibiting sports gambling insofar as they concern[ ] the 'placement and acceptance of wagers' on sporting events by persons 21 years of age or older at a horseracing track or a casino or gambling house in Atlantic City. The new law also specified that the repeal was effective only as to wagers on sporting events not involving a New Jersey college team or a collegiate event taking place in the State." . . .

The 2014 Act was challenged in federal court by the National Collegiate Athletic Association and others as violating PASPA's prohibition on a state "authoriz[ing]" and "licens[ing]" sports gambling. New Jersey defended on the ground that PASPA's prohibitions on authorization and licensing of sports gambling by states and their subdivisions constituted impermissible "commandeering" of state legislatures by the federal government in violation of the Tenth Amendment and the principles laid out under it in New York v. United States, 505 U.S. 144 (1992), and Printz v. United States. 521 U.S. 898 (1997). The lower courts rejected this commandeering argument, but the Supreme Court reversed, 7–2, with Justice Alito writing for the Court:

"Before considering the constitutionality of the PASPA provision prohibiting States from 'author[izing]' sports gambling, we first examine its meaning. The parties advance dueling interpretations, and this dispute has an important bearing on the constitutional issue that we must decide. Neither respondents nor the United States, appearing as an *amicus* in support of respondents, contends that the provision at issue would be constitutional if petitioners' interpretation is correct. Indeed, the United States expressly concedes that the provision is unconstitutional if it means what petitioners claim. Brief for United States 8, 19.

"Petitioners argue that the anti-authorization provision requires States to maintain their existing laws against sports gambling without alteration. One of the accepted meanings of the term 'authorize,' they point out, is 'permit.' . . . They therefore contend that any state law that has the effect of permitting sports gambling, including a law totally or partially repealing a prior prohibition, amounts to an authorization. . . . Respondents interpret the provision more narrowly. They claim that the *primary* definition of 'authorize' requires affirmative action. . . . To authorize, they maintain, means '[t]o empower; to give a right or authority to act; to endow with authority.' . . . And this, they say, is precisely what the 2014 Act does: It empowers a defined group of entities, and it endows them with the authority to conduct sports gambling operations. Respondents do not take the position that PASPA bans all modifications of old laws against sports gambling, Brief for Respondents 20, but just how far they think a modification could go is not clear. They write that a State 'can also repeal or enhance [laws prohibiting sports gambling] without running afoul of PASPA' but that it 'cannot 'partially repeal' a general prohibition for only one or two preferred providers, or only as to sports-gambling schemes conducted by the state. . . .

"The United States makes a similar argument. PASPA, it contends, does not prohibit a State from enacting a complete repeal because 'one would not ordinarily say that private conduct is "authorized by law" simply because the government has not prohibited it.' Brief for United States 17. But the United States claims that '[t]he 2014 Act's selective and conditional permission to engage in conduct that is generally prohibited certainly qualifies' as an authorization. . . .

"In our view, petitioners' interpretation is correct: When a State completely or partially repeals old laws banning sports gambling, it 'authorize[s]' that activity. . . .

. . .

"The respondents and United States argue that even if there is some doubt about the correctness of their interpretation of the anti-authorization provision, that interpretation should be adopted in order to avoid any anti-commandeering problem that would arise if the provision were construed to require States to maintain their laws prohibiting sports gambling. . . . [B]ut even if the law could be interpreted as respondents and the United States suggest, it would still violate the anticommandeering principle, as we now explain.

. . .

"The legislative powers granted to Congress are sizable, but they are not unlimited. The Constitution confers on Congress not plenary legislative power but only certain enumerated powers. Therefore, all other legislative power is reserved for the States, as the Tenth Amendment confirms. And conspicuously absent from the list of powers given to Congress is the power to issue direct orders to the governments of the States. The anticommandeering doctrine simply represents the recognition of this limit on congressional authority.

"Although the anticommandeering principle is simple and basic, it did not emerge in our cases until relatively recently, when Congress attempted in a few isolated instances to extend its authority in unprecedented ways. The pioneering case was *New York*. . . .

"Five years after *New York*, the Court applied the same principles to a federal statute requiring state and local law enforcement officers to perform background checks and related tasks in connection with applications for handgun licenses. *Printz*,. . . .

"Our opinions in *New York* and *Printz* explained why adherence to the anticommandeering principle is important. Without attempting a complete survey, we mention several reasons that are significant here. First, the rule serves as 'one of the Constitution's structural protections of liberty.' . . . 'The Constitution does not protect the sovereignty of States for the benefit of the States or state governments as abstract political entities.' . . . 'To the contrary, the Constitution divides authority between federal and state governments for the protection of individuals.' . . . '[A] healthy balance of power between the States and the Federal Government [reduces] the risk of tyranny and abuse from either front.' . . .

"Second, the anticommandeering rule promotes political accountability. When Congress itself regulates, the responsibility for the benefits and burdens of the regulation is apparent. Voters who like or dislike the effects of the regulation know who to credit or blame. By contrast, if a State imposes regulations only because it has been commanded to do so by Congress, responsibility is blurred.

"Third, the anticommandeering principle prevents Congress from shifting the costs of regulation to the States. If Congress enacts a law and requires enforcement by the Executive Branch, it must appropriate the funds needed to administer the program. It is pressured to weigh the expected benefits of the program against its costs. But if Congress can compel the States to enact and enforce its program, Congress need not engage in any such analysis. . . .

"The PASPA provision at issue here—prohibiting state authorization of sports gambling—violates the anticommandeering rule. That provision unequivocally dictates what a state legislature may and may not do. And this is true under either our interpretation or that advocated by respondents and the United States. In either event, state legislatures are put under the direct control of Congress. It is as if federal officers were installed in state legislative chambers and were armed with the authority to stop legislators from voting on any offending proposals. A more direct affront to state sovereignty is not easy to imagine.

"Neither respondents nor the United States contends that Congress can compel a State to enact legislation, but they say that prohibiting a State from enacting new laws is another matter. Noting that the laws challenged in *New York* and *Printz* 'told states what they must do instead of what they must not do,' respondents contend that commandeering occurs 'only when Congress goes beyond precluding state action and affirmatively commands it.'

"This distinction is empty. It was a matter of happenstance that the laws challenged in *New York* and *Printz* commanded 'affirmative' action as opposed to imposing a prohibition. The basic principle—that Congress cannot issue direct orders to state legislatures—applies in either event.

"Here is an illustration. PASPA includes an exemption for States that permitted sports betting at the time of enactment, but suppose Congress did not adopt such an exemption. Suppose Congress ordered States with legalized sports betting to take the affirmative step of criminalizing that activity and ordered the remaining States to retain their laws prohibiting sports betting. There is no good reason why the former would intrude more deeply on state sovereignty than the latter.

"Respondents and the United States claim that prior decisions of this Court show that PASPA's anti-authorization provision is constitutional, but they misread those cases. In none of them did we uphold the constitutionality of a federal statute that commanded state legislatures to enact or refrain from enacting state law. . . .

". . . Reno v. Condon, 528 U. S. 141 (2000), . . . concerned a federal law restricting the disclosure and dissemination of personal information provided in applications for driver's licenses. The law applied equally to state and private actors. It did not regulate the States' sovereign authority to 'regulate their own citizens.'

. . .

"Respondents and the United States defend the anti-authorization prohibition on the ground that it constitutes a valid preemption provision, but it is no such thing. Preemption is based on the Supremacy Clause, and that Clause is not an independent grant of legislative power to Congress. Instead, it simply provides 'a rule of decision.' It specifies that federal law is supreme in case of a conflict with state law. Therefore, in order for the PASPA provision to preempt state law, it must satisfy two requirements. First, it must represent the exercise of a power conferred on Congress by the Constitution; pointing to the Supremacy Clause will not do. Second, since the Constitution 'confers upon Congress the power to regulate individuals, not States,' the PASPA provision at issue must be best read as one that regulates private actors.

"Our cases have identified three different types of preemption—'conflict,' 'express,' and 'field,'—but all of them work in the same way: Congress enacts a law that imposes restrictions or confers rights on private actors; a state law confers rights or imposes restrictions that conflict with the federal law; and therefore the federal law takes precedence and the state law is preempted.

"This mechanism is shown most clearly in cases involving 'conflict preemption.' . . .

" 'Express preemption' operates in essentially the same way, but this is often obscured by the language used by Congress in framing preemption provisions. The provision at issue in Morales v. Trans World Airlines, Inc., 504 U. S. 374 (1992), is illustrative. The Airline Deregulation Act of 1978 lifted prior federal regulations of airlines, and '[t]o ensure that the States would not undo federal deregulation with regulation of their own,' the Act provided that 'no State or political subdivision thereof . . . shall enact or enforce any law, rule, regulation, standard, or other provision having the force and effect of law relating to rates, routes, or services of any [covered] air carrier.'

"This language might appear to operate directly on the States, but it is a mistake to be confused by the way in which a preemption provision is phrased. As we recently explained, 'we do not require Congress to employ a particular linguistic formulation when preempting state law.' . . . And if we look beyond the phrasing employed in the Airline Deregulation Act's preemption provision, it is clear that this provision operates just like any other federal law with preemptive effect. It confers on private entities (*i.e.*, covered carriers) a federal right to engage in certain conduct subject only to certain (federal) constraints.

"'Field preemption' operates in the same way. . .

. . .

"In sum, regardless of the language sometimes used by Congress and this Court, every form of preemption is based on a federal law that regulates the conduct of private actors, not the States.

"Once this is understood, it is clear that the PASPA provision prohibiting state authorization of sports gambling is not a preemption provision because there is no way in which this provision can be understood as a regulation of private actors. It certainly does not confer any federal rights on private actors interested in conducting sports gambling operations. (It does not give them a federal right to engage in sports gambling.) Nor does it impose any federal restrictions on private actors. If a private citizen or company started a sports gambling operation, either with or without state authorization, § 3702(1) would not be violated and would not provide any ground for a civil action by the Attorney General or any other party. Thus, there is simply no way to understand the provision prohibiting state authorization as anything other than a direct command to the States. And that is exactly what the anticommandeering rule does not allow.

. . .

"Having concluded that § 3702(1) violates the anti-commandeering doctrine, we consider two additional questions: first, whether the decision below should be affirmed on an alternative ground and, second, whether our decision regarding the anti-authorization provision dooms the remainder of PASPA.

"Respondents and the United States argue that, even if we disagree with the Third Circuit's decision regarding the constitutionality of the anti-authorization provision, we should nevertheless affirm based on PASPA's prohibition of state 'licens[ing]' of sports gambling. Although New Jersey's 2014 Act does not expressly provide for the licensing of sports gambling operations, respondents and the United States contend that the law effectively achieves that result because the only entities that it authorizes to engage in that activity, *i.e.*, casinos and racetracks, are already required to be licensed.

"We need not decide whether the 2014 Act violates PASPA's prohibition of state 'licens[ing]' because that provision suffers from the same defect as the prohibition of state authorization. It issues a direct order to the state legislature.[29] Just as Congress lacks the power to order a state legislature not to enact a law authorizing sports gambling, it may not order a state legislature to refrain from enacting a law licensing sports gambling."

---

[29] Even if the prohibition of state licensing were not itself unconstitutional, we do not think it could be severed from the invalid provision forbidding state authorization. . . .

The Court went on to hold all the rest of the provisions of the PASPA inseverable and thus invalid. Justice Thomas, who joined the majority opinion, wrote a separate concurrence to express dissatisfaction with the current state of severability doctrine. Justice Breyer, who joined the Court's opinion except for its severability section, wrote separately to say he would have invalidated only the provision of PASPA dealing with "authoriz[ation]" and licens[ing]," and left intact the rest. Justice Ginsburg, joined by Justice Sotomayor, dissented, criticizing the Court's unwarranted severability analysis used to "deploy a wrecking ball destroying" PASPA. The fact that they dissented rather than concurred in part (as did Justice Breyer) could be read to suggest they disagreed with the majority's commandeering analysis as well (and they did refer to that part of the case as "the alleged 'commandeering'" elements of PASPA), but they never explained any disagreement with the majority on this point.

2. ENFORCEMENT OF FEDERAL RIGHTS IN SUITS AGAINST STATE OFFICERS: THE ELEVENTH AMENDMENT

Page 246. Add at the end of Note, *Congressional Power to Abrogate Eleventh Amendment Immunity and Subject States to Suit in Federal Court*:

The Court found *Florida Prepaid* to be controlling in Allen v. Cooper, 589 U.S. ___, 140 S.Ct. 994 (2020), a case involving Congress's attempt to abrogate state sovereign immunity for breaches of copyright. Writing for a six-member majority, Justice Kagan observed that "there is no difference between copyrights and patents under the [Constitution's Intellectual Property] Clause," and that Congress's attempt to impose damage liability on states for copyright infringement lacked congruence and proportionality, just as its attempt to impose damage liability for patent violations had. For these reasons, Justice Kagan concluded that the Court "would have to overrule *Florida Prepaid* if we were to decide this case Allen's way." The majority declined to do so, observing that "*stare decisis*, this Court has understood, is a 'foundation stone of the rule of law' . . . To reverse a decision, we demand a 'special justification,' *over and above the belief 'that the precedent was wrongly decided.'* . . . [But] Allen offers us nothing special at all; he contends only that if the Court were to use [his approach to constitutional interpretation], it would discover that *Florida Prepaid* was wrong. . . ."

Page 247. Insert after the paragraph discussing Alden v. Maine in the Note on *State Sovereign Immunity in State Court Suits*:

Alden v. Maine involved assertion of a federal claim in a state court of the very state being sued. In Franchise Tax Board v. Hyatt, 587 U.S. ___, 139 S.Ct. 1485 (2019), a closely divided Court relied on *Alden*'s observation that "the bare text of the [Eleventh] Amendment is not an exhaustive description of the States' constitutional immunity from suit" to rule, based on general principles of interstate federalism, that a state enjoys immunity under the Constitution from suits brought against it under state law in state courts of other states. In reaching this outcome, the Court in *Hyatt* overruled Nevada v. Hall, 440 U.S. 410 (1979), prompting the four dissenters to complain that the majority improperly disregarded *stare decisis* without a "special justification" for doing so.

CHAPTER 6

THE SCOPE OF STATE POWER

1. INTRODUCTION

B. TAXATION

Page 252. Replace text (and accompanying footnotes) at the end of Section 1B (Introduction/Taxation) beginning with "Despite *Complete Auto . . .* " with the following:

South Dakota v. Wayfair

585 U.S. ___, 138 S.Ct. 2080, 201 L.Ed.2d 403 (2018).

■ JUSTICE KENNEDY delivered the opinion of the Court.

When a consumer purchases goods or services, the consumer's State often imposes a sales tax. This case requires the Court to determine when an out-of-state seller can be required to collect and remit that tax. All concede that taxing the sales in question here is lawful. The question is whether the out-of-state seller can be held responsible for its payment, and this turns on a proper interpretation of the Commerce Clause, U. S. Const., Art. I, § 8, cl. 3.

In two earlier cases the Court held that an out-of-state seller's liability to collect and remit the tax to the consumer's State depended on whether the seller had a physical presence in that State, but that mere shipment of goods into the consumer's State, following an order from a catalog, did not satisfy the physical presence requirement. National Bellas Hess, Inc. v. Department of Revenue of Ill., 386 U. S. 753 (1967); Quill Corp. v. North Dakota, 504 U. S. 298 (1992). The Court granted certiorari here to reconsider the scope and validity of the physical presence rule mandated by those cases.

I

Like most States, South Dakota has a sales tax. It taxes the retail sales of goods and services in the State. Sellers are generally required to collect and remit this tax to the Department of Revenue. If for some reason the sales tax is not remitted by the seller, then instate consumers are separately responsible for paying a use tax at the same rate.

Many States employ this kind of complementary sales and use tax regime. Under this Court's decisions in *Bellas Hess* and *Quill*, South Dakota may not require a business to collect its sales tax if the business lacks a physical presence in the State. Without that physical presence, South Dakota instead must rely on its residents to pay the use tax owed on their purchases from out-of-state sellers. "[T]he impracticability of [this] collection from the multitude of individual purchasers is obvious." . . . And consumer compliance rates are notoriously low [in the neighborhood of a 4 percent collection rate.] . . . It is estimated that *Bellas Hess* and *Quill* cause the States to lose between $8 and $33 billion every year. . . . In South Dakota alone, the Department of Revenue estimates revenue loss at $48 to $58 million annually. . . . Particularly because South Dakota has no state income tax, it must put substantial reliance on its sales and use taxes for the revenue necessary to fund essential services. Those taxes account for over 60 percent of its general fund.

In 2016, South Dakota confronted the serious inequity *Quill* imposes by enacting S. 106—"An Act to provide for the collection of sales taxes from certain remote sellers, to establish certain Legislative findings, and to declare an emergency." . . . The legislature found that the inability to collect sales tax from remote sellers was "seriously eroding the sales tax base" and "causing revenue losses and imminent harm . . . through the loss of critical funding for state and local services." . . . The legislature also declared an emergency: "Whereas, this Act is necessary for the support of the state government and its existing public institutions, an emergency is hereby declared to exist." . . . Fearing further erosion of the tax base, the legislature expressed its intention to "apply South Dakota's sales and use tax obligations to the limit of federal and state constitutional doctrines" and noted the urgent need for this Court to reconsider its precedents. . . .

To that end, the Act requires out-of-state sellers to collect and remit sales tax "as if the seller had a physical presence in the state." . . . The Act applies only to sellers that, on an annual basis, deliver more than $100,000 of goods or services into the State or engage in 200 or more separate transactions for the delivery of goods or services into the State. The Act also forecloses the retroactive application of this requirement and provides means for the Act to be appropriately stayed until the constitutionality of the law has been clearly established.

Respondents Wayfair, Inc., Overstock.com, Inc., and Newegg, Inc., are merchants with no employees or real estate in South Dakota. Wayfair, Inc., is a leading online retailer of home goods and furniture and had net revenues of over $4.7 billion last year. Overstock.com, Inc., is one of the top online retailers in the United States, selling a wide variety of products from home goods and furniture to clothing and jewelry; and it had net revenues of over $1.7 billion last year. Newegg, Inc., is a major online retailer of consumer electronics in the United States. Each of these three companies ships its goods directly to purchasers throughout the United States, including South Dakota. Each easily meets the minimum sales or transactions requirement of the Act, but none collects South Dakota sales tax.

Pursuant to the Act's provisions for expeditious judicial review, South Dakota filed a declaratory judgment action against respondents in state court, seeking a declaration that the requirements of the Act are valid and applicable to respondents and an injunction requiring respondents to register for licenses to collect and remit sales tax. Respondents moved for summary judgment, arguing that the Act is unconstitutional. South Dakota conceded that the Act cannot survive under *Bellas Hess* and *Quill* but asserted the importance, indeed the necessity, of asking this Court to review those earlier decisions in light of current economic realities.

The trial court granted summary judgment to respondents. The South Dakota Supreme Court affirmed. It stated: "However persuasive the State's arguments on the merits of revisiting the issue, *Quill* has not been overruled [and] remains the controlling precedent on the issue of Commerce Clause limitations on interstate collection of sales and use taxes." This Court granted certiorari. . . .

II

The Constitution grants Congress the power "[t]o regulate Commerce . . . among the several States." Art. I, § 8, cl. 3. The Commerce Clause "reflect[s] a central concern of the Framers that was an immediate reason for calling the Constitutional Convention: the conviction that in order to succeed, the new Union would have to avoid the tendencies toward economic Balkanization that had plagued relations among the Colonies and later among the States under the Articles of Confederation." Hughes v. Oklahoma, 441 U. S. 322, 325–326 (1979). Although the Commerce Clause is written as an affirmative grant of authority to Congress, this Court has long held that in some instances it imposes limitations on the States absent congressional action. Of course, when Congress exercises its power to regulate commerce by enacting legislation, the legislation controls. Southern Pacific Co. v. Arizona ex rel. Sullivan, 325 U. S. 761, 769 (1945). But this Court has observed that "in general Congress has left it to the courts to formulate the rules" to preserve "the free flow of interstate commerce." . . .

To understand the issue presented in this case, it is instructive first to survey the general development of this Court's Commerce Clause principles and then to review the application of those principles to state taxes.

A

From early in its history, a central function of this Court has been to adjudicate disputes that require interpretation of the Commerce Clause in order to determine its meaning, its reach, and the extent to which it limits state regulations of commerce. Gibbons v. Ogden, 9 Wheat. 1 (1824), began setting the course by defining the meaning of commerce. Chief Justice Marshall explained that commerce included both "the interchange of commodities" and "commercial intercourse." . . . A concurring opinion further stated that Congress had the exclusive power to regulate commerce. See id., at 236 (opinion of Johnson, J.). Had that latter submission prevailed and States been denied the power of concurrent regulation, history might have seen sweeping federal regulations at an early date that foreclosed the States from experimentation with laws and policies of their own, or, on the other hand, proposals to reexamine Gibbons' broad definition of commerce to accommodate the necessity of allowing States the power to enact laws to implement the political will of their people.

Just five years after Gibbons, however, in another opinion by Chief Justice Marshall, the Court sustained what in substance was a state regulation of interstate commerce. In Willson v. Black Bird Creek Marsh Co., 2 Pet. 245 (1829), the Court allowed a State to dam and bank a stream that was part of an interstate water system, an action that likely would have been an impermissible intrusion on the national power over commerce had it been the rule that only Congress could regulate in that sphere. . . . Thus, by implication at least, the Court indicated that the power to regulate commerce in some circumstances was held by the States and Congress concurrently. And so both a broad interpretation of interstate commerce and the concurrent regulatory power of the States can be traced to Gibbons and Willson.

Over the next few decades, the Court refined the doctrine to accommodate the necessary balance between state and federal power. In Cooley v. Board of Wardens of Port of Philadelphia ex rel. Soc. for Relief of Distressed Pilots, 12 How. 299 (1852), the Court addressed local laws regulating river pilots who operated in interstate waters and guided many ships on interstate or foreign voyages. The Court held that, while Congress surely could regulate on this subject had it chosen to act, the State, too, could regulate. The Court distinguished between those subjects that by their nature "imperatively deman[d] a single uniform rule, operating equally on the commerce of the United States," and those that "deman[d] th[e] diversity, which alone can meet . . . local necessities." . . . Though considerable uncertainties were yet to be overcome, these precedents still laid the groundwork for the analytical framework that now prevails for Commerce Clause cases.

This Court's doctrine has developed further with time. Modern precedents rest upon two primary principles that mark the boundaries of a State's authority to regulate interstate commerce. First, state regulations may not discriminate against interstate commerce; and second, States may not impose undue burdens on interstate commerce. State laws that discriminate against interstate commerce face "a virtually *per se* rule of invalidity." Granholm v. Heald, 544 U. S. 460, 476 (2005). State laws that "regulat[e] even-handedly to effectuate a legitimate local public interest . . . will be upheld unless the burden imposed on such commerce is clearly excessive in relation to the putative local benefits." Pike v. Bruce Church, Inc., 397 U. S. 137, 142 (1970). Although subject to exceptions and variations, these two principles guide the courts in adjudicating cases challenging state laws under the Commerce Clause.

B

These principles also animate the Court's Commerce Clause precedents addressing the validity of state taxes. The Court explained the now-accepted framework for state taxation in Complete Auto Transit, Inc. v. Brady, 430 U. S. 274 (1977). The Court held that a State "may tax exclusively interstate commerce so long as the tax does not create any effect forbidden by the Commerce Clause." . . . After all, "interstate commerce may be required to pay its fair share of state taxes." D. H. Holmes Co. v. McNamara, 486 U. S. 24, 31 (1988). The Court will sustain a tax so long as it (1) applies to an activity with a substantial nexus with the taxing State, (2) is fairly apportioned, (3) does not discriminate against interstate commerce, and (4) is fairly related to the services the State provides. . . .

Before *Complete Auto*, the Court had addressed a challenge to an Illinois tax that required out-of-state retailers to collect and remit taxes on sales made to consumers who purchased goods for use within Illinois. *Bellas Hess*, 386 U. S., at 754–755. The Court held that a mail-order company "whose only connection with customers in the State is by common carrier or the United States mail" lacked the requisite minimum contacts with the State required by both the Due Process Clause and the Commerce Clause. . . . Unless the retailer maintained a physical presence such as "retail outlets, solicitors, or property within a State," the State lacked the power to require that retailer to collect a local use tax. . . . The dissent disagreed: "There should be no doubt that this large-scale, systematic, continuous solicitation and exploitation of the Illinois consumer market is a sufficient 'nexus' to require Bellas Hess to collect from Illinois customers and to remit the use tax." *Id.*, at 761–762 (opinion of Fortas, J., joined by Black and Douglas, JJ.).

In 1992, the Court reexamined the physical presence rule in *Quill*. That case presented a challenge to North Dakota's "attempt to require an out-of-state mail-order house that has neither outlets nor sales representatives in the State to collect and pay a use tax on goods purchased for use within the State." . . . Despite the fact that *Bellas Hess* linked due process and the Commerce Clause together, the Court in *Quill* overruled the due process holding, but not the Commerce Clause holding; and it thus reaffirmed the physical presence rule. . . .

The Court in *Quill* recognized that intervening precedents, specifically *Complete Auto*, "might not dictate the same result were the issue to arise for the first time today." . . . But, nevertheless, the *Quill* majority concluded that the physical presence rule was necessary to prevent undue burdens on interstate commerce. It grounded the physical presence rule in *Complete Auto*'s requirement that a tax have a " 'substantial nexus' " with the activity being taxed. . . .

Three Justices based their decision to uphold the physical presence rule on *stare decisis* alone. *Id.*, at 320 (Scalia, J., joined by Kennedy and Thomas, JJ., concurring in part and concurring in judgment). Dissenting in relevant part, Justice White argued that "there is no relationship between the physical-presence/nexus rule the Court retains and Commerce Clause considerations that allegedly justify it." *Id.*, at 327 (opinion concurring in part and dissenting in part).

III

The physical presence rule has "been the target of criticism over many years from many quarters." Direct Marketing Assn. v. Brohl, 814 F. 3d 1129, 1148, 1150–1151 (CA10 2016) (Gorsuch, J., concurring). *Quill*, it has been said, was "premised on assumptions that are unfounded" and "riddled with internal inconsistencies." . . . *Quill* created an inefficient "online sales tax loophole" that gives out-of-state businesses an advantage. . . . And "while nexus rules are clearly necessary," the Court "should focus on rules that are appropriate to the twenty-first century, not the nineteenth." . . . Each year, the physical presence rule becomes further removed from economic reality and results in significant revenue losses to the States. These critiques underscore that the physical presence rule, both as first formulated and as applied today, is an incorrect interpretation of the Commerce Clause.

A

Quill is flawed on its own terms. First, the physical presence rule is not a necessary interpretation of the requirement that a state tax must be "applied to an activity with a substantial nexus with the taxing State." *Complete Auto*, 430 U. S., at 279. Second, *Quill* creates rather than resolves market distortions. And third, *Quill* imposes the sort of arbitrary, formalistic distinction that the Court's modern Commerce Clause precedents disavow.

1

All agree that South Dakota has the authority to tax these transactions. S. B. 106 applies to sales of "tangible personal property, products transferred electronically, or services *for delivery into South Dakota*." § 1 (emphasis added). "It has long been settled" that the sale of goods or services "has a sufficient nexus to the State in which the sale is consummated to be treated as a local transaction taxable by that State." Oklahoma Tax Comm'n v. Jefferson Lines, Inc., 514 U. S. 175, 184 (1995); see also 2 C. Trost & P. Hartman, Federal Limitations on State and Local Taxation 2d § 11:1, p. 471 (2003) ("Generally speaking, a sale is attributable to its destination"). The central dispute is whether South Dakota may require remote sellers to collect and remit the tax without some additional connection to the State. The Court has previously stated that "[t]he imposition on the seller of the duty to insure collection of the tax from the purchaser does not violate the [C]ommerce [C]lause." . . . It is a " 'familiar and sanctioned device.' " There just must be "a substantial nexus with the taxing State." *Complete Auto, supra*, at 279.

This nexus requirement is "closely related," *Bellas Hess*, 386 U. S., at 756, to the due process requirement that there be "some definite link, some minimum connection, between a state and the person, property or transaction it seeks to tax." . . . It is settled law that a business need not have a physical presence in a State to satisfy the demands of due process. Burger King Corp. v. Rudzewicz, 471 U. S. 462, 476 (1985). Although physical presence " 'frequently will enhance' " a business' connection with a State, " 'it is an inescapable fact of modern commercial life that a substantial amount of business is transacted . . . [with no] need for physical presence within a State in which business is conducted.' " *Quill*, 504 U. S., at 308. *Quill* itself recognized that "[t]he requirements of due process are met irrespective of a corporation's lack of physical presence in the taxing State." . . .

When considering whether a State may levy a tax, Due Process and Commerce Clause standards may not be identical or coterminous, but there are significant parallels. The reasons given in *Quill* for rejecting the physical presence rule for due process purposes apply as well to the question whether physical presence is a requisite for an out-of-state seller's liability to remit sales taxes. Physical presence is not necessary to create a substantial nexus.

The *Quill* majority expressed concern that without the physical presence rule "a state tax might unduly burden interstate commerce" by subjecting retailers to tax collection obligations in thousands of different taxing jurisdictions. . . . But the administrative costs of compliance, especially in the modern economy with its Internet technology, are largely unrelated to whether a company happens to have a physical presence in a State. For example, a business with one salesperson in each State must collect sales taxes in every jurisdiction in which goods are delivered; but a business with 500 salespersons in one central location and a website accessible in every State need not collect sales taxes on otherwise identical nationwide sales. In other words, under *Quill*, a small company with diverse physical presence might be equally or more burdened by compliance costs than a large remote seller. The physical presence rule is a poor proxy for the compliance costs faced by companies that do business in multiple States. Other aspects of the Court's doctrine can better and more accurately address any potential burdens on interstate commerce, whether or not *Quill*'s physical presence rule is satisfied.

2

The Court has consistently explained that the Commerce Clause was designed to prevent States from engaging in economic discrimination so they would not divide into isolated, separable units. See Philadelphia v. New Jersey, 437 U. S. 617, 623 (1978). But it is "not the purpose of the [C]ommerce [C]lause to relieve those engaged in interstate commerce from their just share of state tax burden." *Complete Auto, supra*, at 288. And it is certainly not the purpose of the Commerce Clause to permit the Judiciary to create market distortions. "If the Commerce Clause was intended to put businesses on an even playing field, the [physical presence] rule is hardly a way to achieve that goal." *Quill, supra*, at 329 (opinion of White, J.). *Quill* puts both local businesses and many interstate businesses with physical presence at a competitive disadvantage relative to remote sellers. Remote sellers can avoid the regulatory burdens of tax collection and can offer *de facto* lower prices caused by the widespread failure of consumers to pay the tax on their own. This "guarantees a competitive benefit to certain firms simply because of the organizational form they choose" while the rest of the Court's jurisprudence "is all about preventing discrimination between firms." *Direct Marketing*, 814 F. 3d, at 1150–1151 (Gorsuch, J., concurring). In effect, *Quill* has come to serve as a judicially created tax shelter for businesses that decide to limit their physical presence and still sell their goods and services to a State's consumers—something that has become easier and more prevalent as technology has advanced.

Worse still, the rule produces an incentive to avoid physical presence in multiple States. Distortions caused by the desire of businesses to avoid tax collection mean that the market may currently lack storefronts, distribution points, and employment centers that otherwise would be efficient or desirable. The Commerce Clause must not prefer interstate commerce only to the point where a merchant physically crosses state borders. Rejecting the physical presence rule is necessary to ensure that artificial competitive advantages are not created by this Court's precedents. This Court should not prevent States from collecting lawful taxes through a physical presence rule that can be satisfied only if there is an employee or a building in the State.

3

The Court's Commerce Clause jurisprudence has "eschewed formalism for a sensitive, case-by-case analysis of purposes and effects." West Lynn Creamery, Inc. v. Healy, 512 U. S. 186, 201 (1994). *Quill*, in contrast, treats economically identical actors differently, and for arbitrary reasons.

Consider, for example, two businesses that sell furniture online. The first stocks a few items of inventory in a small warehouse in North Sioux City, South Dakota. The second uses a major warehouse just across the border in South Sioux City, Nebraska, and maintains a sophisticated website with a virtual showroom accessible in every State, including South Dakota. By reason of its physical presence, the first business must collect and remit a tax on all of its sales to customers from South Dakota, even those sales that have nothing to do with the warehouse. But, under *Quill*, the second, hypothetical seller cannot be subject to the same tax for the sales of the same items made through a pervasive Internet presence. This distinction simply makes no sense. So long as a state law avoids "any effect forbidden by the Commerce Clause," . . . courts should not rely on anachronistic formalisms to invalidate it. The basic principles of the Court's Commerce Clause jurisprudence are grounded in functional, marketplace dynamics; and States can and should consider those realities in enacting and enforcing their tax laws.

B

The *Quill* Court itself acknowledged that the physical presence rule is "artificial at its edges." 504 U. S., at 315. That was an understatement when *Quill* was decided; and when the day-to-day functions of marketing and distribution in the modern economy are considered, it is all the more evident that the physical presence rule is artificial in its entirety. Modern e-commerce does not align analytically with a test that relies on the sort of physical presence defined in *Quill*. In a footnote, *Quill* rejected the argument that "title to 'a few floppy diskettes' present in a State" was sufficient to constitute a "substantial nexus," *id.*, at 315, n. 8. But it is not clear why a single employee or a single warehouse should create a substantial nexus while "physical" aspects of pervasive modern technology should not. For example, a company with a website accessible in South Dakota may be said to have a physical presence in the State via the customers' computers. A website may leave cookies saved to the customers' hard drives, or customers may download the company's app onto their phones. Or a company may lease data storage that is permanently, or even occasionally, located in South Dakota. What may have seemed like a "clear," "bright-line tes[t]" when *Quill* was written now threatens to compound the arbitrary consequences that should have been apparent from the outset. . . .

The "dramatic technological and social changes" of our "increasingly interconnected economy" mean that buyers are "closer to most major retailers" than ever before—"regardless of how close or far the nearest storefront." . . . Between targeted advertising and instant access to most consumers via any internet-enabled device, "a business may be present in a State in a meaningful way without" that presence "being physical in the traditional sense of the term." . . . A virtual showroom can show far more inventory, in far more detail, and with greater opportunities for consumer and seller interaction than might be possible for local stores. Yet the continuous and pervasive virtual presence of retailers today is, under *Quill*, simply irrelevant. This Court should not maintain a rule that ignores these substantial virtual connections to the State.

C

The physical presence rule as defined and enforced in *Bellas Hess* and *Quill* is not just a technical legal problem—it is an extraordinary imposition by the Judiciary on States' authority to collect taxes and perform critical public functions. Forty-one States, two Territories, and the District of Columbia now ask this Court to reject the test formulated in *Quill*. *Quill*'s physical presence rule intrudes on States' reasonable choices in enacting their tax systems. And that it allows remote sellers to escape an obligation to remit a lawful state tax is unfair and unjust. It is unfair and unjust to those competitors, both local and out of State, who must remit the tax; to the consumers who pay the tax; and to the States that seek fair enforcement of the sales tax, a tax many States for many years have considered an indispensable source for raising revenue.

In essence, respondents ask this Court to retain a rule that allows their customers to escape payment of sales taxes—taxes that are essential to create and secure the active market they supply with goods and services. An example may suffice. Wayfair offers to sell a vast selection of furnishings. Its advertising seeks to create an image of beautiful, peaceful homes, but it also says that " '[o]ne of the best things about buying through Wayfair is that we do not have to charge sales tax.' " Brief for Petitioner 55. What Wayfair ignores in its subtle offer to assist in tax evasion is that creating a dream home assumes solvent state and local governments. State taxes fund the police and fire departments that protect the homes containing their customers' furniture and ensure goods are safely delivered; maintain the public roads and municipal services that allow communication with and access to customers; support the "sound local banking institutions to support credit transactions [and] courts to ensure collection of the purchase price," and help create the "climate of consumer confidence" that facilitates sales. According to respondents, it is unfair to stymie their tax-free solicitation of customers. But there is nothing unfair about requiring companies that avail themselves of the States' benefits to bear an equal share of the burden of tax collection. . . .

In the name of federalism and free markets, *Quill* does harm to both. The physical presence rule it defines has limited States' ability to seek long-term prosperity and has prevented market participants from competing on an even playing field.

IV

"Although we approach the reconsideration of our decisions with the utmost caution, *stare decisis* is not an inexorable command." . . . Here, *stare decisis* can no longer support the Court's prohibition of a valid exercise of the States' sovereign power. If it becomes apparent that the Court's Commerce Clause decisions prohibit the States from exercising their lawful sovereign powers in our federal system, the Court should be vigilant in correcting the error. While it can be conceded that Congress has the authority to change the physical presence rule, Congress cannot change the constitutional default rule. It is inconsistent with the Court's proper role to ask Congress to address a false constitutional premise of this Court's own creation. Courts have acted as the front line of review in this limited sphere; and hence it is important that their principles be accurate and logical, whether or not Congress can or will act in response. It is currently the Court, and not Congress, that is limiting the lawful prerogatives of the States.

. . . Though *Quill* was wrong on its own terms when it was decided in 1992, since then the Internet revolution has made its earlier error all the more egregious and harmful.

The *Quill* Court did not have before it the present realities of the interstate marketplace. In 1992, less than 2 percent of Americans had Internet access. Today that number is about 89 percent. When it decided *Quill*, the Court could not have envisioned a world in which the world's largest retailer would be a remote seller, [Amazon]. . . .

. . . Last year, e-commerce grew at four times the rate of traditional retail, and it shows no sign of any slower pace. . . .

This expansion has also increased the revenue shortfall faced by States seeking to collect their sales and use taxes. In 1992, it was estimated that the States were losing between $694 million and $3 billion per year in sales tax revenues as a result of the physical presence rule. Now estimates range from $8 to $33 billion. . . .

The argument, moreover, that the physical presence rule is clear and easy to apply is unsound. Attempts to apply the physical presence rule to online retail sales are proving unworkable. States are already confronting the complexities of defining physical presence in the Cyber Age. For example, Massachusetts proposed a regulation that would have defined physical presence to include making apps available to be downloaded by in-state residents and placing cookies on in-state residents' web browsers. . . . Ohio recently adopted a similar standard. . . . Some States have enacted so-called "click through" nexus statutes, which define nexus to include out-of-state sellers that contract with in-state residents who refer customers for compensation. . . . Others still, like Colorado, have imposed notice and reporting requirements on out-of-state retailers that fall just short of actually collecting and remitting the tax. . . . Statutes of this sort are likely to embroil courts in technical and arbitrary disputes about what counts as physical presence.

Reliance interests are a legitimate consideration when the Court weighs adherence to an earlier but flawed precedent. But even on its own terms, the physical presence rule as defined by *Quill* is no longer a clear or easily applicable standard, so arguments for reliance based on its clarity are misplaced. And, importantly, *stare decisis* accommodates only "legitimate reliance interest[s]." . . . Here, the tax distortion created by *Quill* exists in large part because consumers regularly fail to comply with lawful use taxes. Some remote retailers go so far as to advertise sales as tax free. A business "is in no position to found a constitutional right on the practical opportunities for tax avoidance." . . .

Respondents argue that "the physical presence rule has permitted start-ups and small businesses to use the Internet as a means to grow their companies and access a national market, without exposing them to the daunting complexity and business-development obstacles of nationwide sales tax collection." . . . These burdens may pose legitimate concerns in some instances, particularly for small businesses that make a small volume of sales to customers in many States. State taxes differ, not only in the rate imposed but also in the categories of goods that are taxed and, sometimes, the relevant date of purchase. Eventually, software that is available at a reasonable cost may make it easier for small businesses to cope with these problems. Indeed, as the physical presence rule no longer controls, those systems may well become available in a short period of time, either from private providers or from state taxing agencies themselves. And in all events, Congress may legislate to address these problems if it deems it necessary and fit to do so.

In this case, however, South Dakota affords small merchants a reasonable degree of protection. The law at issue requires a merchant to collect the tax only if it does a considerable amount of business in the State; the law is not retroactive; and South Dakota is a party to the Streamlined Sales and Use Tax Agreement.

Finally, other aspects of the Court's Commerce Clause doctrine can protect against any undue burden on interstate commerce, taking into consideration the small businesses, startups, or others who engage in commerce across state lines. For example, the United States argues that tax-collection requirements should be analyzed under the balancing framework of Pike v. Bruce Church, Inc., 397 U. S. 137. Others have argued that retroactive liability risks a double tax burden in violation of the Court's apportionment jurisprudence because it would make both the buyer and the seller legally liable for collecting and remitting the tax on a transaction intended to be taxed only once. Complex state tax systems could have the effect of discriminating against interstate commerce. Concerns that complex state tax systems could be a burden on small business are answered in part by noting that . . . there are various plans already in place to simplify collection; and since in-state businesses pay the taxes as well, the risk of discrimination against out-of-state sellers is avoided. And, if some small businesses with only *de minimis* contacts seek relief from collection systems thought to be a burden, those entities may still do so under other theories. These issues are not before the Court in the instant case; but their potential to arise in some later case cannot justify retaining this artificial, anachronistic rule that deprives States of vast revenues from major businesses.

For these reasons, the Court concludes that the physical presence rule of *Quill* is unsound and incorrect. The Court's decisions in *Quill* . . . and *National Bellas Hess* . . . should be, and now are, overruled.

V

In the absence of *Quill* and *Bellas Hess*, the first prong of the *Complete Auto* test simply asks whether the tax applies to an activity with a substantial nexus with the taxing State. . . . "[S]uch a nexus is established when the taxpayer [or collector] 'avails itself of the substantial privilege of carrying on business' in that jurisdiction." . . . Here, the nexus is clearly sufficient based on both the economic and virtual contacts respondents have with the State. The Act applies only to sellers that deliver more than $100,000 of goods or services into South Dakota or engage in 200 or more separate transactions for the delivery of goods and services into the State on an annual basis. . . . This quantity of business could not have occurred unless the seller availed itself of the substantial privilege of carrying on business in South Dakota. And respondents are large, national companies that undoubtedly maintain an extensive virtual presence. Thus, the substantial nexus requirement of *Complete Auto* is satisfied in this case.

The question remains whether some other principle in the Court's Commerce Clause doctrine might invalidate the Act. Because the *Quill* physical presence rule was an obvious barrier to the Act's validity, these issues have not yet been litigated or briefed, and so the Court need not resolve them here. That said, South Dakota's tax system includes several features that appear designed to prevent discrimination against or undue burdens upon interstate commerce. First, the Act applies a safe harbor to those who transact only limited business in South Dakota. Second, the Act ensures that no obligation to remit the sales tax may be applied retroactively. . . . Third, South Dakota is one of more than 20 States that have adopted the Streamlined Sales and Use Tax Agreement. This system standardizes taxes to reduce administrative and compliance costs: It requires a single, state level tax administration, uniform definitions of products and services, simplified tax rate structures, and other uniform rules. It also provides sellers access to sales tax administration software paid for by the State. Sellers who choose to use such software are immune from audit liability. Any remaining claims regarding the application of the Commerce Clause in the absence of *Quill* and *Bellas Hess* may be addressed in the first instance on remand.

The judgment of the Supreme Court of South Dakota is vacated, and the case is remanded for further proceedings not inconsistent with this opinion.

. . .

■ JUSTICE THOMAS, concurring.

Justice Byron White joined the majority opinion in *National Bellas Hess*. . . . Twenty-five years later, we had the opportunity to overrule *Bellas Hess* in *Quill*. . . . Only Justice White voted to do so. I should have joined his opinion. Today, I am slightly further removed from *Quill* than Justice White was from *Bellas Hess*. And like Justice White, a quarter century of experience has convinced me that *Bellas Hess* and *Quill* "can no longer be rationally justified." . . . The same is true for this Court's entire negative Commerce Clause jurisprudence. Although I adhered to that jurisprudence in *Quill*, it is never too late to "surrende[r] former views to a better considered position." . . .

■ JUSTICE GORSUCH, concurring.

Our dormant commerce cases usually prevent States from discriminating between in-state and out-of-state firms. *National Bellas Hess* and *Quill* do just the opposite. . . . The Court is right to correct the mistake and I am pleased to join its opinion.

My agreement with the Court's discussion of the history of our dormant commerce clause jurisprudence, however, should not be mistaken for agreement with all aspects of the doctrine. The Commerce Clause is found in Article I and authorizes *Congress* to regulate interstate commerce. Meanwhile our dormant commerce cases suggest Article III *courts* may invalidate state laws that offend no congressional statute. Whether and how much of this can be squared with the text of the Commerce Clause, justified by *stare decisis*, or defended as misbranded products of federalism or antidiscrimination imperatives flowing from Article IV's Privileges and Immunities Clause are questions for another day. . . .

■ CHIEF JUSTICE ROBERTS, with whom JUSTICE BREYER, JUSTICE SOTOMAYOR and JUSTICE KAGAN join, dissenting.

In *National Bellas Hess* . . . this Court held that, under the dormant Commerce Clause, a State could not require retailers without a physical presence in that State to collect taxes on the sale of goods to its residents. A quarter century later, in *Quill* . . . this Court was invited to overrule *Bellas Hess* but declined to do so. Another quarter century has passed, and another State now asks us to abandon the physical-presence rule. I would decline that invitation as well.

I agree that *Bellas Hess* was wrongly decided, for many of the reasons given by the Court. The Court argues in favor of overturning that decision because the "Internet's prevalence and power have changed the dynamics of the national economy." . . . But that is the very reason I oppose discarding the physical-presence rule. E-commerce has grown into a significant and vibrant part of our national economy against the backdrop of established rules, including the physical-presence rule. Any alteration to those rules with the potential to disrupt the development of such a critical segment of the economy should be undertaken by Congress. The Court should not act on this important question of current economic policy, solely to expiate a mistake it made over 50 years ago.

I

This Court "does not overturn its precedents lightly." . . . Departing from the doctrine of *stare decisis* is an "exceptional action" demanding "special justification." . . . The bar is even higher in fields in which Congress "exercises primary authority" and can, if it wishes, override this Court's decisions with contrary legislation. *Bay Mills*, 572 U. S., at ___ (slip op., at 16) (tribal sovereign immunity); see, *e.g.,* Kimble v. Marvel Entertainment, LLC, 576 U. S. ___, ___ (2015) (slip op., at 8) (statutory interpretation); Halliburton Co. v. Erica P. John Fund, Inc., 573 U. S. ___, ___ (2014) (slip op., at 12) (judicially created doctrine implementing a judicially created cause of action). In such cases, we have said that "the burden borne by the party advocating the abandonment of an established precedent" is "greater" than usual. . . . Patterson v. McLean Credit Union, 491 U. S. 164, 172 (1989). That is so "even where the error is a matter of serious concern, provided correction can be had by legislation." . . .

We have applied this heightened form of *stare decisis* in the dormant Commerce Clause context. Under our dormant Commerce Clause precedents, when Congress has not yet legislated on a matter of interstate commerce, it is the province of "the courts to formulate the rules." Southern Pacific Co. v. Arizona ex rel. Sullivan, 325 U. S. 761, 770 (1945). But because Congress "has plenary power to regulate commerce among the States," . . . it may at any time replace such judicial rules with legislation of its own, see Prudential Ins. Co. v. Benjamin, 328 U. S. 408, 424–425 (1946).

In *Quill*, this Court emphasized that the decision to hew to the physical-presence rule on *stare decisis* grounds was "made easier by the fact that the underlying issue is not only one that Congress may be better qualified to resolve, but also one that Congress has the ultimate power to resolve." . . .

II

This is neither the first, nor the second, but the third time this Court has been asked whether a State may obligate sellers with no physical presence within its borders to collect tax on sales to residents. Whatever salience the adage "third time's a charm" has in daily life, it is a poor guide to Supreme Court decisionmaking. If *stare decisis* applied with special force in *Quill*, it should be an even greater impediment to overruling precedent now, particularly since this Court in *Quill* "tossed [the ball] into Congress's court, for acceptance or not as that branch elects." . . .

Congress has in fact been considering whether to alter the rule established in *Bellas Hess* for some time. . . . Nothing in today's decision precludes Congress from continuing to seek a legislative solution. But by suddenly changing the ground rules, the Court may have waylaid Congress's consideration of the issue. . . .

The Court proceeds with an inexplicable sense of urgency. It asserts that the passage of time is only increasing the need to take the extraordinary step of overruling *Bellas Hess* and *Quill*: "Each year, the physical presence rule becomes further removed from economic reality and results in significant revenue losses to the States." . . . But evidence . . . indicates that the pendulum is swinging in the opposite direction, and has been for some time. States and local governments are already able to collect approximately 80 percent of the tax revenue that would be available if there were no physical-presence rule. Some companies, including the online behemoth Amazon, now voluntarily collect and remit sales tax in every State that assesses one—even those in which they have no physical presence. To the extent the physical-presence rule is harming States, the harm is apparently receding with time.

. . .

The Court [also] breezily disregards the costs that its decision will impose on retailers. . . .

The burden will fall disproportionately on small businesses. One vitalizing effect of the Internet has been connecting small, even "micro" businesses to potential buyers across the Nation. . . . The Court's decision today will surely have the effect of dampening opportunities for commerce in a broad range of new markets.

A good reason to leave these matters to Congress is that legislators may more directly consider the competing interests at stake. Unlike this Court,

Congress has the flexibility to address these questions in a wide variety of ways. As we have said in other dormant Commerce Clause cases, Congress "has the capacity to investigate and analyze facts beyond anything the Judiciary could match." . . .

    . . .

I respectfully dissent.

2. DISCRIMINATION AGAINST INTERSTATE COMMERCE

Page 257. Insert a footnote (using a * mark) at the end of the first sentence in the Note:

*   This is true even where the regulation of alcohol sales is involved and a State invokes the Twenty-First Amendment. In Tennessee Wine and Spirits Retailers Assn. v. Thomas, 588 U.S. ___, 139 S.Ct. 2449 (2019), the Court struck down a multi-year durational-residency requirement Tennessee imposed on persons and companies wishing to operate retail liquor stores in the state. The Court held that such a law violated the Commerce Clause and was not saved by the Twenty-First Amendment, which the Court held to give states only those powers they enjoyed prior to the Eighteenth Amendment and Prohibition. The Court noted that it had invalidated many state liquor regulations before the Eighteenth Amendment's ratification, and that by the late 19th century it had concluded that the Commerce Clause prevented states from discriminating against citizens and products of other states.

6. PREEMPTION OF STATE LEGISLATION BY FEDERAL LEGISLATION—THE IMPACT OF THE SUPREMACY CLAUSE

Page 321. Insert the following paragraphs directly before the principal-case treatment of Arizona v. United States:

Almost two decades later, the Court continues as a general matter to adhere to the same preemption-doctrine framework, albeit with some of the Justices interested in particular refinements. Virginia Uranium, Inc. v. Warren, 587 U.S. ___, 139 S.Ct. 1894 (2019), is a good example. Petitioner, who sought to mine raw uranium ore from a site near Coles Hill, Virginia, went to court to argue that Virginia's law completely prohibiting uranium mining in the State is preempted by the Atomic Energy Act (AEA), which, petitioner argued, gives the Nuclear Regulatory Commission (NRC) exclusive power to regulate uranium mining based on nuclear safety concerns. The Court rejected this argument, 6–3, but the case failed to generate a majority opinion. All six Justices in the majority rejected express preemption based on the text and structure of the AEA. As Justice Gorsuch, writing for himself and Justices Thomas and Kavanagh (and making arguments agreed to by concurring Justices Ginsburg, Sotomayor and Kagan) explained, the AEA contains no provision expressly preempting state law. And perhaps more importantly, the AEA grants the NRC extensive and sometimes exclusive authority to regulate nearly every aspect of the nuclear fuel life cycle *except* mining, expressly stating that the NRC's regulatory powers arise only "after [uranium's] removal from its place of deposit in nature," 42 U. S. C. § 2092. Indeed, another part of the AEA confirms this reading by providing that if the federal government wants to control uranium mining on private land, it must purchase or seize the land by eminent domain and make it federal land, § 2096, indicating that state authority remains untouched.

Moving from express to field preemption, Justice Gorsuch's opinion took on petitioner's reliance upon Pacific Gas & Elec. Co. v. State Energy Resources Conservation and Development Comm'n, 461 U. S. 190, where the Court rejected a preemption challenge to a California law prohibiting the construction of new nuclear power plants, but, said petitioner, only because California's law—unlike the Virginia law in question in the present case—was motivated by concerns other than safety, which is the exclusive domain of the NRC. Justice Gorsuch conceded that the Court reached its result in *Pacific Gas & Electric* only after observing that the California law was enacted out of concern with economic development and not for the purpose of addressing radiation safety hazards. But, Justice Gorsuch pointed out, *Pacific Gas* concerned a state moratorium on construction of new nuclear power plants, and nuclear plant construction has always been an area exclusively regulated by the federal government. It is one thing, he said, to inquire exactingly into state legislative purposes when state law comes close to trenching on core federal powers; it is another thing altogether to insist on the same exacting scrutiny for state laws far removed from core NRC powers. More generally, Justice Gorsuch observed, later cases confirm the propriety of restraint in looking at state legislative intent to determine preemption. See, *e.g.*, Silkwood v. Kerr-McGee Corp., 464 U.S. 238; English v. General Elec. Co., 496 U.S. 72. His reading of relevant case law led him to conclude that the Court generally has treated field preemption as dependent on *what* the State did, not *why* it did it. Justice Gorsuch went on to highlight the dangers of an approach that looks to state legislative intent to determine preemption:

"Our field preemption cases proceed as they do, moreover, for good reasons. Consider just some of the costs to cooperative federalism and individual liberty we would invite by inquiring into state legislative purpose too precipitately. The natural tendency of regular federal judicial inquiries into state legislative intentions would be to stifle deliberation in state legislatures and encourage resort to secrecy and subterfuge. That would inhibit the sort of open and vigorous legislative debate that our Constitution recognizes as vital to testing ideas and improving laws. In Virginia Uranium's vision as well, federal courts would have to allow depositions of state legislators and governors, and perhaps hale them into court for cross-examination at trial about their subjective motivations in passing a mining statute. And at the end of it all, federal courts would risk subjecting similarly situated persons to radically different legal rules as judges uphold and strike down materially identical state regulations based only on the happenstance of judicial assessments of the 'true' intentions lurking behind them. In light of all this, it can surprise no one that our precedents have long warned against undertaking potential misadventures into hidden state legislative intentions without a clear statutory mandate for the project. . . .

        . . .

"Beyond these concerns . . . lie well-known conceptual and practical ones this Court has also advised against inviting unnecessarily. State legislatures are composed of individuals who often pursue legislation for multiple and unexpressed purposes, so what legal rules should determine when and how to ascribe a particular intention to a particular legislator? What if an impermissible intention existed but wasn't necessary to her vote? And what percentage of the legislature must harbor the impermissible intention before we can impute it to the collective institution? Putting all that aside, how are courts supposed to conduct a reasonable inquiry into these questions when recorded state legislative history materials are often not as readily available or complete as their federal counterparts? And if trying to peer inside legislators' skulls is too fraught an enterprise, shouldn't we limit ourselves to trying to glean legislative purposes from the statutory text where we began? Even *Pacific Gas* warned future courts against too hastily accepting a litigant's invitation to 'become embroiled in attempting to ascertain' state legislative 'motive[s],' acknowledging that such inquiries 'often' prove 'unsatisfactory venture[s]. What motivates one legislator to vote for a statute is not necessarily what motivates scores of others to enact it.' . . . We think these warnings wise, and we heed them today."

Moving beyond express and field preemption, Justice Gorsuch's opinion had this to say:

". . . . [Petitioner suggests] Virginia's mining law stands as an impermissible 'obstacle to the accomplishment and execution of the full purposes and objectives of Congress.' . . . On [petitioner's] account, Congress sought to capture the benefits of developing nuclear power while mitigating its safety and environmental costs. And, the company contends, Virginia's moratorium disrupts the delicate 'balance' Congress sought to achieve between these benefits and costs. Maybe the text of the AEA doesn't touch on mining in so many words, but its authority to regulate later stages of the nuclear fuel life cycle would be effectively undermined if mining laws like Virginia's were allowed.

"A sound preemption analysis cannot be as simplistic as that. No more than in field preemption can the Supremacy Clause be deployed here to elevate abstract and unenacted legislative desires above state law; only federal laws 'made in pursuance of' the Constitution, through its prescribed processes of bicameralism and presentment, are entitled to preemptive effect. Pre-emptive purpose, whether express or implied, must therefore be 'sought in the text and structure of the statute at issue.' . . .

"Sound and well-documented reasons underlie this rule too. Efforts to ascribe unenacted purposes and objectives to a federal statute face many of the same challenges as inquiries into state legislative intent. Trying to discern what motivates legislators individually and collectively invites speculation and risks overlooking the reality that individual Members of Congress often pursue multiple and competing purposes, many of which are compromised to secure a law's passage and few of which are fully realized in the final product. Hefty inferences may be required, as well, when trying to estimate whether Congress would have wanted to prohibit States from pursuing regulations that may happen to touch, in various degrees and different ways, on unenacted federal purposes and objectives. Worse yet, in piling inference upon inference about hidden legislative wishes we risk displacing the legislative compromises actually reflected in the statutory text—compromises that sometimes may seem irrational to an outsider coming to the statute cold, but whose genius lies in having won the broad support our Constitution demands of any new law. In disregarding these legislative compromises, we may only wind up displacing perfectly legitimate state laws on the strength of 'purposes' that only we can see, that may seem perfectly logical to us, but that lack the democratic provenance the Constitution demands before a federal law may be declared supreme. . . .

"So it may be that Congress meant the AEA to promote the development of nuclear power. It may be that Congress meant the AEA to balance that goal against various safety concerns. But it also may be that Members of Congress held many other disparate or conflicting goals in mind when they voted to enact and amend the AEA, and many different views on exactly how to manage the competing costs and benefits. If polled, they might have reached very different assessments, as well, about the consistency of Virginia's law with their own purposes and objectives. The only thing a court can be sure of is what can be found in the law itself. And every indication in the law before us suggests that Congress elected to leave mining regulation on private land to the States and grant the NRC regulatory authority only *after* uranium is removed from the earth. That compromise may not be the only permissible or even the most rationally attractive one, but it is surely both permissible and rational to think that Congress might have chosen to regulate the more novel aspects of nuclear power while leaving to States their traditional function of regulating mining activities on private lands within their boundaries."

Justice Ginsburg, joined by Justices Sotomayor and Kagan, agreed with Justice Gorsuch that Virginia's flat ban on uranium mining is not preempted, but felt that his discussion of the perils of legislative-motive inquiry went well beyond what was needed to say to decide this case. Moreover, because petitioner's obstacle-preemption arguments fail under existing doctrine, she saw little reason to question, as Justice Gorsuch might be interpreted as doing, whether that doctrine should be retained.

Chief Justice Roberts, joined by Justices Breyer and Alito, dissented, accusing the majority of answering different questions than those on which review had been granted, and arguing that a state-legislative-purpose analysis is permissible, and indeed required under the *Pacific Gas & Electric* case, and that it doomed Virginia's mining ban.

CHAPTER 7

SEPARATION OF POWERS

1. THE PRESIDENT'S POWER TO DETERMINE NATIONAL POLICY

B. INTERNATIONAL RELATIONS

Page 348. Add after Zivotofsky v. Kerry:

Trump v. Hawaii
585 U.S. ___, 138 S.Ct. 2392, 201 L.Ed.2d 775 (2018).

[The report of this case appears infra, at p. 233.]

C. WAR AND NATIONAL DEFENSE

Page 361. Add after Boumediene v. Bush:

In Department of Homeland Security v. Thuraissigiam, 591 U.S. ___, 140 S.Ct. 1959 (2020), the Court considered whether a provision of the Illegal Immigration Reform and Immigrant Responsibility Act (IIRIRA), which provides for the expedited removal of certain "applicants" seeking admission into the United States, whether at a designated port of entry or elsewhere, 8 U. S. C. § 1225(a)(1), violated the Suspension Clause. Under the IIRIRA, an applicant may avoid expedited removal by making a showing to an asylum officer of a "credible fear of persecution," which in turn is defined as "a significant possibility . . . that the alien could establish eligibility for asylum." § 1225(b)(1)(B)(v). If an applicant makes such a demonstration, the applicant is offered "full consideration" of the asylum claim in a standard removal hearing. If an asylum officer concludes an applicant has not made a credible-fear claim, that determination is reviewed by a supervisor, whose decision can then be appealed by the applicant to an immigration judge. But under IIRIRA federal courts may not review determinations that applicants lack a credible fear of persecution on a petition for a writ of habeas corpus. Respondent was a Sri Lankan national who was detained for expedited removal 25 yards after crossing the southern border of the United States without an entry document. After an asylum officer rejected his credible-fear claim—and a supervising officer agreed and an Immigration Judge affirmed—he filed a federal habeas petition. The Ninth Circuit Court of Appeals reversed the District Court's dismissal of the petition, holding that, as applied here, § 1252(e)(2) violates the Suspension Clause (and also the Due Process Clause). The Supreme Court reversed, concluding that § 1252(e)(2) does not violate the Suspension Clause because Respondent did not seek release from custody, but an additional opportunity to obtain asylum. Accordingly, his claims were not within the scope of the writ as it existed when the Constitution was adopted, and therefore Congress's decision to bar federal courts from considering these claims did not run afoul of evils the Suspension Clause sought to prevent. As the Court put it: "Respondent's Suspension Clause argument fails because it would extend the writ of habeas corpus far beyond its scope 'when the Constitution was drafted and ratified.' Boumediene v. Bush, 553 U. S. 723, 746 (2008). Indeed, respondent's use of the writ would have been unrecognizable at that time. Habeas has traditionally been a means to secure release from unlawful detention, but respondent invokes the writ to achieve an entirely different end, namely, to obtain additional administrative review of his asylum claim and ultimately to obtain authorization to stay in this country." Justice Alito wrote the opinion for the Court, joined by Chief Justice Roberts and Justices Thomas, Gorsuch and Kavanaugh. Justice Thomas wrote a concurring opinion. Justice Breyer wrote an opinion (joined by Justice Ginsburg) concurring in the judgment. Justice Sotomayor filed a dissenting opinion, in which Justice Kagan joined.

D. THE LINE ITEM VETO

Page 362. Insert the following paragraph before the paragraph beginning with the words "The non-delegation idea is said. . . ." in the Note on *Delegation of Legislative Power to the Executive*:

In one noteworthy recent case three Justices (and maybe more) would have invalidated a congressional enactment on non-delegation grounds. The federal Sex Offender Registration and Notification Act (SORNA) seeks to create a relatively uniform and comprehensive registration system for individuals convicted of various sexual offenses. But for sex offenders convicted prior to SORNA's enactment, the statute gives the Attorney General "the authority" to "specify the applicability" of SORNA's registration requirements and "to prescribe rules for [their] registration." 34 U.S.C. § 20913(d). Under that delegated authority, the Attorney General issued a rule providing that SORNA's registration requirements apply in full to pre-Act offenders. When the rule was challenged, in Gundy v. United States, 588 U.S. ___, 139 S.Ct. 2116 (2019), on the ground that Congress unconstitutionally delegated legislative power when it authorized the Attorney General to "specify the applicability" of SORNA's registration requirements to pre-Act offenders, a 4-Justice plurality (Justices Kagan, Ginsburg, Breyer and Sotomayor) construed the overall structure and language of SORNA implicitly to direct the Attorney General to register all pre-Act offenders as soon as practicable, and concluded that this implicit directive created a sufficiently intelligible standard to defeat a non-delegation argument. Justice Alito concurred in the judgment on the ground that SORNA is permissible under the approach the Court has taken since the New Deal, which permits Congress to authorize executive authority that is limited only by "extraordinarily capacious standards." But he added: "If a majority of this Court were willing to reconsider the approach we have taken for the past 84 years, I would support that effort." Three dissenting Justices (Chief Justice Roberts and Justices Thomas and Gorsuch) would have done just that. Justice Kavanaugh did not participate in the case.

2. CONGRESSIONAL INTERFERENCE WITH PRESIDENTIAL PREROGATIVES

B. APPOINTMENT, DISCHARGE, AND SUPERVISION OF "OFFICERS OF THE UNITED STATES"

Page 387. Add after Free Enterprise Fund v. Public Company Accounting Oversight Board:

Seila Law, LLC v. Consumer Financial Protection Bureau

591 U.S. ___, 140 S.Ct. 2183 (2020).

■ CHIEF JUSTICE ROBERTS delivered the opinion of the Court with respect to Parts I, II, and III.

In the wake of the 2008 financial crisis, Congress established the Consumer Financial Protection Bureau (CFPB), an independent regulatory agency tasked with ensuring that consumer debt products are safe and transparent. In organizing the CFPB, Congress deviated from the structure of nearly every other independent administrative agency in our history. Instead of placing the agency under the leadership of a board with multiple members, Congress provided that the CFPB would be led by a single Director, who serves for a longer term than the President and cannot be removed by the President except for inefficiency, neglect, or malfeasance. The CFPB Director has no boss, peers, or voters to report to. Yet the Director wields vast rulemaking, enforcement, and adjudicatory authority over a significant portion of the U. S. economy. The question before us is whether this arrangement violates the Constitution's separation of powers.

Under our Constitution, the "executive Power"—all of it—is "vested in a President," who must "take Care that the Laws be faithfully executed." Art. II, § 1, cl. 1; id., § 3. Because no single person could fulfill that responsibility alone, the Framers expected that the President would rely on subordinate officers for assistance. Ten years ago, in Free Enterprise Fund v. Public Company Accounting Oversight Bd., 561 U. S. 477 (2010), we reiterated that, "as a general matter," the Constitution gives the President "the authority to remove those who assist him in carrying out his duties," . . . . "Without such power, the President could not be held fully accountable for discharging his own responsibilities; the buck would stop somewhere else." . . .

The President's power to remove—and thus supervise—those who wield executive power on his behalf follows from the text of Article II, was settled by the First Congress, and was confirmed in the landmark decision Myers v. United States, 272 U. S. 52 (1926). Our precedents have recognized only two exceptions to the President's unrestricted removal power. In Humphrey's Executor v. United States, 295 U. S. 602 (1935), we held that Congress could create expert agencies led by a group of principal officers removable by the President only for good cause. And in United States v. Perkins, 116 U. S. 483 (1886), and Morrison v. Olson, 487 U. S. 654 (1988), we held that Congress could provide tenure protections to certain inferior officers with narrowly defined duties.

We are now asked to extend these precedents to a new configuration: an independent agency that wields significant executive power and is run by a single individual who cannot be removed by the President unless certain statutory criteria are met. We decline to take that step. While we need not and do not revisit our prior decisions allowing certain limitations on the President's removal power, there are compelling reasons not to extend those precedents to the novel context of an independent agency led by a single Director. Such an agency lacks a foundation in historical practice and clashes with constitutional structure by concentrating power in a unilateral actor insulated from Presidential control.

We therefore hold that the structure of the CFPB violates the separation of powers. We go on to hold that the CFPB Director's removal protection is severable from the other statutory provisions bearing on the CFPB's authority. The agency may therefore continue to operate, but its Director, in light of our decision, must be removable by the President at will.

I

A

In the summer of 2007, then-Professor Elizabeth Warren called for the creation of a new, independent federal agency focused on regulating consumer financial products. Warren, Unsafe at Any Rate, Democracy (Summer 2007). Professor Warren believed the financial products marketed to ordinary American households—credit cards, student loans, mortgages, and the like—had grown increasingly unsafe due to a "regulatory jumble" that paid too much attention to banks and too little to consumers. . . . To remedy the lack of "coherent, consumer-oriented" financial regulation, she proposed "concentrat[ing] the review of financial products in a single location"—an independent agency modeled after the multimember Consumer Product Safety Commission. . . .

That proposal soon met its moment. Within months of Professor Warren's writing, the subprime mortgage market collapsed, precipitating a financial crisis that wiped out over $10 trillion in American household wealth and cost millions of Americans their jobs, their retirements, and their homes. In the aftermath, the Obama administration embraced Professor Warren's recommendation. Through the Treasury Department, the administration encouraged Congress to establish an agency with a mandate to ensure that "consumer protection regulations" in the financial sector "are written fairly and enforced vigorously." . . . Like Professor Warren, the administration envisioned a traditional independent agency, run by a multimember board with a "diverse set of viewpoints and experiences." . . .

In 2010, Congress acted on these proposals and created the Consumer Financial Protection Bureau (CFPB) as an independent financial regulator within the Federal Reserve System. Dodd-Frank Wall Street Reform and Consumer Protection Act (Dodd-Frank), 124 Stat. 1376. Congress tasked the CFPB with "implement[ing]" and "enforc[ing]" a large body of financial consumer protection laws to "ensur[e] that all consumers have access to markets for consumer financial products and services and that markets for consumer financial products and services are fair, transparent, and competitive." 12 U. S. C. § 5511(a). Congress transferred the administration of 18 existing federal statutes to the CFPB, including the Fair Credit Reporting Act, the Fair Debt Collection Practices Act, and the Truth in Lending Act. See §§ 5512(a), 5481(12), (14). In addition, Congress enacted a new prohibition on "any unfair, deceptive, or abusive act or practice" by certain participants in the consumer-finance sector.

§ 5536(a)(1)(B). Congress authorized the CFPB to implement that broad standard (and the 18 pre-existing statutes placed under the agency's purview) through binding regulations. §§ 5531(a)–(b), 5581(a)(1)(A), (b).

Congress also vested the CFPB with potent enforcement powers. The agency has the authority to conduct investigations, issue subpoenas and civil investigative demands, initiate administrative adjudications, and prosecute civil actions in federal court. §§ 5562, 5564(a), (f). To remedy violations of federal consumer financial law, the CFPB may seek restitution, disgorgement, and injunctive relief, as well as civil penalties of up to $1,000,000 (inflation adjusted) for each day that a violation occurs. §§ 5565(a), (c)(2); 12 CFR § 1083.1(a), Table (2019). Since its inception, the CFPB has obtained over $11 billion in relief for over 25 million consumers, including a $1 billion penalty against a single bank in 2018. . . .

The CFPB's rulemaking and enforcement powers are coupled with extensive adjudicatory authority. The agency may conduct administrative proceedings to "ensure or enforce compliance with" the statutes and regulations it administers. 12 U. S. C. § 5563(a). When the CFPB acts as an adjudicator, it has "jurisdiction to grant any appropriate legal or equitable relief." § 5565(a)(1). The "hearing officer" who presides over the proceedings may issue subpoenas, order depositions, and resolve any motions filed by the parties. 12 CFR § 1081.104(b). At the close of the proceedings, the hearing officer issues a "recommended decision," and the CFPB Director considers that recommendation and "issue[s] a final decision and order." §§ 1081.400(d), 1081.402(b); see also § 1081.405.

Congress's design for the CFPB differed from the proposals of Professor Warren and the Obama administration in one critical respect. Rather than create a traditional independent agency headed by a multimember board or commission, Congress elected to place the CFPB under the leadership of a single Director. 12 U. S. C. § 5491(b)(1). The CFPB Director is appointed by the President with the advice and consent of the Senate. § 5491(b)(2). The Director serves for a term of five years, during which the President may remove the Director from office only for "inefficiency, neglect of duty, or malfeasance in office." §§ 5491(c)(1), (3).

Unlike most other agencies, the CFPB does not rely on the annual appropriations process for funding. Instead, the CFPB receives funding directly from the Federal Reserve, which is itself funded outside the appropriations process through bank assessments. Each year, the CFPB requests an amount that the Director deems "reasonably necessary to carry out" the agency's duties, and the Federal Reserve grants that request so long as it does not exceed 12% of the total operating expenses of the Federal Reserve (inflation adjusted). §§ 5497(a)(1), (2)(A)(iii), 2(B). In recent years, the CFPB's annual budget has exceeded half a billion dollars. . . .

B

Seila Law LLC is a California-based law firm that provides debt-related legal services to clients. In 2017, the CFPB issued a civil investigative demand to Seila Law to determine whether the firm had "engag[ed] in unlawful acts or practices in the advertising, marketing, or sale of debt relief services." . . . The demand (essentially a subpoena) directed Seila Law to produce information and documents related to its business practices.

Seila Law asked the CFPB to set aside the demand, objecting that the agency's leadership by a single Director removable only for cause violated the separation of powers. The CFPB declined to address that claim and directed Seila Law to comply with the demand.

When Seila Law refused, the CFPB filed a petition to enforce the demand in the District Court. . . . In response, Seila Law renewed its defense that the demand was invalid and must be set aside because the CFPB's structure violated the Constitution. The District Court disagreed and ordered Seila Law to comply with the demand (with one modification not relevant here).

The Court of Appeals affirmed. . . . The Court observed that the "arguments for and against" the constitutionality of the CFPB's structure had already been "thoroughly canvassed" in majority, concurring, and dissenting opinions by the en banc Court of Appeals for the District of Columbia Circuit in PHH Corp. v. CFPB, 881 F. 3d 75 (2018), which had rejected a challenge similar to the one presented here. . . . The Court saw "no need to re-plow the same ground." . . . Instead, it provided a brief explanation for why it agreed with the PHH Court's core holding. The Court took as its starting point Humphrey's Executor, which had approved for-cause removal protection for the Commissioners of the Federal Trade Commission (FTC). In applying that precedent, the Court recognized that the CFPB wields "substantially more executive power than the FTC did back in 1935" and that the CFPB's leadership by a single Director (as opposed to a multimember commission) presented a "structural difference" that some jurists had found "dispositive." . . . But the Court felt bound to disregard those differences in light of our decision in Morrison, which permitted a single individual (an independent counsel) to exercise a core executive power (prosecuting criminal offenses) despite being insulated from removal except for cause. Because the Court found Humphrey's Executor and Morrison "controlling," it affirmed the District Court's order requiring compliance with the demand. . . .

We granted certiorari to address the constitutionality of the CFPB's structure. . . . We also requested argument on an additional question: whether, if the CFPB's structure violates the separation of powers, the CFPB Director's removal protection can be severed from the rest of the Dodd-Frank Act. Because the Government agrees with petitioner on the merits of the constitutional question, we appointed Paul Clement to defend the judgment below as amicus curiae. He has ably discharged his responsibilities.

II

We first consider three threshold arguments raised by the appointed amicus for why we may not or should not reach the merits. Each is unavailing. . . .

. . .

[In the third threshold argument], amicus contends that we should dismiss the case because the parties agree on the merits of the constitutional question and the case therefore lacks "adverseness." . . . That contention, however, is foreclosed by United States v. Windsor, 570 U. S. 744 (2013). There, we explained that a lower court order that presents real-world consequences for the Government and its adversary suffices to support Article III jurisdiction—even if "the Executive may welcome" an adverse order that "is accompanied by the constitutional ruling it wants." . . . Here, petitioner and the Government disagree about whether petitioner must comply with the civil investigative demand. The lower courts sided with the Government, and the Government has not volunteered to relinquish that victory and withdraw the demand. To the contrary, while the Government agrees that the agency is unconstitutionally structured, it believes it may nevertheless enforce the demand on remand. . . . Accordingly, our "decision will have real meaning" for the parties. INS v. Chadha, 462 U. S. 919, 939 (1983). And, as in *Windsor*, any prudential concerns with deciding an important legal question in this posture can be addressed by "the practice of entertaining arguments made by an *amicus* when the Solicitor General confesses error with respect to a judgment below," which we have done. . . .

We therefore turn to the merits of petitioner's constitutional challenge.

III

We hold that the CFPB's leadership by a single individual removable only for inefficiency, neglect, or malfeasance violates the separation of powers.

A

Article II provides that "[t]he executive Power shall be vested in a President," who must "take Care that the Laws be faithfully executed." Art. II, § 1, cl. 1; id., § 3. The entire "executive Power" belongs to the President alone. But because it would be "impossib[le]" for "one man" to "perform all the great business of the State," the Constitution assumes that lesser executive officers will "assist the supreme Magistrate in discharging the duties of his trust." 30 Writings of George Washington 334 (J. Fitzpatrick ed. 1939).

These lesser officers must remain accountable to the President, whose authority they wield. As Madison explained, "[I]f any power whatsoever is in its nature Executive, it is the power of appointing, overseeing, and controlling those who execute the laws." 1 Annals of Cong. 463 (1789). That power, in turn, generally includes the ability to remove executive officials, for it is "only the authority that can remove" such officials that they "must fear and, in the performance of [their] functions, obey." . . .

The President's removal power has long been confirmed by history and precedent. It "was discussed extensively in Congress when the first executive departments were created" in 1789. . . . "The view that 'prevailed, as most consonant to the text of the Constitution' and 'to the requisite responsibility and harmony in the Executive Department,' was that the executive power included a power to oversee executive officers through removal." . . . The First Congress's recognition of the President's removal power in 1789 "provides contemporaneous and weighty evidence of the Constitution's meaning,". . . , and has long been the "settled and well understood construction of the Constitution," . . . .

The Court recognized the President's prerogative to remove executive officials in Myers v. United States, 272 U.S. 52. Chief Justice Taft, writing for the Court, conducted an exhaustive examination of the First Congress's determination in 1789, the views of the Framers and their contemporaries, historical practice, and our precedents up until that point. He concluded that Article II "grants to the President" the "general administrative control of those executing the laws, including the power of appointment *and removal* of executive officers." Id., at 163–164 (emphasis added). Just as the President's "selection of administrative officers is essential to the execution of the laws by him, so must be his power of removing those for whom he cannot continue to be responsible." . . . "[T]o hold otherwise," the Court reasoned, "would make it impossible for the President . . . to take care that the laws be faithfully executed." . . . .

We recently reiterated the President's general removal power in *Free Enterprise Fund*. "Since 1789," we recapped, "the Constitution has been understood to empower the President to keep these officers accountable—by removing them from office, if necessary." . . . Although we had previously sustained congressional limits on that power in certain circumstances, we declined to extend those limits to "a new situation not yet encountered by the Court"—an official insulated by two layers of for-cause removal protection. . . . In the face of that novel impediment to the President's oversight of the Executive Branch, we adhered to the general rule that the President possesses "the authority to remove those who assist him in carrying out his duties." . . .

Free Enterprise Fund left in place two exceptions to the President's unrestricted removal power. First, in *Humphrey's Executor*, decided less than a decade after *Myers*, the Court upheld a statute that protected the Commissioners of the FTC from removal except for "inefficiency, neglect of duty, or malfeasance in office." . . . In reaching that conclusion, the Court stressed that Congress's ability to impose such removal restrictions "will depend upon the character of the office." . . .

Because the Court limited its holding "to officers of the kind here under consideration,". . . , the contours of the *Humphrey's Executor* exception depend upon the characteristics of the agency before the Court. Rightly or wrongly, the Court viewed the FTC (as it existed in 1935) as exercising "no part of the executive power." . . . Instead, it was "an administrative body" that performed "specified duties as a legislative or as a judicial aid." . . . It acted "as a legislative agency" in "making investigations and reports" to Congress and "as an agency of the judiciary" in making recommendations to courts as a master in chancery. . . . "To the extent that [the FTC] exercise[d] any executive function[,] as distinguished from executive power in the constitutional sense," it did so only in the discharge of its "quasi-legislative or quasi-judicial powers." . . .

The Court identified several organizational features that helped explain its characterization of the FTC as non-executive. Composed of five members—no more than three from the same political party—the Board was designed to be "non-partisan" and to "act with entire impartiality." . . . The FTC's duties were "neither political nor executive," but instead called for "the trained judgment of a body of experts" "informed by experience." . . . And the Commissioners' staggered, seven-year terms enabled the agency to accumulate technical expertise and avoid a "complete change" in leadership "at any one time." . . .

In short, *Humphrey's Executor* permitted Congress to give for-cause removal protections to a multimember body of experts, balanced along partisan lines, that performed legislative and judicial functions and was said not to exercise any executive power. Consistent with that understanding, the Court later applied "[t]he philosophy of *Humphrey's Executor*" to uphold for-cause removal protections for the members of the War Claims Commission—a three-member "adjudicatory body" tasked with resolving claims for compensation arising from World War II. Wiener v. United States, 357 U. S. 349, 356 (1958).

While recognizing an exception for multimember bodies with "quasi-judicial" or "quasi-legislative" functions, *Humphrey's Executor* reaffirmed the core holding of *Myers* that the President has "unrestrictable power . . . to remove purely executive officers." . . . The Court acknowledged that between purely executive officers on the one hand, and officers that closely resembled the FTC

Commissioners on the other, there existed "a field of doubt" that the Court left "for future consideration.". . .

We have recognized a second exception for inferior officers in two cases, United States v. Perkins and Morrison v. Olson.[3] In *Perkins*, we upheld tenure protections for a naval cadet-engineer. . . . And, in *Morrison*, we upheld a provision granting good-cause tenure protection to an independent counsel appointed to investigate and prosecute particular alleged crimes by high-ranking Government officials. . . . Backing away from the reliance in *Humphrey's Executor* on the concepts of "quasi-legislative" and "quasi-judicial" power, we viewed the ultimate question as whether a removal restriction is of "such a nature that [it] impede[s] the President's ability to perform his constitutional duty." . . . Although the independent counsel was a single person and performed "law enforcement functions that typically have been undertaken by officials within the Executive Branch," we concluded that the removal protections did not unduly interfere with the functioning of the Executive Branch because "the independent counsel [was] an inferior officer under the Appointments Clause, with limited jurisdiction and tenure and lacking policymaking or significant administrative authority." . . .

These two exceptions—one for multimember expert agencies that do not wield substantial executive power, and one for inferior officers with limited duties and no policymaking or administrative authority—"represent what up to now have been the outermost constitutional limits of permissible congressional restrictions on the President's removal power." *PHH*, 881 F. 3d, at 196 (Kavanaugh, J., dissenting) (internal quotation marks omitted).

B

Neither *Humphrey's Executor* nor *Morrison* resolves whether the CFPB Director's insulation from removal is constitutional. Start with *Humphrey's Executor*. Unlike the New Deal-era FTC upheld there, the CFPB is led by a single Director who cannot be described as a "body of experts" and cannot be considered "non-partisan" in the same sense as a group of officials drawn from both sides of the aisle. . . . Moreover, while the staggered terms of the FTC Commissioners prevented complete turnovers in agency leadership and guaranteed that there would always be some Commissioners who had accrued significant expertise, the CFPB's single-Director structure and five-year term guarantee abrupt shifts in agency leadership and with it the loss of accumulated expertise.

In addition, the CFPB Director is hardly a mere legislative or judicial aid. Instead of making reports and recommendations to Congress, as the 1935 FTC did, the Director possesses the authority to promulgate binding rules fleshing out 19 federal statutes, including a broad prohibition on unfair and deceptive practices in a major segment of the U. S. economy. And instead of submitting recommended dispositions to an Article III court, the Director may unilaterally issue final decisions awarding legal and equitable relief in administrative

---

[3]   Article II distinguishes between two kinds of officers—principal officers (who must be appointed by the President with the advice and consent of the Senate) and inferior officers (whose appointment Congress may vest in the President, courts, or heads of Departments). § 2, cl. 2. While "[o]ur cases have not set forth an exclusive criterion for distinguishing between principal and inferior officers," we have in the past examined factors such as the nature, scope, and duration of an officer's duties. Edmond v. United States, 520 U. S. 651, 661 (1997). More recently, we have focused on whether the officer's work is "directed and supervised" by a principal officer. Id., at 663.

adjudications. Finally, the Director's enforcement authority includes the power to seek daunting monetary penalties against private parties on behalf of the United States in federal court—a quintessentially executive power not considered in *Humphrey's Executor*.

The logic of *Morrison* also does not apply. Everyone agrees the CFPB Director is not an inferior officer, and her duties are far from limited. Unlike the independent counsel, who lacked policymaking or administrative authority, the Director has the sole responsibility to administer 19 separate consumer-protection statutes that cover everything from credit cards and car payments to mortgages and student loans. It is true that the independent counsel in *Morrison* was empowered to initiate criminal investigations and prosecutions, and in that respect wielded core executive power. But that power, while significant, was trained inward to high-ranking Governmental actors identified by others and was confined to a specified matter in which the Department of Justice had a potential conflict of interest. By contrast, the CFPB Director has the authority to bring the coercive power of the state to bear on millions of private citizens and businesses, imposing even billion-dollar penalties through administrative adjudications and civil actions.

In light of these differences, the constitutionality of the CFPB Director's insulation from removal cannot be settled by *Humphrey's Executor* or *Morrison* alone.

C

The question instead is whether to extend those precedents to the "new situation" before us, namely an independent agency led by a single Director and vested with significant executive power. . . . We decline to do so. Such an agency has no basis in history and no place in our constitutional structure.

1

"Perhaps the most telling indication of [a] severe constitutional problem" with an executive entity "is [a] lack of historical precedent" to support it. An agency with a structure like that of the CFPB is almost wholly unprecedented.

After years of litigating the agency's constitutionality, the Courts of Appeals, parties, and *amici* have identified "only a handful of isolated" incidents in which Congress has provided good-cause tenure to principal officers who wield power alone rather than as members of a board or commission. . . . "[T]hese few scattered examples"—four to be exact—shed little light. . . .

First, the CFPB's defenders point to the Comptroller of the Currency, who enjoyed removal protection for one year during the Civil War. That example has rightly been dismissed as an aberration. It was "adopted without discussion" during the heat of the Civil War and abandoned before it could be "tested by executive or judicial inquiry." . . .

Second, the supporters of the CFPB point to the Office of the Special Counsel (OSC), which has been headed by a single officer since 1978. But this first enduring single-leader office, created nearly 200 years after the Constitution was ratified, drew a contemporaneous constitutional objection from the Office of Legal Counsel under President Carter and a subsequent veto on constitutional grounds by President Reagan. . . . In any event, the OSC exercises only limited jurisdiction to enforce certain rules governing Federal Government employers and employees. See 5 U. S. C. § 1212. It does not bind private parties at all or wield regulatory authority comparable to the CFPB.

Third, the CFPB's defenders note that the Social Security Administration (SSA) has been run by a single Administrator since 1994. That example, too, is comparatively recent and controversial. President Clinton questioned the constitutionality of the SSA's new single-Director structure upon signing it into law. . . . In addition, unlike the CFPB, the SSA lacks the authority to bring enforcement actions against private parties. Its role is largely limited to adjudicating claims for Social Security benefits.

The only remaining example is the Federal Housing Finance Agency (FHFA), created in 2008 to assume responsibility for Fannie Mae and Freddie Mac. That agency is essentially a companion of the CFPB, established in response to the same financial crisis. . . . It regulates primarily Government-sponsored enterprises, not purely private actors. And its single-Director structure is a source of ongoing controversy. Indeed, it was recently held unconstitutional by the Fifth Circuit, sitting en banc. . . .

With the exception of the one-year blip for the Comptroller of the Currency, these isolated examples are modern and contested. And they do not involve regulatory or enforcement authority remotely comparable to that exercised by the CFPB. The CFPB's single-Director structure is an innovation with no foothold in history or tradition.

2

In addition to being a historical anomaly, the CFPB's single-Director configuration is incompatible with our constitutional structure. Aside from the sole exception of the Presidency, that structure scrupulously avoids concentrating power in the hands of any single individual.

"The Framers recognized that, in the long term, structural protections against abuse of power were critical to preserving liberty." . . . Their solution to governmental power and its perils was simple: divide it. To prevent the "gradual concentration" of power in the same hands, they enabled "[a]mbition . . . to counteract ambition" at every turn. The Federalist No. 51, p. 349 (J. Cooke ed. 1961) (J. Madison). At the highest level, they "split the atom of sovereignty" itself into one Federal Government and the States. . . . They then divided the "powers of the new Federal Government into three defined categories, Legislative, Executive, and Judicial." . . .

They did not stop there. Most prominently, the Framers bifurcated the federal legislative power into two Chambers: the House of Representatives and the Senate, each composed of multiple Members and Senators. Art. I, §§ 2, 3.

The Executive Branch is a stark departure from all this division. The Framers viewed the legislative power as a special threat to individual liberty, so they divided that power to ensure that "differences of opinion" and the "jarrings of parties" would "promote deliberation and circumspection" and "check excesses in the majority." See The Federalist No. 70, at 475 (A. Hamilton); see also id., No. 51, at 350. By contrast, the Framers thought it necessary to secure the authority of the Executive so that he could carry out his unique responsibilities. See id., No. 70, at 475–478. As Madison put it, while "the weight of the legislative authority requires that it should be . . . divided, the weakness of the executive may require, on the other hand, that it should be fortified." Id., No. 51, at 350.

The Framers deemed an energetic executive essential to "the protection of the community against foreign attacks," "the steady administration of the laws," "the protection of property," and "the security of liberty." Id., No. 70, at 471. Accordingly, they chose not to bog the Executive down with the "habitual feebleness and dilatoriness" that comes with a "diversity of views and opinions." Id., at 476. Instead, they gave the Executive the "[d]ecision, activity, secrecy, and dispatch" that "characterise the proceedings of one man." Id., at 472.

To justify and check *that* authority—unique in our constitutional structure—the Framers made the President the most democratic and politically accountable official in Government. Only the President (along with the Vice President) is elected by the entire Nation. And the President's political accountability is enhanced by the solitary nature of the Executive Branch, which provides "a single object for the jealousy and watchfulness of the people." Id., at 479. The President "cannot delegate ultimate responsibility or the active obligation to supervise that goes with it," because Article II "makes a single President responsible for the actions of the Executive Branch." . . .

The resulting constitutional strategy is straightforward: divide power everywhere except for the Presidency, and render the President directly accountable to the people through regular elections. In that scheme, individual executive officials will still wield significant authority, but that authority remains subject to the ongoing supervision and control of the elected President. Through the President's oversight, "the chain of dependence [is] preserved," so that "the lowest officers, the middle grade, and the highest" all "depend, as they ought, on the President, and the President on the community." . . .

The CFPB's single-Director structure contravenes this carefully calibrated system by vesting significant governmental power in the hands of a single individual accountable to no one. The Director is neither elected by the people nor meaningfully controlled (through the threat of removal) by someone who is. The Director does not even depend on Congress for annual appropriations. . . . Yet the Director may *unilaterally*, without meaningful supervision, issue final regulations, oversee adjudications, set enforcement priorities, initiate prosecutions, and determine what penalties to impose on private parties. With no colleagues to persuade, and no boss or electorate looking over her shoulder, the Director may dictate and enforce policy for a vital segment of the economy affecting millions of Americans.

The CFPB Director's insulation from removal by an accountable President is enough to render the agency's structure unconstitutional. But several other features of the CFPB combine to make the Director's removal protection even more problematic. In addition to lacking the most direct method of presidential control—removal at will—the agency's unique structure also forecloses certain indirect methods of Presidential control.

Because the CFPB is headed by a single Director with a five-year term, some Presidents may not have any opportunity to shape its leadership and thereby influence its activities. A President elected in 2020 would likely not appoint a CFPB Director until 2023, and a President elected in 2028 may *never* appoint one. That means an unlucky President might get elected on a consumer-protection platform and enter office only to find herself saddled with a holdover Director from a competing political party who is dead set *against* that agenda. To make matters worse, the agency's single-Director structure means the President will not have the opportunity to appoint any other leaders—such as a chair or fellow members of a Commission or Board—who can serve as a check on the Director's authority and help bring the agency in line with the President's preferred policies.

The CFPB's receipt of funds outside the appropriations process further aggravates the agency's threat to Presidential control. The President normally has the opportunity to recommend or veto spending bills that affect the operation of administrative agencies. See Art. I, § 7, cl. 2; Art. II, § 3. And, for the past century, the President has annually submitted a proposed budget to Congress for approval. . . . Presidents frequently use these budgetary tools "to influence the policies of independent agencies." . . . But no similar opportunity exists for the President to influence the CFPB Director. Instead, the Director receives over $500 million per year to fund the agency's chosen priorities. And the Director receives that money from the Federal Reserve, which is itself funded outside of the annual appropriations process. This financial freedom makes it even more likely that the agency will "slip from the Executive's control, and thus from that of the people."

3

Amicus raises three principal arguments in the agency's defense. At the outset, *amicus* questions the textual basis for the removal power and highlights statements from Madison, Hamilton, and Chief Justice Marshall expressing "heterodox" views on the subject. But those concerns are misplaced. It is true that "there is no 'removal clause' in the Constitution," id., at 1, but neither is there a "separation of powers clause" or a "federalism clause." These foundational doctrines are instead evident from the Constitution's vesting of certain powers in certain bodies. As we have explained many times before, the President's removal power stems from Article II's vesting of the "executive Power" in the President. . . . As for the opinions of Madison, Hamilton, and Chief Justice Marshall, we have already considered the statements cited by *amicus* and discounted them in light of their context (Madison), the fact they reflect initial impressions later abandoned by the speaker (Hamilton), or their subsequent rejection as ill-considered dicta (Chief Justice Marshall). See *Free Enterprise Fund*, 561 U. S., at 500, n. 6 (Madison); *Myers*, 272 U. S., at 136–139, 142–144 (Hamilton and Chief Justice Marshall).

Next, *amicus* offers a grand theory of our removal precedents that, if accepted, could leave room for an agency like the CFPB—and many other innovative intrusions on Article II. According to *amicus*, *Humphrey's Executor* and *Morrison* establish a general rule that Congress may impose "modest" restrictions on the President's removal power, with only two limited exceptions. Congress may not reserve a role *for itself* in individual removal decisions (as it attempted to do in *Myers* and *Bowsher*). And it may not eliminate the President's removal power altogether (as it effectively did in *Free Enterprise Fund*). Outside those two situations, *amicus* argues, Congress is generally free to constrain the President's removal power. . . .

But text, first principles, the First Congress's decision in 1789, *Myers*, and *Free Enterprise Fund* all establish that the President's removal power is the rule, not the exception. While we do not revisit *Humphrey's Executor* or any other precedent today, we decline to elevate it into a freestanding invitation for Congress to impose additional restrictions on the President's removal authority.

Finally, *amicus* contends that if we identify a constitutional problem with the CFPB's structure, we should avoid it by broadly construing the statutory grounds for removing the CFPB Director from office. . . .The Dodd-Frank Act provides that the Director may be removed for "inefficiency, neglect of duty, or malfeasance in office." 12 U. S. C. § 5491(c)(3). In *amicus'* view, that language could be interpreted to reserve substantial discretion to the President.

We are not persuaded. For one, *Humphrey's Executor* implicitly rejected an interpretation that would leave the President free to remove an officer based on disagreements about agency policy. . . . In addition, while both *amicus* and the House of Representatives invite us to adopt whatever construction would cure the constitutional problem, they have not advanced any workable standard derived from the statutory language. *Amicus* suggests that the proper standard might permit removals based on *general* policy disagreements, but not *specific* ones; the House suggests that the permissible bases for removal might vary depending on the context and the Presidential power involved. . . . They do not attempt to root either of those standards in the statutory text. Further, although nearly identical language governs the removal of some two-dozen multimember independent agencies, *amicus* suggests that the standard should vary from agency to agency, morphing as necessary to avoid constitutional doubt. . . . We decline to embrace such an uncertain and elastic approach to the text.

Amicus and the House also fail to engage with the Dodd-Frank Act as a whole, which makes plain that the CFPB is an "independent bureau." 12 U. S. C. § 5491(a); see also 44 U. S. C. § 3502(5) (listing the CFPB as an "independent regulatory agency"). Neither *amicus* nor the House explains how the CFPB would be "independent" if its head were required to implement the President's policies upon pain of removal. See Black's Law Dictionary 838 (9th ed. 2009) (defining "independent" as "[n]ot subject to the control or influence of another"). The Constitution might of course compel the agency to be dependent on the President notwithstanding Congress's contrary intent, but that result cannot fairly be inferred from the statute Congress enacted.

Constitutional avoidance is not a license to rewrite Congress's work to say whatever the Constitution needs it to say in a given situation. Without a proffered interpretation that is rooted in the statutory text and structure, and would avoid the constitutional violation we have identified, we take Congress at its word that it meant to impose a meaningful restriction on the President's removal authority.

The dissent, for its part, largely reprises points that the Court has already considered and rejected: It notes the lack of an express removal provision, invokes Congress's general power to create and define executive offices, highlights isolated statements from individual Framers, downplays the decision of 1789, minimizes *Myers*, brainstorms methods of Presidential control short of removal, touts the need for creative congressional responses to technological and economic change, and celebrates a pragmatic, flexible approach to American governance. . . .

If these arguments sound familiar, it's because they are. They were raised by the dissent in *Free Enterprise Fund*. . . . The answers to these repeated concerns (beyond those we have already covered) are the same today as they were ten years ago. Today, as then, Congress's "plenary control over the salary, duties, and even existence of executive offices" makes "Presidential oversight" *more* critical—not less—as the "[o]nly" tool to "counter [Congress's] influence." . . .

Today, as then, the various "bureaucratic minutiae" a President might use to corral agency personnel is no substitute for at will removal. . . .Ibid. And today, as always, the urge to meet new technological and societal problems with novel governmental structures must be tempered by constitutional restraints that are not known—and were not chosen—for their efficiency or flexibility. . . .

As we explained in *Free Enterprise Fund*, "One can have a government that functions without being ruled by functionaries, and a government that benefits from expertise without being ruled by experts.". . . While "[n]o one doubts Congress's power to create a vast and varied federal bureaucracy," the expansion of that bureaucracy into new territories the Framers could scarcely have imagined only sharpens our duty to ensure that the Executive Branch is overseen by a President accountable to the people. . . .

IV

[CHIEF JUSTICE ROBERTS, joined by JUSTICES ALITO AND KAVANAUGH, explained why he believed the CFPB Director's removal protection is severable from the other statutory provisions bearing on the CFPB's authority. In light of the views of four Justices that the removal protection was itself constitutionally permissible, a majority of Justices took the view that the agency may therefore continue to operate, even though its Director, in light of the decision by the five Justices in the majority, must be removable by the President at will.]

. . .

* * *

The judgment of the United States Court of Appeals for the Ninth Circuit is vacated, and the case is remanded for further proceedings consistent with this opinion.

■ JUSTICE THOMAS, with whom JUSTICE GORSUCH joins, concurring in part and dissenting in part.

The Court's decision today takes a restrained approach on the merits by limiting Humphrey's Executor v. United States, 295 U. S. 602 (1935), rather than overruling it. At the same time, the Court takes an aggressive approach on severability by severing a provision when it is not necessary to do so. I would do the opposite. Because the Court takes a step in the right direction by limiting *Humphrey's Executor* to "multimember expert agencies that *do not wield substantial executive power*," . . . (emphasis added), I join Parts I, II, and III of its opinion. I respectfully dissent from the Court's severability analysis, however, because I do not believe that we should address severability in this case.

I

. . .

* * *

Continued reliance on *Humphrey's Executor* to justify the existence of independent agencies creates a serious, ongoing threat to our Government's design. Leaving these unconstitutional agencies in place does not enhance this Court's legitimacy; it subverts political accountability and threatens individual liberty. We have a "responsibility to 'examin[e] without fear, and revis[e] without reluctance,' any 'hasty and crude decisions' rather than leaving 'the character of [the] law impaired, and the beauty and harmony of the [American constitutional] system destroyed by the perpetuity of error.' " . . . We simply cannot compromise when it comes to our Government's structure. Today, the Court does enough to resolve this case, but in the future, we should reconsider . And I hope that we will have the will to do so.

II

While I think that the Court correctly resolves the merits of the constitutional question, I do not agree with its decision to sever the removal restriction in 12 U. S. C. § 5491(c)(3). To resolve this case, I would simply deny the Consumer Financial Protection Bureau (CFPB) petition to enforce the civil investigative demand.

. . .

■ JUSTICE KAGAN, with whom JUSTICES GINSBURG, BREYER and SOTOMAYOR join, concurring in the judgment with respect to severability and dissenting in part.

Throughout the Nation's history, this Court has left most decisions about how to structure the Executive Branch to Congress and the President, acting through legislation they both agree to. In particular, the Court has commonly allowed those two branches to create zones of administrative independence by limiting the President's power to remove agency heads. The Federal Reserve Board. The Federal Trade Commission (FTC). The National Labor Relations Board. Statute after statute establishing such entities instructs the President that he may not discharge their directors except for cause—most often phrased as inefficiency, neglect of duty, or malfeasance in office. Those statutes, whose language the Court has repeatedly approved, provide the model for the removal restriction before us today. If precedent were any guide, that provision would have survived its encounter with this Court—and so would the intended independence of the Consumer Financial Protection Bureau (CFPB).

Our Constitution and history demand that result. The text of the Constitution allows these common for-cause removal limits. Nothing in it speaks of removal. And it grants Congress authority to organize all the institutions of American governance, provided only that those arrangements allow the President to perform his own constitutionally assigned duties. Still more, the Framers' choice to give the political branches wide discretion over administrative offices has played out through American history in ways that have settled the constitutional meaning. From the first, Congress debated and enacted measures to create spheres of administration—especially of financial affairs—detached from direct presidential control. As the years passed, and governance became ever more complicated, Congress continued to adopt and adapt such measures— confident it had latitude to do so under a Constitution meant to "endure for ages to come." McCulloch v. Maryland, 4 Wheat. 316, 415 (1819) (approving the Second Bank of the United States). Not every innovation in governance—not every experiment in administrative independence—has proved successful. And debates about the prudence of limiting the President's control over regulatory agencies, including through his removal power, have never abated. But the Constitution—both as originally drafted and as practiced—mostly leaves disagreements about administrative structure to Congress and the President, who have the knowledge and experience needed to address them. Within broad bounds, it keeps the courts—who do not—out of the picture.

The Court today fails to respect its proper role. It recognizes that this Court has approved limits on the President's removal power over heads of agencies much like the CFPB. Agencies possessing similar powers, agencies charged with similar missions, agencies created for similar reasons. The majority's explanation is that the heads of those agencies fall within an "exception"—one for multimember bodies and another for inferior officers—to a "general rule" of unrestricted presidential removal power. . . . And the majority says the CFPB Director does not. That account, though, is wrong in every respect. The majority's general rule does not exist. Its exceptions, likewise, are made up for the occasion—gerrymandered so the CFPB falls outside them. And the distinction doing most of the majority's work—between multimember bodies and single directors—does not respond to the constitutional values at stake. If a removal provision violates the separation of powers, it is because the measure so deprives the President of control over an official as to impede his own constitutional functions. But with or without a for-cause removal provision, the President has at least as much control over an individual as over a commission—and possibly more. That means the constitutional concern is, if anything, ameliorated when the agency has a single head. Unwittingly, the majority shows why courts should stay their hand in these matters. "Compared to Congress and the President, the Judiciary possesses an inferior understanding of the realities of administration" and the way "political power[ ] operates." . . .

In second-guessing the political branches, the majority second-guesses as well the wisdom of the Framers and the judgment of history. It writes in rules to the Constitution that the drafters knew well enough not to put there. It repudiates the lessons of American experience, from the 18th century to the present day. And it commits the Nation to a static version of governance, incapable of responding to new conditions and challenges. Congress and the President established the CFPB to address financial practices that had brought on a devastating recession, and could do so again. Today's decision wipes out a feature of that agency its creators thought fundamental to its mission—a measure of independence from political pressure. I respectfully dissent.

. . .

NOTE ON WHO COUNTS AS AN "OFFICER OF THE UNITED STATES" SUBJECT TO THE APPOINTMENTS CLAUSE

In Lucia v. Securities and Exchange Commission, 585 U.S. ___, 138 S.Ct. 2044 (2018), the Court confronted the question whether administrative law judges (ALJs) within the Securities and Exchange Commission (SEC) constitute "Officers of the United States"—who, by the terms of the Appointments Clause, can be appointed only by "the President," "Courts of Law," or "Heads of Departments"—or instead employees, who can be appointed by other persons. ALJs within the SEC are not appointed by the Commissioners themselves, but by others within the agency. ALJs are typically given the task of presiding over administrative disciplinary proceedings, and have "authority to do all things necessary and appropriate" to ensure a "fair and orderly" adversarial proceeding. After a hearing is concluded, an ALJ issues an initial decision that the entire Commission may but need not review. If the Commission decides not to review an ALJ's initial decision, that decision becomes final and is "deemed the action of the Commission."

Raymond Lucia was charged by the Commission with various securities laws violations, and his case was assigned to an ALJ who, after a hearing, found a violation and imposed sanctions. Lucia appealed to the Commission, arguing that having an ALJ preside over his hearings violated the Appointments Clause. He lost this argument at the Commission and before the U.S. Court of Appeals for the D.C. Circuit, but prevailed in the Supreme Court 6–3. Writing for the Court, Justice Kagan relied heavily on Freytag v. Commissioner, 501 U.S. 868 (1991), in which the Court had ruled that special trial judges (STJs) within the United States Tax Court constituted "Officers of the United States" whose appointment needed to comply with the Appointments Clause. Justice Kagan wrote:

"The sole question here is whether the Commission's ALJs are 'Officers of the United States' or simply employees of the Federal Government. The Appointments Clause prescribes the exclusive means of appointing 'Officers.' Only the President, a court of law, or a head of department can do so. See Art. II, § 2, cl. 2. And as all parties agree, none of those actors appointed [the ALJ who] heard Lucia's case; instead, SEC staff members gave him an ALJ slot. So if the Commission's ALJs are constitutional officers, Lucia raises a valid Appointments Clause claim. The only way to defeat his position is to show that those ALJs are not officers at all, but instead non-officer employees—part of the broad swath of 'lesser functionaries' in the Government's workforce. For if that is true, the Appointments Clause cares not a whit about who named them.

"Two decisions set out this Court's basic framework for distinguishing between officers and employees. [United States v. Germaine, 99 U.S. 508 (1879),] held that 'civil surgeons' (doctors hired to perform various physical exams) were mere employees because their duties were 'occasional or temporary' rather than 'continuing and permanent.' Stressing 'ideas of tenure [and] duration,' the Court there made clear that an individual must occupy a 'continuing' position established by law to qualify as an officer. [Buckley v. Valeo, 424 U.S. 1 (1976),] then set out another requirement, central to this case. It determined that members of a federal commission were officers only after finding that they 'exercis[ed] significant authority pursuant to the laws of the United States.' The inquiry thus focused on the extent of power an individual wields in carrying out his assigned functions.

"Both the *amicus* and the Government urge us to elaborate on *Buckley*'s 'significant authority' test, but another of our precedents makes that project unnecessary. The standard is no doubt framed in general terms, tempting advocates to add whatever glosses best suit their arguments. And maybe one day we will see a need to refine or enhance the test *Buckley* set out so concisely. But that day is not this one, because in Freytag v. Commissioner, 501 U. S. 868 (1991), we applied the unadorned 'significant authority' test to adjudicative officials who are near-carbon copies of the Commission's ALJs. [O]ur analysis there (sans any more detailed legal criteria) necessarily decides this case.

. . .

"*Freytag* says everything necessary to decide this case. To begin, the Commission's ALJs, like the Tax Court's STJs, hold a continuing office established by law. . . . Far from serving temporarily or episodically, SEC ALJs 'receive[ ] a career appointment.' . . .

"Still more, the Commission's ALJs exercise the same 'significant discretion' when carrying out the same 'important functions' as STJs do. Both sets of officials have all the authority needed to ensure fair and orderly adversarial hearings—indeed, nearly all the tools of federal trial judges. Consider in order the four specific (if overlapping) powers *Freytag* mentioned. First, the Commission's ALJs (like the Tax Court's STJs) 'take testimony.' More precisely, they '[r]eceiv[e] evidence' and '[e]xamine witnesses' at hearings, and may also take pre-hearing depositions. Second, the ALJs (like STJs) 'conduct trials.' . . . Third, the ALJs (like STJs) 'rule on the admissibility of evidence.' . . . And fourth, the ALJs (like STJs) 'have the power to enforce compliance with discovery orders.' . . . So point for point—straight from *Freytag*'s list—the Commission's ALJs have equivalent duties and powers as STJs in conducting adversarial inquiries.

"And at the close of those proceedings, ALJs issue decisions much like that in *Freytag*—except with potentially more independent effect. As the *Freytag* Court recounted, STJs 'prepare proposed findings and an opinion' adjudicating charges and assessing tax liabilities. Similarly, the Commission's ALJs issue decisions containing factual findings, legal conclusions, and appropriate remedies. And what happens next reveals that the ALJ can play the more autonomous role. In a major case like *Freytag*, a regular Tax Court judge must always review an STJ's opinion. And that opinion counts for nothing unless the regular judge adopts it as his own. By contrast, the SEC can decide against reviewing an ALJ decision at all. And when the SEC declines review (and issues an order saying so), the ALJ's decision itself 'becomes final' and is 'deemed the action of the Commission.' That last-word capacity makes this an *a fortiori* case: If the Tax Court's STJs are officers, as *Freytag* held, then the Commission's ALJs must be too."

Justice Thomas, who joined the majority opinion, wrote a separate concurrence joined by Justice Gorsuch (who also joined the majority) elaborating on situations that might not so easily be covered by *Freytag*. Justice Breyer wrote separately to say he would rule in Lucia's favor on statutory rather than constitutional grounds, and Justice Sotomayor wrote a dissent, joined by Justice Ginsburg.

The Court distinguished *Lucia*, *Freytag* and *Buckley*, and chose not to apply the framework they used, in Financial Oversight Board for Puerto Rico v. Aurelius Investment, LLC, 590 U.S. ___, 140 S.Ct. 1649 (2020). The case involved a challenge to the method by which members of the Financial Oversight and Management Board—an entity created by Congress in 2016 to oversee Puerto Rico's budget and bankruptcy filings—were appointed. In rejecting the notion that Board-member appointment was regulated by Article II's Appointments Clause, the Court drew a distinction between appointees who exercise essentially local powers (in this case, with respect to a territory), and those who exercise federal or national powers. Because the Board members in question in *Aurelius* fell into the former category, they were not "officers of the United States," and thus the Appointments Clause did not govern their selection. The Court did state, however, that selection of officers of the United States who do exercise national or federal (rather than local) powers is subject to the Appointments Clause, even though these officers may be located in Puerto Rico or their duties may relate to Puerto Rico. The result in the case was unanimous; Justice Breyer wrote a majority opinion in which six other Justices joined, and Justices Thomas and Sotomayor each wrote an opinion concurring in the judgment.

3. PRESIDENTIAL IMMUNITIES

Page 402. Add after Clinton v. Jones:

Trump v. Vance

591 U.S. ___, 140 S.Ct. 2412 (2020).

■ CHIEF JUSTICE ROBERTS delivered the opinion of the Court.

In our judicial system, "the public has a right to every man's evidence." Since the earliest days of the Republic, "every man" has included the President of the United States. Beginning with Jefferson and carrying on through Clinton, Presidents have uniformly testified or produced documents in criminal proceedings when called upon by federal courts. This case involves—so far as we and the parties can tell—the first *state* criminal subpoena directed to a President. The President contends that the subpoena is unenforceable. We granted certiorari to decide whether Article II and the Supremacy Clause categorically preclude, or require a heightened standard for, the issuance of a state criminal subpoena to a sitting President.

I

In the summer of 2018, the New York County District Attorney's Office opened an investigation into what it opaquely describes as "business transactions involving multiple individuals whose conduct may have violated state law." . . . A year later, the office—acting on behalf of a grand jury—served a subpoena *duces tecum* (essentially a request to produce evidence) on Mazars USA, LLP, the personal accounting firm of President Donald J. Trump. The subpoena directed Mazars to produce financial records relating to the President and business organizations affiliated with him, including "[t]ax returns and related schedules," from "2011 to the present." . . .

The President, acting in his personal capacity, sued the district attorney and Mazars in Federal District Court to enjoin enforcement of the subpoena. He argued that, under Article II and the Supremacy Clause, a sitting President enjoys absolute immunity from state criminal process. He asked the court to issue a "declaratory judgment that the subpoena is invalid and unenforceable while the President is in office" and to permanently enjoin the district attorney "from taking any action to enforce the subpoena." . . . Mazars, concluding that the dispute was between the President and the district attorney, took no position on the legal issues raised by the President.

The District Court abstained from exercising jurisdiction and dismissed the case based on Younger v. Harris, 401 U. S. 37 (1971), which generally precludes federal courts from intervening in ongoing state criminal prosecutions. . . . In an alternative holding, the court ruled that the President was not entitled to injunctive relief. . . .

The Second Circuit met the District Court halfway. As to the dismissal, the Court of Appeals held that *Younger* abstention was inappropriate because that doctrine's core justification—"preventing friction" between States and the Federal Government—is diminished when state and federal actors are already in conflict, as the district attorney and the President were. . . .

On the merits, the Court of Appeals agreed with the District Court's denial of a preliminary injunction. Drawing on the 200-year history of Presidents being subject to federal judicial process, the Court of Appeals concluded that "presidential immunity does not bar the enforcement of a state grand jury subpoena directing a third party to produce non-privileged material, even when the subject matter under investigation pertains to the President.". . . It also rejected the argument raised by the United States as *amicus curiae* that a state grand jury subpoena must satisfy a heightened showing of need. The court reasoned that the proposed test, derived from cases addressing privileged Executive Branch communications, "ha[d] little bearing on a subpoena" seeking "information relating solely to the President in his private capacity and disconnected from the discharge of his constitutional obligations." . . .

We granted certiorari. . . .

II

In the summer of 1807, all eyes were on Richmond, Virginia. Aaron Burr, the former Vice President, was on trial for treason. Fallen from political grace after his fatal duel with Alexander Hamilton, and with a murder charge pending in New Jersey, Burr followed the path of many down-and-out Americans of his day—he headed West in search of new opportunity. But Burr was a man with outsized ambitions. Together with General James Wilkinson, the Governor of the Louisiana Territory, he hatched a plan to establish a new territory in Mexico, then controlled by Spain. Both men anticipated that war between the United States and Spain was imminent, and when it broke out they intended to invade Spanish territory at the head of a private army.

But while Burr was rallying allies to his cause, tensions with Spain eased and rumors began to swirl that Burr was conspiring to detach States by the Allegheny Mountains from the Union. Wary of being exposed as the principal co-conspirator, Wilkinson took steps to ensure that any blame would fall on Burr. He sent a series of letters to President Jefferson accusing Burr of plotting to attack New Orleans and revolutionize the Louisiana Territory.

Jefferson, who despised his former running mate Burr for trying to steal the 1800 presidential election from him, was predisposed to credit Wilkinson's version of events. The President sent a special message to Congress identifying Burr as the "prime mover" in a plot "against the peace and safety of the Union." . . . According to Jefferson, Burr contemplated either the "severance of the Union" or an attack on Spanish territory. . . . Jefferson acknowledged that his sources contained a "mixture of rumors, conjectures, and suspicions" but, citing Wilkinson's letters, he assured Congress that Burr's guilt was "beyond question." . . .

The trial that followed was "the greatest spectacle in the short history of the republic," complete with a Founder-studded cast. . . . People flocked to Richmond to watch, massing in tents and covered wagons along the banks of the James River, nearly doubling the town's population of 5,000. Burr's defense team included Edmund Randolph and Luther Martin, both former delegates at the Constitutional Convention and renowned advocates. Chief Justice John Marshall, who had recently squared off with the Jefferson administration in Marbury v. Madison, . . . presided as Circuit Justice for Virginia. Meanwhile Jefferson, intent on conviction, orchestrated the prosecution from afar, dedicating Cabinet meetings to the case, peppering the prosecutors with directions, and spending nearly $100,000 from the Treasury on the five-month proceedings.

In the lead-up to trial, Burr, taking aim at his accusers, moved for a subpoena *duces tecum* directed at Jefferson. The draft subpoena required the President to produce an October 21, 1806 letter from Wilkinson and accompanying documents, which Jefferson had referenced in his message to Congress. The prosecution opposed the request, arguing that a President could not be subjected to such a subpoena and that the letter might contain state secrets. Following four days of argument, Marshall announced his ruling to a packed chamber.

The President, Marshall declared, does not "stand exempt from the general provisions of the constitution" or, in particular, the Sixth Amendment's guarantee that those accused have compulsory process for obtaining witnesses for their defense. . . . At common law the "single reservation" to the duty to testify in response to a subpoena was "the case of the king," whose "dignity" was seen as "incompatible" with appearing "under the process of the court." . . . But, as Marshall explained, a king is born to power and can "do no wrong." . . . The President, by contrast, is "of the people" and subject to the law. . . . According to Marshall, the sole argument for exempting the President from testimonial obligations was that his "duties as chief magistrate demand his whole time for national objects." . . . But, in Marshall's assessment, those demands were "not unremitting." . . . And should the President's duties preclude his attendance at a particular time and place, a court could work that out upon return of the subpoena. . . .

Marshall also rejected the prosecution's argument that the President was immune from a subpoena *duces tecum* because executive papers might contain state secrets. "A subpoena duces tecum," he said, "may issue to any person to whom an ordinary subpoena may issue.". . . As he explained, no "fair construction" of the Constitution supported the conclusion that the right "to compel the attendance of witnesses[ ] does not extend" to requiring those witnesses to "bring[ ] with them such papers as may be material in the defence.". . . And, as a matter of basic fairness, permitting such information to be withheld would "tarnish the reputation of the court.". . . As for "the propriety of introducing any papers," that would "depend on the character of the paper, not on the character of the person who holds it.". . . Marshall acknowledged that the papers sought by Burr could contain information "the disclosure of which would endanger the public safety," but stated that, again, such concerns would have "due consideration" upon the return of the subpoena. . . .

While the arguments unfolded, Jefferson, who had received word of the motion, wrote to the prosecutor indicating that he would—subject to the prerogative to decide which executive communications should be withheld—"furnish on all occasions, whatever the purposes of justice may require." . . . His "personal attendance," however, was out of the question, for it "would leave the nation without" the "sole branch which the constitution requires to be always in function." . . .

Before Burr received the subpoenaed documents, Marshall rejected the prosecution's core legal theory for treason and Burr was accordingly acquitted. Jefferson, however, was not done. Committed to salvaging a conviction, he directed the prosecutors to proceed with a misdemeanor (yes, misdemeanor) charge for inciting war against Spain. Burr then renewed his request for Wilkinson's October 21 letter, which he later received a copy of, and subpoenaed a second letter, dated November 12, 1806, which the prosecutor claimed was privileged. Acknowledging that the President may withhold information to protect public safety, Marshall instructed that Jefferson should "state the particular reasons" for withholding the letter. . . . The court, paying "all proper respect" to those reasons, would then decide whether to compel disclosure. . . . But that decision was averted when the misdemeanor trial was cut short after it became clear that the prosecution lacked the evidence to convict.

In the two centuries since the Burr trial, successive Presidents have accepted Marshall's ruling that the Chief Executive is subject to subpoena. In 1818, President Monroe received a subpoena to testify in a court-martial against one of his appointees. . . . His Attorney General, William Wirt—who had served as a prosecutor during Burr's trial—advised Monroe that, per Marshall's ruling, a subpoena to testify may "be properly awarded to the President." . . . Monroe offered to sit for a deposition and ultimately submitted answers to written interrogatories.

Following Monroe's lead, his successors have uniformly agreed to testify when called in criminal proceedings, provided they could do so at a time and place of their choosing. In 1875, President Grant submitted to a three-hour deposition in the criminal prosecution of a political appointee embroiled in a network of tax-evading whiskey distillers. . . . A century later, President Ford's attempted assassin subpoenaed him to testify in her defense. . . . Ford obliged—from a safe distance—in the first videotaped deposition of a President. President Carter testified via the same means in the trial of two local officials who, while Carter was Governor of Georgia, had offered to contribute to his campaign in exchange for advance warning of any state gambling raids. . . . Two years later, Carter gave videotaped testimony to a federal grand jury investigating whether a fugitive financier had entreated the White House to quash his extradition proceedings. . . . President Clinton testified three times, twice via deposition pursuant to subpoenas in federal criminal trials of associates implicated during the Whitewater investigation, and once by video for a grand jury investigating possible perjury. . . .

The bookend to Marshall's ruling came in 1974 when the question he never had to decide—whether to compel the disclosure of official communications over the objection of the President—came to a head. That spring, the Special Prosecutor appointed to investigate the break-in of the Democratic National Committee Headquarters at the Watergate complex filed an indictment charging seven defendants associated with President Nixon and naming Nixon as an unindicted co-conspirator. As the case moved toward trial, the Special Prosecutor secured a subpoena *duces tecum* directing Nixon to produce, among other things, tape recordings of Oval Office meetings. Nixon moved to quash the subpoena, claiming that the Constitution provides an absolute privilege of confidentiality to all presidential communications. This Court rejected that argument in United States v. Nixon, 418 U. S. 683 (1974), a decision we later described as "unequivocally and emphatically endors[ing] Marshall's" holding that Presidents are subject to subpoena. Clinton v. Jones, 520 U. S. 681, 704 (1997).

The *Nixon* Court readily acknowledged the importance of preserving the confidentiality of communications "between high Government officials and those who advise and assist them." . . . "Human experience," the Court explained, "teaches that those who expect public dissemination of their remarks may well temper candor with a concern for appearances and for their own interests to the detriment of the decisionmaking process." . . . Confidentiality thus promoted the "public interest in candid, objective, and even blunt or harsh opinions in Presidential decisionmaking." . . .

But, like Marshall two centuries prior, the Court recognized the countervailing interests at stake. Invoking the common law maxim that "the public has a right to every man's evidence," the Court observed that the public interest in fair and accurate judicial proceedings is at its height in the criminal setting, where our common commitment to justice demands that "guilt shall not escape" nor "innocence suffer." . . . Because these dual aims would be "defeated if judgments" were "founded on a partial or speculative presentation of the facts," the *Nixon* Court recognized that it was "imperative" that "compulsory process be available for the production of evidence needed either by the prosecution or the defense." . . .

The Court thus concluded that the President's "generalized assertion of privilege must yield to the demonstrated, specific need for evidence in a pending criminal trial." . . . Two weeks later, President Nixon dutifully released the tapes.

III

The history surveyed above all involved *federal* criminal proceedings. Here we are confronted for the first time with a subpoena issued to the President by a local grand jury operating under the supervision of a *state* court.

In the President's view, that distinction makes all the difference. He argues that the Supremacy Clause gives a sitting President absolute immunity from state criminal subpoenas because compliance with those subpoenas would categorically impair a President's performance of his Article II functions. The Solicitor General, arguing on behalf of the United States, agrees with much of the President's reasoning but does not commit to his bottom line. Instead, the Solicitor General urges us to resolve this case by holding that a state grand jury subpoena for a sitting President's personal records must, at the very least, "satisfy a heightened standard of need," which the Solicitor General contends was not met here. . . .

A

We begin with the question of absolute immunity. No one doubts that Article II guarantees the independence of the Executive Branch. As the head of that branch, the President "occupies a unique position in the constitutional scheme." Nixon v. Fitzgerald, 457 U. S. 731, 749 (1982). His duties, which range from faithfully executing the laws to commanding the Armed Forces, are of unrivaled gravity and breadth. Quite appropriately, those duties come with protections that safeguard the President's ability to perform his vital functions. See, *e.g.*, *ibid.* (concluding that the President enjoys "absolute immunity from damages liability predicated on his official acts"); *Nixon*, 418 U. S., at 708 (recognizing that presidential communications are presumptively privileged).

In addition, the Constitution guarantees "the entire independence of the General Government from any control by the respective States." . . . As we have often repeated, "States have no power . . . to retard, impede, burden, or in any manner control the operations of the constitutional laws enacted by Congress." McCulloch v. Maryland, 4 Wheat. 316, 436 (1819). It follows that States also lack the power to impede the President's execution of those laws.

Marshall's ruling in *Burr*, entrenched by 200 years of practice and our decision in *Nixon*, confirms that *federal* criminal subpoenas do not "rise to the level of constitutionally forbidden impairment of the Executive's ability to perform its constitutionally mandated functions." *Clinton*, 520 U. S., at 702–703. But the President, joined in part by the Solicitor General, argues that *state* criminal subpoenas pose a unique threat of impairment and thus demand greater protection. To be clear, the President does not contend here that *this* subpoena, in particular, is impermissibly burdensome. Instead he makes a *categorical* argument about the burdens generally associated with state criminal subpoenas, focusing on three: diversion, stigma, and harassment. We address each in turn.

1

The President's primary contention, which the Solicitor General supports, is that complying with state criminal subpoenas would necessarily divert the Chief Executive from his duties. He grounds that concern in Nixon v. Fitzgerald, which recognized a President's "absolute immunity from damages liability predicated on his official acts.". . . In explaining the basis for that immunity, this Court observed that the prospect of such liability could "distract a President from his public duties, to the detriment of not only the President and his office but also the Nation that the Presidency was designed to serve.". . . The President contends that the diversion occasioned by a state criminal subpoena imposes an equally intolerable burden on a President's ability to perform his Article II functions.

But *Fitzgerald* did not hold that distraction was sufficient to confer absolute immunity. We instead drew a careful analogy to the common law absolute immunity of judges and prosecutors, concluding that a President, like those officials, must "deal fearlessly and impartially with the duties of his office"—not be made "unduly cautious in the discharge of [those] duties" by the prospect of civil liability for official acts. . . . Indeed, we expressly rejected immunity based on distraction alone 15 years later in Clinton v. Jones. There, President Clinton argued that the risk of being "distracted by the need to participate in litigation" entitled a sitting President to absolute immunity from civil liability, not just for official acts, as in *Fitzgerald*, but for private conduct as well. . . . We disagreed with that rationale, explaining that the "dominant concern" in *Fitzgerald* was not mere distraction but the distortion of the Executive's "decisionmaking process" with respect to official acts that would stem from "worry as to the possibility of damages." . . . The Court recognized that Presidents constantly face myriad demands on their attention, "some private, some political, and some as a result of official duty." . . . But, the Court concluded, "[w]hile such distractions may be vexing to those subjected to them, they do not ordinarily implicate constitutional . . . concerns." . . .

The same is true of criminal subpoenas. Just as a "properly managed" civil suit is generally "unlikely to occupy any substantial amount of " a President's time or attention, . . . two centuries of experience confirm that a properly tailored criminal subpoena will not normally hamper the performance of the President's constitutional duties. If anything, we expect that in the mine run of cases, where a President is subpoenaed during a proceeding targeting someone else, as Jefferson was, the burden on a President will ordinarily be lighter than the burden of defending against a civil suit.

The President, however, believes the district attorney is investigating him and his businesses. In such a situation, he contends, the "toll that criminal process . . . exacts from the President is even heavier" than the distraction at issue in *Fitzgerald* and *Clinton*, because "criminal litigation" poses unique burdens on the President's time and will generate a "considerable if not overwhelming degree of mental preoccupation." . . .

But the President is not seeking immunity from the diversion occasioned by the prospect of future criminal *liability*. Instead he concedes—consistent with the position of the Department of Justice—that state grand juries are free to investigate a sitting President with an eye toward charging him after the completion of his term. . . . The President's objection therefore must be limited to the *additional* distraction caused by the subpoena itself. But that argument runs up against the 200 years of precedent establishing that Presidents, and their official communications, are subject to judicial process, see *Burr*, 25 F. Cas., at 34, even when the President is under investigation, see *Nixon*, 418 U. S., at 706.

2

The President next claims that the stigma of being subpoenaed will undermine his leadership at home and abroad. Notably, the Solicitor General does not endorse this argument, perhaps because we have twice denied absolute immunity claims by Presidents in cases involving allegations of serious misconduct. See *Clinton*, . . .; *Nixon*, ... But even if a tarnished reputation were a cognizable impairment, there is nothing inherently stigmatizing about a President performing "the citizen's normal duty of . . . furnishing information relevant" to a criminal investigation. . . . Nor can we accept that the risk of association with persons or activities under criminal investigation can absolve a President of such an important public duty. Prior Presidents have weathered these associations in federal cases . . . and there is no reason to think any attendant notoriety is necessarily greater in state court proceedings.

To be sure, the consequences for a President's public standing will likely increase if he is the one under investigation. But, again, the President concedes that such investigations are permitted under Article II and the Supremacy Clause, and receipt of a subpoena would not seem to categorically magnify the harm to the President's reputation.

Additionally, while the current suit has cast the Mazars subpoena into the spotlight, longstanding rules of grand jury secrecy aim to prevent the very stigma the President anticipates. . . . Of course, disclosure restrictions are not perfect. See *Nixon*, 418 U. S., at 687, n. 4 (observing that news media reporting made the protective order shielding the fact that the President had been named as an unindicted co-conspirator "no longer meaningful"). But those who make unauthorized disclosures regarding a grand jury subpoena do so at their peril. See, *e.g.*, N. Y. Penal Law Ann. § 215.70 (West 2010) (designating unlawful grand jury disclosure as a felony).

3

Finally, the President and the Solicitor General warn that subjecting Presidents to state criminal subpoenas will make them "easily identifiable target[s]" for harassment. *Fitzgerald*, ... But we rejected a nearly identical argument in *Clinton*, where then-President Clinton argued that permitting civil liability for unofficial acts would "generate a large volume of politically motivated harassing and frivolous litigation." . . . The President and the Solicitor General nevertheless argue that state criminal subpoenas pose a heightened risk and could undermine the President's ability to "deal fearlessly and impartially" with the States. . . . They caution that, while federal prosecutors are accountable to and removable by the President, the 2,300 district attorneys in this country are responsive to local constituencies, local interests, and local prejudices, and might "use criminal process to register their dissatisfaction with" the President. . . . What is more, we are told, the state courts supervising local grand juries may not exhibit the same respect that federal courts show to the President as a coordinate branch of Government.

We recognize, as does the district attorney, that harassing subpoenas could, under certain circumstances, threaten the independence or effectiveness of the Executive. . . . Even so, in *Clinton* we found that the risk of harassment was not "serious" because federal courts have the tools to deter and, where necessary, dismiss vexatious civil suits. . . . And, while we cannot ignore the possibility that state prosecutors may have political motivations, see . . . (Alito, J., dissenting), here again the law already seeks to protect against the predicted abuse.

First, grand juries are prohibited from engaging in "arbitrary fishing expeditions" and initiating investigations "out of malice or an intent to harass." United States v. R. Enterprises, Inc., 498 U. S. 292, 299 (1991). See also, *e.g.*, Virag v. Hynes, 54 N. Y. 2d 437, 442–443, 430 N. E. 2d 1249, 1252 (1981) (recognizing that grand jury subpoenas can be "challenged by an affirmative showing of impropriety," including "bad faith". . .). These protections, as the district attorney himself puts it, "apply with special force to a President, in light of the office's unique position as the head of the Executive Branch." . . . And, in the event of such harassment, a President would be entitled to the protection of federal courts. The policy against federal interference in state criminal proceedings, while strong, allows "intervention in those cases where the District Court properly finds that the state proceeding is motivated by a desire to harass or is conducted in bad faith." . . .

Second, contrary to Justice Alito's characterization, our holding does not allow States to "run roughshod over the functioning of [the Executive B]ranch." . . . The Supremacy Clause prohibits state judges and prosecutors from interfering with a President's official duties. . . . Any effort to manipulate a President's policy decisions or to "retaliat[e]" against a President for official acts through issuance of a subpoena . . . would thus be an unconstitutional attempt to "influence" a superior sovereign "exempt" from such obstacles, see *McCulloch*, ... We generally "assume[ ] that state courts and prosecutors will observe constitutional limitations." . . . Failing that, federal law allows a President to challenge any allegedly unconstitutional influence in a federal forum, as the President has done here. See 42 U. S. C. § 1983; Ex parte Young, 209 U. S. 123, 155–156 (1908) (holding that federal courts may enjoin state officials to conform their conduct to federal law).

Given these safeguards and the Court's precedents, we cannot conclude that absolute immunity is necessary or appropriate under Article II or the Supremacy Clause. Our dissenting colleagues agree. . . . On that point the Court is unanimous.

B

We next consider whether a state grand jury subpoena seeking a President's private papers must satisfy a heightened need standard. The Solicitor General would require a threshold showing that the evidence sought is "critical" for "specific charging decisions" and that the subpoena is a "last resort," meaning the evidence is "not available from any other source" and is needed "now, rather than at the end of the President's term." . . . Justice Alito, largely embracing those criteria, agrees that a state criminal subpoena to a President "should not be allowed unless a heightened standard is met." . . .

We disagree, for three reasons. First, such a heightened standard would extend protection designed for official documents to the President's private papers. As the Solicitor General and Justice Alito acknowledge, their proposed test is derived from executive privilege cases that trace back to *Burr*. . . . There, Marshall explained that if Jefferson invoked presidential privilege over executive communications, the court would not "proceed against the president as against an ordinary individual" but would instead require an affidavit from the defense that "would clearly show the paper to be essential to the justice of the case.". . . The Solicitor General and Justice Alito would have us apply a similar standard to a President's personal papers. But this argument does not account for the relevant passage from *Burr*: "If there be a paper in the possession of the executive, which is *not of an official nature*, he must stand, as respects that paper, in nearly the same situation with any other individual." (emphasis added). . . And it is only "nearly"—and not "entirely"—because the President retains the right to assert privilege over documents that, while ostensibly private, "partake of the character of an official paper." . . .

Second, neither the Solicitor General nor Justice Alito has established that heightened protection against state subpoenas is necessary for the Executive to fulfill his Article II functions. Beyond the risk of harassment, which we addressed above, the only justification they offer for the heightened standard is protecting Presidents from "unwarranted burdens." . . . In effect, they argue that even if federal subpoenas to a President are warranted whenever evidence is material, state subpoenas are warranted "only when [the] evidence is essential." . . . But that double standard has no basis in law. For if the state subpoena is not issued to manipulate, the documents themselves are not protected, and the Executive is not impaired, then nothing in Article II or the Supremacy Clause supports holding state subpoenas to a higher standard than their federal counterparts.

Finally, in the absence of a need to protect the Executive, the public interest in fair and effective law enforcement cuts in favor of comprehensive access to evidence. Requiring a state grand jury to meet a heightened standard of need would hobble the grand jury's ability to acquire "all information that might possibly bear on its investigation." . . . And, even assuming the evidence withheld under that standard were preserved until the conclusion of a President's term, in the interim the State would be deprived of investigative leads that the evidence might yield, allowing memories to fade and documents to disappear. This could frustrate the identification, investigation, and indictment of third parties (for whom applicable statutes of limitations might lapse). More troubling, it could prejudice the innocent by depriving the grand jury of *exculpatory* evidence.

Rejecting a heightened need standard does not leave Presidents with "no real protection." To start, a President may avail himself of the same protections available to every other citizen. These include the right to challenge the subpoena on any grounds permitted by state law, which usually include bad faith and undue burden or breadth. . . . And, as in federal court, "[t]he high respect that is owed to the office of the Chief Executive . . . should inform the conduct of the entire proceeding, including the timing and scope of discovery." *Clinton*, 520 U. S., at 707. See *id.*, at 724 (Breyer, J., concurring in judgment) (stressing the need for courts presiding over suits against the President to "schedule proceedings so as to avoid significant interference with the President's ongoing discharge of his official responsibilities"); *Nixon*, 418 U. S., at 702 ("[W]here a subpoena is directed to a President . . . appellate review . . . should be particularly meticulous.").

Furthermore, although the Constitution does not entitle the Executive to absolute immunity or a heightened standard, he is not "relegate[d]" only to the challenges available to private citizens. . . . A President can raise subpoena-specific constitutional challenges, in either a state or federal forum. As previously noted, he can challenge the subpoena as an attempt to influence the performance of his official duties, in violation of the Supremacy Clause. . . . This avenue protects against local political machinations "interposed as an obstacle to the effective operation of a federal constitutional power." . . .

In addition, the Executive can—as the district attorney concedes—argue that compliance with a particular subpoena would impede his constitutional duties. . . . Incidental to the functions confided in Article II is "the power to perform them, without obstruction or impediment." 3 J. Story, Commentaries on the Constitution of the United States § 1563, pp. 418–419 (1833). As a result, "once the President sets forth and explains a conflict between judicial proceeding and public duties," or shows that an order or subpoena would "significantly interfere with his efforts to carry out" those duties, "the matter changes." *Clinton*, . . . (opinion of Breyer, J.). At that point, a court should use its inherent authority to quash or modify the subpoena, if necessary to ensure that such "interference with the President's duties would not occur." . . . (opinion of the Court).

* * *

Two hundred years ago, a great jurist of our Court established that no citizen, not even the President, is categorically above the common duty to produce evidence when called upon in a criminal proceeding. We reaffirm that principle today and hold that the President is neither absolutely immune from state criminal subpoenas seeking his private papers nor entitled to a heightened standard of need. The "guard[ ] furnished to this high officer" lies where it always has—in "the conduct of a court" applying established legal and constitutional principles to individual subpoenas in a manner that preserves both the independence of the Executive and the integrity of the criminal justice system. . . .

The arguments presented here and in the Court of Appeals were limited to absolute immunity and heightened need. The Court of Appeals, however, has directed that the case be returned to the District Court, where the President may raise further arguments as appropriate.

We affirm the judgment of the Court of Appeals and remand the case for further proceedings consistent with this opinion.

■ JUSTICE KAVANAUGH, with whom JUSTICE GORSUCH joins, concurring in the judgment.

The Court today unanimously concludes that a President does not possess absolute immunity from a state criminal subpoena, but also unanimously agrees that this case should be remanded to the District Court, where the President may raise constitutional and legal objections to the subpoena as appropriate. . . . I agree with those two conclusions.

* * *

The dispute over this grand jury subpoena reflects a conflict between a State's interest in criminal investigation and a President's Article II interest in performing his or her duties without undue interference. Although this case involves personal information of the President and is therefore not an executive privilege case, the majority opinion correctly concludes based on precedent that Article II and the Supremacy Clause of the Constitution supply some protection for the Presidency against state criminal subpoenas of this sort.

In our system of government, as this Court has often stated, no one is above the law. That principle applies, of course, to a President. At the same time, in light of Article II of the Constitution, this Court has repeatedly declared—and the Court indicates again today—that a court may not proceed against a President as it would against an ordinary litigant. See Cheney v. United States Dist. Court for D. C., 542 U. S. 367, 381–382 (2004) ("In no case would a court be required to proceed against the president as against an ordinary individual" . . .); Clinton v. Jones, 520 U. S. 681, 704, n. 39 (1997) (a court may not "proceed against the president as against an ordinary individual" . . .); United States v. Nixon, 418 U. S. 683, 715 (1974) ("In no case of this kind would a court be required to proceed against the president as against an ordinary individual" . . .); United States v. Burr, 25 F. Cas. 187, 192 (No. 14,694) (CC Va. 1807) (Marshall, C. J.) ("In no case of this kind would a court be required to proceed against the president as against an ordinary individual").

The question here, then, is how to balance the State's interests and the Article II interests. The longstanding precedent that has applied to federal criminal subpoenas for official, privileged Executive Branch information is United States v. Nixon, ... That landmark case requires that a prosecutor establish a "demonstrated, specific need" for the President's information. . . . see also In re Sealed Case, 121 F. 3d 729, 753–757 (CADC 1997); cf. Senate Select Committee on Presidential Campaign Activities v. Nixon, 498 F. 2d 725, 730–731 (CADC 1974) (en banc) (similar standard for congressional subpoenas to the Executive Branch).

The Nixon "demonstrated, specific need" standard is a tried-and-true test that accommodates both the interests of the criminal process and the Article II interests of the Presidency. The Nixon standard ensures that a prosecutor's interest in subpoenaed information is sufficiently important to justify an intrusion on the Article II interests of the Presidency. The Nixon standard also reduces the risk of subjecting a President to unwarranted burdens, because it provides that a prosecutor may obtain a President's information only in certain defined circumstances.

Although the Court adopted the Nixon standard in a different Article II context—there, involving the confidentiality of official, privileged information—the majority opinion today recognizes that there are also important Article II (and Supremacy Clause) interests at stake here. A state criminal subpoena to a President raises Article II and Supremacy Clause issues because of the potential for a state prosecutor to use the criminal process and issue subpoenas in a way that interferes with the President's duties, through harassment or diversion. Cf. Nixon v. Fitzgerald, 457 U. S. 731, 751–753 (1982).

Because this case again entails a clash between the interests of the criminal process and the Article II interests of the Presidency, I would apply the longstanding *Nixon* "demonstrated, specific need" standard to this case. The majority opinion does not apply the *Nixon* standard in this distinct Article II context, as I would have done. That said, the majority opinion appropriately takes account of some important concerns that also animate *Nixon* and the Constitution's balance of powers. The majority opinion explains that a state prosecutor may not issue a subpoena for a President's personal information out of bad faith, malice, or an intent to harass a President; as a result of prosecutorial impropriety; to seek information that is not relevant to an investigation; that is overly broad or unduly burdensome; to manipulate, influence, or retaliate against a President's official acts or policy decisions; or in a way that would impede, conflict with, or interfere with a President's official duties. . . All nine Members of the Court agree, moreover, that a President may raise objections to a state criminal subpoena not just in state court but also in federal court. And the majority opinion indicates that, in light of the "high respect that is owed to the office of the Chief Executive," courts "should be particularly meticulous" in assessing a subpoena for a President's personal records. . . .

In the end, much may depend on how the majority opinion's various standards are applied in future years and decades. It will take future cases to determine precisely how much difference exists between (i) the various standards articulated by the majority opinion, (ii) the overarching *Nixon* "demonstrated, specific need" standard that I would adopt, and (iii) Justice Thomas's and Justice Alito's other proposed standards. In any event, in my view, lower courts in cases of this sort involving a President will almost invariably have to begin by delving into why the State wants the information; why and how much the State needs the information, including whether the State could obtain the information elsewhere; and whether compliance with the subpoena would unduly burden or interfere with a President's official duties.

. . .

■ JUSTICE THOMAS, dissenting.

. . .

The President argues that he is absolutely immune from the issuance of any subpoena, but that if the Court disagrees, we should remand so that the District Court can develop a record about this particular subpoena. I agree with the majority that the President is not entitled to absolute immunity from *issuance* of the subpoena. But he may be entitled to relief against its *enforcement*. I therefore agree with the President that the proper course is to vacate and remand. If the President can show that "his duties as chief magistrate demand his whole time for national objects,". . . he is entitled to relief from enforcement of the subpoena.

. . .

■ JUSTICE ALITO, dissenting.

This case is almost certain to be portrayed as a case about the current President and the current political situation, but the case has a much deeper significance. While the decision will of course have a direct effect on President Trump, what the Court holds today will also affect all future Presidents—which is to say, it will affect the Presidency, and that is a matter of great and lasting importance to the Nation.

The event that precipitated this case is unprecedented. Respondent Vance, an elected state prosecutor, launched a criminal investigation of a sitting

President and obtained a grand jury subpoena for his records. The specific question before us—whether the subpoena may be enforced—cannot be answered adequately without considering the broader question that frames it: whether the Constitution imposes restrictions on a State's deployment of its criminal law enforcement powers against a sitting President. If the Constitution sets no such limits, then a local prosecutor may prosecute a sitting President. And if that is allowed, it follows *a fortiori* that the subpoena at issue can be enforced. On the other hand, if the Constitution does not permit a State to prosecute a sitting President, the next logical question is whether the Constitution restrains any other prosecutorial or investigative weapons.

These are important questions that go to the very structure of the Government created by the Constitution. In evaluating these questions, two important structural features must be taken into account.

I

A

The first is the nature and role of the Presidency. The Presidency, like Congress and the Supreme Court, is a permanent institution created by the Constitution. All three of these institutions are distinct from the human beings who serve in them at any point in time. In the case of Congress or the Supreme Court, the distinction is easy to perceive, since they have multiple Members. But because "[t]he President is the only person who alone composes a branch of government . . . , there is not always a clear line between his personal and official affairs." . . . As a result, the law's treatment of the person who serves as President can have an important effect on the institution, and the institution of the Presidency plays an indispensable role in our constitutional system.

The Constitution entrusts the President with responsibilities that are essential to the country's safety and wellbeing. . . .

. . .

"Constitutionally speaking, the President never sleeps. The President must be ready, at a moment's notice, to do whatever it takes to preserve, protect, and defend the Constitution and the American people." . . . Without a President who is able at all times to carry out the responsibilities of the office, our constitutional system could not operate, and the country would be at risk. That is why the Twenty-fifth Amendment created a mechanism for temporarily transferring the responsibilities of the office to the Vice President if the President is incapacitated for even a brief time. The Amendment has been explicitly invoked on only two occasions, each time for a period of about two hours. This mechanism reflects an appreciation that the Nation cannot be safely left without a functioning President for even a brief time.

B

The second structural feature is the relationship between the Federal Government and the States. Just as our Constitution balances power against power among the branches of the Federal Government, it also divides power between the Federal Government and the States. The Constitution permitted the States to retain many of the sovereign powers that they previously possessed, see, *e.g.*, Murphy v. National Collegiate Athletic Assn., 584 U. S. ___ (2018), but it gave the Federal Government powers that were deemed essential for the Nation's well-being and, indeed, its survival. And it provided for the Federal

Government to be independent of and, within its allotted sphere, supreme over the States. Art. VI, cl. 2. Accordingly, a State may not block or interfere with the lawful work of the National Government.

This was an enduring lesson of Chief Justice Marshall's landmark opinion for the Court in McCulloch v. Maryland, 4 Wheat. 316 (1819). As is well known, the case concerned the attempt by the State of Maryland to regulate and tax the federally chartered Second Bank of the United States. After holding that Congress had the authority to establish the bank, . . . Marshall's opinion went on to conclude that the State could not tax it. Marshall recognized that the States retained the "sovereign" power to tax persons and entities within their jurisdiction, . . . but this power, he explained, "is subordinate to, and may be controlled by the constitution of the United States.". . . . Noting the potency of the taxing power ("[a] right to tax without limit or control, is essentially a power to destroy," . . . he concluded that a State's power to tax had to give way to Congress's authority to charter the bank. In his words, the state power to tax could not be used to "defeat the legitimate operations,". . . of the Federal Government or "to retard, impede, burden, or in any manner control" it . . . . Marshall thus held, not simply that Maryland was barred from assessing a crushing tax that threatened the bank's ability to operate, but that the State could not tax the bank at all. . . .

. . .

II

A

In *McCulloch*, Maryland's sovereign taxing power had to yield, and in a similar way, a State's sovereign power to enforce its criminal laws must accommodate the indispensable role that the Constitution assigns to the Presidency. This must be the rule with respect to a state prosecution of a sitting President. Both the structure of the Government established by the Constitution and the Constitution's provisions on the impeachment and removal of a President make it clear that the prosecution of a sitting President is out of the question. It has been aptly said that the President is the "sole indispensable man in government," and subjecting a sitting President to criminal prosecution would severely hamper his ability to carry out the vital responsibilities that the Constitution puts in his hands.

Justice Joseph Story endorsed this reasoning in his famous treatise. He wrote that a President's responsibilities necessarily entail "the power to perform [those duties], without any obstruction or impediment whatsoever," and that, as a result, a President is not "liable to arrest, imprisonment, or detention" while in office. 3 Commentaries on the Constitution of the United States § 1563, pp. 418–419 (1833).

The constitutional provisions on impeachment provide further support for the rule that a President may not be prosecuted while in office. The Framers foresaw the need to provide for the possibility that a President might be implicated in the commission of a serious offense, and they did not want the country to be forced to endure such a President for the remainder of his term in office. But when a President has been elected by the people pursuant to the procedures set out in the Constitution, it is no small thing to overturn that choice. The Framers therefore crafted a special set of procedures to deal with that contingency. They put the charging decision in the hands of a body that represents all the people (the House of Representatives), not a single prosecutor or the members of a local grand jury. And they entrusted the weighty decision whether to remove a President to a supermajority of Senators, who were expected to exercise reasoned judgment and not the political passions of the day or the sentiments of a particular region.

The Constitution not only sets out the procedures for dealing with a President who is suspected of committing a serious offense; it also specifies the consequences of a judgment adverse to the President. After providing that the judgment cannot impose any punishment beyond removal from the Presidency and disqualification from holding any other federal office, the Constitution states that "the Party convicted shall nevertheless be liable and subject to Indictment, Trial, Judgment, and Punishment, according to Law." Art. I, § 3, cl. 7. The plain implication is that criminal prosecution, like removal from the Presidency and disqualification from other offices, is a consequence that can come about only after the Senate's judgment, not during or prior to the Senate trial.

. . .

In the proceedings below, neither respondent, nor the District Court, nor the Second Circuit was willing to concede the fundamental point that a sitting President may not be prosecuted by a local district attorney. Respondent has said that he is investigating the President and, until oral argument in this Court, he never foreswore an intention to charge the President while he is still in office. The District Court conceded only that "perhaps" a sitting President could not be prosecuted for an offense punishable by "lengthy imprisonment" but that an offense requiring only a short trial would be another matter. . . . And the Second Circuit was silent on the question.

The scenario apparently contemplated by the District Court is striking. If a sitting President were charged in New York County, would he be arrested and fingerprinted? He would presumably be required to appear for arraignment in criminal court, where the judge would set the conditions for his release. Could he be sent to Rikers Island or be required to post bail? Could the judge impose restrictions on his travel? If the President were scheduled to travel abroad—perhaps to attend a G–7 meeting—would he have to get judicial approval? If the President were charged with a complicated offense requiring a long trial, would he have to put his Presidential responsibilities aside for weeks on end while sitting in a Manhattan courtroom? While the trial was in progress, would aides be able to approach him and whisper in his ear about pressing matters? Would he be able to obtain a recess whenever he needed to speak with an aide at greater length or attend to an urgent matter, such as speaking with a foreign leader? Could he effectively carry out all his essential Presidential responsibilities after the trial day ended and at the same time adequately confer with his trial attorneys regarding his defense? Or should he be expected to give up the right to attend his own trial and be tried in absentia? And if he were convicted, could he be imprisoned? Would aides be installed in a nearby cell?

. . .

B

While the prosecution of a sitting President provides the most dramatic example of a clash between the indispensable work of the Presidency and a State's exercise of its criminal law enforcement powers, other examples are easy to imagine. Suppose state officers obtained and sought to execute a search warrant for a sitting President's private quarters in the White House. Suppose a state court authorized surveillance of a telephone that a sitting President was known to use. Or suppose that a sitting President was subpoenaed to testify before a state grand jury and, as is generally the rule, no Presidential aides, even those carrying the so-called "nuclear football," were permitted to enter the grand jury room. What these examples illustrate is a principle that this Court has recognized: legal proceedings involving a sitting President must take the responsibilities and demands of the office into account. See Clinton v. Jones, 520 U. S. 681, 707 (1997).

It is not enough to recite sayings like "no man is above the law" and "the public has a right to every man's evidence." . . . These sayings are true—and important—but they beg the question. The law applies equally to all persons, including a person who happens for a period of time to occupy the Presidency. But there is no question that the nature of the office demands in some instances that the application of laws be adjusted at least until the person's term in office ends.

C

I now come to the specific investigative weapon at issue in the case before us—a subpoena for a sitting President's records. This weapon is less intrusive in an immediate sense than those mentioned above. Since the records are held by, and the subpoena was issued to, a third party, compliance would not require much work on the President's part. And after all, this is just one subpoena.

But we should heed the "great jurist," who rejected a similar argument in *McCulloch*. If we say that a subpoena to a third party is insufficient to undermine a President's performance of his duties, what about a subpoena served on the President himself? Surely in that case, the President could turn over the work of gathering the requested documents to attorneys or others recruited to perform the task. And if one subpoena is permitted, what about two? Or three? Or ten? Drawing a line based on such factors would involve the same sort of "perplexing inquiry, so unfit for the judicial department" that Marshall rejected in *McCulloch* . . . .

The Court faced a similar issue when it considered whether a President can be sued for an allegedly unlawful act committed in the performance of official duties. See Nixon v. Fitzgerald, 457 U. S. 731 (1982). We did not ask whether the particular suit before us would have interfered with the carrying out of Presidential duties. (It could not have had that effect because President Nixon had already left office.)

Instead, we adopted a rule for all such suits, and we should take a similar approach here. The rule should take into account both the effect of subpoenas on the functioning of the Presidency and the risk that they will be used for harassment.

I turn first to the question of the effect of a state grand jury subpoena for a President's records. When the issuance of such a subpoena is part of an investigation that regards the President as a "target" or "subject," the subpoena can easily impair a President's "energetic performance of [his] constitutional duties." Cheney v. United States Dist. Court for D. C., 542 U. S. 367, 382 (2004). Few individuals will simply brush off an indication that they may be within a prosecutor's crosshairs. Few will put the matter out of their minds and go about their work unaffected. For many, the prospect of prosecution will be the first and last thing on their minds every day.

We have come to expect our Presidents to shoulder burdens that very few people could bear, but it is unrealistic to think that the prospect of possible criminal prosecution will not interfere with the performance of the duties of the office. . . .

As for the potential use of subpoenas to harass, we need not " 'exhibit a naiveté from which ordinary citizens are free.' " . . . As we have recognized, a President is "an easily identifiable target." *Fitzgerald*, ... There are more than 2,300 local prosecutors and district attorneys in the country. Many local prosecutors are elected, and many prosecutors have ambitions for higher elected office. (Respondent's famous predecessor Thomas E. Dewey used the office of District Attorney for New York County as a springboard to the governorship of New York and to the Republican nomination for President in 1944 and 1948.) If a sitting President is intensely unpopular in a particular district—and that is a common condition—targeting the President may be an alluring and effective electoral strategy. But it is a strategy that would undermine our constitutional structure.

. . .

D

In light of the above, a subpoena like the one now before us should not be enforced unless it meets a test that takes into account the need to prevent interference with a President's discharge of the responsibilities of the office. I agree with the Court that not all such subpoenas should be barred. There may be situations in which there is an urgent and critical need for the subpoenaed information. The situation in the Burr trial, where the documents at issue were sought by a criminal defendant to defend against a charge of treason, is a good example. But in a case like the one at hand, a subpoena should not be allowed unless a heightened standard is met.

. . .

The Presidency deserves greater protection [than ordinary citizens]. Thus, in a case like this one, a prosecutor should be required (1) to provide at least a general description of the possible offenses that are under investigation, (2) to outline how the subpoenaed records relate to those offenses, and (3) to explain why it is important that the records be produced and why it is necessary for production to occur while the President is still in office. . . .

. . .

Trump v. Mazars USA, LLP
591 U.S. ___, 140 S.Ct. 2019 (2020).

■ CHIEF JUSTICE ROBERTS delivered the opinion of the Court.

Over the course of five days in April 2019, three committees of the U. S. House of Representatives issued four subpoenas seeking information about the finances of President Donald J. Trump, his children, and affiliated businesses. We have held that the House has authority under the Constitution to issue subpoenas to assist it in carrying out its legislative responsibilities. The House asserts that the financial information sought here—encompassing a decade's worth of transactions by the President and his family—will help guide legislative reform in areas ranging from money laundering and terrorism to foreign involvement in U. S. elections. The President contends that the House lacked a valid legislative aim and instead sought these records to harass him, expose personal matters, and conduct law enforcement activities beyond its authority. The question presented is whether the subpoenas exceed the authority of the House under the Constitution.

We have never addressed a congressional subpoena for the President's information. Two hundred years ago, it was established that Presidents may be subpoenaed during a federal criminal proceeding, United States v. Burr, 25 F.Cas. 30 (No. 14,692d) (CC Va. 1807) (Marshall, Cir. J.), and earlier today we extended that ruling to state criminal proceedings, Trump v. Vance . . . . Nearly fifty years ago, we held that a federal prosecutor could obtain information from a President despite assertions of executive privilege, United States v. Nixon, 418 U.S. 683 (1974), and more recently we ruled that a private litigant could subject a President to a damages suit and appropriate discovery obligations in federal court, Clinton v. Jones, 520 U.S. 681 (1997).

This case is different. Here the President's information is sought not by prosecutors or private parties in connection with a particular judicial proceeding, but by committees of Congress that have set forth broad legislative objectives. Congress and the President—the two political branches established by the Constitution—have an ongoing relationship that the Framers intended to feature both rivalry and reciprocity. See The Federalist No. 51, p. 349 (J. Cooke ed. 1961) (J. Madison); Youngstown Sheet & Tube Co. v. Sawyer, 343 U.S. 579, 635 (1952) (Jackson, J., concurring). That distinctive aspect necessarily informs our analysis of the question before us.

I

A

Each of the three committees sought overlapping sets of financial documents, but each supplied different justifications for the requests.

The House Committee on Financial Services issued two subpoenas, both on April 11, 2019. . . . The first, issued to Deutsche Bank, seeks the financial information of the President, his children, their immediate family members, and several affiliated business entities. . . . The second, issued to Capital One, demands similar financial information with respect to more than a dozen business entities associated with the President. . . .

According to the House, the Financial Services Committee issued these subpoenas pursuant to House Resolution 206, which called for "efforts to close loopholes that allow corruption, terrorism, and money laundering to infiltrate our country's financial system." . . . Such loopholes, the resolution explained, had allowed "illicit money, including from Russian oligarchs," to flow into the United States through "anonymous shell companies" using investments such as "luxury high-end real estate." . . . The House also invokes the oversight plan of the Financial Services Committee, which stated that the Committee intends to review banking regulation and "examine the implementation, effectiveness, and enforcement" of laws designed to prevent money laundering and the financing of terrorism. . . . The plan further provided that the Committee would "consider proposals to prevent the abuse of the financial system" and "address any vulnerabilities identified" in the real estate market. . . .

On the same day as the Financial Services Committee, the Permanent Select Committee on Intelligence issued an identical subpoena to Deutsche Bank—albeit for different reasons. According to the House, the Intelligence Committee subpoenaed Deutsche Bank as part of an investigation into foreign efforts to undermine the U. S. political process. Committee Chairman Adam Schiff had described that investigation in a previous statement, explaining that the Committee was examining alleged attempts by Russia to influence the 2016 election; potential links between Russia and the President's campaign; and whether the President and his associates had been compromised by foreign actors or interests. Press Release, House Permanent Select Committee on Intelligence, Chairman Schiff Statement on House Intelligence Committee Investigation (Feb. 6, 2019). Chairman Schiff added that the Committee planned "to develop legislation and policy reforms to ensure the U. S. government is better positioned to counter future efforts to undermine our political process and national security." . . .

Four days after the Financial Services and Intelligence Committees, the House Committee on Oversight and Reform issued another subpoena, this time to the President's personal accounting firm, Mazars USA, LLP. The subpoena demanded information related to the President and several affiliated business entities from 2011 through 2018, including statements of financial condition, independent auditors' reports, financial reports, underlying source documents, and communications between Mazars and the President or his businesses. The subpoena also requested all engagement agreements and contracts "[w]ithout regard to time."

Chairman Elijah Cummings explained the basis for the subpoena in a memorandum to the Oversight Committee. According to the chairman, recent testimony by the President's former personal attorney Michael Cohen, along with several documents prepared by Mazars and supplied by Cohen, raised questions about whether the President had accurately represented his financial affairs. Chairman Cummings asserted that the Committee had "full authority to investigate" whether the President: (1) "may have engaged in illegal conduct before and during his tenure in office," (2) "has undisclosed conflicts of interest that may impair his ability to make impartial policy decisions," (3) "is complying with the Emoluments Clauses of the Constitution," and (4) "has accurately reported his finances to the Office of Government Ethics and other federal entities." . . . "The Committee's interest in these matters," Chairman Cummings concluded, "informs its review of multiple laws and legislative proposals under our jurisdiction." . . .

B

Petitioners—the President in his personal capacity, along with his children and affiliated businesses—filed two suits challenging the subpoenas. They contested the subpoena issued by the Oversight Committee in the District Court for the District of Columbia . . . and the subpoenas issued by the Financial Services and Intelligence Committees in the Southern District of New York . . . . In both cases, petitioners contended that the subpoenas lacked a legitimate legislative purpose and violated the separation of powers. The President did not, however, resist the subpoenas by arguing that any of the requested records were protected by executive privilege. For relief, petitioners asked for declaratory judgments and injunctions preventing Mazars and the banks from complying with the subpoenas. Although named as defendants, Mazars and the banks took no positions on the legal issues in these cases, and the House committees intervened to defend the subpoenas.

Petitioners' challenges failed. . . .

We granted certiorari in both cases and stayed the judgments below pending our decision. . . .

II

A

The question presented is whether the subpoenas exceed the authority of the House under the Constitution. Historically, disputes over congressional demands for presidential documents have not ended up in court. Instead, they have been hashed out in the "hurly-burly, the give-and-take of the political process between the legislative and the executive." . . .

That practice began with George Washington and the early Congress. In 1792, a House committee requested Executive Branch documents pertaining to General St. Clair's campaign against the Indians in the Northwest Territory, which had concluded in an utter rout of federal forces when they were caught by surprise near the present-day border between Ohio and Indiana. . . . Since this was the first such request from Congress, President Washington called a Cabinet meeting, wishing to take care that his response "be rightly conducted" because it could "become a precedent." . . .

The meeting, attended by the likes of Alexander Hamilton, Thomas Jefferson, Edmund Randolph, and Henry Knox, ended with the Cabinet of "one mind": The House had authority to "institute inquiries" and "call for papers" but the President could "exercise a discretion" over disclosures, "communicat[ing] such papers as the public good would permit" and "refus[ing]" the rest. . . . President Washington then dispatched Jefferson to speak to individual congressmen and "bring them by persuasion into the right channel." . . . The discussions were apparently fruitful, as the House later narrowed its request and the documents were supplied without recourse to the courts. . . .

Jefferson, once he became President, followed Washington's precedent. In early 1807, after Jefferson had disclosed that "sundry persons" were conspiring to invade Spanish territory in North America with a private army, . . . the House requested that the President produce any information in his possession touching on the conspiracy (except for information that would harm the public interest). . . . Jefferson chose not to divulge the entire "voluminous" correspondence on the subject, explaining that much of it was "private" or mere "rumors" and "neither safety nor justice" permitted him to "expos[e] names" apart from identifying the conspiracy's "principal actor": Aaron Burr. . . . Instead of the entire correspondence, Jefferson sent Congress particular documents and a special message summarizing the conspiracy. . . . Neither Congress nor the President asked the Judiciary to intervene.

Ever since, congressional demands for the President's information have been resolved by the political branches without involving this Court. The Reagan and Clinton presidencies provide two modern examples:

During the Reagan administration, a House subcommittee subpoenaed all documents related to the Department of the Interior's decision whether to designate Canada a reciprocal country for purposes of the Mineral Lands Leasing Act. President Reagan directed that certain documents be withheld because they implicated his confidential relationship with subordinates. While withholding those documents, the administration made "repeated efforts" at accommodation through limited disclosures and testimony over a period of several months. . . . Unsatisfied, the subcommittee and its parent committee eventually voted to hold the Secretary of the Interior in contempt, and an innovative compromise soon followed: All documents were made available, but only for one day with no photocopying, minimal notetaking, and no participation by non-Members of Congress. . . .

In 1995, a Senate committee subpoenaed notes taken by a White House attorney at a meeting with President Clinton's personal lawyers concerning the Whitewater controversy. The President resisted the subpoena on the ground that the notes were protected by attorney-client privilege, leading to "long and protracted" negotiations and a Senate threat to seek judicial enforcement of the subpoena. . . . Eventually the parties reached an agreement, whereby President Clinton avoided the threatened suit, agreed to turn over the notes, and obtained the Senate's concession that he had not waived any privileges. . . .

Congress and the President maintained this tradition of negotiation and compromise—without the involvement of this Court—until the present dispute. Indeed, from President Washington until now, we have never considered a dispute over a congressional subpoena for the President's records. And, according to the parties, the appellate courts have addressed such a subpoena only once, when a Senate committee subpoenaed President Nixon during the Watergate scandal. Senate Select Committee on Presidential Campaign Activities v. Nixon, 498 F.2d 725 (CADC 1974) (en banc). In that case, the [Court of Appeals for the D.C. Circuit] refused to enforce the subpoena, and the Senate did not seek review by this Court.

This dispute therefore represents a significant departure from historical practice. Although the parties agree that this particular controversy is justiciable, we recognize that it is the first of its kind to reach this Court; that disputes of this sort can raise important issues concerning relations between the branches; that related disputes involving congressional efforts to seek official Executive Branch information recur on a regular basis, including in the context of deeply partisan controversy; and that Congress and the Executive have nonetheless managed for over two centuries to resolve such disputes among themselves without the benefit of guidance from us. Such longstanding practice " 'is a consideration of great weight' " in cases concerning "the allocation of power between [the] two elected branches of Government," and it imposes on us a duty of care to ensure that we not needlessly disturb "the compromises and working arrangements that [those] branches . . . themselves have reached." . . . With that in mind, we turn to the question presented.

B

Congress has no enumerated constitutional power to conduct investigations or issue subpoenas, but we have held that each House has power "to secure needed information" in order to legislate. McGrain v. Daugherty, 273 U.S. 135, 161 (1927). This "power of inquiry—with process to enforce it—is an essential and appropriate auxiliary to the legislative function." . . . Without information, Congress would be shooting in the dark, unable to legislate "wisely or effectively." . . . The congressional power to obtain information is "broad" and "indispensable." Watkins v. United States, 354 U.S. 178, 187, 215 (1957). It encompasses inquiries into the administration of existing laws, studies of proposed laws, and "surveys of defects in our social, economic or political system for the purpose of enabling the Congress to remedy them.". . .

Because this power is "justified solely as an adjunct to the legislative process," it is subject to several limitations. . . . Most importantly, a congressional subpoena is valid only if it is "related to, and in furtherance of, a legitimate task of the Congress.". . . The subpoena must serve a "valid legislative purpose," Quinn v. United States, 349 U.S. 155, 161(1955); it must "concern[ ] a subject on which legislation 'could be had,'" Eastland v. United States Servicemen's Fund, 421 U.S. 491, 506 (1975) (quoting *McGrain*, 273 U.S. at 177).

Furthermore, Congress may not issue a subpoena for the purpose of "law enforcement," because "those powers are assigned under our Constitution to the Executive and the Judiciary." *Quinn*, ... Thus Congress may not use subpoenas to "try" someone "before [a] committee for any crime or wrongdoing." . . . Congress has no " 'general' power to inquire into private affairs and compel disclosures,". . . and "there is no congressional power to expose for the sake of exposure,". . . . "Investigations conducted solely for the personal aggrandizement of the investigators or to 'punish' those investigated are indefensible.". . .

Finally, recipients of legislative subpoenas retain their constitutional rights throughout the course of an investigation. . . . And recipients have long been understood to retain common law and constitutional privileges with respect to certain materials, such as attorney-client communications and governmental communications protected by executive privilege. . . .

C

The President contends, as does the Solicitor General appearing on behalf of the United States, that the usual rules for congressional subpoenas do not govern here because the President's papers are at issue. They argue for a more demanding standard based in large part on cases involving the Nixon tapes— recordings of conversations between President Nixon and close advisers discussing the break-in at the Democratic National Committee's headquarters at the Watergate complex. The tapes were subpoenaed by a Senate committee and the Special Prosecutor investigating the break-in, prompting President Nixon to invoke executive privilege and leading to two cases addressing the showing necessary to require the President to comply with the subpoenas. See *Nixon*, 418 U.S. 683; *Senate Select Committee*, 498 F.2d 725.

Those cases, the President and the Solicitor General now contend, establish the standard that should govern the House subpoenas here. Quoting *Nixon*, the President asserts that the House must establish a "demonstrated, specific need" for the financial information, just as the Watergate special prosecutor was required to do in order to obtain the tapes. . . . And drawing on *Senate Select Committee*—the D. C. Circuit case refusing to enforce the Senate subpoena for the tapes—the President and the Solicitor General argue that the House must show that the financial information is "demonstrably critical" to its legislative purpose. . . .

We disagree that these demanding standards apply here. Unlike the cases before us, *Nixon* and *Senate Select Committee* involved Oval Office communications over which the President asserted executive privilege. That privilege safeguards the public interest in candid, confidential deliberations within the Executive Branch; it is "fundamental to the operation of Government." *Nixon*, 418 U.S. at 708. As a result, information subject to executive privilege deserves "the greatest protection consistent with the fair administration of justice.". . . . We decline to transplant that protection root and branch to cases involving nonprivileged, private information, which by definition does not implicate sensitive Executive Branch deliberations.

The standards proposed by the President and the Solicitor General—if applied outside the context of privileged information—would risk seriously impeding Congress in carrying out its responsibilities. The President and the Solicitor General would apply the same exacting standards to *all* subpoenas for the President's information, without recognizing distinctions between privileged and nonprivileged information, between official and personal information, or between various legislative objectives. Such a categorical approach would represent a significant departure from the longstanding way of doing business between the branches, giving short shrift to Congress's important interests in conducting inquiries to obtain the information it needs to legislate effectively. Confounding the legislature in that effort would be contrary to the principle that:

> "It is the proper duty of a representative body to look diligently into every affair of government and to talk much about what it sees. It is meant to be the eyes and the voice, and to embody the wisdom and will of its constituents. Unless Congress have and use every means of acquainting itself with the acts and the disposition of the administrative agents of the government, the country must be helpless to learn how it is being served." United States v. Rumely, 345 U.S. 41, 43 (1953) . . . .

Legislative inquiries might involve the President in appropriate cases; as noted, Congress's responsibilities extend to "every affair of government." . . . Because the President's approach does not take adequate account of these significant congressional interests, we do not adopt it.

D

The House meanwhile would have us ignore that these suits involve the President. Invoking our precedents concerning investigations that did not target the President's papers, the House urges us to uphold its subpoenas because they "relate[ ] to a valid legislative purpose" or "concern[ ] a subject on which legislation could be had." . . . That approach is appropriate, the House argues, because the cases before us are not "momentous separation-of-powers disputes." . . .

. . .

The House's approach fails to take adequate account of the significant separation of powers issues raised by congressional subpoenas for the President's information. Congress and the President have an ongoing institutional relationship as the "opposite and rival" political branches established by the Constitution. The Federalist No. 51, at 349. As a result, congressional subpoenas directed at the President differ markedly from congressional subpoenas we have previously reviewed . . . and they bear little resemblance to criminal subpoenas issued to the President in the course of a specific investigation, see *Vance. . .* ; *Nixon.* . . . Unlike those subpoenas, congressional subpoenas for the President's information unavoidably pit the political branches against one another. . . .

Far from accounting for separation of powers concerns, the House's approach aggravates them by leaving essentially no limits on the congressional power to subpoena the President's personal records. Any personal paper possessed by a President could potentially "relate to" a conceivable subject of legislation, for Congress has broad legislative powers that touch a vast number of subjects. . . . The President's financial records could relate to economic reform, medical records to health reform, school transcripts to education reform, and so on. Indeed, at argument, the House was unable to identify *any* type of information that lacks some relation to potential legislation. . . .

Without limits on its subpoena powers, Congress could "exert an imperious controul" over the Executive Branch and aggrandize itself at the President's expense, just as the Framers feared. The Federalist No. 71, at 484 (A. Hamilton); see *id.*, No. 48, at 332–333 (J. Madison); . . . . And a limitless subpoena power would transform the "established practice" of the political branches. . . . Instead of negotiating over information requests, Congress could simply walk away from the bargaining table and compel compliance in court.

The House and the courts below suggest that these separation of powers concerns are not fully implicated by the particular subpoenas here, but we disagree. We would have to be "blind" not to see what "[a]ll others can see and understand": that the subpoenas do not represent a run-of-the-mill legislative effort but rather a clash between rival branches of government over records of intense political interest for all involved. . . .

The interbranch conflict here does not vanish simply because the subpoenas seek personal papers or because the President sued in his personal capacity. The President is the only person who alone composes a branch of government. As a result, there is not always a clear line between his personal and official affairs. "The interest of the man" is often "connected with the constitutional rights of the place." The Federalist No. 51, at 349. Given the close connection between the Office of the President and its occupant, congressional demands for the President's papers can implicate the relationship between the branches regardless whether those papers are personal or official. Either way, a demand may aim to harass the President or render him "complaisan[t] to the humors of the Legislature." *Id.*, No. 71, at 483. In fact, a subpoena for personal papers may pose a heightened risk of such impermissible purposes, precisely because of the documents' personal nature and their less evident connection to a legislative task. No one can say that the controversy here is less significant to the relationship between the branches simply because it involves personal papers. Quite the opposite. That appears to be what makes the matter of such great consequence to the President and Congress.

In addition, separation of powers concerns are no less palpable here simply because the subpoenas were issued to third parties. Congressional demands for the President's information present an interbranch conflict no matter where the information is held—it is, after all, the President's information. Were it otherwise, Congress could sidestep constitutional requirements any time a President's information is entrusted to a third party—as occurs with rapidly increasing frequency. . . . Indeed, Congress could declare open season on the President's information held by schools, archives, internet service providers, e-mail clients, and financial institutions. The Constitution does not tolerate such ready evasion; it "deals with substance, not shadows.". . .

E

Congressional subpoenas for the President's personal information implicate weighty concerns regarding the separation of powers. Neither side, however, identifies an approach that accounts for these concerns. For more than two centuries, the political branches have resolved information disputes using the wide variety of means that the Constitution puts at their disposal. The nature of such interactions would be transformed by judicial enforcement of either of the approaches suggested by the parties, eroding a "[d]eeply embedded traditional way[ ] of conducting government." *Youngstown Sheet & Tube Co.*, 343 U.S. at 610 (Frankfurter, J., concurring).

A balanced approach is necessary, one that takes a "considerable impression" from "the practice of the government" . . . and "resist[s]" the "pressure inherent within each of the separate Branches to exceed the outer limits of its power,". . . We therefore conclude that, in assessing whether a subpoena directed at the President's personal information is "related to, and in furtherance of, a legitimate task of the Congress,". . . courts must perform a careful analysis that takes adequate account of the separation of powers principles at stake, including both the significant legislative interests of Congress and the "unique position" of the President. . . . Several special considerations inform this analysis.

First, courts should carefully assess whether the asserted legislative purpose warrants the significant step of involving the President and his papers. " '[O]ccasion[s] for constitutional confrontation between the two branches' should be avoided whenever possible." Cheney v. United States Dist. Court for D. C., 542 U.S. 367, 389–390 (2004) (quoting *Nixon*, 418 U.S. at 692). Congress may not rely on the President's information if other sources could reasonably provide Congress the information it needs in light of its particular legislative objective. The President's unique constitutional position means that Congress may not look to him as a "case study" for general legislation. . . .

Unlike in criminal proceedings, where "[t]he very integrity of the judicial system" would be undermined without "full disclosure of all the facts,". . . efforts to craft legislation involve predictive policy judgments that are "not hamper[ed] . . . in quite the same way" when every scrap of potentially relevant evidence is not available. . . . While we certainly recognize Congress's important interests in obtaining information through appropriate inquiries, those interests are not sufficiently powerful to justify access to the President's personal papers when other sources could provide Congress the information it needs.

Second, to narrow the scope of possible conflict between the branches, courts should insist on a subpoena no broader than reasonably necessary to support Congress's legislative objective. The specificity of the subpoena's request "serves as an important safeguard against unnecessary intrusion into the operation of the Office of the President." *Cheney*, ...

Third, courts should be attentive to the nature of the evidence offered by Congress to establish that a subpoena advances a valid legislative purpose. The more detailed and substantial the evidence of Congress's legislative purpose, the better. . . . That is particularly true when Congress contemplates legislation that raises sensitive constitutional issues, such as legislation concerning the Presidency. In such cases, it is "impossible" to conclude that a subpoena is designed to advance a valid legislative purpose unless Congress adequately identifies its aims and explains why the President's information will advance its consideration of the possible legislation. . . .

Fourth, courts should be careful to assess the burdens imposed on the President by a subpoena. We have held that burdens on the President's time and attention stemming from judicial process and litigation, without more, generally do not cross constitutional lines. See *Vance*; *Clinton* . . . . But burdens imposed by a congressional subpoena should be carefully scrutinized, for they stem from a rival political branch that has an ongoing relationship with the President and incentives to use subpoenas for institutional advantage.

Other considerations may be pertinent as well; one case every two centuries does not afford enough experience for an exhaustive list.

When Congress seeks information "needed for intelligent legislative action," it "unquestionably" remains "the duty of *all* citizens to cooperate." . . . Congressional subpoenas for information from the President, however, implicate special concerns regarding the separation of powers. The courts below did not take adequate account of those concerns. The judgments of the Courts of Appeals for the D. C. Circuit and the Second Circuit are vacated, and the cases are remanded for further proceedings consistent with this opinion.

■ JUSTICE THOMAS, dissenting.

. . .

[Justice Thomas argued that history from England and from 18th and 19th century America demonstrated that Presidents were not susceptible to these kinds of Congressional subpoenas.]

* * *

Congress' legislative powers do not authorize it to engage in a nationwide inquisition with whatever resources it chooses to appropriate for itself. The majority's solution—a nonexhaustive four-factor test of uncertain origin—is better than nothing. But the power that Congress seeks to exercise here has even less basis in the Constitution than the majority supposes. I would reverse in full because the power to subpoena private, nonofficial documents is not a necessary implication of Congress' legislative powers. If Congress wishes to obtain these documents, it should proceed through the impeachment power. Accordingly, I respectfully dissent.

■ JUSTICE ALITO, dissenting.

Justice Thomas makes a valuable argument about the constitutionality of congressional subpoenas for a President's personal documents. In these cases, however, I would assume for the sake of argument that such subpoenas are not categorically barred. Nevertheless, legislative subpoenas for a President's personal documents are inherently suspicious. Such documents are seldom of any special value in considering potential legislation, and subpoenas for such documents can easily be used for improper non-legislative purposes. Accordingly, courts must be very sensitive to separation of powers issues when they are asked to approve the enforcement of such subpoenas.

In many cases, disputes about subpoenas for Presidential documents are fought without judicial involvement. If Congress attempts to obtain such documents by subpoenaing a President directly, those two heavyweight institutions can use their considerable weapons to settle the matter. . . . But when Congress issues such a subpoena to a third party, Congress must surely appreciate that the Judiciary may be pulled into the dispute, and Congress should not expect that the courts will allow the subpoena to be enforced without seriously examining its legitimacy.

Whenever such a subpoena comes before a court, Congress should be required to make more than a perfunctory showing that it is seeking the documents for a legitimate legislative purpose and not for the purpose of exposing supposed Presidential wrongdoing. . . . The House can inquire about possible Presidential wrongdoing pursuant to its impeachment power[, as Justice Thomas suggests,] . . . but the Committees do not defend these subpoenas as ancillary to that power.

Instead, they claim that the subpoenas were issued to gather information that is relevant to legislative issues, but[, as a dissenting judge in the lower court suggested,] there is disturbing evidence of an improper law enforcement purpose. See 940 F.3d 710, 767–771 (CADC 2019) (Rao, J., dissenting). In addition, the sheer volume of documents sought calls out for explanation. . . .

The Court recognizes that the decisions below did not give adequate consideration to separation of powers concerns. Therefore, after setting out a non-exhaustive list of considerations for the lower courts to take into account, the Court vacates the judgments of the Courts of Appeals and sends the cases back for reconsideration. I agree that the lower courts erred and that these cases must be remanded, but I do not think that the considerations outlined by the Court can be properly satisfied unless the House is required to show more than it has put forward to date.

Specifically, the House should provide a description of the type of legislation being considered, and while great specificity is not necessary, the description should be sufficient to permit a court to assess whether the particular records sought are of any special importance. The House should also spell out its constitutional authority to enact the type of legislation that it is contemplating, and it should justify the scope of the subpoenas in relation to the articulated legislative needs. In addition, it should explain why the subpoenaed information, as opposed to information available from other sources, is needed. Unless the House is required to make a showing along these lines, I would hold that enforcement of the subpoenas cannot be ordered. Because I find the terms of the Court's remand inadequate, I must respectfully dissent.

Page 403. Change the title of *NOTE ON THE IMPEACHMENT OF PRESIDENT WILLIAM CLINTON* **to** *NOTE ON THE IMPEACHMENTS OF PRESIDENTS WILLIAM CLINTON AND DONALD TRUMP*, **and add the following at the end of the Note:**

Two decades later, Donald Trump became the third U.S. President to be impeached. After an inquiry that took place between September and November 2019, the House of Representatives on December 18, 2019 passed two Articles of Impeachment, charging President Trump with abuse of power and obstruction of Congress. The allegations dealt with, among other things, the propriety of and motivations behind President Trump's communications with the President of Ukraine concerning U.S. military aid to that country. About a month after the House's vote, on January 21, 2020, the Republican majority in the Senate rebuffed several attempts by Democratic impeachment managers from the House to exercise subpoena authority to adduce testimony from current and former White House officials, and to compel production of Trump administration documents which had not been provided to House investigators during the inquiry. The House impeachment managers made their opening arguments from January 22–24; the defense made its arguments the following three days, from January 25–28. After ensuing rounds of questions, answers, and debate from January 29–31, on January 31 a Senate majority of 51 Republican senators conclusively voted against allowing subpoenas to call witnesses or documents.

Less than a week later, on February 5, 2020, the Senate acquitted President Trump on both impeachment articles, as neither article garnered the votes of two thirds of the Senators. On the obstruction of Congress charge, all fifty-three Republican Senators voted not guilty, with all 45 Democrats and both independents voting guilty. On the abuse of power charge, all 45 Democrats and the two independents voted guilty again, but this time they were joined by one Republican Senator, Mitt Romney of Utah. Because 52 Republicans voted not guilty, the charge failed, but Senator Romney's vote marked the first time in American history a Senator cast a vote to convict and remove a President of the same political party. For a general discussion of many of the constitutional issues presented by the Trump impeachment and trial, see Vikram David Amar and Jason Mazzone, "The Power to 'Try' 'Cases of Impeachment:' Some Reflections on the Finality, Transparency and Integrity of Senate Adjudications of Presidential Impeachments (Including that of Donald J. Trump)," 95 CHI-KENT L. REV. ___ (forthcoming 2020).

PART 3

GOVERNMENT AND THE INDIVIDUAL: THE PROTECTION OF LIBERTY AND PROPERTY UNDER THE DUE PROCESS AND EQUAL PROTECTION CLAUSES

CHAPTER 8

THE BILL OF RIGHTS, THE CIVIL WAR AMENDMENTS AND THEIR INTER-RELATIONSHIP

3. APPLICATION OF THE BILL OF RIGHTS TO THE STATES

Page 441. Replace last paragraph of Note, *Incorporation and the Jury Trial Cases* with the following:

Although the Court, without a majority opinion, at first upheld an Oregon statute providing for conviction in criminal cases by a vote of 10 persons out of a jury of twelve, Apodaca v. Oregon, 406 U.S. 404 (1972), 48 years later the Court changed course and held unconstitutional an identical Louisiana statute. Ramos v. Louisiana, 590 U.S. ___, 140 S.Ct. 1390 (2020). In doing so, the Court referenced "the historical meaning of the Sixth Amendment's jury trial right, this Court's long-repeated statements that it demands unanimity, [and] the racist origins of Louisiana's and Oregon's laws." Oregon and Louisiana were the only two states that allowed for convictions of serious offenses by nonunanimous juries and both originally adopted those laws in the Jim Crow era to undermine the possibility that African American jurors might vote for acquittals of African American defendants. Justice Gorsuch's majority opinion also noted the Anglo-American 400 year history assuming that the jury trial right required unanimity and the volume of Court precedents that also had articulated that requirement. Solely on the basis of the doctrine of *stare decisis*, a dissent by Justice Alito, joined by Chief Justice Roberts and Justice Kagan, would not have overruled *Apodaca*.*

---

* The Court, in Burch v. Louisiana, 441 U.S. 130 (1979), already had held invalid a statute providing for trial "before a jury of six persons, five of whom must concur to render a verdict." Even given *Apodaca* as the then prevailing ruling, the Court there noted that "having already departed from the strictly historical requirements of jury trial, it is inevitable that lines must be drawn somewhere if the substance of the jury trial right is to be preserved."

Page 461. Add after McDonald v. City of Chicago:

Timbs v. Indiana, 586 U.S. ___, 139 S.Ct. 682 (2019). Timbs pled guilty to dealing in a controlled substance and conspiracy to commit theft. He was sentenced to a year of home detention, five years of probation that included a court-supervised addiction treatment program, and the payment of $1,203 in fees and costs. When he was arrested, police seized his Land Rover SUV, for which he had paid $42,000 from his father's life insurance. After Timbs' guilty plea, the State sought civil forfeiture of the SUV, which had been used to transport heroin, but the Indiana trial court denied the forfeiture demand, finding it a violation of the Excessive Fines Clause of the Eighth Amendment, because the SUV cost more than four times the maximum $10,000 monetary fine assessable against him for his drug conviction. The intermediate appellate court affirmed, but the

Indiana Supreme Court reversed, holding "that the Excessive Fines Clause constrains only federal action and is inapplicable to state impositions."

Applying the approach used in *McDonald*, the Court vacated the judgment and remanded the case, holding that the Eighth Amendment's "Excessive Fines Clause is . . . incorporated by the Due Process Clause of the Fourteenth Amendment." Justice Ginsburg's opinion for the Court began by noting that a "Bill of Rights protection is incorporated, we have explained, if it is 'fundamental to our scheme of ordered liberty,' or 'deeply rooted in this Nation's history and tradition.' " She traced the "venerable lineage" of the Excessive Fines Clause "back to at least 1215" when "Magna Carta required that economic sanctions 'be proportioned to the wrong' and 'not be so large as to deprive [an offender] of his livelihood.' " The "English Bill of Rights [of 1689] reaffirmed Magna Carta's guarantee by providing that 'excessive Bail ought not to be required, nor excessive Fines imposed; nor cruel and unusual Punishments inflicted.' " In 1787, even before its adoption in the Bill of Rights, "the constitutions of eight States—accounting for 70% of the U. S. population—forbade excessive fines." By the time the Fourteenth Amendment was ratified in 1868, "the constitutions of 35 of the 37 States—accounting for over 90% of the U. S. population—expressly prohibited excessive fines." Justice Ginsburg continued:

"Today, acknowledgment of the right's fundamental nature remains widespread. As Indiana itself reports, all 50 States have a constitutional provision prohibiting the imposition of excessive fines either directly or by requiring proportionality. . . .

"For good reason, the protection against excessive fines has been a constant shield throughout Anglo-American history: Exorbitant tolls undermine other constitutional liberties. Excessive fines can be used, for example, to retaliate against or chill the speech of political enemies . . . . Even absent a political motive, fines may be employed 'in a measure out of accord with the penal goals of retribution and deterrence,' for 'fines are a source of revenue,' while other forms of punishment 'cost a State money.' "

Justice Ginsburg rejected Indiana's argument that "the Clause does not apply to its use of civil *in rem* forfeitures because . . . the Clause's specific application to such forfeitures is neither fundamental nor deeply rooted." In "Austin v. United States, 509 U. S. 602 (1993), . . . this Court held that civil *in rem* forfeitures fall within the Clause's protection when they are at least partially punitive." The Court found Indiana's "invitation to reconsider our unanimous judgment in *Austin*" not properly before them. And the Court disagreed with Indiana's argument "that the Excessive Fines Clause cannot be incorporated if it applies to civil *in rem* forfeitures": "In considering whether the Fourteenth Amendment incorporates a protection contained in the Bill of Rights, we ask whether the right guaranteed—not each and every particular application of that right—is fundamental or deeply rooted."

Justice Gorsuch concurred, writing that "[a]s an original matter, . . . the appropriate vehicle for incorporation may well be the Fourteenth Amendment's Privileges or Immunities Clause, rather than, as this Court has long assumed, the Due Process Clause. . . . But nothing in this case turns on that question, and, regardless of the precise vehicle, there can be no serious doubt that the Fourteenth Amendment requires the States to respect the freedom from excessive fines enshrined in the Eighth Amendment."

Justice Thomas concurred in the judgment, taking the position that "[i]nstead of reading the Fourteenth Amendment's Due Process Clause to encompass a substantive right that has nothing to do with 'process,' I would hold that the right to be free from excessive fines is one of the 'privileges or immunities of citizens of the United States' protected by the Fourteenth Amendment."

CHAPTER 9

THE DUE PROCESS, CONTRACT, AND JUST COMPENSATION CLAUSES AND THE REVIEW OF THE REASONABLENESS OF LEGISLATION

1. ECONOMIC REGULATORY LEGISLATION

B. THE CONTRACT CLAUSE—WHAT DOES IT ADD TO THE DUE PROCESS LIMITATION?

Page 498. Add the following after Exxon Corp. v. Eagerton:

Sveen v. Melin, 584 U.S. ___, 138 S.Ct. 1815 (2018). A Minnesota law passed in 2002, similar to recent statutory changes in 25 other States, changed the former rule—that divorce did not affect an insured's designation of his or her spouse as the beneficiary of the insurance policy—to a default rule that "the dissolution or annulment of a marriage revokes any revocable[ ] beneficiary designation[ ] made by an individual to the individual's former spouse." The statute is premised on the theory that the policyholder would want that result, but if that is not the case it allows the policyholder after divorce to rename the ex-spouse as beneficiary. With only Justice Gorsuch dissenting, the Court held that the Contracts Clause did not prevent application of the current "revocation-on-divorce law" to a spousal beneficiary designation made before the statute was enacted that the insured, later divorced and now deceased, never changed. Justice Kagan's opinion for the Court included the following:

"[N]ot all laws affecting pre-existing contracts violate the Clause. See El Paso v. Simmons, 379 U.S. 497, 506–507 (1965). To determine when such a law crosses the constitutional line, this Court has long applied a two-step test. The threshold issue is whether the state law has 'operated as a substantial impairment of a contractual relationship.' *Allied Structural Steel Co.*, 438 U.S., at 244. In answering that question, the Court has considered the extent to which the law undermines the contractual bargain, interferes with a party's reasonable expectations, and prevents the party from safeguarding or reinstating his rights. See *id.*, at 246; *El Paso*, 379 U.S., at 514–515; Texaco, Inc. v. Short, 454 U.S. 516, 531 (1982). If such factors show a substantial impairment, the inquiry turns to the means and ends of the legislation. In particular, the Court has asked whether the state law is drawn in an 'appropriate' and 'reasonable' way to advance 'a significant and legitimate public purpose.' Energy Reserves Group, Inc. v. Kansas Power & Light Co., 459 U.S. 400, 411–412 (1983).

"Here, we may stop after step one because Minnesota's revocation-on-divorce statute does not substantially impair pre-existing contractual arrangements. True enough that in revoking a beneficiary designation, the law makes a significant change. As Melin says, the 'whole point' of buying life insurance is to provide the proceeds to the named beneficiary. . . . But three aspects of Minnesota's law, taken together, defeat Melin's argument that the change it effected 'severely impaired' her ex-husband's contract. . . . First, the statute is designed to reflect a policyholder's intent—and so to support, rather than impair, the contractual scheme. Second, the law is unlikely to disturb any policyholder's expectations because it does no more than a divorce court could always have done. And third, the statute supplies a mere default rule, which the policyholder can undo in a moment. . . ."

In her elaboration of these points, Justice Kagan emphasized that "[a]lthough there are exceptions, most divorcees do not aspire to enrich their former partners" and that "the insured's failure to change the beneficiary after a divorce is more likely the result of neglect than choice." Moreover, the statute "is unlikely to upset a policyholder's expectations at the time of contracting . . . because an insured cannot reasonably rely on a beneficiary designation remaining in place after a divorce" given that "divorce courts have wide discretion to divide property between spouses when a marriage ends." And "[f]inally, a policyholder can reverse the effect of the Minnesota statute with the stroke of a pen . . . by the simple act of sending a change-of-beneficiary form to his insurer" or more permanently by "agree[ing] to a divorce settlement continuing his ex-spouse's beneficiary status."

Justice Gorsuch's lone dissent first argued that the "Contracts Clause categorically prohibits states from passing 'any . . . Law impairing the Obligation of Contracts.' Art. I, § 10, cl. 1 (emphasis added)." He asserted that "[f]or much of its history, this Court construed the Contracts Clause in this light." He then argued that "[e]ven under our modern precedents, . . . when a state alters life insurance contracts by undoing their beneficiary designations it surely 'substantially impairs' them." And he concluded that "[n]o one can offer any reasonable justification for this impairment in light of readily available alternatives." Among such alternatives, "the state could have easily achieved [its] goal without impairing contracts *at all*. It could have required courts to confirm that divorcing couples have reviewed their life insurance designations. . . . It could have instructed insurance companies to notify policyholders of their right to change beneficiary designations. It could have disseminated information on its own. Or it could have required attorneys in divorce proceedings to address the question with affected parties. . . . Yet there's no evidence Minnesota investigated any of them, let alone found them wanting."

C. THE JUST COMPENSATION CLAUSE OF THE FIFTH AMENDMENT—WHAT DOES IT ADD TO DUE PROCESS?

1. RESTRICTIONS ON PROPERTY USE

Page 515. Add the following before Horne v. Department of Agriculture:

Murr v. Wisconsin, 582 U.S. ___, 137 S.Ct. 1933 (2017). Petitioners, family members who owned two adjacent undeveloped lots (known as Lots "E" and "F") along the St. Croix river in Wisconsin, brought suit contending that state governmental entities took their property by enacting burdensome regulations that forbid separate improvement or sale of the parcels. For the area where petitioners' property is located, Wisconsin law contains a "merger" provision specifying that adjacent lots under common ownership may not be "sold or developed as separate lots" unless they meet a certain size requirement.

A decade later after assuming common ownership of the two lots, petitioners became interested in moving a cabin that was located on Lot F to a different portion of the lot and selling Lot E to fund the project. Because of their insufficient size, under state law the lots could not be sold or developed separately, so petitioners then sought variances from the St. Croix County Board of Adjustment to enable the building and improvement plan, including a variance to allow the separate sale or use of the lots. The Board denied the requests, and the state courts affirmed in relevant part. In particular, the Wisconsin Court of Appeals agreed with the Board's interpretation that the local ordinance "effectively merged" Lots E and F, so petitioners "could only sell or build on the single larger [merged] lot."

Petitioners then filed an action in state court, contending that the state and county regulations worked a regulatory taking by depriving them of "all, or practically all, of the use of Lot E because the lot cannot be sold or developed as a separate lot." Both sides submitted appraisal numbers to the trial court. "Respondents' appraisal included values of $698,300 for the lots together as regulated; $771,000 for the lots as two distinct buildable properties; and $373,000 for Lot F as a single lot with improvements[, whereas] Petitioners' appraisal included an unrebutted, estimated value of $40,000 for Lot E as an undevelopable lot, based on the counterfactual assumption that it could be sold as a separate property."

The trial court granted summary judgment to respondents on the ground that notwithstanding the regulations in place petitioners retained "several available options for the use and enjoyment of their property," including preserving or relocating the existing cabin, and eliminating the cabin and building a new residence on Lot E, on Lot F, or across both lots. The court specifically found petitioners had not been deprived of all economic value of their property, because the difference in value between treating the property as two lots versus a single larger lot was less than 10 percent.

The Wisconsin Court of Appeals—observing that it first had to "determine what, precisely, is the property at issue" and observing that the takings analysis should "properly focus[ ] . . . on the Murrs' property as a whole"—affirmed the grant of summary judgment, the Wisconsin Supreme Court denied review, and the Court granted certiorari.

In a 5–3 majority opinion written by Justice Kennedy, and joined by Justices Ginsburg, Breyer, Sotomayor and Kagan, the Court affirmed. Justice Kennedy began the Court's analysis laying out the broader regulatory takings framework:

". . . This area of the law has been characterized by 'ad hoc, factual inquiries, designed to allow careful examination and weighing of all the relevant circumstances.' . . . The Court has, however, stated two guidelines relevant here for determining when government regulation is so onerous that it constitutes a taking. First, 'with certain qualifications . . . a regulation which "denies all economically beneficial or productive use of land" will require compensation under the Takings Clause.' . . . Second, when a regulation impedes the use of property without depriving the owner of all economically beneficial use, a taking still may be found based on 'a complex of factors,' including (1) the economic impact of the regulation on the claimant; (2) the extent to which the regulation has interfered with distinct investment-backed expectations; and (3) the character of the governmental action. . . .

. . .

"A central dynamic of the Court's regulatory takings jurisprudence, then, is its flexibility. This has been and remains a means to reconcile two competing objectives central to regulatory takings doctrine. One is the individual's right to retain the interests and exercise the freedoms at the core of private property ownership. . . . Property rights are necessary to preserve freedom, for property ownership empowers persons to shape and to plan their own destiny in a world where governments are always eager to do so for them.

"The other persisting interest is the government's well-established power to 'adjus[t] rights for the public good.' . . . As Justice Holmes declared, 'Government hardly could go on if to some extent values incident to property could not be diminished without paying for every such change in the general law.' . . . In adjudicating regulatory takings cases a proper balancing of these principles requires a careful inquiry informed by the specifics of the case.

"This case presents a question that is linked to the ultimate determination whether a regulatory taking has occurred: What is the proper unit of property against which to assess the effect of the challenged governmental action? Put another way, '[b]ecause our test for regulatory taking requires us to compare the value that has been taken from the property with the value that remains in the property, one of the critical questions is determining how to define the unit of property "whose value is to furnish the denominator of the fraction." ' . . . This Court . . . has explained that the question is important to the regulatory takings inquiry. 'To the extent that any portion of property is taken, that portion is always taken in its entirety; the relevant question, however, is whether the property taken is all, or only a portion of, the parcel in question.'

. . .

"While the Court has not set forth specific guidance on how to identify the relevant parcel for the regulatory taking inquiry, there are two concepts which the Court has indicated can be unduly narrow.

"First, the Court has declined to limit the parcel in an artificial manner to the portion of property targeted by the challenged regulation. . . .

. . .

"The second concept about which the Court has expressed caution is the view that property rights under the Takings Clause should be coextensive with those under state law. . . . The Court [has] explained that States do not have the unfettered authority to 'shape and define property rights and reasonable investment-backed expectations,' leaving landowners without recourse against unreasonable regulations. . . .

. . .

"As the foregoing discussion makes clear, no single consideration can supply the exclusive test for determining the denominator. Instead, courts must consider a number of factors. These include the treatment of the land under state and local law; the physical characteristics of the land; and the prospective value of the regulated land. The endeavor should determine whether reasonable expectations about property ownership would lead a landowner to anticipate that his holdings would be treated as one parcel, or, instead, as separate tracts. The inquiry is objective, and the reasonable expectations at issue derive from background customs and the whole of our legal tradition. . . .

"First, courts should give substantial weight to the treatment of the land, in particular how it is bounded or divided, under state and local law. The reasonable expectations of an acquirer of land must acknowledge legitimate restrictions affecting his or her subsequent use and dispensation of the property. . . . A valid takings claim will not evaporate just because a purchaser took title after the law was enacted. . . . A reasonable restriction that predates a landowner's acquisition, however, can be one of the objective factors that most landowners would reasonably consider in forming fair expectations about their property. . . .

"Second, courts must look to the physical characteristics of the landowner's property. These include the physical relationship of any distinguishable tracts, the parcel's topography, and the surrounding human and ecological environment. In particular, it may be relevant that the property is located in an area that is subject to, or likely to become subject to, environmental or other regulation. . . .

"Third, courts should assess the value of the property under the challenged regulation, with special attention to the effect of burdened land on the value of other holdings. Though a use restriction may decrease the market value of the property, the effect may be tempered if the regulated land adds value to the remaining property, such as by increasing privacy, expanding recreational space, or preserving surrounding natural beauty. A law that limits use of a landowner's small lot in one part of the city by reason of the landowner's nonadjacent holdings elsewhere may decrease the market value of the small lot in an unmitigated fashion. The absence of a special relationship between the holdings may counsel against consideration of all the holdings as a single parcel, making the restrictive law susceptible to a takings challenge. On the other hand, if the landowner's other property is adjacent to the small lot, the market value of the properties may well increase if their combination enables the expansion of a structure, or if development restraints for one part of the parcel protect the unobstructed skyline views of another part. That, in turn, may counsel in favor of treatment as a single parcel and may reveal the weakness of a regulatory takings challenge to the law.

. . .

"The State of Wisconsin and petitioners each ask this Court to adopt a formalistic rule to guide the parcel inquiry. Neither proposal suffices to capture the central legal and factual principles that inform reasonable expectations about property interests. Wisconsin would tie the definition of the parcel to state law, considering the two lots here as a single whole due to their merger under the challenged regulations. That approach, as already noted, simply assumes the answer to the question: May the State define the relevant parcel in a way that permits it to escape its responsibility to justify regulation in light of legitimate property expectations? It is, of course, unquestionable that the law must recognize those legitimate expectations in order to give proper weight to the rights of owners and the right of the State to pass reasonable laws and regulations. . . .

"Petitioners propose a different test that is also flawed. They urge the Court to adopt a presumption that lot lines define the relevant parcel in every instance, making Lot E the necessary denominator. Petitioners' argument, however, ignores the fact that lot lines are themselves creatures of state law, which can be overridden by the State in the reasonable exercise of its power. In effect, petitioners ask this Court to credit the aspect of state law that favors their preferred result (lot lines) and ignore that which does not (merger provision).

"This approach contravenes the Court's case law, which recognizes that reasonable land-use regulations do not work a taking. . . . Among other cases, Agins v. City of Tiburon, 447 U. S. 255 (1980), demonstrates the validity of this proposition because it upheld zoning regulations as a legitimate exercise of the government's police power. . . .

"The merger provision here is likewise a legitimate exercise of government power, as reflected by its consistency with a long history of state and local merger regulations that originated nearly a century ago. . . . Merger provisions often form part of a regulatory scheme that establishes a minimum lot size in order to preserve open space while still allowing orderly development. . . .

. . .

"Petitioners' reliance on lot lines also is problematic for another reason. Lot lines have varying degrees of formality across the States, so it is difficult to make them a standard measure of the reasonable expectations of property owners. Indeed, in some jurisdictions, lot lines may be subject to informal adjustment by property owners, with minimal government oversight. . . . The ease of modifying lot lines also creates the risk of gamesmanship by landowners, who might seek to alter the lines in anticipation of regulation that seems likely to affect only part of their property.

"Under the appropriate multifactor standard, it follows that for purposes of determining whether a regulatory taking has occurred here, petitioners' property should be evaluated as a single parcel consisting of Lots E and F together. First, the treatment of the property under state and local law indicates petitioners' property should be treated as one when considering the effects of the restrictions. As the Wisconsin courts held, the state and local regulations merged Lots E and F. . . . The decision to adopt the merger provision at issue here was for a specific and legitimate purpose, consistent with the widespread understanding that lot lines are not dominant or controlling in every case. . . . Petitioners' land was subject to this regulatory burden, moreover, only because of voluntary conduct in bringing the lots under common ownership after the regulations were enacted. As a result, the valid merger of the lots under state law informs the reasonable expectation they will be treated as a single property.

"Second, the physical characteristics of the property support its treatment as a unified parcel. The lots are contiguous along their longest edge. Their rough terrain and narrow shape make it reasonable to expect their range of potential uses might be limited. . . . The land's location along the river is also significant. Petitioners could have anticipated public regulation might affect their enjoyment of their property, as the Lower St. Croix was a regulated area under federal, state, and local law long before petitioners possessed the land.

"Third, the prospective value that Lot E brings to Lot F supports considering the two as one parcel for purposes of determining if there is a regulatory taking. Petitioners are prohibited from selling Lots E and F separately or from building separate residential structures on each. Yet this restriction is mitigated by the benefits of using the property as an integrated whole, allowing increased privacy and recreational space, plus the optimal location of any improvements. . . .

"The special relationship of the lots is further shown by their combined valuation. Were Lot E separately saleable but still subject to the development restriction, petitioners' appraiser would value the property at only $40,000. We express no opinion on the validity of this figure. We also note the number is not particularly helpful for understanding petitioners' retained value in the properties because Lot E, under the regulations, cannot be sold without Lot F. The point that is useful for these purposes is that the combined lots are valued at $698,300, which is far greater than the summed value of the separate regulated lots (Lot F with its cabin at $373,000, according to respondents' appraiser, and Lot E as an undevelopable plot at $40,000, according to petitioners' appraiser). The value added by the lots' combination shows their complementarity and supports their treatment as one parcel.

"The State Court of Appeals was correct in analyzing petitioners' property as a single unit. Petitioners allege that in doing so, the state court applied a categorical rule that all contiguous, commonly owned holdings must be combined for Takings Clause analysis. . . . This does not appear to be the case, however, for the precedent relied on by the Court of Appeals addressed multiple factors before treating contiguous properties as one parcel. . . . The judgment below, furthermore, may be affirmed on any ground permitted by the law and record. . . . To the extent the state court treated the two lots as one parcel based on a bright-line rule, nothing in this opinion approves that methodology, as distinct from the result.

"Considering petitioners' property as a whole, the state court was correct to conclude that petitioners cannot establish a compensable taking in these circumstances. Petitioners have not suffered a taking under *Lucas*, as they have not been deprived of all economically beneficial use of their property. . . . They can use the property for residential purposes, including an enhanced, larger residential improvement. The property has not lost all economic value, as its value has decreased by less than 10 percent. . . .

"Petitioners furthermore have not suffered a taking under the more general test of *Penn Central*. . . . The expert appraisal relied upon by the state courts refutes any claim that the economic impact of the regulation is severe. Petitioners cannot claim that they reasonably expected to sell or develop their lots separately given the regulations which predated their acquisition of both lots. Finally, the governmental action was a reasonable land-use regulation, enacted as part of a coordinated federal, state, and local effort to preserve the river and surrounding land."

. . .

Chief Justice Roberts, joined by Justices Thomas and Alito, dissented, saying that the Court's "bottom-line conclusion [finding no taking] does not trouble me; the majority presents a fair case that the Murrs can still make good use of both lots, and that the ordinance is a commonplace tool to preserve scenic areas, such as the Lower St. Croix River, for the benefit of landowners and the public alike.

"Where the majority goes astray, however, is in concluding that the definition of the 'private property' at issue in a case such as this turns on an elaborate test looking not only to state and local law, but also to (1) 'the physical characteristics of the land,' (2) 'the prospective value of the regulated land,' (3) the 'reasonable expectations' of the owner, and (4) 'background customs and the whole of our legal tradition.' . . . Our decisions have, time and again, declared that the Takings Clause protects private property rights as state law creates and defines them. By securing such *established* property rights, the Takings Clause protects individuals from being forced to bear the full weight of actions that should be borne by the public at large. The majority's new, malleable definition of 'private property'—adopted solely 'for purposes of th[e] takings inquiry,' " . . .— undermines that protection.

"I would stick with our traditional approach: State law defines the boundaries of distinct parcels of land, and those boundaries should determine the 'private property' at issue in regulatory takings cases. Whether a regulation effects a taking of that property is a separate question, one in which common ownership of adjacent property may be taken into account. Because the majority departs from these settled principles, I respectfully dissent.

  . . .

"Staying with a state law approach to defining 'private property' would make our job in this case fairly easy. The Murr siblings acquired Lot F in 1994 and Lot E a year later. Once the lots fell into common ownership, the challenged ordinance prevented them from being 'sold or developed as separate lots' because neither contained a sufficiently large area of buildable land. . . . The Murrs argued that the ordinance amounted to a taking of Lot E, but the State of Wisconsin and St. Croix County proposed that both lots together should count as the relevant 'parcel.' The trial court sided with the State and County, and the Wisconsin Court of Appeals affirmed. Rather than considering whether Lots E and F are separate parcels under Wisconsin law, however, the Court of Appeals adopted a takings-specific approach to defining the relevant parcel. . . . Relying on what it called a 'well-established rule' for 'regulatory takings cases,' the court explained "that contiguous property under common ownership is considered as a whole regardless of the number of parcels contained therein.' . . . And because Lots E and F were side by side and owned by the Murrs, the case was straightforward: The two lots were one 'parcel' for the regulatory takings analysis. The court therefore evaluated the effect of the ordinance on the two lots considered together.

"As I see it, the Wisconsin Court of Appeals was wrong to apply a takings-specific definition of the property at issue. Instead, the court should have asked whether, under general state law principles, Lots E and F are legally distinct parcels of land. I would therefore vacate the judgment below and remand for the court to identify the relevant property using ordinary principles of Wisconsin property law.

"After making that state law determination, the next step would be to determine whether the challenged ordinance amounts to a 'taking.' . . . "

Justice Thomas wrote a separate dissent, expressing agreement with Chief Justice Roberts' dissent but also urging the Court "to take a fresh look at our regulatory takings jurisprudence, to see whether it can be grounded in the original public meaning of the Takings Clause of the Fifth Amendment or the Privileges or Immunities Clause of the Fourteenth Amendment."

Justice Gorsuch took no part in the consideration or decision of this case.

3.   REMEDIES FOR TAKINGS

Page 533. Add after First English Evangelical Lutheran Church of Glendale v. County of Los Angeles:

Knick v. Township of Scott, 588 U.S. ___, 139 S.Ct. 2162 (2019). The Court, in a 5–4 decision, overruled "Williamson County Regional Planning Comm'n v. Hamilton Bank of Johnson City, 473 U. S. 172 (1985), [which had] held that a property owner whose property has been taken by a local government has not suffered a violation of his Fifth Amendment rights—and thus cannot bring a federal takings claim in federal court—until a state court has denied his claim for just compensation under state law." For the majority, Chief Justice Roberts wrote in part:

"A property owner has an actionable Fifth Amendment takings claim when the government takes his property without paying for it. That does not mean that the government must provide compensation in advance of a taking or risk having its action invalidated: So long as the property owner has some way to obtain compensation after the fact, governments need not fear that courts will enjoin their activities. But it does mean that the property owner has suffered a violation of his Fifth Amendment rights when the government takes his property without just compensation, and therefore may bring his claim in federal court under § 1983 at that time.

. . .

"The Fifth Amendment right to full compensation arises at the time of the taking, regardless of post-taking remedies that may be available to the property owner.

. . .

". . . The fact that the State has provided a property owner with a procedure that may subsequently result in just compensation cannot deprive the owner of his Fifth Amendment right to compensation under the Constitution, leaving only the state law right. And that is key because it is the existence of the Fifth Amendment right that allows the owner to proceed directly to federal court under § 1983.

. . .

"A later payment of compensation may remedy the constitutional violation that occurred at the time of the taking, but that does not mean the violation never took place. . . .

"In sum, because a taking without compensation violates the self-executing Fifth Amendment at the time of the taking, the property owner can bring a federal suit at that time. . . .

. . .

". . . Certainly it is correct that a fully compensated plaintiff has no further claim, but that is because the taking has been *remedied* by compensation, not because there was *no taking* in the first place. . . .

. . .

"Today, because the federal and nearly all state governments provide just compensation remedies to property owners who have suffered a taking, equitable relief is generally unavailable. As long as an adequate provision for obtaining just compensation exists, there is no basis to enjoin the government's action effecting a taking. But that is because, as the Court explained in *First English*, such a procedure is a remedy for a taking that violated the Constitution, not because the availability of the procedure somehow prevented the violation from occurring in the first place.

. . .

"We conclude that a government violates the Takings Clause when it takes property without compensation, and that a property owner may bring a Fifth Amendment claim under § 1983 at that time. That does not as a practical matter mean that government action or regulation may not proceed in the absence of contemporaneous compensation. Given the availability of post-taking compensation, barring the government from acting will ordinarily not be appropriate. But because the violation is complete at the time of the taking, pursuit of a remedy in federal court need not await any subsequent state action. Takings claims against local governments should be handled the same as other claims under the Bill of Rights. *Williamson County* erred in holding otherwise.

. . .

". . . Our holding that uncompensated takings violate the Fifth Amendment will not expose governments to new liability; it will simply allow into federal court takings claims that otherwise would have been brought as inverse condemnation suits in state court."[a]

Justice Kagan, joined by Justices Ginsburg, Breyer, and Sotomayor dissented. She wrote in part:

". . . *Williamson County* was rooted in an understanding of the Fifth Amendment's Takings Clause stretching back to the late 1800s. . . . The majority today holds, in conflict with precedent after precedent, that a government violates the Constitution whenever it takes property without advance compensation—no matter how good its commitment to pay. That conclusion has no basis in the Takings Clause. Its consequence is to channel a mass of quintessentially local cases involving complex state-law issues into federal courts. . . .

. . .

". . . [T]he Takings Clause . . . does not prohibit takings; to the contrary, it permits them provided the government gives just compensation. So when the government 'takes and pays,' it is not violating the Constitution at all. Put another way, a Takings Clause violation has two necessary elements. First, the government must take the property. Second, it must deny the property owner just compensation. . . . If the government has not done both, no constitutional violation has happened. . . .

"Similarly[,] . . . [f]or over a hundred years, this Court held that advance or contemporaneous payment was not required, so long as the government had

---

[a] A concurring opinion by Justice Thomas is omitted.

established reliable procedures for an owner to later obtain just compensation (including interest for any time elapsed). . . .

. . .

". . . Everyone agrees that a § 1983 suit cannot be brought before a constitutional violation has occurred. And according to the Court's repeated decisions, a Takings Clause violation does not occur until an owner has used the government's procedures and failed to obtain just compensation. . . .

. . .

". . . The majority's overruling of *Williamson County* will have two damaging consequences. It will inevitably turn even well-meaning government officials into lawbreakers. And it will subvert important principles of judicial federalism.

". . . A government actor usually cannot know in advance whether implementing a regulatory program will effect a taking, much less of whose property. Until today, such an official could do his work without fear of wrongdoing, in any jurisdiction that had set up a reliable means for property owners to obtain compensation. Even if some regulatory action turned out to take someone's property, the official would not have violated the Constitution. But no longer. Now, when a government undertakes land-use regulation . . ., the responsible employees will almost inescapably become constitutional malefactors. That is not a fair position in which to place persons carrying out their governmental duties.

"Still more important, the majority's ruling channels to federal courts a (potentially massive) set of cases that more properly belongs, at least in the first instance, in state courts—where *Williamson County* put them. . . .

. . .

". . . Today's decision sends a flood of complex state-law issues to federal courts. It makes federal courts a principal player in local and state land-use disputes. It betrays judicial federalism."

2. PROTECTION OF PERSONAL LIBERTIES

B. FAMILY AND MARITAL RELATIONSHIPS

Page 572. Add after Obergefell v. Hodges:

Pavan v. Smith, 582 U.S. __, 137 S.Ct. 2075 (2017). In a per curiam opinion, the Court summarily reversed an Arkansas Supreme Court judgment upholding an Arkansas regulatory scheme that "generally requires the name of the mother's male spouse to appear on the child's birth certificate—regardless of his biological relationship to the child"—but does not require the State to "issue birth certificates including the female spouses of women who give birth in the State." In the majority's view, "that differential treatment infringes *Obergefell*'s commitment to provide same-sex couples 'the constellation of benefits that the States have linked to marriage,' " . . . .

The suit was brought by "two married same-sex couples who conceived children through anonymous sperm donation." When they sought birth certificates for their newborns, "the Arkansas Department of Health issued certificates bearing only the birth mother's name." The Court noted that "all parties agree [that] the requirement that a married woman's husband appear on her child's birth certificate applies in cases where the couple conceived by means of artificial insemination with the help of an anonymous sperm donor." The Court's opinion contained these passages:

". . . [S]ame-sex parents in Arkansas lack the same right as opposite-sex parents to be listed on a child's birth certificate, a document often used for important transactions like making medical decisions for a child or enrolling a child in school. . . .

"*Obergefell* proscribes such disparate treatment. As we explained there, a State may not 'exclude same-sex couples from civil marriage on the same terms and conditions as opposite-sex couples.' . . . Indeed, in listing those terms and conditions—the 'rights, benefits, and responsibilities' to which same-sex couples, no less than opposite-sex couples, must have access—we expressly identified 'birth and death certificates.' . . . That was no accident: Several of the plaintiffs in *Obergefell* challenged a State's refusal to recognize their same-sex spouses on their children's birth certificates. . . . In considering those challenges, we held the relevant state laws unconstitutional to the extent they treated same-sex couples differently from opposite-sex couples. . . . That holding applies with equal force [here].

"Echoing the court below, the State defends its birth-certificate law on the ground that being named on a child's birth certificate is not a benefit that attends marriage. Instead, the State insists, a birth certificate is simply a device for recording biological parentage—regardless of whether the child's parents are married. But Arkansas law makes birth certificates about more than just genetics. As already discussed, when an opposite-sex couple conceives a child by way of anonymous sperm donation—just as the petitioners did here—state law requires the placement of the birth mother's husband on the child's birth certificate. . . . And that is so even though (as the State concedes) the husband 'is definitely not the biological father' in those circumstances. . . .* Arkansas has thus chosen to make its birth certificates more than a mere marker of biological relationships: The State uses those certificates to give married parents a form of legal recognition that is not available to unmarried parents. Having made that choice, Arkansas may not, consistent with *Obergefell*, deny married same-sex couples that recognition."

Justice Gorsuch, joined by Justices Thomas and Alito dissented, finding this case inappropriate for the "strong medicine of summary reversal." He wrote in pertinent part:

". . . [N]othing in *Obergefell* spoke (let alone clearly) to . . . whether [the Arkansas law], or a state supreme court decision upholding it, must go. The statute in question establishes a set of rules designed to ensure that the biological parents of a child are listed on the child's birth certificate. Before the state supreme court, the State argued that rational reasons exist for a biology based birth registration regime, reasons that in no way offend *Obergefell*—like ensuring government officials can identify public health trends and helping individuals determine their biological lineage, citizenship, or susceptibility to genetic disorders. In an opinion that did not in any way seek to defy but rather

---

* [O]ther factual scenarios (beyond those present in this case) similarly show that the State's birth certificates are about more than genetic parentage. For example, when an Arkansas child is adopted, the State places the child's original birth certificate under seal and issues a new birth certificate—unidentifiable as an amended version—listing the child's (nonbiological) adoptive parents.

earnestly engage *Obergefell*, the state supreme court agreed. And it is very hard to see what is wrong with this conclusion for, just as the state court recognized, nothing in *Obergefell* indicates that a birth registration regime based on biology, one no doubt with many analogues across the country and throughout history, offends the Constitution. . . . Neither does anything in today's opinion purport to identify any constitutional problem with a biology based birth registration regime. So whatever else we might do with this case, summary reversal would not exactly seem the obvious course.

. . .

"[I]f the artificial insemination statute [§ 9–10–201] is the concern, it's still hard to see how summary reversal should follow for at least a few reasons. First, petitioners didn't actually challenge [it] in their lawsuit. Instead, petitioners sought and the trial court granted relief eliminating the State's authority . . . to enforce a birth registration regime generally based on biology. On appeal, the state supreme court simply held that this overbroad remedy wasn't commanded by *Obergefell* or the Constitution. And, again, nothing in today's opinion for the Court identifies anything wrong, let alone clearly wrong, in that conclusion. Second, though petitioners' lawsuit didn't challenge § 9–10–201, the State has repeatedly conceded that the benefits afforded nonbiological parents under § 9–10–201 must be afforded equally to both same-sex and opposite-sex couples. So that in this particular case and all others of its kind, the State agrees, the female spouse of the birth mother must be listed on birth certificates too. Third, further proof still of the state of the law in Arkansas today is the fact that, when it comes to adoption (a situation not present in this case but another one in which Arkansas departs from biology based registration), the State tells us that adopting parents are eligible for placement on birth certificates without respect to sexual orientation.

". . . [I]t is not even clear what the Court expects to happen on remand that hasn't happened already. . . . Perhaps the state supreme court could memorialize the State's concession on § 9–10–201, even though that law wasn't fairly challenged and such a chore is hardly the usual reward for seeking faithfully to apply, not evade, this Court's mandates."

C. PERSONAL AUTONOMY

Page 608. Add after Planned Parenthood of Southeastern Pennsylvania v. Casey:

National Institute of Family and Life Advocates v. Becerra

585 U.S. ___, 138 S.Ct. 2361, 201 L.Ed.2d 835 (2018).

[The report of this case appears infra, at p. 182.]

Page 627. Add after Whole Woman's Health v. Hellerstedt:

June Medical Services L.L.C. v. Russo, 591 U.S. ___, 140 S.Ct. 2103 (2020). The Court, 5–4, held unconstitutional—in the words of Justice Breyer's plurality opinion that was joined by Justices Ginsburg, Sotomayor, and Kagan— "a Louisiana statute, Act 620, that is almost word-for-word identical to Texas' admitting-privileges law" that it had invalidated in *Whole Woman's Health*. Justice Breyer wrote in part:

". . . As in *Whole Woman's Health*, the District Court found that the statute offers no significant health benefit. It found that conditions on admitting privileges common to hospitals throughout the State have made and will continue to make it impossible for abortion providers to obtain conforming privileges for reasons that have nothing to do with the State's asserted interests in promoting women's health and safety. And it found that this inability places a substantial obstacle in the path of women seeking an abortion. As in *Whole Woman's Health*, the substantial obstacle the Act imposes, and the absence of any health-related benefit, led the District Court to conclude that the law imposes an undue burden and is therefore unconstitutional. . . ."

The Fifth Circuit Court of Appeals, 2–1, though applying the standards set forth in *Whole Woman's Health*, had rejected the District Court's findings, but the Supreme Court had issued a stay of the Circuit's judgment, "thereby allowing the District Court's injunction to remain in effect[,]" and after plenary review it reversed the judgment of the Court of Appeals.

The plurality first concluded that the State had waived its contention, first raised in its cross-petition for certiorari, that the plaintiffs—abortion providers and clinics—should not be allowed to rely on the abortion access rights of their patients. Justice Breyer wrote that "the State's strategic waiver and a long line of well-established precedents foreclose its belated challenge to the plaintiffs' standing."

Addressing the merits, Justice Breyer emphasized that the Court had "reviewed the record in detail ourselves[,]" and that it "start[ed] from the premise that a district court's findings of fact, 'whether based on oral or other evidence, must not be set aside unless clearly erroneous, and the reviewing court must give due regard to the trial court's opportunity to judge the witnesses' credibility.' Fed. Rule Civ. Proc. 52(a)(6)." Applying that standard, "we find that the testimony and other evidence contained in the extensive record developed over the 6-day trial support the District Court's ultimate conclusion that, '[e]ven if Act 620 could be said to further women's health to some marginal degree, the burdens it imposes far outweigh any such benefit, and thus the Act imposes an unconstitutional undue burden.'"

Included in Justice Breyer's extensive review of the record are the following passages:

"The evidence on which the District Court relied in this case is even stronger and more detailed [than that in *Whole Woman's Health*],. . .

"The evidence shows, among other things, that the fact that hospital admissions for abortion are vanishingly rare means that, unless they also maintain active OB/GYN practices, abortion providers in Louisiana are unlikely to have any recent in-hospital experience. 250 F. Supp. 3d, at 49. Yet such experience can well be a precondition to obtaining privileges. . . .

"The evidence also shows that many providers, even if they could initially obtain admitting privileges, would be unable to keep them. That is because, unless they have a practice that requires regular in-hospital care, they will lose the privileges for failing to use them. . . .

"The evidence also shows that opposition to abortion played a significant role in some hospitals' decisions to deny admitting privileges. 250 F. Supp. 3d, at 48–49, 51–53 (collecting evidence). . . .

"Still other hospitals have requirements that abortion providers cannot satisfy because of the hostility they face in Louisiana. . . .

"Just as in *Whole Woman's Health*, the experiences of the individual doctors in this case support the District Court's factual finding that Louisiana's admitting-privileges requirement, like that in Texas' law, serves no ' "relevant credentialing function.' " . . ."

With respect to Act 620's impact on abortion access, Justice Breyer reviewed the District Court's finding that enforcing the hospital admitting privileges requirement would effectively leave only one doctor in Louisiana to provide abortions. As to that provider:

". . . [his] inability to obtain privileges in the Baton Rouge area would leave Louisiana with just one clinic with one provider to serve the 10,000 women annually who seek abortions in the State.

"Working full time in New Orleans, [he] would be able to absorb no more than about 30% of the annual demand for abortions in Louisiana. . . . And because [he] does not perform abortions beyond 18 weeks, women between 18 weeks and the state legal limit of 20 weeks would have little or no way to exercise their constitutional right to an abortion. . . .

"Those women not altogether prevented from obtaining an abortion would face other burdens. As in *Whole Woman's Health*, the reduction in abortion providers caused by Act 620 would inevitably mean 'longer waiting times, and increased crowding.' . . . The District Court heard testimony that delays in obtaining an abortion increase the risk that a woman will experience complications from the procedure and may make it impossible for her to choose a noninvasive medication abortion. . . .

"Even if they obtain an appointment at a clinic, women who might previously have gone to a clinic in Baton Rouge or Shreveport would face increased driving distances. New Orleans is nearly a five hour drive from Shreveport; it is over an hour from Baton Rouge; and Baton Rouge is more than four hours from Shreveport. The impact of those increases would be magnified by Louisiana's requirement that every woman undergo an ultrasound and receive mandatory counseling at least 24 hours before an abortion. . . . A Shreveport resident seeking an abortion who might previously have obtained care at one of that city's local clinics would either have to spend nearly 20 hours driving back and forth to [his] clinic twice, or else find overnight lodging in New Orleans. As the District Court stated, both experts and laypersons testified that the burdens of this increased travel would fall disproportionately on poor women, who are least able to absorb them.

. . .

"Taken together, we think that these findings and the evidence that underlies them are sufficient to support the District Court's conclusion that Act 620 would place substantial obstacles in the path of women seeking an abortion in Louisiana."

V

Benefits

"We turn finally to the law's asserted benefits. The District Court found that there was ' "no significant health-related problem that the new law helped to cure." ' 250 F. Supp. 3d, at 86 (quoting *Whole Woman's Health*, 579 U. S., at ___ (slip op., at 22)). It found that the admitting privileges requirement '[d]oes [n]ot [p]rotect [w]omen's [h]ealth,' provides 'no significant health benefits,' and makes no improvement to women's health 'compared to prior law.' . . . Our examination of the record convinces us that these findings are not 'clearly erroneous.'

"First, the District Court found that the admitting-privileges requirement serves no 'relevant credentialing function.' . . .

"[W]hile 'competency is a factor' in credentialing decisions, . . . hospitals primarily focus upon a doctor's ability to perform the inpatient, hospital based procedures for which the doctor seeks privileges—not outpatient abortions. . . . And nothing in the record indicates that the background vetting for admitting privileges adds significantly to the vetting that the State Board of Medical Examiners already provides. . . .

"Second, the District Court found that the admitting-privileges requirement 'does not conform to prevailing medical standards and will not improve the safety of abortion in Louisiana.' . . .

"As in *Whole Woman's Health*, the State introduced no evidence 'showing that patients have better outcomes when their physicians have admitting privileges' or 'of any instance in which an admitting privileges requirement would have helped even one woman obtain better treatment.' "

VI

Conclusion

"We conclude, in light of the record, that the District Court's significant factual findings—both as to burdens and as to benefits—have ample evidentiary support. None is 'clearly erroneous.' Given the facts found, we must also uphold the District Court's related factual and legal determinations. These include its determination that Louisiana's law poses a 'substantial obstacle' to women seeking an abortion; its determination that the law offers no significant health-related benefits; and its determination that the law consequently imposes an 'undue burden' on a woman's constitutional right to choose to have an abortion. We also agree with its ultimate legal conclusion that, in light of these findings and our precedents, Act 620 violates the Constitution."

In a postscript, Justice Breyer also observed, relying on *Casey*, that the "record here establishes that Act 620's admitting-privileges requirement places a substantial obstacle in the path of a large fraction of those women seeking an abortion for whom it is a relevant restriction."

Chief Justice Roberts also voted to invalidate Act 620, but he concurred only in the judgment. His separate opinion contained the following:

"I joined the dissent in *Whole Woman's Health* and continue to believe that the case was wrongly decided. The question today however is not whether *Whole Woman's Health* was right or wrong, but whether to adhere to it in deciding the present case. . . .

. . .

"The legal doctrine of stare decisis requires us, absent special circumstances, to treat like cases alike. The Louisiana law imposes a burden on access to abortion just as severe as that imposed by the Texas law, for the same reasons. Therefore Louisiana's law cannot stand under our precedents.

. . .

"Both Louisiana and the providers agree that the undue burden standard announced in *Casey* provides the appropriate framework to analyze Louisiana's law. . . . Neither party has asked us to reassess the constitutional validity of that standard.

. . .

"Under *Casey*, the State may not impose an undue burden on the woman's ability to obtain an abortion. . . . Laws that do not pose a substantial obstacle to abortion access are permissible, so long as they are 'reasonably related' to a legitimate state interest. . . .

"After faithfully reciting this standard, the Court in *Whole Woman's Health* added the following observation: "The rule announced in *Casey* . . . requires that courts consider the burdens a law imposes on abortion access together with the benefits those laws confer." 579 U. S., at ___–___ . . . . The plurality repeats today that the undue burden standard requires courts 'to weigh the law's asserted benefits against the burdens it imposes on abortion access.'

"Read in isolation from *Casey*, such an inquiry could invite a grand 'balancing test in which unweighted factors mysteriously are weighed.' Marrs v. Motorola, Inc., 577 F. 3d 783, 788 (CA7 2009). Under such tests, 'equality of treatment is . . . impossible to achieve; predictability is destroyed; judicial arbitrariness is facilitated; judicial courage is impaired.' Scalia, The Rule of Law as a Law of Rules, 56 U. Chi. L. Rev. 1175, 1182 (1989).

"In this context, courts applying a balancing test would be asked in essence to weigh the State's interests in 'protecting the potentiality of human life' and the health of the woman, on the one hand, against the woman's liberty interest in defining her 'own concept of existence, of meaning, of the universe, and of the mystery of human life' on the other. *Casey*, ... There is no plausible sense in which anyone, let alone this Court, could objectively assign weight to such imponderable values and no meaningful way to compare them if there were. Attempting to do so would be like 'judging whether a particular line is longer than a particular rock is heavy,' Bendix Autolite Corp. v. Midwesco Enterprises, Inc., 486 U. S. 888, 897 (1988) (Scalia, J., concurring in judgment). Pretending that we could pull that off would require us to act as legislators, not judges, and would result in nothing other than an 'unanalyzed exercise of judicial will' in the guise of a 'neutral utilitarian calculus.' . . . .

"Nothing about *Casey* suggested that a weighing of costs and benefits of an abortion regulation was a job for the courts. . . . *Casey* instead focuses on the existence of a substantial obstacle, the sort of inquiry familiar to judges across a variety of contexts. . . .

. . .

"The upshot of *Casey* is clear: The several restrictions that did not impose a substantial obstacle were constitutional, while the restriction that did impose a substantial obstacle was unconstitutional.

"To be sure, the Court at times discussed the benefits of the regulations, including when it distinguished spousal notification from parental consent. . . . But in the context of *Casey's* governing standard, these benefits were not placed on a scale opposite the law's burdens. Rather, *Casey* discussed benefits in considering the threshold requirement that the State have a 'legitimate purpose' and that the law be 'reasonably related to that goal.' . . .

"So long as that showing is made, the only question for a court is whether a law has the 'effect of placing a substantial obstacle in the path of a woman seeking an abortion of a nonviable fetus.' . . .[2]

. . .

"Here the plurality expressly acknowledges that we are not considering how to analyze an abortion regulation that does not present a substantial obstacle. . . . In this case, *Casey's* requirement of finding a substantial obstacle before invalidating an abortion regulation is therefore a sufficient basis for the decision, as it was in *Whole Woman's Health*. In neither case, nor in *Casey* itself, was there call for consideration of a regulation's benefits, and nothing in *Casey* commands such consideration. Under principles of stare decisis, I agree with the plurality that the determination in *Whole Woman's Health* that Texas's law imposed a substantial obstacle requires the same determination about Louisiana's law. Under those same principles, I would adhere to the holding of *Casey*, requiring a substantial obstacle before striking down an abortion regulation.

". . . Because Louisiana's admitting privileges requirement would restrict women's access to abortion to the same degree as Texas's law, it also cannot stand under our precedent.[4]

"To begin, the two laws are nearly identical. . . .

. . .

"Crucially, the District Court findings indicate that Louisiana's law would restrict access to abortion in just the same way as Texas's law, to the same degree or worse. . . .

. . .

" . . .[6]

. . .

---

[2] Justice Gorsuch correctly notes that *Casey* "expressly disavowed any test as strict as strict scrutiny." But he certainly is wrong to suggest that my position is in any way inconsistent with that disavowal. Applying strict scrutiny would require "any regulation touching upon the abortion decision" to be the least restrictive means to further a compelling state interest. . . . *Casey* however recognized that such a test would give "too little acknowledgement and implementation" to the State's "legitimate interests in the health of the woman and in protecting the potential life within her." . . . Under *Casey*, abortion regulations are valid so long as they do not pose a substantial obstacle and meet the threshold requirement of being "reasonably related" to a "legitimate purpose." . . .

[4] For the reasons the plurality explains, I agree that the abortion providers in this case have standing to assert the constitutional rights of their patients.

[6] I agree with Justice Alito that the validity of admitting privileges laws "depend[s] on numerous factors that may differ from State to State." And I agree with Justice Gorsuch that "[w]hen it comes to the factual record, litigants normally start the case on a clean slate." Appreciating that others may in good faith disagree, however, I cannot view the record here as in any pertinent respect sufficiently different from that in *Whole Woman's Health* to warrant a different outcome.

"The question is not whether we would reach the same findings from the same record. These District Court findings "entail[ed] primarily . . . factual work" and therefore are "review[ed] only for clear error." . . .

". . . In my view, the District Court's work reveals no such clear error, for the reasons the plurality explains. . . ."

Each of the remaining four Justices filed a dissent. In his, Justice Thomas first argued that because "this suit was brought by abortionists and abortion clinics[, whose] sole claim . . . is that Louisiana's law violates the purported substantive due process right of a woman to abort her unborn child[,] . . . [u]nder a proper understanding of Article III, these plaintiffs lack standing to invoke our jurisdiction." Then he contended that "[e]ven if the plaintiffs had standing, the Court would still lack the authority to enjoin Louisiana's law," not just because in his view "[f]or the detailed reasons explained by Justice Alito," it was "not true"—as the plurality and the Chief Justice claimed—"that the Court's judgment is dictated by 'our precedents,' particularly *Whole Woman's Health*[,] but because, far more simply, the "Constitution does not constrain the States' ability to regulate or even prohibit abortion." In his view, "the putative right to abortion is a creation that should be undone." For Justice Thomas, "the idea that the Framers of the Fourteenth Amendment understood the Due Process Clause to protect a right to abortion is farcical. . . . In 1868, when the Fourteenth Amendment was ratified, a majority of the States and numerous Territories had laws on the books that limited (and in many cases nearly prohibited) abortion. . . . It would no doubt shock the public at that time to learn that one of the new constitutional Amendments contained hidden within the interstices of its text a right to abortion. The fact that it took this Court over a century to find that right all but proves that it was more than hidden—it simply was not (and is not) there." He concluded that "[b]ecause we can reconcile neither *Roe* nor its progeny with the text of our Constitution, those decisions should be overruled."

Justice Alito authored the principal dissent, joined in full by Justice Gorsuch and mostly by Justices Thomas and Kavanaugh. His dissent includes these passages:

". . . The plurality concludes that the Louisiana law does nothing to protect the health of women, but that is disproved by substantial evidence in the record. And the plurality upholds the District Court's finding that the Louisiana law would cause a drastic reduction in the number of abortion providers in the State even though this finding was based on an erroneous legal standard and a thoroughly inadequate factual inquiry.

"The Chief Justice stresses the importance of *stare decisis* and thinks that precedent, namely *Whole Woman's Health*, dooms the Louisiana law. But at the same time, he votes to overrule *Whole Woman's Health* insofar as it changed the *Casey* test.

"Both the plurality and The Chief Justice hold that abortion providers can invoke a woman's abortion right when they attack state laws that are enacted to protect a woman's health. Neither waiver nor *stare decisis* can justify this holding, which clashes with our general rule on third-party standing. And the idea that a regulated party can invoke the right of a third party for the purpose of attacking legislation enacted to protect the third party is stunning. Given the apparent conflict of interest, that concept would be rejected out of hand in a case not involving abortion.

". . . I would remand the case to the District Court and instruct that court, before proceeding any further, to require the joinder of a plaintiff with standing. If a proper plaintiff is added, the District Court should conduct a new trial and determine, based on proper evidence, whether enforcement of Act 620 would diminish the number of abortion providers in the State to such a degree that women's access to abortions would be substantially impaired. In making that determination, the court should jettison the nebulous 'good faith' test that it used in judging whether the physicians who currently lack admitting privileges would be able to obtain privileges and thus continue to perform abortions if Act 620 were permitted to take effect. Because the doctors in question (many of whom are or were plaintiffs in this case) stand to lose, not gain, by obtaining privileges, the court should require the plaintiffs to show that these doctors sought admitting privileges with the degree of effort that they would expend if their personal interests were at stake."

. . .

"*Casey* . . . rules out the balancing test adopted in *Whole Woman's Health*. *Whole Woman's Health* simply misinterpreted *Casey*, and I agree that *Whole Woman's Health* should be overruled insofar as it changed the *Casey* test. Unless *Casey* is reexamined—and Louisiana has not asked us to do that—the test it adopted should remain the governing standard.

. . .

"[C]ontrary to the view taken by the plurality and (seemingly) by The Chief Justice, there is ample evidence in the record showing that admitting privileges help to protect the health of women by ensuring that physicians who perform abortions meet a higher standard of competence than is shown by the mere possession of a license to practice. . . .

. . .

"The record shows that the vetting conducted by hospitals goes far beyond what is done at Louisiana abortion clinics. . . .

. . .

"In sum, contrary to the plurality's assertion, there is ample evidence in the record showing that requiring admitting privileges has health and safety benefits. There is certainly room for debate about the need for this requirement, but under our case law, this Court's task is not to ascertain whether a law 'adds significantly' to the existing regulatory framework. Instead, when confronted with a genuine dispute about a law's benefits, we have afforded legislatures 'wide discretion' in assessing whether a regulation serves a legitimate medical need and is medically reasonable even in the face of medical and scientific uncertainty. Gonzales v. Carhart, 550 U. S. 124, 163 (2007); Mazurek v. Armstrong, 520 U. S. 968, 973 (1997) (per curiam) . . . . Louisiana easily satisfied this standard.

. . .

"[The plurality and The Chief Justice] also err in their assessment of Act 620's likely effect on access to abortion. . . .

"While it is certainly true that the Texas and Louisiana *statutes* are largely the same, the two cases are not. The decision in *Whole Woman's Health* was not based on the face of the Texas statute, but on an empirical question, namely, the effect of the statute on access to abortion in that State. . . . The Court's answer to that question depended on numerous factors that may differ from State to

State, including the demand for abortions, the number and location of abortion clinics and physicians, the geography of the State, the distribution of the population, and the ability of physicians to obtain admitting privileges. There is no reason to think that a law requiring admitting privileges will necessarily have the same effect in every state. . . .

"The suggestion that *Whole Woman's Health* is materially identical to this case is ironic, since the two cases differ in a way that was critical to the Court's reasoning in *Whole Woman's Health*, i.e., the difference between a pre-enforcement facial challenge and a post-enforcement challenge based on evidence of the law's effects. . . .

. . .

"Aside from suggesting that *Whole Woman's Health* is dispositive, the plurality and the Chief Justice provide one other reason for concluding that Act 620, if allowed to go into effect, would create a substantial obstacle for women seeking abortions. Pointing to the District Court's finding that the Louisiana law would have a drastic effect on abortion access, . . . the plurality and the Chief Justice note that findings of fact may be overturned only if clearly erroneous, and they see no such error here. In taking this approach, they overlook the flawed legal standard on which the District Court's finding depends, and they ignore the gross deficiencies of the evidence in the record.

"Because the Louisiana law was not allowed to go into effect for any appreciable time, it was necessary for the District Court to predict what its effects would be. Attempting to do that, the court apparently concluded that none of the doctors who currently perform abortions in the State would be replaced if the admitting privileges requirement forced them to leave abortion practice. . . . That inference is debatable, as it primarily rests on . . . anecdotal testimony . . . . Neither the plurality nor the Chief Justice explains why it should be accepted. That alone casts doubt on the finding to which the majority defers, but the problems with the finding do not stop there.

"The finding was based on a fundamentally flawed test. . . .

"[T]he factual finding on which the plurality and the Chief Justice rely— that the Louisiana law would drastically reduce access to abortion in the State— depends on the District Court's finding that the doctors in question exercised 'good faith' in their quest for privileges, but that test is woefully deficient.

". . . The District Court ignored a factor of the utmost importance, the incentives of the doctors in question.

". . . If these doctors had secured privileges, that would have tended to defeat the lawsuit. Not only that, acquiring privileges would have subjected all the doctors to . . . hospital monitoring, as well as any other obligations that a hospital imposed on doctors with privileges, such as providing unpaid care for the indigent. Thus, in light of the situation at the time when the doctors made their attempts to get privileges, they had an incentive to do as little as they thought the District Court would demand, not as much as they would if they stood to benefit from success.

. . .

"In light of the doctors' incentives, . . . [t]he court should have asked whether the doctors' efforts to acquire privileges were equal to the efforts they would have made if they knew that their ability to continue to perform abortions was at stake. The District Court did not do that, and because its finding on abortion access rests on the wrong legal standard, it cannot stand. A finding based on an erroneous legal test is invalid; it cannot be sustained under the 'clearly erroneous' rule. . . .

"Not only did the District Court apply the wrong test, but the evidence in the record fails to show that the doctors made anything more than perfunctory efforts to obtain privileges.

[After Justice Alito's extensive review of the record from his perspective concerning this point, he concluded as follows:]

". . . In short, the record does not show that Act 620 would drive any of these doctors out of abortion practice, and . . . [i]t follows that the District Court's finding on Act 620's likely effects cannot stand.

"The Court should remand this case for a new trial under the correct legal standards. The District Court should apply *Casey*'s 'substantial obstacle' test, not the *Whole Woman's Health* balancing test. And it should require those challenging Act 620 to demonstrate that the doctors who lack admitting privileges attempted to obtain them with the same zeal they would have exhibited if the Act were in effect and they stood to lose by failing in those efforts.

"[Also, o]n remand, the District Court should not permit June Medical to assert the rights of women wishing to obtain an abortion. The court should require the joinder of a plaintiff whose own rights are at stake. Our precedents rarely permit a plaintiff to assert the rights of a third party, and June Medical cannot satisfy our established test for third-party standing. Indeed, what June Medical seeks is something we have never allowed. It wants to rely on the rights of third parties whose interests conflict with its own.

. . .

"This case features a blatant conflict of interest between an abortion provider and its patients. Like any other regulated entity, an abortion provider has a financial interest in avoiding burdensome regulations such as Act 620's admitting privileges requirement. Applying for privileges takes time and energy, and maintaining privileges may impose additional burdens. Women seeking abortions, on the other hand, have an interest in the preservation of regulations that protect their health. The conflict inherent in such a situation is glaring.

. . .

". . .The parties have not brought to our attention any other situation in which a party is allowed to invoke the right of a third party with blatantly adverse interests. The rule that the majority applies here is an abortion-only rule.

. . .

"On remand, the District Court should permit the joinder of a plaintiff with standing and should not proceed until such a plaintiff appears."

Justice Gorsuch's dissent focused on perceived failures by the majority to abide by, among others, "[r]ules about the deference due the legislative process, the standing of the parties before us, the use of facial challenges to invalidate democratically enacted statutes, and the award of prospective relief." He asserted: "In truth, Roe v. Wade . . . is not even at issue here. The real question we face concerns our willingness to follow the traditional constraints of the judicial process when a case touching on abortion enters the courtroom."

He concluded, with elaboration, that "the Louisiana legislature passed Act 620 only after extensive hearings at which experts detailed how the Act would promote safer abortion treatment—by providing 'a more thorough evaluation mechanism of physician competency,' promoting 'continuity of care' following abortion, enhancing inter-physician communication, and preventing patient abandonment." And he wrote: "Nor did the legislature neglect to consider the law's potential burdens."

Then he wrote that "[a]fter overlooking so many facts and the deference owed to the legislative process, today's decision misapplies many of the rules that normally constrain the judicial process"—such as general rules against third party standing and rules about facial challenges ("the standard for facial challenges has been flipped on its head: Rather than requiring that a law be unconstitutional in all its applications to fall, today's decision requires that Louisiana's law be constitutional in all its applications to stand."),

He also faulted the Court for its "remarkably static view of the market":

". . . Today's decision . . . appears to assume that, if Louisiana's law took effect, not a single hospital would amend its rules to permit abortion providers easier access to admitting privileges; no clinic would choose to relocate closer to a hospital that offers admitting privileges rather than permanently close its doors; the prospect of significant unmet demand would not prompt a single Louisiana doctor with established admitting privileges to begin performing abortions; and unmet demand would not induce even one out-of-state abortion provider to relocate to Louisiana."

He found those assumptions "[n]ot only questionable, [but] already contradicted by emerging evidence." And he continued with additional criticisms:

". . . From beginning to end, the plurality treats *Whole Woman's Health*'s fact-laden predictions about how a Texas law would impact the availability of abortion in that State in 2016 as if they obviously and necessarily applied to Louisiana in 2020. Most notably, the plurality cites *Whole Woman's Health* for the proposition that admitting privileges requirements offer no benefit when it comes to patient safety or otherwise. But *Whole Woman's Health* found an absence of benefit based only on the particular factual record before it. Nothing in the decision suggested that its conclusions about the costs and benefits of the Texas statute were universal principles of law, medicine, or economics true in all places and at all times. . . . Yet that is exactly how the plurality treats those conclusions—all while leaving unmentioned the facts Louisiana amassed in an effort to show that its law promises patient benefits in this place at this time.

"Not only does today's decision treat factual questions as if they were legal ones, it treats legal questions as if they were facts. . . . [T]he plurality today reviews for clear error not only the district court's findings about how the law will affect abortion access, but also the lower court's judgment that the law's effects impose a 'substantial obstacle.' The plurality defers not only to the district court's findings about the extent of the law's benefits, but also to the lower court's judgment that the benefits are so limited that the law's burden on abortion access is 'undue.' By declining to apply our normal *de novo* standard of review to questions of law like these, today's decision proceeds on the remarkable premise that, even if the district court was wrong on the law, a duly enacted statute must fall because the lower court wasn't *clearly* wrong."

Justice Gorsuch also faulted the plurality for failing to apply an "administrable legal rule." He argued that "as today's concurrence recognizes, the legal standard the plurality applies when it comes to admitting privileges for abortion clinics turns out to be exactly the sort of all-things-considered balancing of benefits and burdens this Court has long rejected." But Chief Justice Roberts' approach in his concurrence did not solve the problem either:

"Start with the concurrence's discussion of *Whole Woman's Health*. Immediately after paying homage to *stare decisis*, the concurrence *refuses* to follow the all-things-considered balancing test that decision employed when striking down Texas's admitting privileges law. In the process, the concurrence rightly recounts many of the problems with raw balancing tests. But then, switching directions again, the concurrence insists we are bound by an *alternative* holding in *Whole Woman's Health*. According to the concurrence, this alternative holding declared that the Texas law imposed an impermissible 'substantial obstacle' to abortion access in light *only* of the burdens the law imposed—'independent of [any] discussion of [the law's] benefits.' And, the concurrence concludes, because the facts of this suit look like those in *Whole Woman's Health*, we must find an impermissible substantial obstacle here too.

"But in this footwork lie at least two missteps. For one, the facts of this suit cannot be so neatly reduced to *Whole Woman's Health* redux. . . . For another, *Whole Woman's Health* nowhere issued the alternative holding on which the concurrence pins its argument. . . .

"The concurrence's fallback argument doesn't solve the problem either. So what if *Whole Woman's Health* rejected the benefits-free version of the 'substantial obstacle' test the concurrence endorses? . . .

". . . [U]nder the concurrence's test it seems possible that even the most compelling and narrowly tailored medical regulation would have to fail if it placed a substantial obstacle in the way of abortion access. Such a result would appear to create yet another discontinuity with *Casey*, which expressly disavowed any test as strict as strict scrutiny. . . ."

Finally, Justice Kavanaugh's brief dissent said in relevant part:

"Today, five Members of the Court reject the *Whole Woman's Health* cost-benefit standard. (Roberts, C. J., concurring in judgment); (Thomas, J., dissenting); (Alito, J., joined by Thomas, Gorsuch, and Kavanaugh, JJ., dissenting); (Gorsuch, J., dissenting). A different five Members of the Court conclude that Louisiana's admitting-privileges law is unconstitutional because it 'would restrict women's access to abortion to the same degree as' the Texas law in *Whole Woman's Health*. (opinion of ROBERTS, C. J.); see also (opinion of Breyer, J., joined by Ginsburg, Sotomayor, and Kagan, JJ.).

"I agree with the first of those two conclusions. But I respectfully dissent from the second because, in my view, additional factfinding is necessary to properly evaluate Louisiana's law. . . . In short, I agree with Justice Alito that the Court should remand the case for a new trial and additional factfinding under the appropriate legal standards.[2]"

---

[2]   In my view, the District Court on remand should also address the State's new argument (raised for the first time in this Court) that these doctors and clinics lack third-party standing.

Page 636. Add after Obergefell v. Hodges:

Pavan v. Smith, 582 U.S. ___, 137 S.Ct. 2075 (2017).

[The report of this case appears supra, p. 103.]

CHAPTER 10

THE EQUAL PROTECTION CLAUSE AND THE REVIEW OF THE REASONABLENESS OF LEGISLATION

3. SUSPECT CLASSIFICATIONS

A. CLASSIFICATIONS DISADVANTAGING RACIAL MINORITIES

Page 691. Add footnote a after Korematsu v. United States:

ᵃ In Trump v. Hawaii, 585 U.S. ___, 138 S.Ct. 2392 (2018), the Court, 5–4, rejected an Establishment Clause challenge to an Executive Order signed by President Trump (who had made a number of disparaging statements about Muslims during his presidential campaign and after he took office) that imposed restrictions on entry into the United States by foreign nationals from a number of mostly Muslim-majority countries. The Court concluded that "because there is persuasive evidence that the entry suspension has a legitimate grounding in national security concerns, quite apart from any religious hostility, we must accept that independent justification." At the end of his opinion for the Court, responding to the dissent's invocation of *Korematsu*, Chief Justice Roberts wrote this:

"... *Korematsu* has nothing to do with this case. The forcible relocation of U. S. citizens to concentration camps, solely and explicitly on the basis of race, is objectively unlawful and outside the scope of Presidential authority. But it is wholly inapt to liken that morally repugnant order to a facially neutral policy denying certain foreign nationals the privilege of admission. . . .

"The dissent's reference to *Korematsu*, however, affords this Court the opportunity to make express what is already obvious: *Korematsu* was gravely wrong the day it was decided, has been overruled in the court of history, and—to be clear—'has no place in law under the Constitution.' 323 U.S., at 248 (Jackson, J., dissenting)."

For the full report of Trump v. Hawaii, see infra, at p. 1697.

C. CLASSIFICATIONS BASED ON GENDER

Page 755. Add after Nguyen v. Immigration and Naturalization Service:

Sessions v. Morales-Santana, 582 U.S. ___, 137 S.Ct. 1678 (2017). Under 8 U. S. C. § 1401(a)(7), a child born abroad to married parents, only one of whom is a U.S. citizen, may acquire citizenship at birth only if the citizen parent had resided in the United States for at least a certain period of time before the child was born. (When Morales-Santana was born the requirement was 10 years, at least five of them after the age of 14, but now the residence requirement is 5 years total, two after 14). Those same rules apply to unwed U.S. citizen fathers under § 1409(a), but § 1409(c) creates an exception in the case of an unwed U.S. citizen mother, who can transmit her citizenship to her child if she has lived in the U.S. for just one year before the birth. In a deportation proceeding, Morales-Santana—who has lived most of his life in the U.S.—claimed citizenship through his biological father's U.S. citizenship, even though his father left Puerto Rico, which is part of the United States, for the Dominican Republic, which is not, 20 days shy of his 19th birthday (and therefore just shy of the 5 year after-turning-14 requirement). Morales-Santana contended that the differential treatment of unwed citizen fathers and mothers reflected in the comparison of §§ 1409(a) and 1409(c) violated the equal protection component of the Fifth Amendment's due process clause. He lost in the Board of Immigration Appeals, but the Second Circuit reversed and also held that he derived citizenship from his father. The Supreme Court affirmed on the merits of the equal protection ruling, but reversed as to the remedy. Justice Ginsburg's opinion for the Court included the following:

III

"Sections 1401 and 1409. . . date from an era when the lawbooks of our Nation were rife with overbroad generalizations about the way men and women are. . . .

"Laws granting or denying benefits 'on the basis of the sex of the qualifying parent,' our post-1970 decisions affirm, differentiate on the basis of gender, and therefore attract heightened review under the Constitution's equal protection guarantee. . . .

"Prescribing one rule for mothers, another for fathers, § 1409 is of the same genre as the classifications we declared unconstitutional in *Reed*, *Frontiero*, *Wiesenfeld*, *Goldfarb*, and *Westcott*. . . . Successful defense of legislation that differentiates on the basis of gender . . . requires an 'exceedingly persuasive justification.' *Virginia*, ...

A

"The defender of legislation that differentiates on the basis of gender must show 'at least that the [challenged] classification serves important governmental objectives and that the discriminatory means employed are substantially related to the achievement of those objectives.' *Virginia*, . . . Moreover, the classification must substantially serve an important governmental interest *today*, for 'in interpreting the [e]qual [p]rotection [guarantee], [we have] recognized that new insights and societal understandings can reveal unjustified inequality . . . that once passed unnoticed and unchallenged.' Obergefell v. Hodges, ...

1

"History reveals what lurks behind § 1409. Enacted in the Nationality Act of 1940 . . ., § 1409 ended a century and a half of congressional silence on the citizenship of children born abroad to unwed parents. During this era, two once habitual, but now untenable, assumptions pervaded our Nation's citizenship laws and underpinned judicial and administrative rulings: In marriage, husband is dominant, wife subordinate; unwed mother is the natural and sole guardian of a non-marital child.

". . . [F]rom 1790 until 1934, the foreign-born child of a married couple gained U. S. citizenship only through the father.

"For unwed parents, the father-controls tradition never held sway. Instead, the mother was regarded as the child's natural and sole guardian. . . .

"In the 1940 Act, Congress discarded the father-controls assumption concerning married parents, but codified the mother-as-sole-guardian perception regarding unmarried parents. . . .

"This unwed-mother-as-natural-guardian notion renders § 1409's gender-based residency rules understandable. Fearing that a foreign-born child could turn out 'more alien than American in character,' the administration believed that a citizen parent with lengthy ties to the United States would counteract the influence of the alien parent. . . . Concern about the attachment of foreign-born children to the United States explains the treatment of unwed citizen fathers, who, according to the familiar stereotype, would care little about, and have scant contact with, their nonmarital children. For unwed citizen mothers, however, there was no need for a prolonged residency prophylactic. The alien father, who might transmit foreign ways, was presumptively out of the picture. . . .

2

. . .

". . . [T]he Court has held that no 'important [governmental] interest' is served by laws grounded, as § 1409(a) and (c) are, in the obsolescing view that 'unwed fathers [are] invariably less qualified and entitled than mothers' to take responsibility for nonmarital children. Caban v. Mohammed, 441 U. S. 380, 382, 394 (1979). Overbroad generalizations of that order, the Court has come to comprehend, have a constraining impact, descriptive though they may be of the way many people still order their lives. . . . In light of the equal protection jurisprudence this Court has developed since 1971, . . . § 1409(a) and (c)'s discrete duration-of-residence requirements for unwed mothers and fathers who have accepted parental responsibility is stunningly anachronistic."

Justice Ginsburg distinguished the *Nguyen* case, on which the Government sought to rely, by first noting that this case did not "renew the contest over § 1409's paternal-acknowledgment requirement[,]" given that "the Government does not dispute that Morales-Santana's father, by marrying Morales-Santana's mother, satisfied that requirement[,]" and also by noting as follows:

"Unlike the paternal-acknowledgment requirement at issue in *Nguyen* . . ., the physical-presence requirements now before us relate solely to the duration of the parent's prebirth residency in the United States, not to the parent's filial tie to the child. As the Court of Appeals observed . . ., a man needs no more time in the United States than a woman 'in order to have assimilated citizenship-related values to transmit to [his] child.' . . . And unlike *Nguyen*'s parental-acknowledgment requirement, § 1409(a)'s age-calibrated physical-presence requirements cannot fairly be described as 'minimal.' "

The Government argued "that the statute serves two important objectives: (1) ensuring a connection between the child to become a citizen and the United States and (2) preventing 'statelessness,' *i.e.*, a child's possession of no citizenship at all." But "[e]ven indulging the assumption that Congress intended § 1409 to serve these interests, . . . neither rationale survives heightened scrutiny." Justice Ginsburg's response included this analysis:

1

". . . The Government does not contend, nor could it, that unmarried men take more time to absorb U. S. values than unmarried women do. Instead, it presents a novel argument . . . .

"An unwed mother, the Government urges, is the child's only 'legally recognized' parent at the time of childbirth. . . . An unwed citizen father enters the scene later, as a second parent. A longer physical connection to the United

States is warranted for the unwed father, the Government maintains, because of the 'competing national influence' of the alien mother. . . .

"Underlying this apparent design is the assumption that the alien father of a nonmarital child born abroad to a U. S.-citizen mother will not accept parental responsibility. For an actual affiliation between alien father and nonmarital child would create the 'competing national influence' that, according to the Government, justifies imposing on unwed U. S.-citizen fathers, but not unwed U. S.-citizen mothers, lengthy physical-presence requirements. Hardly gender neutral, that assumption conforms to the long-held view that unwed fathers care little about, indeed are strangers to, their children. Lump characterization of that kind, however, no longer passes equal protection inspection.

"Accepting, *arguendo*, that Congress intended the diverse physical-presence prescriptions to serve an interest in ensuring a connection between the foreign-born nonmarital child and the United States, the gender-based means scarcely serve the posited end. The scheme permits the transmission of citizenship to children who have no tie to the United States so long as their mother was a U. S. citizen continuously present in the United States for one year at any point in her life *prior* to the child's birth. The transmission holds even if the mother marries the child's alien father immediately after the child's birth and never returns with the child to the United States. At the same time, the legislation precludes citizenship transmission by a U. S.-citizen father who falls a few days short of meeting § 1401(a)(7)'s longer physical-presence requirements, even if the father acknowledges paternity on the day of the child's birth and raises the child in the United States. One cannot see in this driven-by-gender scheme the close means-end fit required to survive heightened scrutiny. . . .

2

"The Government maintains that Congress established the gender-based residency differential in § 1409(a) and (c) to reduce the risk that a foreign-born child of a U. S. citizen would be born stateless. . . . But there is little reason to believe that a statelessness concern prompted the diverse physical-presence requirements. Nor has the Government shown that the risk of statelessness disproportionately endangered the children of unwed mothers.

". . . [N]othing in the congressional hearings and reports on the 1940 and 1952 Acts 'refer[s] to the problem of statelessness for children born abroad.' . . . The justification for § 1409's gender-based dichotomy . . . was not the child's plight, it was the mother's role as the 'natural guardian' of a nonmarital child. . . . It will not do to 'hypothesiz[e] or inven[t]' governmental purposes for gender classifications '*post hoc* in response to litigation.' *Virginia*, ..."

Justice Ginsburg also found "the Government's risk-of-statelessness argument" infected by "an assumption without foundation." Because foreign laws placed "formidable impediments . . . on an unwed mother's transmission of citizenship to her child[,]" experts had concluded that " 'the risk of parenting stateless children abroad was, as of [1940 and 1952], and remains today, substantial for unmarried U. S. fathers, a risk perhaps greater than that for unmarried U. S. mothers.' " Thus, "[o]ne can hardly characterize as gender neutral a scheme allegedly attending to the risk of statelessness for children of unwed U. S. citizen mothers while ignoring the same risk for children of unwed U. S.-citizen fathers.

. . .

"In sum, the Government has advanced no 'exceedingly persuasive' justification for § 1409(a) and (c)'s gender-specific residency and age criteria. Those disparate criteria, we hold, cannot withstand inspection under a Constitution that requires the Government to respect the equal dignity and stature of its male and female citizens."[21]

Despite that holding, the Court decided it was "not equipped to grant the relief Morales-Santana seeks, *i.e.*, extending to his father (and, derivatively, to him) the benefit of the one-year physical-presence term § 1409(c) reserves for unwed mothers." Equal treatment could be achieved either by extending the favorable treatment provided to unwed citizen mothers as an exception, as he requested, or by lengthening the physical-presence requirement for unwed citizen mothers to be the same as that for unwed citizen fathers. The "choice . . . is governed by the legislature's intent, as revealed by the statute[,]" and "striking the discriminatory exception . . . leads here to extending the general rule of longer physical-presence requirements to cover the previously favored group." In general, "a court should ' "measure the intensity of commitment to the residual policy" '—the main rule, not the exception—' "and consider the degree of potential disruption of the statutory scheme that would occur by extension as opposed to abrogation." ' " Justice Ginsburg continued:

"The residual policy here, the longer physical-presence requirement stated in §§ 1401(a)(7) and 1409, evidences Congress' recognition of 'the importance of residence in this country as the talisman of dedicated attachment.' . . . And the potential for 'disruption of the statutory scheme' is large. For if § 1409(c)'s one-year dispensation were extended to unwed citizen fathers, would it not be irrational to retain the longer term when the U. S.-citizen parent is married? Disadvantageous treatment of marital children in comparison to nonmarital children is scarcely a purpose one can sensibly attribute to Congress.

"Although extension of benefits is customary in federal benefit cases, . . . all indicators in this case point in the opposite direction. Put to the choice, Congress, we believe, would have abrogated § 1409(c)'s exception, preferring preservation of the general rule.

". . . Going forward, Congress may address the issue and settle on a uniform prescription that neither favors nor disadvantages any person on the basis of gender. In the interim, as the Government suggests, § 1401(a)(7)'s now-five-year requirement should apply, prospectively, to children born to unwed U. S.-citizen mothers. . . ."

Justice Thomas, joined by Justice Alito, concurred in the judgment in part, taking the position that because the "Court's remedial holding resolves this case[,] . . . it is unnecessary for us to decide whether the 1952 version of the INA was constitutional, . . . or whether other immigration laws (such as the current versions of §§ 1401(g) and 1409) are constitutional."

Justice Gorsuch took no part in the consideration or decision of this case.

---

[21] Justice Thomas, joined by Justice Alito, sees our equal protection ruling as "unnecessary," given our remedial holding. But, "as we have repeatedly emphasized, discrimination itself . . . perpetuat[es] 'archaic and stereotypic notions' " incompatible with the equal treatment guaranteed by the Constitution. Heckler v. Mathews, 465 U. S. 728, 739 (1984) (quoting Mississippi Univ. for Women v. Hogan, 458 U. S. 718, 725 (1982)).

G. WHAT OTHER CLASSIFICATIONS WILL PROVOKE HEIGHTENED SCRUTINY?

2. CLASSIFICATIONS DISADVANTAGING THE RETARDED, HOMOSEXUALS, THE ELDERLY, THE POOR, ETC.

Page 889. Add after Obergefell v. Hodges:

Pavan v. Smith, 582 U.S. ___, 137 S.Ct. 2075 (2017).

[The report of this case appears supra, p. 103.]

4. PROTECTION OF PERSONAL LIBERTIES

B. VOTING AND ELECTIONS

2. LEGISLATIVE DISTRICTING

Page 927. Add after Alabama Legislative Black Caucus v. Alabama:

Bethune-Hill v. Virginia State Board of Elections, 580 U.S. ___, 137 S.Ct. 788 (2017). Once again, the Court found that a three-judge District Court had used incorrect legal standards when evaluating claims of impermissible racial gerrymandering. In the process of redistricting "to ensure proper numerical apportionment for the Virginia House of Delegates" after the 2010 census, the Virginia legislature also drew new district boundaries for 12 districts "with a goal of ensuring that each district would have a black voting age population (BVAP) of at least 55%." Voters in those districts challenged each of them as an unconstitutional racial gerrymander, but the District Court found that as to 11 of them "race did not predominate" in the line-drawing. On appeal, the Supreme Court agreed with the challengers "that the District Court misunderstood the relevant precedents when it required the[m] to establish, as a prerequisite to showing racial predominance, an actual conflict between the enacted plan and traditional redistricting principles." Justice Kennedy's majority opinion elaborated:

"The State's theory in this case is irreconcilable with *Miller* and *Shaw II*. The State insists, for example, that the harm from racial gerrymandering lies not in racial line-drawing *per se* but in grouping voters of the same race together when they otherwise lack shared interests. But 'the constitutional violation' in racial gerrymandering cases stems from the 'racial purpose of state action, not its stark manifestation.' *Miller*, ... The Equal Protection Clause does not prohibit misshapen districts. It prohibits unjustified racial classifications.

"The State contends further that race does not have a prohibited effect on a district's lines if the legislature could have drawn the same lines in accordance with traditional criteria. That argument parallels the District Court's reasoning that a reapportionment plan is not an express racial classification unless a racial purpose is apparent from the face of the plan based on the irregular nature of the lines themselves. . . . This is incorrect. The racial predominance inquiry concerns the actual considerations that provided the essential basis for the lines drawn, not *post hoc* justifications the legislature in theory could have used but in reality did not.

"Traditional redistricting principles, moreover, are numerous and malleable. The District Court here identified no fewer than 11 race-neutral redistricting factors a legislature could consider, some of which are 'surprisingly ethereal' and 'admi[t] of degrees.' . . . By deploying those factors in various combinations and permutations, a State could construct a plethora of potential maps that look consistent with traditional, race-neutral principles. But if race for its own sake is the overriding reason for choosing one map over others, race still may predominate.

"For these reasons, a conflict or inconsistency between the enacted plan and traditional redistricting criteria is not a threshold requirement or a mandatory precondition in order for a challenger to establish a claim of racial gerrymandering. Of course, a conflict or inconsistency may be persuasive circumstantial evidence tending to show racial predomination, but there is no rule requiring challengers to present this kind of evidence in every case.

"As a practical matter, in many cases, perhaps most cases, challengers will be unable to prove an unconstitutional racial gerrymander without evidence that the enacted plan conflicts with traditional redistricting criteria. . . . [Still,] there may be cases where challengers will be able to establish racial predominance in the absence of an actual conflict by presenting direct evidence of the legislative purpose and intent or other compelling circumstantial evidence."

The Court also agreed with the challengers "that the District Court erred . . . when it considered the legislature's racial motive only to the extent that the challengers identified deviations from traditional redistricting criteria that were attributable to race and not to some other factor[, thereby] foreclos[ing] a holistic analysis of each district [that] led the District Court to give insufficient weight to the 55% BVAP target and other relevant evidence that race predominated." Because the "ultimate . . . inquiry . . . is the legislature's predominant motive for the design of the district as a whole[, a] court faced with a racial gerrymandering claim . . . must consider all of the lines of the district at issue; any explanation for a particular portion of the lines, moreover, must take account of the districtwide context. Concentrating on particular portions in isolation may obscure the significance of relevant districtwide evidence, such as stark splits in the racial composition of populations moved into and out of disparate parts of the district, or the use of an express racial target. A holistic analysis is necessary to give that kind of evidence its proper weight."

As to these 11 districts, the Court remanded for the District Court "to determine in the first instance the extent to which, under the proper standard, race directed the[ir] shape . . . . And if race did predominate, it is proper for the District Court to determine in the first instance whether strict scrutiny is satisfied."

The District Court had found that the challenge to the remaining district—District 75—also failed, despite its conclusion that race did predominate in its configuration, because "the State's predominant use of race in District 75 was narrowly tailored to achieve compliance with § 5" of the Voting Rights Act. The Court upheld that ruling. First, the challengers "do not dispute that compliance with § 5 was a compelling interest at the relevant time. As in previous cases, therefore, the Court assumes, without deciding, that the State's interest in complying with the Voting Rights Act was compelling." Second, under the *Alabama* case, the State is not required "to show that its action was 'actually . . . necessary' to avoid a statutory violation, so that, but for its use of race, the State would have lost in court. . . . Rather, the requisite strong basis in evidence exists when the legislature has '*good reasons* to believe' it must use race in order to satisfy the Voting Rights Act, 'even if a court does not find that the actions were necessary for statutory compliance.'" And third, "[u]nder the facts found by the District Court, the legislature performed th[e right] kind of functional analysis of District 75 when deciding upon the 55% BVAP target." Given the "careful assessment of local conditions and structures, the State had a strong basis in evidence to believe a 55% BVAP floor was required to avoid retrogression." In these cases, "the District Court's factual findings are reviewed only for clear error[,]" and the "record here supports the legislature's conclusion that this was one instance where a 55% BVAP was necessary for black voters to have a functional working majority."

Justice Alito concurred in part and concurred in the judgment, "join[ing] the opinion of the Court insofar as it upholds the constitutionality of District 75" and "concur[ring] in the judgment of the Court insofar as it vacates and remands the judgment below with respect to all the remaining districts." He emphasized, however, that "[u]nlike the Court, . . . I would hold that all these districts must satisfy strict scrutiny."

Justice Thomas concurred in the judgment in part and dissented in part. He "concur[red] in the Court's judgment reversing the District Court's decision to uphold 11 of the 12 districts[,]" but did "not agree . . . with the Court's decision to leave open the question whether race predominated in those districts and, thus, whether they are subject to strict scrutiny." He reiterated his view that once a legislature concedes it has intentionally drawn districts as majority-black districts, strict scrutiny is mandated. And he "disagree[d] with the majority's determination that District 75 satisfies strict scrutiny[, because] . . . the State has neither asserted a compelling state interest nor narrowly tailored its use of race." He "would hold that complying with § 5 of the Voting Rights Act is not a compelling interest" since he has concluded that § 5 is unconstitutional. He retained "serious doubts about the Court's standard for narrow tailoring, as characterized today and in Alabama Legislative Black Caucus v. Alabama, 575 U. S. ___ (2015)[,]" finding "[t]hat approach to narrow tailoring—deferring to a State's belief that it has good reasons to use race—. . . 'strict' in name only. . . ." Accordingly, in his view the State's "efforts fall far short of establishing that a 55% black voting-age population bears a more ' "exact connection" ' to the State's interest than any alternative percentage."

Cooper v. Harris, 581 U.S. ___, 137 S.Ct. 1455 (2017). Again applying a deferential standard of review to the factual findings of a three-judge District Court in its resolution of a racial gerrymandering claim, the Court affirmed a judgment holding unconstitutional North Carolina's drawing, after the 2010 census, of two congressional districts with long time "substantial populations of black voters[.]" Under the never-challenged 2001 redistricting map required by population changes revealed in the 2000 census, "neither District 1 nor District 12 had a black voting-age population (called a 'BVAP') that was a majority of the whole: The former had a BVAP of around 48%, the latter a BVAP of around 43%. . . . Nonetheless, in five successive general elections conducted in those reconfigured districts, all the candidates preferred by most African-American voters won their contests—and by some handy margins." When the 2010 census again required redistricting to conform to the one-person, one-vote standard, the "new map . . . significantly altered both District 1 and District 12":

"The 2010 census had revealed District 1 to be substantially underpopulated: To comply with the Constitution's one-person-one-vote principle, the State needed to place almost 100,000 new people within the district's boundaries. . . . [The Republican mapmakers] chose to take most of those people from heavily black areas of Durham, requiring a finger-like extension of the district's western line. . . . With that addition, District 1's BVAP rose from 48.6% to 52.7%. . . . District 12 . . . had no need for significant total-population changes: It was overpopulated by fewer than 3,000 people out of over 730,000. . . . Still, [they] decided to reconfigure the district, further narrowing its already snakelike body while adding areas at either end . . . . Those changes appreciably shifted the racial composition of District 12: As the district gained some 35,000 African-Americans of voting age and lost some 50,000 whites of that age, its BVAP increased from 43.8% to 50.7%."

With respect to District 1, Justice Kagan's majority opinion first concluded that "[u]ncontested evidence in the record shows that the State's mapmakers, in considering District 1, purposefully established a racial target: African-Americans should make up no less than a majority of the voting-age population." Given the "body of evidence—showing an announced racial target that subordinated other districting criteria and produced boundaries amplifying divisions between blacks and whites—the District Court did not clearly err in finding that race predominated in drawing District 1. Indeed, as all three judges recognized, the court could hardly have concluded anything but."

The "more substantial question" was "whether District 1 can survive the strict scrutiny applied to racial gerrymanders." It could not, despite the continued assumption "that complying with the VRA is a compelling interest." The District's "electoral history provided no evidence that a § 2 plaintiff could demonstrate the third *Gingles* prerequisite—effective white bloc-voting." And, to North Carolina's contention that past experience was of limited value concerning a new district with nearly 100,000 additional people, Justice Kagan responded by stating:

". . . True enough, a legislature undertaking a redistricting must assess whether the new districts it contemplates (not the old ones it sheds) conform to the VRA's requirements. And true too, an inescapable influx of additional voters into a district may suggest the possibility that its former track record of compliance can continue only if the legislature intentionally adjusts its racial composition. Still, North Carolina too far downplays the significance of a longtime pattern of white crossover voting in the area that would form the core of the redrawn District 1. . . . And even more important, North Carolina can point to no meaningful legislative inquiry into what it now rightly identifies as the key issue: whether a new, enlarged District 1, created without a focus on race but however else the State would choose, could lead to § 2 liability. The prospect of a significant population increase in a district only raises—it does not answer—the question whether § 2 requires deliberate measures to augment the district's BVAP. (Indeed, such population growth could cut in either direction, depending on who comes into the district.) To have a strong basis in evidence to conclude that § 2 demands such race-based steps, the State must carefully evaluate whether a plaintiff could establish the *Gingles* preconditions—including effective white bloc-voting—in a new district created without those measures. We see nothing in the legislative record that fits that description."

That was "no accident" said Justice Kagan, because the redistricters had effectively (and erroneously) "concluded [that] whenever a legislature *can* draw a majority-minority district, it *must* do so—even if a crossover district would also allow the minority group to elect its favored candidates." Finding that idea "at war with our § 2 jurisprudence[,]" the Court refused to "approve a racial gerrymander whose necessity is supported by no evidence and whose *raison d'être* is a legal mistake."

With respect to North Carolina's District 12, which was before the Court for the fifth time starting in 1992, the State did not defend its line-drawing as an effort to comply with § 5 of the VRA, but claimed rather that the district lines were drawn "to 'pack' District 12 with Democrats, not African-Americans"—an account the District Court rejected. Justice Kagan acknowledged the "special challenges" such a defense raises for a trial court:

"In the more usual case alleging a racial gerrymander—where no one has raised a partisanship defense—the court can make real headway by exploring the challenged district's conformity to traditional districting principles, such as compactness and respect for county lines. . . . But such evidence loses much of its value when the State asserts partisanship as a defense, because a bizarre shape—as of the new District 12—can arise from a 'political motivation' as well as a racial one. *Cromartie I*, 526 U. S., at 547, n. 3. And crucially, political and racial reasons are capable of yielding similar oddities in a district's boundaries. That is because, of course, 'racial identification is highly correlated with political affiliation.' *Cromartie II*, 532 U. S., at 243. As a result of those redistricting realities, a trial court has a formidable task: It must make 'a sensitive inquiry' into all 'circumstantial and direct evidence of intent' to assess whether the plaintiffs have managed to disentangle race from politics and prove that the former drove a district's lines. . . .

"Our job is different—and generally easier. [W]e review a district court's finding as to racial predominance only for clear error, except when the court made a legal mistake. . . . [W]e give singular deference to a trial court's judgments about the credibility of witnesses. . . .[7]

"In light of those principles, we uphold the District Court's finding of racial predominance respecting District 12. The evidence offered at trial, including live witness testimony subject to credibility determinations, adequately supports the conclusion that race, not politics, accounted for the district's reconfiguration. And no error of law infected that judgment: Contrary to North Carolina's view, the District Court had no call to dismiss this challenge just because the plaintiffs did not proffer an alternative design for District 12 as circumstantial evidence of the legislature's intent."

Justice Kagan reviewed the evidence before the District Court, and its conclusions, and then said:

---

[7] . . . [I]f legislators use race as their predominant districting criterion with the end goal of advancing their partisan interests—perhaps thinking that a proposed district is more 'sellable' as a race-based VRA compliance measure than as a political gerrymander and will accomplish much the same thing—their action still triggers strict scrutiny. . . . In other words, the sorting of voters on the grounds of their race remains suspect even if race is meant to function as a proxy for other (including political) characteristics. . . .

". . . Maybe we would have evaluated the testimony differently had we presided over the trial; or then again, maybe we would not have. Either way— and it is only *this* which matters—we are far from having a 'definite and firm conviction' that the District Court made a mistake in concluding from the record before it that racial considerations predominated in District 12's design."

As for North Carolina's contention (which the "dissent echoes") that "[w]hen race and politics are competing explanations of a district's lines, . . . the party challenging the district must introduce . . . 'an alternative [map] that achieves the legislature's political objectives while improving racial balance' "—something the challengers here did not do—the majority disagreed:

"We have no doubt that an alternative districting plan, of the kind North Carolina describes, can serve as key evidence in a race-versus-politics dispute. One, often highly persuasive way to disprove a State's contention that politics drove a district's lines is to show that the legislature had the capacity to accomplish all its partisan goals without moving so many members of a minority group into the district."

But "with or without an alternative map" challengers can satisfy "the plaintiff's burden of proof":

". . . In Bush v. Vera, for example, this Court upheld a finding of racial predominance based on 'substantial direct evidence of the legislature's racial motivations'—including credible testimony from political figures and statements made in a § 5 preclearance submission—plus circumstantial evidence that redistricters had access to racial, but not political, data at the 'block-by-block level' needed to explain their 'intricate' designs. . . . Not a single Member of the Court thought that the absence of a counter-map made any difference. Similarly, it does not matter in this case, where the plaintiffs' introduction of mostly direct and some circumstantial evidence—documents issued in the redistricting process, testimony of government officials, expert analysis of demographic patterns—gave the District Court a sufficient basis, sans any map, to resolve the race-or-politics question.

"A plaintiff's task, in other words, is simply to persuade the trial court— without any special evidentiary prerequisite—that race (not politics) was the 'predominant consideration in deciding to place a significant number of voters within or without a particular district.' *Alabama*, . . .; cf. *Bethune-Hill*, ... The Equal Protection Clause prohibits the unjustified drawing of district lines based on race. An alternative map is merely an evidentiary tool to show that such a substantive violation has occurred; neither its presence nor its absence can itself resolve a racial gerrymandering claim."

The State's, and the dissent's, reliance on Easley v. Cromartie (Cromartie II) was misplaced:

". . . In a case like *Cromartie II*—that is, one in which the plaintiffs had meager direct evidence of a racial gerrymander and needed to rely on evidence of forgone alternatives—only maps of that kind could carry the day.

"But this case is most unlike *Cromartie II*, even though it involves the same electoral district some twenty years on. This case turned not on the possibility of creating more optimally constructed districts, but on direct evidence of the General Assembly's intent in creating the actual District 12, including many hours of trial testimony subject to credibility determinations. That evidence, the District Court plausibly found, itself satisfied the plaintiffs' burden of debunking

North Carolina's 'it was really politics' defense; there was no need for an alternative map to do the same job."

Justice Thomas concurred in the majority opinion and wrote briefly "to explain the additional grounds on which [he] would affirm . . . and to note [his] agreement, in particular, with the Court's clear-error analysis." As to District 1, "North Carolina's concession that it created the district as a majority-black district is by itself sufficient to trigger strict scrutiny[,]" and that could not be satisfied based on "efforts to comply with § 2 of the VRA[,]" because in his view "§ 2 does not apply to redistricting and therefore cannot justify a racial gerrymander." As to District 12, "I agree with the Court that the District Court did not clearly err when it determined that race was North Carolina's predominant motive in drawing the district. This is the same conclusion I reached when we last reviewed District 12" in *Cromartie II*: "The Court reached the contrary conclusion in *Cromartie II* only by misapplying our deferential standard for reviewing factual findings. . . . Today's decision does not repeat *Cromartie II's* error, and indeed it confines that case to its particular facts. It thus represents a welcome course correction to this Court's application of the clear-error standard."

Justice Alito, joined by Chief Justice Roberts and Justice Kennedy, concurred in the judgment with respect to District 1 and dissented with respect to District 12.* As to the latter, he argued that the "failure to produce an alternative map doomed the challengers in *Cromartie II*, and the same should be true now." And his assessment was that the "record shows" that District 12 was not drawn predominantly because of race. He emphasized that because of " 'the intrusive potential of judicial intervention into the legislative realm,' " *Miller*, . . . we have warned that courts must be very cautious about imputing a racial motive to a State's redistricting plan." His insistence that *Cromartie II* mandated the presentation of an alternative map as "a logical response to the difficult problem of distinguishing between racial and political motivations when race and political party preference closely correlate" was premised on the perception that this "is a problem with serious institutional and federalism implications." Among them is that "if a court mistakes a political gerrymander for a racial gerrymander, it illegitimately invades a traditional domain of state authority, usurping the role of a State's elected representatives." And he warned of "a final, often-unstated danger where race and politics correlate: that the federal courts will be transformed into weapons of political warfare." Moreover, "even if there are cases in which a plaintiff could prove a racial gerrymandering claim without an alternative map, they would be exceptional ones in which the evidence of racial predominance is overwhelming. This most definitely is not one of those cases, . . . and the plaintiffs' failure to produce an alternative map mandates reversal. Moreover, even in an exceptional case, the absence of such a map would still be strong evidence that a district's boundaries were determined by politics rather than race."

Justice Alito also argued that even "set[ting] aside the challengers' failure to submit an alternative map, the District Court's finding that race predominated in the drawing of District 12 is clearly erroneous. The State offered strong and coherent evidence that politics, not race, was the legislature's predominant aim, and the evidence supporting the District Court's contrary

---

*   Justice Gorsuch did not participate in this case.

finding is weak and manifestly inadequate in light of the high evidentiary standard that our cases require challengers to meet in order to prove racial predominance." His lengthy review of the record led him to conclude that there was "strong evidence . . . that the changes made to the 2001 map were designed to maximize Republican opportunities"; that "so long as the legislature chose to retain the basic shape of District 12 and to increase the number of Democrats in the district, it was inevitable that the Democrats brought in would be disproportionately black"; that "the increase in the black voting age population of District 12 is easily explained by a coherent (and generally successful) political strategy"; and that the references to racial considerations in the record were too weak to support a finding that race was the "predominant" factor in the drawing of District 12's boundaries. He also offered this summary:

"Reviewing the evidence . . ., two themes emerge. First, District 12's borders and racial composition are readily explained by political considerations and the effects of the legislature's political strategy on the demographics of District 12. Second, the majority largely ignores this explanation, as did the court below, and instead adopts the most damning interpretation of all available evidence.

"Both of these analytical maneuvers violate our clearly established precedent. . . ."[a]

---

[a] In North Carolina v. Covington, 581 U.S. ___, 137 S.Ct. 1624 (2017), the Court's per curiam opinion—which noted that the Court had separately summarily affirmed the District Court's ruling that 28 majority-black state legislative districts drawn by the North Carolina General Assembly in 2011 were unconstitutional racial gerrymanders—vacated and remanded for further proceedings the District Court's remedial order in the case. The District Court's ruling on the merits came in August 2016, and that court "declined to require changes in time for the then-impending November 2016 election, but ordered the General Assembly to redraw the map before North Carolina holds any future elections for that body." Shortly after the election, the court set a March 2017 deadline for the drawing of new districts and ordered that "[t]he term of any legislator elected in 2016" from a district later modified by that remedial plan "shall be shortened to one year" (rather than the regular two):

"Those legislators would then be replaced by new ones, to be chosen in court-ordered special elections in the fall of 2017. The legislators elected in those special elections, too, were then to 'serve a one year term.' . . . Finally, in order to make this regime workable, the court also suspended provisions of the North Carolina Constitution requiring prospective legislators to reside within a district for one year before they may be elected to represent it. To explain why these measures were warranted, the court stated: 'While special elections have costs, those costs pale in comparison to the injury caused by allowing citizens to continue to be represented by legislators elected pursuant to a racial gerrymander.'"

The Court's per curiam response to the State's appeal stated in relevant part:

". . . [I]n the context of deciding whether to truncate existing legislators' terms and order a special election, there is much for a court to weigh. Although this Court has never addressed whether or when a special election may be a proper remedy for a racial gerrymander, obvious considerations include the severity and nature of the particular constitutional violation, the extent of the likely disruption to the ordinary processes of governance if early elections are imposed, and the need to act with proper judicial restraint when intruding on state sovereignty. We do not suggest anything about the relative weight of these factors (or others), but they are among the matters a court would generally be expected to consider in its 'balancing of the individual and collective interests' at stake. Swann v. Charlotte-Mecklenburg Bd. of Ed., 402 U. S. 1, 16 (1971).

". . . [T]he District Court addressed the balance of equities in only the most cursory fashion. . . . [Its] minimal reasoning would appear to justify a special election in *every* racial-gerrymandering case—a result clearly at odds with our demand for careful case-specific analysis. For that reason, we cannot have confidence that the court adequately grappled with the interests on both sides of the remedial question before us."

Page 928. Replace Vieth v. Jubelirer with the following:

Rucho v. Common Cause

588 U.S. ___, 139 S.Ct. 2484, 204 L.Ed.2d 931 (2019).

■ CHIEF JUSTICE ROBERTS delivered the opinion of the Court.

Voters and other plaintiffs in North Carolina and Maryland challenged their States' congressional districting maps as unconstitutional partisan gerrymanders. The North Carolina plaintiffs complained that the State's districting plan discriminated against Democrats; the Maryland plaintiffs complained that their State's plan discriminated against Republicans. The plaintiffs alleged that the gerrymandering violated the First Amendment, the Equal Protection Clause of the Fourteenth Amendment, the Elections Clause, and Article I, § 2, of the Constitution. The District Courts in both cases ruled in favor of the plaintiffs, and the defendants appealed directly to this Court.

These cases require us to consider once again whether claims of excessive partisanship in districting are "justiciable"—that is, properly suited for resolution by the federal courts. This Court has not previously struck down a districting plan as an unconstitutional partisan gerrymander, and has struggled without success over the past several decades to discern judicially manageable standards for deciding such claims. The districting plans at issue here are highly partisan, by any measure. The question is whether the courts below appropriately exercised judicial power when they found them unconstitutional as well.

I

A

The first case involves a challenge to the congressional redistricting plan enacted by the Republican-controlled North Carolina General Assembly in 2016. . . . The Republican legislators leading the redistricting effort instructed their mapmaker to use political data to draw a map that would produce a congressional delegation of ten Republicans and three Democrats. . . . As one of the two Republicans chairing the redistricting committee stated, "I think electing Republicans is better than electing Democrats. So I drew this map to help foster what I think is better for the country." . . . He further explained that the map was drawn with the aim of electing ten Republicans and three Democrats because he did "not believe it [would be] possible to draw a map with 11 Republicans and 2 Democrats." . . . One Democratic state senator objected that entrenching the 10–3 advantage for Republicans was not "fair, reasonable, [or] balanced" because, as recently as 2012, "Democratic congressional candidates had received more votes on a statewide basis than Republican candidates." . . . The General Assembly was not swayed . . . and approved the 2016 Plan by a party-line vote. . . .

In November 2016, North Carolina conducted congressional elections using the 2016 Plan, and Republican candidates won 10 of the 13 congressional districts. . . . In the 2018 elections, Republican candidates won nine congressional districts, while Democratic candidates won three. The Republican candidate narrowly prevailed in the remaining district, but the State Board of Elections called a new election after allegations of fraud.

[T]he North Carolina Democratic Party, Common Cause (a nonprofit organization), and 14 individual North Carolina voters sued[, as did the League of Women Voters and other voters in a similar suit that was consolidated with this one.]

The plaintiffs . . . [first] alleged that the Plan violated the Equal Protection Clause . . . by intentionally diluting the electoral strength of Democratic voters. Second, they claimed that the Plan violated their First Amendment rights by retaliating against supporters of Democratic candidates on the basis of their political beliefs. Third, they asserted that the Plan usurped the right of "the People" to elect their preferred candidates for Congress, in violation of the requirement in Article I, § 2, of the Constitution that Members of the House of Representatives be chosen "by the People of the several States." Finally, they alleged that the Plan violated the Elections Clause by exceeding the State's delegated authority to prescribe the "Times, Places and Manner of holding Elections" for Members of Congress.

[T]he three-judge District Court unanimously concluded that the 2016 Plan violated the Equal Protection Clause and Article I of the Constitution[, and, with one dissenter,] that the Plan violated the First Amendment. . . . The defendants appealed directly to this Court under 28 U. S. C. § 1253.

While that appeal was pending, we decided Gill v. Whitford, 585 U. S. ___ (2018), [where] we held that a plaintiff asserting a partisan gerrymandering claim based on a theory of vote dilution must establish standing by showing he lives in an allegedly "cracked" or "packed" district. . . . A "cracked" district is one in which a party's supporters are divided among multiple districts, so that they fall short of a majority in each; a "packed" district is one in which a party's supporters are highly concentrated, so they win that district by a large margin, "wasting" many votes that would improve their chances in others. . . .

After deciding *Gill*, we remanded the present case for further consideration . . . . On remand, the District Court again struck down the 2016 Plan. . . . It found standing and concluded that the case was appropriate for judicial resolution. On the merits, the court found that "the General Assembly's predominant intent was to discriminate against voters who supported or were likely to support non-Republican candidates," and to "entrench Republican candidates" through widespread cracking and packing of Democratic voters. . . . [T]he District Court held that 12 of the 13 districts constituted partisan gerrymanders that violated the Equal Protection Clause. . . .

The court also agreed with the plaintiffs that the 2016 Plan discriminated against them because of their political speech and association, in violation of the First Amendment. . . . Finally, the District Court concluded that the 2016 Plan violated the Elections Clause and Article I, § 2[, and it] enjoined the State from using the 2016 Plan in any election after the November 2018 general election. . . .

. . .

B

. . . In 2011, the Maryland Legislature—dominated by Democrats—undertook to redraw the lines of that State's eight congressional districts. The Governor . . ., Democrat Martin O'Malley, led the process. He appointed a redistricting committee . . . and asked Congressman Steny Hoyer, who has described himself as a "serial gerrymanderer," to advise the committee. . . . The Governor later testified that his aim was to "use the redistricting process to change the overall composition of Maryland's congressional delegation to 7 Democrats and 1 Republican by flipping" one district. . . . "[A] decision was made to go for the Sixth," . . . which had been held by a Republican for nearly two decades. To achieve the required equal population among districts, only about 10,000 residents needed to be removed from that district. . . . The 2011 Plan accomplished that by moving roughly 360,000 voters out of the Sixth District and moving 350,000 new voters in. Overall, the Plan reduced the number of registered Republicans in the Sixth District by about 66,000 and increased the number of registered Democrats by about 24,000. . . . The map was adopted by a party-line vote. . . . It was used in the 2012 election and succeeded in flipping the Sixth District. A Democrat has held the seat ever since.

. . . Maryland voters [sued,] alleg[ing] that the 2011 Plan violated the First Amendment, the Elections Clause, and Article I, § 2,of the Constitution. . . . [T]he District Court . . . concluded that the plaintiffs' claims were justiciable, and that the Plan violated the First Amendment by diminishing their "ability to elect their candidate of choice" because of their party affiliation and voting history, and by burdening their associational rights. . . . On the latter point, the court relied upon findings that Republicans in the Sixth District "were burdened in fundraising, attracting volunteers, campaigning, and generating interest in voting in an atmosphere of general confusion and apathy." . . .

The District Court permanently enjoined the State from using the 2011 Plan and ordered it to promptly adopt a new plan for the 2020 election. . . . The defendants appealed directly to this Court . . . .

II

A

. . .

Chief Justice Marshall famously wrote that it is "the province and duty of the judicial department to say what the law is." Marbury v. Madison . . . . Sometimes, however, "the law is that the judicial department has no business entertaining the claim of unlawfulness—because the question is entrusted to one of the political branches or involves no judicially enforceable rights." Vieth v. Jubelirer, 541 U. S. 267, 277 (2004) (plurality opinion). In such a case the claim is said to present a "political question" and to be nonjusticiable—outside the courts' competence and therefore beyond the courts' jurisdiction. Baker v. Carr, 369 U. S. 186, 217 (1962). Among the political question cases the Court has identified are those that lack "judicially discoverable and manageable standards for resolving [them]." . . .

Last Term in Gill v. Whitford, we reviewed our partisan gerrymandering cases and concluded that those cases "leave unresolved whether such claims may be brought." . . . The question here is whether there is an "appropriate role for the Federal Judiciary" in remedying the problem of partisan gerrymandering— whether such claims are claims of *legal* right, resolvable according to *legal* principles, or political questions that must find their resolution elsewhere. . . .

B

Partisan gerrymandering is nothing new. Nor is frustration with it. The practice was known in the Colonies prior to Independence, and the Framers were familiar with it at the time of the drafting and ratification of the Constitution. See *Vieth*, 541 U. S., at 274 (plurality opinion). During the very first congressional elections, George Washington and his Federalist allies accused Patrick Henry of trying to gerrymander Virginia's districts against their candidates—in particular James Madison, who ultimately prevailed over fellow future President James Monroe. . . .

In 1812, Governor of Massachusetts and future Vice President Elbridge Gerry notoriously approved congressional districts that the legislature had drawn to aid the Democratic-Republican Party. The moniker "gerrymander" was born when an outraged Federalist newspaper observed that one of the misshapen districts resembled a salamander. . . .

The Framers addressed the election of Representatives to Congress in the Elections Clause. Art. I, § 4, cl. 1. That provision assigns to state legislatures the power to prescribe the "Times, Places and Manner of holding Elections" for Members of Congress, while giving Congress the power to "make or alter" any such regulations. Whether to give that supervisory authority to the National Government was debated at the Constitutional Convention. When those opposed to such congressional oversight moved to strike the relevant language, Madison came to its defense:

> "[T]he State Legislatures will sometimes fail or refuse to consult the common interest at the expense of their local coveniency or prejudices. . . . Whenever the State Legislatures had a favorite measure to carry, they would take care so to mould their regulations as to favor the candidates they wished to succeed." 2 Records of the Federal Convention of 1787, at 240–241.

During the subsequent fight for ratification, the provision remained a subject of debate. Antifederalists predicted that Congress's power under the Elections Clause would allow Congress to make itself "omnipotent," setting the "time" of elections as never or the "place" in difficult to reach corners of the State. Federalists responded that, among other justifications, the revisionary power was necessary to counter state legislatures set on undermining fair representation, including through malapportionment. . . .

Congress has regularly exercised its Elections Clause power, including to address partisan gerrymandering. The Apportionment Act of 1842, which required single-member districts for the first time, specified that those districts be "composed of contiguous territory," . . . in "an attempt to forbid the practice of the gerrymander," . . . . Later statutes added requirements of compactness and equality of population. . . . (Only the single member district requirement remains in place today. . . .) . . . Congress also used its Elections Clause power in 1870, enacting the first comprehensive federal statute dealing with elections as a way to enforce the Fifteenth Amendment. . . . Starting in the 1950s, Congress enacted a series of laws to protect the right to vote through measures such as the suspension of literacy tests and the prohibition of English-only elections. . . .

Appellants suggest that, through the Elections Clause, the Framers set aside electoral issues such as the one before us as questions that only Congress can resolve. . . . We do not agree. In two areas—one-person, one-vote and racial gerrymandering—our cases have held that there is a role for the courts with respect to at least some issues that could arise from a State's drawing of congressional districts. See Wesberry v. Sanders, 376 U. S. 1 (1964); Shaw v. Reno, 509 U. S. 630 (1993) (*Shaw I*).

But the history is not irrelevant. The Framers . . . settled on a characteristic approach, assigning the issue to the state legislatures, expressly checked and balanced by the Federal Congress. As Alexander Hamilton explained, "it will . . . not be denied that a discretionary power over elections ought to exist somewhere. It will, I presume, be as readily conceded that there were only three ways in which this power could have been reasonably modified and disposed: that it must either have been lodged wholly in the national legislature, or wholly in the State legislatures, or primarily in the latter, and ultimately in the former." The Federalist No. 59, p. 362 (C. Rossiter ed. 1961). At no point was there a suggestion that the federal courts had a role to play. Nor was there any indication that the Framers had ever heard of courts doing such a thing.

C

Courts have nevertheless been called upon to resolve a variety of questions surrounding districting. . . .

In the leading case of Baker v. Carr, . . . [the] Court concluded that the claim of population inequality among districts did not fall into [the] category [of nonjusticiable political questions], because such a claim could be decided under basic equal protection principles. . . .

Another line of challenges to districting plans has focused on race. Laws that explicitly discriminate on the basis of race, as well as those that are race neutral on their face but are unexplainable on grounds other than race, are of course presumptively invalid. The Court applied those principles to electoral boundaries in Gomillion v. Lightfoot, concluding that a challenge to an "uncouth twenty-eight sided" municipal boundary line that excluded black voters from city elections stated a constitutional claim. 364 U. S. 339, 340 (1960). In Wright v. Rockefeller, 376 U. S. 52 (1964), the Court extended the reasoning of *Gomillion* to congressional districting. See *Shaw I*, 509 U. S., at 645.

Partisan gerrymandering claims have proved far more difficult to adjudicate. The basic reason is that, while it is illegal for a jurisdiction to depart from the one-person, one-vote rule, or to engage in racial discrimination in districting, "a jurisdiction may engage in constitutional political gerrymandering." Hunt v. Cromartie, 526 U. S. 541, 551 (1999) (citing Bush v. Vera, 517 U. S. 952, 968 (1996); Shaw v. Hunt, 517 U. S. 899, 905 (1996) (*Shaw II*); Miller v. Johnson, 515 U. S. 900, 916 (1995); *Shaw I*, 509 U. S., at 646). See also Gaffney v. Cummings, 412 U. S. 735, 753 (1973) (recognizing that "[p]olitics and political considerations are inseparable from districting and apportionment").

To hold that legislators cannot take partisan interests into account when drawing district lines would essentially countermand the Framers' decision to entrust districting to political entities. The "central problem" is not determining whether a jurisdiction has engaged in partisan gerrymandering. It is "determining when political gerrymandering has gone too far." *Vieth*, 541 U. S., at 296 (plurality opinion). See League of United Latin American Citizens v. Perry, 548 U. S. 399, 420 (2006) (*LULAC*) (opinion of Kennedy, J.) (difficulty is "providing a standard for deciding how much partisan dominance is too much").

We first considered a partisan gerrymandering claim in Gaffney v. Cummings in 1973. . . . In upholding the State's plan, we reasoned that districting "inevitably has and is intended to have substantial political consequences." . . .

Thirteen years later, in Davis v. Bandemer, we addressed a claim that Indiana Republicans had cracked and packed Democrats in violation of the Equal Protection Clause. . . . A majority of the Court agreed that the case was justiciable, but the Court splintered over the proper standard to apply. . . . [T]here was "no 'Court' for a standard that properly should be applied in determining whether a challenged redistricting plan is an unconstitutional partisan political gerrymander." . . .

Eighteen years later, in *Vieth*, the plaintiffs complained that Pennsylvania's legislature "ignored all traditional redistricting criteria, including the preservation of local government boundaries," in order to benefit Republican congressional candidates. . . . Justice Scalia[,] for a four-Justice plurality[,] would have held that the plaintiffs' claims were nonjusticiable because there was no "judicially discernible and manageable standard" for deciding them. . . . Justice Kennedy, concurring in the judgment, noted "the lack of comprehensive and neutral principles for drawing electoral boundaries [and] the absence of rules to limit and confine judicial intervention." . . . . He nonetheless left open the possibility that "in another case a standard might emerge." . . . Four Justices dissented.

In *LULAC*, the plaintiffs challenged a mid-decade redistricting map approved by the Texas Legislature. Once again a majority of the Court could not find a justiciable standard for resolving the plaintiffs' partisan gerrymandering claims. . . .

As we summed up last Term in *Gill*, our "considerable efforts in *Gaffney*, *Bandemer*, *Vieth*, and *LULAC* leave unresolved whether . . . claims [of legal right] may be brought in cases involving allegations of partisan gerrymandering." . . . Two "threshold questions" remained: standing, which we addressed in *Gill*, and "whether [such] claims are justiciable." . . .

III

A

In considering whether partisan gerrymandering claims are justiciable, we are mindful of Justice Kennedy's counsel in *Vieth*: Any standard for resolving such claims must be grounded in a "limited and precise rationale" and be "clear, manageable, and politically neutral." 541 U. S., at 306–308 (opinion concurring in judgment). An important reason for those careful constraints is that, as a Justice with extensive experience in state and local politics put it, "[t]he opportunity to control the drawing of electoral boundaries through the legislative process of apportionment is a critical and traditional part of politics in the United States." *Bandemer*, 478 U. S., at 145 (opinion of O'Connor, J.). See *Gaffney*, 412 U. S., at 749 (observing that districting implicates "fundamental 'choices about the nature of representation'" (quoting Burns v. Richardson, 384 U. S. 73, 92 (1966))). An expansive standard requiring "the correction of all election district lines drawn for partisan reasons would commit federal and state courts to unprecedented intervention in the American political process," *Vieth*, 541 U. S., at 306 (opinion of Kennedy, J.).

As noted, the question is one of degree: How to "provid[e] a standard for deciding how much partisan dominance is too much." *LULAC*, 548 U. S., at 420 (opinion of Kennedy, J.). And it is vital in such circumstances that the Court act only in accord with especially clear standards: "With uncertain limits, intervening courts—even when proceeding with best intentions—would risk assuming political, not legal, responsibility for a process that often produces ill will and distrust." *Vieth*, 541 U. S., at 307 (opinion of Kennedy, J.). If federal courts are to "inject [themselves] into the most heated partisan issues" by adjudicating partisan gerrymandering claims, *Bandemer*, 478 U. S., at 145 (opinion of O'Connor, J.), they must be armed with a standard that can reliably differentiate unconstitutional from "constitutional political gerrymandering." . . .

B

Partisan gerrymandering claims rest on an instinct that groups with a certain level of political support should enjoy a commensurate level of political power and influence. Explicitly or implicitly, a districting map is alleged to be unconstitutional because it makes it too difficult for one party to translate statewide support into seats in the legislature. But such a claim is based on a "norm that does not exist" in our electoral system—"statewide elections for representatives along party lines." *Bandemer*, 478 U. S., at 159 (opinion of O'Connor, J.).

Partisan gerrymandering claims invariably sound in a desire for proportional representation. As Justice O'Connor put it, such claims are based on "a conviction that the greater the departure from proportionality, the more suspect an apportionment plan becomes." *Ibid.* "Our cases, however, clearly foreclose any claim that the Constitution requires proportional representation or that legislatures in reapportioning must draw district lines to come as near as possible to allocating seats to the contending parties in proportion to what their anticipated statewide vote will be." *Id.*, at 130 (plurality opinion). See Mobile v. Bolden, 446 U. S. 55, 75–76 (1980) (plurality opinion) ("The Equal Protection Clause of the Fourteenth Amendment does not require proportional representation as an imperative of political organization.").

The Founders certainly did not think proportional representation was required. For more than 50 years after ratification of the Constitution, many States elected their congressional representatives through at-large or "general ticket" elections. Such States typically sent single-party delegations to Congress. . . . That meant that a party could garner nearly half of the vote statewide and wind up without any seats in the congressional delegation. . . .

Unable to claim that the Constitution requires proportional representation outright, plaintiffs inevitably ask the courts to make their own political judgment about how much representation particular political parties *deserve*—based on the votes of their supporters—and to rearrange the challenged districts to achieve that end. But federal courts are not equipped to apportion political power as a matter of fairness, nor is there any basis for concluding that they were authorized to do so. As Justice Scalia put it for the plurality in *Vieth*:

> " 'Fairness' does not seem to us a judicially manageable standard. . . .
> Some criterion more solid and more demonstrably met than that seems
> to us necessary to enable the state legislatures to discern the limits of
> their districting discretion, to meaningfully constrain the discretion of
> the courts, and to win public acceptance for the courts' intrusion into a
> process that is the very foundation of democratic decisionmaking." . . .

The initial difficulty in settling on a "clear, manageable and politically neutral" test for fairness is that it is not even clear what fairness looks like in this context. There is a large measure of "unfairness" in any winner-take-all system. Fairness may mean a greater number of competitive districts. Such a claim seeks to undo packing and cracking so that supporters of the disadvantaged party have a better shot at electing their preferred candidates. But making as many districts as possible more competitive could be a recipe for disaster for the disadvantaged party. As Justice White has pointed out, "[i]f all or most of the districts are competitive . . . even a narrow statewide preference for either party would produce an overwhelming majority for the winning party in the state legislature." *Bandemer*, . . . (plurality opinion).

On the other hand, perhaps the ultimate objective of a "fairer" share of seats in the congressional delegation is most readily achieved by yielding to the gravitational pull of proportionality and engaging in cracking and packing, to ensure each party its "appropriate" share of "safe" seats. . . . Such an approach, however, comes at the expense of competitive districts and of individuals in districts allocated to the opposing party.

Or perhaps fairness should be measured by adherence to "traditional" districting criteria, such as maintaining political subdivisions, keeping communities of interest together, and protecting incumbents. . . . But protecting incumbents, for example, enshrines a particular partisan distribution. And the "natural political geography" of a State—such as the fact that urban electoral districts are often dominated by one political party—can itself lead to inherently packed districts. . . .

Deciding among just these different visions of fairness (you can imagine many others) poses basic questions that are political, not legal. There are no legal standards discernible in the Constitution for making such judgments, let alone limited and precise standards that are clear, manageable, and politically neutral. Any judicial decision on what is "fair" in this context would be an "unmoored determination" of the sort characteristic of a political question beyond the competence of the federal courts. Zivotofsky v. Clinton, 566 U. S. 189, 196 (2012).

And it is only after determining how to define fairness that you can even begin to answer the determinative question: "How much is too much?" At what point does permissible partisanship become unconstitutional? If compliance with traditional districting criteria is the fairness touchstone, for example, how much deviation from those criteria is constitutionally acceptable and how should mapdrawers prioritize competing criteria? Should a court "reverse gerrymander" other parts of a State to counteract "natural" gerrymandering caused, for example, by the urban concentration of one party? If a districting plan protected half of the incumbents but redistricted the rest into head to head races, would that be constitutional? A court would have to rank the relative importance of those traditional criteria and weigh how much deviation from each to allow.

If a court instead focused on the respective number of seats in the legislature, it would have to decide the ideal number of seats for each party and determine at what point deviation from that balance went too far. If a 5–3 allocation corresponds most closely to statewide vote totals, is a 6–2 allocation permissible, given that legislatures have the authority to engage in a certain degree of partisan gerrymandering? Which seats should be packed and which cracked? Or if the goal is as many competitive districts as possible, how close does the split need to be for the district to be considered competitive? . . . Even assuming the court knew which version of fairness to be looking for, there are no discernible and manageable standards for deciding whether there has been a violation. . . .

Appellees contend that if we can adjudicate one-person, one-vote claims, we can also assess partisan gerrymandering claims. But the one-person, one-vote rule is relatively easy to administer as a matter of math. The same cannot be said of partisan gerrymandering claims, because the Constitution supplies no objective measure for assessing whether a districting map treats a political party fairly. . .

More fundamentally, "vote dilution" in the one-person, one-vote cases refers to the idea that each vote must carry equal weight. . . . That requirement . . . does not mean that each party must be influential in proportion to its number of supporters. . . .[1]

Nor do our racial gerrymandering cases provide an appropriate standard for assessing partisan gerrymandering. . . . Unlike partisan gerrymandering claims, a racial gerrymandering claim does not ask for a fair share of political power and influence, with all the justiciability conundrums that entails. It asks instead for the elimination of a racial classification. A partisan gerrymandering claim cannot ask for the elimination of partisanship.

IV

Appellees and the dissent propose a number of "tests" for evaluating partisan gerrymandering claims, but none meets the need for a limited and precise standard that is judicially discernible and manageable. And none provides a solid grounding for judges to take the extraordinary step of reallocating power and influence between political parties.

The *Common Cause* District Court concluded that all but one of the districts in North Carolina's 2016 Plan violated the Equal Protection Clause by intentionally diluting the voting strength of Democrats. . . . In reaching that result the court first required the plaintiffs to prove "that a legislative mapdrawer's predominant purpose in drawing the lines of a particular district was to 'subordinate adherents of one political party and entrench a rival party in power.' " . . . The District Court next required a showing "that the dilution of the votes of supporters of a disfavored party in a particular district—by virtue of cracking or packing—is likely to persist in subsequent elections such that an elected representative from the favored party in the district will not feel a need to be responsive to constituents who support the disfavored party." . . . Finally, after a prima facie showing of partisan vote dilution, the District Court shifted the burden to the defendants to prove that the discriminatory effects are "attributable to a legitimate state interest or other neutral explanation." . . .

The District Court's "predominant intent" prong is borrowed from the racial gerrymandering context. . . . If district lines were drawn for the purpose of separating racial groups, then they are subject to strict scrutiny because "race-based decisionmaking is inherently suspect." *Miller*, ... But determining that lines were drawn on the basis of partisanship does not indicate that the districting was improper. A permissible intent—securing partisan advantage—does not become constitutionally impermissible, like racial discrimination, when that permissible intent "predominates."

---

[1]   The dissent's observation that the Framers viewed political parties "with deep suspicion, as fomenters of factionalism and symptoms of disease in the body politic" . . . is exactly right. Its inference from that fact is exactly wrong. The Framers would have been amazed at a constitutional theory that guarantees a certain degree of representation to political parties.

The District Court tried to limit the reach of its test by requiring plaintiffs to show, in addition to predominant partisan intent, that vote dilution "is likely to persist" to such a degree that the elected representative will feel free to ignore the concerns of the supporters of the minority party. . . . But "[t]o allow district courts to strike down apportionment plans on the basis of their prognostications as to the outcome of future elections . . . invites 'findings' on matters as to which neither judges nor anyone else can have any confidence." *Bandemer*, 478 U. S., at 160 (opinion of O'Connor, J.). . . . Judges [would have to] forecast with unspecified certainty whether a prospective winner will have a margin of victory sufficient to permit him to ignore the supporters of his defeated opponent (whoever that may turn out to be). Judges not only have to pick the winner— they have to beat the point spread.

. . . Experience proves that accurately predicting electoral outcomes is not so simple, either because the plans are based on flawed assumptions about voter preferences and behavior or because demographics and priorities change over time. In our two leading partisan gerrymandering cases themselves, the predictions of durability proved to be dramatically wrong. In 1981, Republicans controlled both houses of the Indiana Legislature as well as the governorship. Democrats challenged the state legislature districting map enacted by the Republicans. This Court in *Bandemer* rejected that challenge, and just months later the Democrats increased their share of House seats in the 1986 elections. Two years later the House was split 50–50 between Democrats and Republicans, and the Democrats took control of the chamber in 1990. Democrats also challenged the Pennsylvania congressional districting plan at issue in *Vieth*. Two years after that challenge failed, they gained four seats in the delegation, going from a 12–7 minority to an 11–8 majority. At the next election, they flipped another Republican seat.

Even the most sophisticated districting maps cannot reliably account for some of the reasons voters prefer one candidate over another, or why their preferences may change. Voters elect individual candidates in individual districts, and their selections depend on the issues that matter to them, the quality of the candidates, the tone of the candidates' campaigns, the performance of an incumbent, national events or local issues that drive voter turnout, and other considerations. Many voters split their tickets. Others never register with a political party, and vote for candidates from both major parties at different points during their lifetimes. For all of those reasons, asking judges to predict how a particular districting map will perform in future elections risks basing constitutional holdings on unstable ground outside judicial expertise.

It is hard to see what the District Court's third prong . . . adds to the inquiry. . . . The first prong already requires the plaintiff to prove that partisan advantage predominates. Asking whether a legitimate purpose other than partisanship was the motivation for a particular districting map just restates the question.

B

The District Courts also found partisan gerrymandering claims justiciable under the First Amendment, coalescing around a basic three-part test: proof of intent to burden individuals based on their voting history or party affiliation; an actual burden on political speech or associational rights; and a causal link between the invidious intent and actual burden. . . .

To begin, there are no restrictions on speech, association, or any other First Amendment activities in the districting plans at issue. The plaintiffs are free to engage in those activities no matter what the effect of a plan may be on their district.

The plaintiffs' argument is that partisanship in districting should be regarded as simple discrimination against supporters of the opposing party on the basis of political viewpoint. . . . But . . . [that] test simply describes the act of districting for partisan advantage. It provides no standard for determining when partisan activity goes too far.

As for actual burden, the slight anecdotal evidence found sufficient by the District Courts in these cases shows that this too is not a serious standard for separating constitutional from unconstitutional partisan gerrymandering. The District Courts relied on testimony about difficulty drumming up volunteers and enthusiasm. How much of a decline in voter engagement is enough to constitute a First Amendment burden? How many door knocks must go unanswered? How many petitions unsigned? How many calls for volunteers unheeded? . . .

These cases involve blatant examples of partisanship driving districting decisions. But the First Amendment analysis below offers no "clear" and "manageable" way of distinguishing permissible from impermissible partisan motivation. . . . The decisions below prove the prediction of the *Vieth* plurality that "a First Amendment claim, if it were sustained, would render unlawful *all* consideration of political affiliation in districting," . . . contrary to our established precedent.

C

The dissent proposes using a State's own districting criteria as a neutral baseline from which to measure how extreme a partisan gerrymander is. The dissent would have us line up all the possible maps drawn using those criteria according to the partisan distribution they would produce. Distance from the "median" map would indicate whether a particular districting plan harms supporters of one party to an unconstitutional extent. . . .

As an initial matter, it does not make sense to use criteria that will vary from State to State and year to year as the baseline for determining whether a gerrymander violates the Federal Constitution. The degree of partisan advantage that the Constitution tolerates should not turn on criteria offered by the gerrymanderers themselves. . . . [T]he same map could be constitutional or not depending solely on what the mapmakers said they set out to do. That possibility illustrates that the dissent's proposed constitutional test is indeterminate and arbitrary.

Even if we were to accept the dissent's proposed baseline, it would return us to "the original unanswerable question (How much political motivation and effect is too much?)." . . . Would twenty percent away from the median map be okay? Forty percent? Sixty percent? Why or why not? . . . The dissent's answer says it all: "This much is too much." That is not even trying to articulate a standard or rule.

The dissent argues that there are other instances in law where matters of degree are left to the courts. True enough. But those instances typically involve constitutional or statutory provisions or common law confining and guiding the exercise of judicial discretion. . . . Here, on the other hand, the Constitution provides no basis whatever to guide the exercise of judicial discretion. Common experience gives content to terms such as "substantial risk" or "substantial harm," but the same cannot be said of substantial deviation from a median map. There is no way to tell whether the prohibited deviation from that map should kick in at 25 percent or 75 percent or some other point. The only provision in the Constitution that specifically addresses the matter assigns it to the political branches. See Art. I, § 4, cl. 1.

D

The North Carolina District Court further concluded that the 2016 Plan violated the Elections Clause and Article I, § 2. We are unconvinced by that novel approach.

. . .

. . . [T]he plurality in *Vieth* concluded—without objection from any other Justice—that neither § 2 nor § 4 of Article I "provides a judicially enforceable limit on the political considerations that the States and Congress may take into account when districting." . . .

The District Court nevertheless asserted that partisan gerrymanders violate "the core principle of [our] republican government" preserved in Art. I, § 2, "namely, that the voters should choose their representatives, not the other way around." . . . That seems like an objection more properly grounded in the Guarantee Clause of Article IV, § 4, which "guarantee[s] to every State in [the] Union a Republican Form of Government." This Court has several times concluded, however, that the Guarantee Clause does not provide the basis for a justiciable claim. See, *e.g.*, Pacific States Telephone & Telegraph Co. v. Oregon, 223 U. S. 118 (1912).

V

Excessive partisanship in districting leads to results that reasonably seem unjust. But the fact that such gerrymandering is "incompatible with democratic principles," . . . does not mean that the solution lies with the federal judiciary. We conclude that partisan gerrymandering claims present political questions beyond the reach of the federal courts. Federal judges have no license to reallocate political power between the two major political parties, with no plausible grant of authority in the Constitution, and no legal standards to limit and direct their decisions. "[J]udicial action must be governed by *standard*, by *rule*," and must be "principled, rational, and based upon reasoned distinctions" found in the Constitution or laws. *Vieth* . . . (plurality opinion). Judicial review of partisan gerrymandering does not meet those basic requirements.

. . .

What the appellees and dissent seek is an unprecedented expansion of judicial power. We have never struck down a partisan gerrymander as unconstitutional—despite various requests over the past 45 years. The expansion of judicial authority would not be into just any area of controversy, but into one of the most intensely partisan aspects of American political life. That intervention would be unlimited in scope and duration—it would recur over and over again around the country with each new round of districting, for state as well as federal representatives. Consideration of the impact of today's ruling on democratic principles cannot ignore the effect of the unelected and politically unaccountable branch of the Federal Government assuming such an extraordinary and unprecedented role.

Our conclusion does not condone excessive partisan gerrymandering. Nor does our conclusion condemn complaints about districting to echo into a void. The States, for example, are actively addressing the issue on a number of fronts. In 2015, the Supreme Court of Florida struck down that State's congressional districting plan as a violation of the Fair Districts Amendment to the Florida Constitution. . . . The dissent wonders why we can't do the same. The answer is that there is no "Fair Districts Amendment" to the Federal Constitution. Provisions in state statutes and state constitutions can provide standards and guidance for state courts to apply. . . . Indeed, numerous other States are restricting partisan considerations in districting through legislation. One way they are doing so is by placing power to draw electoral districts in the hands of independent commissions. . . .

Other States have mandated at least some of the traditional districting criteria for their mapmakers. Some have outright prohibited partisan favoritism in redistricting. . . .

As noted, the Framers gave Congress the power to do something about partisan gerrymandering in the Elections Clause. The first bill introduced in the 116th Congress would require States to create 15-member independent commissions to draw congressional districts and would establish certain redistricting criteria, including protection for communities of interest, and ban partisan gerrymandering. H. R. 1, 116th Cong., 1st Sess., §§ 2401, 2411 (2019).

Dozens of other bills have been introduced to limit reliance on political considerations in redistricting. . . .

. . .

We express no view on any of these pending proposals. We simply note that the avenue for reform established by the Framers, and used by Congress in the past, remains open.

* * *

. . . [W]e have no commission to allocate political power and influence in the absence of a constitutional directive or legal standards to guide us in the exercise of such authority. "It is emphatically the province and duty of the judicial department to say what the law is." Marbury v. Madison . . . . In this rare circumstance, that means our duty is to say "this is not law."

The judgments . . . are vacated, and the cases are remanded with instructions to dismiss for lack of jurisdiction.

■ JUSTICE KAGAN, with whom JUSTICE GINSBURG, JUSTICE BREYER, and JUSTICE SOTOMAYOR join, dissenting.

For the first time ever, this Court refuses to remedy a constitutional violation because it thinks the task beyond judicial capabilities.

And not just any constitutional violation. The partisan gerrymanders in these cases deprived citizens of the most fundamental of their constitutional rights: the rights to participate equally in the political process, to join with others to advance political beliefs, and to choose their political representatives. In so doing, the partisan gerrymanders here debased and dishonored our democracy, turning upside-down the core American idea that all governmental power derives from the people. These gerrymanders enabled politicians to entrench themselves in office as against voters' preferences. They promoted partisanship above respect for the popular will. They encouraged a politics of polarization and dysfunction. If left unchecked, gerrymanders like the ones here may irreparably damage our system of government.

And checking them is *not* beyond the courts. The majority's abdication comes just when courts across the country, including those below, have coalesced around manageable judicial standards to resolve partisan gerrymandering claims. Those standards satisfy the majority's own benchmarks. They do not require—indeed, they do not permit—courts to rely on their own ideas of electoral fairness, whether proportional representation or any other. And they limit courts to correcting only egregious gerrymanders, so judges do not become omnipresent players in the political process. But yes, the standards used here do allow—as well they should—judicial intervention in the worst-of-the-worst cases of democratic subversion, causing blatant constitutional harms. In other words, they allow courts to undo partisan gerrymanders of the kind we face today from North Carolina and Maryland. In giving such gerrymanders a pass from judicial review, the majority goes tragically wrong.

I

[Following a detailed, critical "recount[ing of] exactly what politicians in North Carolina and Maryland did to entrench their parties in political office, whatever the electorate might think[,]" Justice Kagan continued:]

"Governments," the Declaration of Independence states, "deriv[e] their just Powers from the Consent of the Governed." The Constitution begins: "We the People of the United States." The Gettysburg Address (almost) ends: "[G]overnment of the people, by the people, for the people." If there is a single idea that made our Nation (and that our Nation commended to the world), it is this one: The people are sovereign. The "power," James Madison wrote, "is in the people over the Government, and not in the Government over the people." 4 Annals of Cong. 934 (1794).

Free and fair and periodic elections are the key to that vision. . . . Madison again: "[R]epublican liberty" demands "not only, that all power should be derived from the people; but that those entrusted with it should be kept in dependence on the people." 2 The Federalist No. 37 . . . . Election day . . . is what links the people to their representatives, and gives the people their sovereign power. That day is the foundation of democratic governance.

And partisan gerrymandering can make it meaningless. At its most extreme—as in North Carolina and Maryland—the practice amounts to "rigging elections." . . . By drawing districts to maximize the power of some voters and minimize the power of others, a party in office at the right time can entrench itself there for a decade or more, no matter what the voters would prefer. . . . The "core principle of republican government," this Court has recognized, is "that the voters should choose their representatives, not the other way around." Arizona State Legislature v. Arizona Independent Redistricting Comm'n, ... Partisan gerrymandering turns it the other way around. By that mechanism, politicians can cherry-pick voters to ensure their reelection. And the power becomes, as Madison put it, "in the Government over the people." . . .

The majority disputes [nothing] . . . about how gerrymanders undermine democracy. . . . The majority offers two ideas [for not responding to that recognition]. One is that the political process can deal with the problem—a proposition so dubious on its face that I feel secure in delaying my answer . . . . The other is that political gerrymanders have always been with us. To its credit, the majority does not frame that point as an originalist constitutional argument. . . .[1] The majority's idea instead seems to be that if we have lived with partisan gerrymanders so long, we will survive.

That complacency has no cause. Yes, partisan gerrymandering goes back to the Republic's earliest days. (As does vociferous opposition to it.) But big data and modern technology—of just the kind that the mapmakers in North Carolina and Maryland used—make today's gerrymandering altogether different from the crude linedrawing of the past. Old-time efforts, based on little more than guesses, sometimes led to so-called dummymanders—gerrymanders that went spectacularly wrong. Not likely in today's world. Mapmakers now have access to more granular data about party preference and voting behavior than ever before. County-level voting data has given way to precinct-level or city-block-level data; and increasingly, mapmakers avail themselves of data sets providing wide-ranging information about even individual voters. . . . Just as important, advancements in computing technology have enabled mapmakers to put that information to use with unprecedented efficiency and precision. . . . While bygone mapmakers may have drafted three or four alternative districting plans, today's mapmakers can generate thousands of possibilities at the touch of a key—and then choose the one giving their party maximum advantage (usually while still meeting traditional districting requirements). The effect is to make gerrymanders far more effective and durable than before, insulating politicians against all but the most titanic shifts in the political tides. . . .

The proof is in the 2010 pudding. . . . Take Pennsylvania. In the three congressional elections occurring under the State's original districting plan (before the State Supreme Court struck it down), Democrats received between 45% and 51% of the statewide vote, but won only 5 of 18 House seats. . . . Or go next door to Ohio. There, in four congressional elections, Democrats tallied between 39% and 47% of the statewide vote, but never won more than 4 of 16 House seats. . . . And gerrymanders will only get worse . . . as data becomes ever more fine-grained and data analysis techniques continue to improve. . . . And someplace along this road, "we the people" become sovereign no longer.

C

Partisan gerrymandering of the kind before us not only subverts democracy. . . . It violates individuals' constitutional rights as well. . . .

Partisan gerrymandering operates through vote dilution—the devaluation of one citizen's vote as compared to others. . . . Whether the person is packed or cracked, his vote carries less weight—has less consequence—than it would under a neutrally drawn (non-partisan) map. . . . In short, the mapmaker has made some votes count for less, because they are likely to go for the other party.

That practice implicates the Fourteenth Amendment's Equal Protection Clause. . . . The constitutional injury in a partisan gerrymandering case is much the same [as in the one-person, one-vote cases involving districts created with significantly different populations], except that the dilution is based on party affiliation. . . . As Justice Kennedy (in a controlling opinion) once hypothesized: If districters declared that they were drawing a map "so as most to burden [the

---

[1] And . . . any originalist argument would have to deal with an inconvenient fact. The Framers originally viewed political parties themselves (let alone their most partisan actions) with deep suspicion, as fomenters of factionalism and "symptom[s] of disease in the body politic." G. Wood, Empire of Liberty: A History of the Early Republic, 1789–1815, p. 140 (2009).

votes of] Party X's" supporters, it would violate the Equal Protection Clause. *Vieth*, ... For (in the language of the one-person-one-vote decisions) it would infringe those voters' rights to "equal [electoral] participation." . . .

And partisan gerrymandering implicates the First Amendment too. That Amendment gives its greatest protection to political beliefs, speech, and association. Yet partisan gerrymanders subject certain voters to "disfavored treatment"—again, counting their votes for less—precisely because of "their voting history [and] their expression of political views." *Vieth*, . . . (opinion of Kennedy, J.). And added to that strictly personal harm is an associational one. Representative democracy is "unimaginable without the ability of citizens to band together in [support of] candidates who espouse their political views." California Democratic Party v. Jones, 530 U. S. 567, 574 (2000). By diluting the votes of certain citizens, the State frustrates their efforts to translate those affiliations into political effectiveness. . . .

Though different Justices have described the constitutional harm in diverse ways, nearly all have agreed on this much: Extreme partisan gerrymandering (as happened in North Carolina and Maryland) violates the Constitution. . . . [T]he majority never disagrees; it appears to accept the "principle that each person must have an equal say in the election of representatives." . . .

II

So the only way to understand the majority's opinion is as follows: In the face of grievous harm to democratic governance and flagrant infringements on individuals' rights—in the face of escalating partisan manipulation whose compatibility with this Nation's values and law no one defends—the majority declines to provide any remedy. For the first time in this Nation's history, the majority declares that it can do nothing about an acknowledged constitutional violation because it has searched high and low and cannot find a workable legal standard to apply.

The majority gives two reasons for thinking that the adjudication of partisan gerrymandering claims is beyond judicial capabilities. First and foremost, the majority says, it cannot find a neutral baseline—one not based on contestable notions of political fairness—from which to measure injury. . . . And second, the majority argues that even after establishing a baseline, a court would have no way to answer "the determinative question: 'How much is too much?' " . . .

I'll give the majority this one—and important—thing: It identifies some dangers everyone should want to avoid. Judges should not be apportioning political power based on their own vision of electoral fairness, whether proportional representation or any other. And judges should not be striking down maps left, right, and center, on the view that every smidgen of politics is a smidgen too much. Respect for state legislative processes—and restraint in the exercise of judicial authority—counsels intervention in only egregious cases.

But in throwing up its hands, the majority misses [that w]hat it says can't be done *has* been done. Over the past several years, federal courts across the country—including, but not exclusively, in the decisions below—have largely converged on a standard for adjudicating partisan gerrymandering claims (striking down both Democratic and Republican districting plans in the process) . . . . And that standard does what the majority says is impossible. The standard does not use any judge-made conception of electoral fairness—either proportional representation or any other; instead, it takes as its baseline a State's *own* criteria of fairness, apart from partisan gain. And by requiring plaintiffs to make difficult showings relating to both purpose and effects, the standard invalidates the most extreme, but only the most extreme, partisan gerrymanders.

. . .

A

Start with the standard the lower courts used. . . . Both courts focused on the harm of vote dilution, though the North Carolina court mostly grounded its analysis in the Fourteenth Amendment and the Maryland court in the First. And both courts (like others around the country) used basically the same three-part test to decide whether the plaintiffs had made out a vote dilution claim. As many legal standards do, that test has three parts: (1) intent; (2) effects; and (3) causation. First, the plaintiffs challenging a districting plan must prove that state officials' "predominant purpose" in drawing a district's lines was to "entrench [their party] in power" by diluting the votes of citizens favoring its rival. . . . Second, the plaintiffs must establish that the lines drawn in fact have the intended effect by "substantially" diluting their votes. . . . And third, if the plaintiffs make those showings, the State must come up with a legitimate, non-partisan justification to save its map.

Turn now to the test's application. First, did the North Carolina and Maryland districters have the predominant purpose of entrenching their own party in power? Here, the two District Courts catalogued the overwhelming direct evidence that they did. . . .

The majority's response to the District Courts' purpose analysis is discomfiting. The majority does not contest the lower courts' findings; how could it? Instead, the majority says that state officials' intent to entrench their party in power is perfectly "permissible," even when it is the predominant factor in drawing district lines. But that is wrong. True enough, that the intent to inject "political considerations" into districting may not raise any constitutional concerns. . . . But when political actors have a specific and predominant intent to entrench themselves in power by manipulating district lines, that goes too far. . . . Consider again Justice Kennedy's hypothetical of mapmakers who set out to maximally burden (*i.e.*, make count for as little as possible) the votes going to a rival party. Does the majority really think that goal is permissible? But why even bother with hypotheticals? Just consider the purposes here. It cannot be permissible and thus irrelevant, as the majority claims, that state officials have as their purpose the kind of grotesquely gerrymandered map that, according to all this Court has ever said, violates the Constitution.

On to the second step of the analysis, where the plaintiffs must prove that the districting plan substantially dilutes their votes. The majority fails to discuss most of the evidence the District Courts relied on to find that the plaintiffs had done so. . . . But that evidence—particularly from North Carolina—is the key to understanding both the problem these cases present and the solution to it they offer. The evidence reveals just how bad the two gerrymanders were . . . . And it shows how the same technologies and data that today facilitate extreme partisan gerrymanders also enable courts to discover them, by exposing just how much they dilute votes. . . .

Consider the sort of evidence used in North Carolina first. There, the plaintiffs demonstrated the districting plan's effects mostly by relying on what might be called the "extreme outlier approach." . . . The approach—which also has recently been used in Michigan and Ohio litigation—begins by using advanced computing technology to randomly generate a large collection of districting plans that incorporate the State's physical and political geography and meet its declared districting criteria, *except for* partisan gain. For each of those maps, the method then uses actual precinct-level votes from past elections to determine a partisan outcome (*i.e.,* the number of Democratic and Republican seats that map produces). Suppose we now have 1,000 maps, each with a partisan outcome attached to it. We can line up those maps on a continuum—the most favorable to Republicans on one end, the most favorable to Democrats on the other. We can then find the median outcome . . . in a world with no partisan manipulation. And we can see where the State's actual plan falls on the spectrum—at or near the median or way out on one of the tails? The further out on the tail, the more extreme the partisan distortion and the more significant the vote dilution. . . .

Using that approach, the North Carolina plaintiffs offered a boatload of alternative districting plans—all showing that the State's map was an out-out-out-outlier. One expert produced 3,000 maps, adhering in the way described above to the districting criteria that the North Carolina redistricting committee had used, other than partisan advantage. . . . Every single one of the 3,000 maps would have produced at least one more Democratic House Member than the State's actual map, and 77% would have elected three or four more. . . . A second expert obtained essentially the same results with maps conforming to more generic districting criteria (*e.g.,* compactness and contiguity of districts). Over 99% of that expert's 24,518 simulations would have led to the election of at least one more Democrat, and over 70% would have led to two or three more. . . . Based on those and other findings, the District Court determined that the North Carolina plan substantially dilutes the plaintiffs' votes.

Because the Maryland gerrymander involved just one district, the evidence in that case was far simpler—but no less powerful for that. . . . The 2010 census required only a minimal change in the Sixth District's population—the subtraction of about 10,000 residents from more than 700,000. But instead of making a correspondingly minimal adjustment, Democratic officials reconfigured the entire district. They moved 360,000 residents out and another 350,000 in, while splitting some counties for the first time in almost two centuries. . . . [The] reversal of the district's partisan composition translated into four consecutive Democratic victories, including in a wave election year for Republicans (2014). In what was once a party stronghold, Republicans now have little or no chance to elect their preferred candidate. The District Court thus found that the gerrymandered Maryland map substantially dilutes Republicans' votes. . . .

The majority claims all these findings are mere "prognostications" about the future, in which no one "can have any confidence." . . . But the courts below did not gaze into crystal balls . . . . Their findings about these gerrymanders' effects on voters—both in the past and predictably in the future—were evidence-based, data-based, statistics-based. . . . They looked at the evidence—at the facts about how these districts operated—and they could reach only one conclusion. By substantially diluting the votes of citizens favoring their rivals, the politicians of one party had succeeded in entrenching themselves in office. They had beat democracy.

B

The majority's broadest claim . . . is that this is a price we must pay because judicial oversight of partisan gerrymandering cannot be "politically neutral" or "manageable." . . . But it never tries to analyze . . . whether the kind of standard developed below . . . allows for neutral and manageable oversight. . . . That kind of oversight is not only possible; it's been done.

Consider neutrality first. Contrary to the majority's suggestion, the District Courts did not have to—and in fact did not—choose among competing visions of electoral fairness. [T]hey did not try to compare the State's actual map to an "ideally fair" one (whether based on proportional representation or some other criterion). Instead, they looked at the difference between what the State did and what the State would have done if politicians hadn't been intent on partisan gain. Or put differently, the comparator (or baseline or touchstone) is the result not of a judge's philosophizing but of the State's own characteristics and judgments. The effects evidence in these cases accepted as a given the State's physical geography (*e.g.,* where does the Chesapeake run?) and political geography (*e.g.,* where do the Democrats live on top of each other?). . . . Under their approach, . . . the State selected its own fairness baseline in the form of its other districting criteria. All the courts did was determine how far the State had gone off that track because of its politicians' effort to entrench themselves in office.

. . .

The majority's sole response misses the point. According to the majority, "it does not make sense to use" a State's own (non-partisan) districting criteria as the baseline from which to measure partisan gerrymandering because those criteria "will vary from State to State and year to year." But that is a virtue, not a vice—a feature, not a bug. Using the criteria the State itself has chosen at the relevant time prevents any judicial predilections from affecting the analysis— exactly what the majority claims it wants. At the same time, using those criteria enables a court to measure just what it should: the extent to which the pursuit of partisan advantage—by these legislators at this moment—has distorted the State's districting decisions. Sure, different non-partisan criteria could result, as the majority notes, in different partisan distributions to serve as the baseline. But that in itself raises no issue: Everyone agrees that state officials using non-partisan criteria (*e.g.,* must counties be kept together? should districts be compact?) have wide latitude in districting. The problem arises only when legislators or mapmakers substantially deviate from the baseline distribution by manipulating district lines for partisan gain. So once again, the majority's analysis falters because it equates the demand to eliminate partisan gerrymandering with a demand for a single partisan distribution—the one reflecting proportional representation. But those two demands are different, and only the former is at issue here.

The majority's "how much is too much" critique fares no better than its neutrality argument. How about the following for a first-cut answer: This much is too much. By any measure, a map that produces a greater partisan skew than any of 3,000 randomly generated maps (all with the State's political geography and districting criteria built in) reflects "too much" partisanship. . . . The absolute worst of 3,001 possible maps. The *only one* that could produce a 10–3 partisan split even as Republicans got a bare majority of the statewide vote. And again: How much is too much? This much is too much: A map that without any evident non-partisan districting reason (to the contrary) shifted the composition of a district from 47% Republicans and 36% Democrats to 33% Republicans and 42% Democrats. A map that in 2011was responsible for the largest partisan swing of a congressional district in the country. . . . Even the majority acknowledges that "[t]hese cases involve blatant examples of partisanship driving districting decisions." If the majority had done nothing else, it could have set the line here. How much is too much? At the least, any gerrymanders as bad as these.

And if the majority thought that approach too case-specific, it could have used the lower courts' general standard—focusing on "predominant" purpose and "substantial" effects—without fear of indeterminacy. . . . Although purpose inquiries carry certain hazards (which courts must attend to), they are a common form of analysis in constitutional cases. See, *e.g.,* Miller v. Johnson, 515 U. S. 900, 916 (1995); Church of Lukumi Babalu Aye, Inc. v. Hialeah, 508 U. S. 520, 533 (1993); Washington v. Davis, 426 U. S. 229, 239 (1976). Those inquiries would be no harder here than in other contexts.

Nor is there any reason to doubt, as the majority does, the competence of courts to determine whether a district map "substantially" dilutes the votes of a rival party's supporters from the everything-but-partisanship baseline described above. . . . As this Court recently noted, "the law is full of instances" where a judge's decision rests on "estimating rightly . . . some matter of degree"— including the "substantial[ity]" of risk or harm. . . . To the extent additional guidance has developed over the years (as under the Sherman Act), courts themselves have been its author—as they could be in this context too. And contrary to the majority's suggestion, courts all the time make judgments about the substantiality of harm without reducing them to particular percentages. . . .

And the combined inquiry used in these cases set the bar high, so that courts could intervene in the worst partisan gerrymanders, but no others. . . . That the two courts below found constitutional violations does not mean their tests were unrigorous; it means that the conduct they confronted was constitutionally appalling—by even the strictest measure, inordinately partisan.

. . .

III

. . .

The majority . . . conclud[es] its opinion with a paean to congressional bills limiting partisan gerrymanders. . . . [W]hat all these *bills* have in common is that they are not *laws*. The politicians who benefit from partisan gerrymandering are unlikely to change partisan gerrymandering. And because those politicians maintain themselves in office through partisan gerrymandering, the chances for legislative reform are slight.

. . . The majority notes that voters themselves have recently approved ballot initiatives to put power over districting in the hands of independent commissions or other nonpartisan actors. . . . [Yet f]ewer than half the States offer voters an opportunity to put initiatives to direct vote; in all the rest (including North Carolina and Maryland), voters are dependent on legislators to make electoral changes . . . . And even when voters have a mechanism they can work themselves, legislators often fight their efforts tooth and nail. . . .

The majority's most perplexing "solution" is to look to state courts. . . . But what do those courts know that this Court does not? If they can develop and apply neutral and manageable standards to identify unconstitutional gerrymanders, why couldn't we?[6]

. . .

. . . [T]hese cases have great political consequence. . . . [A] bipartisan group of current and former Members of the House of Representatives . . . describe all the ways partisan gerrymandering harms our political system—what they call "a cascade of negative results." . . . These artificially drawn districts shift influence from swing voters to party-base voters who participate in primaries; make bipartisanship and pragmatic compromise politically difficult or impossible; and drive voters away from an ever more dysfunctional political process. . . . Last year, we heard much the same from current and former state legislators. In their view, partisan gerrymandering has "sounded the death-knell of bipartisanship," creating a legislative environment that is "toxic" and "tribal." Brief as *Amicus Curiae* in Gill v. Whitford, ... Gerrymandering, in short, helps create the polarized political system so many Americans loathe.

And gerrymandering is, as so many Justices have emphasized before, anti-democratic in the most profound sense. . . .

Of all times to abandon the Court's duty to declare the law, this was not the one. The practices challenged in these cases imperil our system of government. Part of the Court's role in that system is to defend its foundations. None is more important than free and fair elections. With respect but deep sadness, I dissent.

---

[6] Contrary to the majority's suggestion, state courts do not typically have more specific "standards and guidance" to apply than federal courts have. . . . [E]ven the Florida "Free Districts Amendment," which the majority touts, says nothing more than that no districting plan "shall be drawn with the intent to favor or disfavor a political party." Fla. Const., Art. III, § 20(a). If the majority wants the kind of guidance that will keep courts from intervening too far in the political sphere, that Amendment does not provide it: The standard is in fact a good deal less exacting than the one the District Courts below applied. In any event, only a few States have a constitutional provision like Florida's, so the majority's state-court solution does not go far.

CHAPTER 12

APPLICATION OF THE POST-CIVIL WAR AMENDMENTS TO PRIVATE CONDUCT: CONGRESSIONAL POWER TO ENFORCE THE AMENDMENTS

2. APPLICATION OF THE CONSTITUTION TO PRIVATE CONDUCT

A. PRIVATE PERFORMANCE OF "GOVERNMENT" FUNCTIONS

Page 1079. Add at the end of the Section:

Manhattan Community Access Corporation v. Halleck

587 U.S. ___, 139 S.Ct. 1921, 204 L.Ed.2d 405 (2019).

■ JUSTICE KAVANAUGH delivered the opinion of the Court.

The Free Speech Clause of the First Amendment constrains governmental actors and protects private actors. To draw the line between governmental and private, this Court applies what is known as the state-action doctrine. Under that doctrine, as relevant here, a private entity may be considered a state actor when it exercises a function "traditionally exclusively reserved to the State." Jackson v. Metropolitan Edison Co., 419 U. S. 345, 352 (1974).

This state-action case concerns the public access channels on Time Warner's cable system in Manhattan. Public access channels are available for private citizens to use. The public access channels on Time Warner's cable system in Manhattan are operated by a private nonprofit corporation known as MNN. The question here is whether MNN—even though it is a private entity—nonetheless is a state actor when it operates the public access channels. In other words, is operation of public access channels on a cable system a traditional, exclusive public function? If so, then the First Amendment would restrict MNN's exercise of editorial discretion over the speech and speakers on the public access channels.

Under the state-action doctrine as it has been articulated and applied by our precedents, we conclude that operation of public access channels on a cable system is not a traditional, exclusive public function. Moreover, a private entity such as MNN who opens its property for speech by others is not transformed by that fact alone into a state actor. In operating the public access channels, MNN is a private actor, not a state actor, and MNN therefore is not subject to First Amendment constraints on its editorial discretion. We reverse in relevant part

154

APPLICATION OF THE POST-CIVIL WAR AMENDMENTS TO PRIVATE
CONDUCT: CONGRESSIONAL POWER TO ENFORCE THE AMENDMENTS   CHAPTER 12

the judgment of the Second Circuit, and we remand the case for further proceedings consistent with this opinion.

I

A

Since the 1970s, public access channels have been a regular feature on cable television systems throughout the United States. In the 1970s, Federal Communications Commission regulations required certain cable operators to set aside channels on their cable systems for public access. In 1979, however, this Court ruled that the FCC lacked statutory authority to impose that mandate. . . . A few years later, Congress passed and President Reagan signed the Cable Communications Policy Act of 1984. 98 Stat. 2779. The Act authorized state and local governments to require cable operators to set aside channels on their cable systems for public access. 47 U. S. C. § 531(b).

The New York State Public Service Commission regulates cable franchising in New York State and requires cable operators in the State to set aside channels on their cable systems for public access. 16 N. Y. Codes, Rules & Regs. §§ 895.1(f), 895.4(b) (2018). State law requires that use of the public access channels be free of charge and first-come, first-served. §§ 895.4(c)(4) and (6). Under state law, the cable operator operates the public access channels unless the local government in the area chooses to itself operate the channels or designates a private entity to operate the channels. § 895.4(c)(1).

Time Warner (now known as Charter) operates a cable system in Manhattan. Under state law, Time Warner must set aside some channels on its cable system for public access. New York City (the City) has designated a private nonprofit corporation named Manhattan Neighborhood Network, commonly referred to as MNN, to operate Time Warner's public access channels in Manhattan. This case involves a complaint against MNN regarding its management of the public access channels.

B

. . .

DeeDee Halleck and Jesus Papoleto Melendez produced public access programming in Manhattan. They made a film about MNN's alleged neglect of the East Harlem community. Halleck submitted the film to MNN for airing on MNN's public access channels, and MNN later televised the film. Afterwards, MNN fielded multiple complaints about the film's content. In response, MNN temporarily suspended Halleck from using the public access channels.

Halleck and Melendez soon became embroiled in another dispute with MNN staff. In the wake of that dispute, MNN ultimately suspended Halleck and Melendez from all MNN services and facilities.

Halleck and Melendez then sued MNN, among other parties, in Federal District Court. The two producers claimed that MNN violated their First Amendment free-speech rights when MNN restricted their access to the public access channels because of the content of their film.

MNN moved to dismiss the producers' First Amendment claim on the ground that MNN is not a state actor and therefore is not subject to First Amendment restrictions on its editorial discretion. The District Court agreed with MNN and dismissed the producers' First Amendment claim. The Second Circuit reversed in relevant part. . . . In the majority opinion . . . the court stated that the public access channels in Manhattan are a public forum for purposes of the First Amendment. Reasoning that "public forums are usually operated by governments," the court concluded that MNN is a state actor subject to First Amendment constraints. . . . [One judge] added a concurring opinion, explaining that MNN also qualifies as a state actor for the independent reason that "New York City delegated to MNN the traditionally public function of administering and regulating speech in the public forum of Manhattan's public access channels." . . .

. . .

We granted certiorari to resolve disagreement among the Courts of Appeals on the question whether private operators of public access cable channels are state actors subject to the First Amendment. . . .

II

. . .

In accord with the text and structure of the Constitution, this Court's state-action doctrine distinguishes the government from individuals and private entities. . . . By enforcing that constitutional boundary between the governmental and the private, the state-action doctrine protects a robust sphere of individual liberty.

Here, the producers claim that MNN, a private entity, restricted their access to MNN's public access channels because of the content of the producers' film. The producers have advanced a First Amendment claim against MNN. The threshold problem with that First Amendment claim is a fundamental one: MNN is a private entity.

Relying on this Court's state-action precedents, the producers assert that MNN is nonetheless a state actor subject to First Amendment constraints on its editorial discretion. Under this Court's cases, a private entity can qualify as a state actor in a few limited circumstances—including, for example, (i) when the private entity performs a traditional, exclusive public function, see, *e.g., Jackson*, 419 U. S., at 352–354; (ii) when the government compels the private entity to take a particular action, see, *e.g.,* Blum v. Yaretsky, 457 U. S. 991, 1004–1005 (1982); or (iii) when the government acts jointly with the private entity, see, *e.g.,* Lugar v. Edmondson Oil Co., 457 U. S. 922, 941–942 (1982).

The producers' primary argument here falls into the first category: The producers contend that MNN exercises a traditional, exclusive public function when it operates the public access channels on Time Warner's cable system in Manhattan. We disagree.

A

Under the Court's cases, a private entity may qualify as a state actor when it exercises "powers traditionally exclusively reserved to the State." . . . It is not enough that the federal, state, or local government exercised the function in the past, or still does. And it is not enough that the function serves the public good or the public interest in some way. Rather, to qualify as a traditional, exclusive public function within the meaning of our state-action precedents, the government must have traditionally *and* exclusively performed the function. . . .

The Court has stressed that "very few" functions fall into that category. Flagg Bros., Inc. v. Brooks, 436 U. S. 149, 158 (1978). Under the Court's cases, those functions include, for example, running elections and operating a company

156

APPLICATION OF THE POST-CIVIL WAR AMENDMENTS TO PRIVATE CONDUCT: CONGRESSIONAL POWER TO ENFORCE THE AMENDMENTS   **CHAPTER 12**

town. See Terry v. Adams, 345 U. S. 461, 468–470 (1953) (elections); Marsh v. Alabama, 326 U. S. 501, 505–509 (1946) (company town); Smith v. Allwright, 321 U. S. 649, 662–666 (1944) (elections); Nixon v. Condon, 286 U. S. 73, 84–89 (1932) (elections).[1] The Court has ruled that a variety of functions do not fall into that category, including, for example: running sports associations and leagues, administering insurance payments, operating nursing homes, providing special education, representing indigent criminal defendants, resolving private disputes, and supplying electricity. See American Mfrs. Mut. Ins. Co. v. Sullivan, 526 U. S. 40, 55–57 (1999) (insurance payments); National Collegiate Athletic Assn. v. Tarkanian, 488 U. S. 179, 197, n. 18 (1988) (college sports); San Francisco Arts & Athletics, Inc. v. United States Olympic Comm., 483 U. S. 522, 544–545 (1987) (amateur sports); *Blum*, 457 U. S., at 1011–1012 (nursing home); *Rendell-Baker*, 457 U. S., at 842 (special education); Polk County v. Dodson, 454 U. S. 312, 318–319 (1981) (public defender); *Flagg Bros.*, 436 U. S., at 157–163 (private dispute resolution); *Jackson*, 419 U. S., at 352–354 (electric service).

The relevant function in this case is operation of public access channels on a cable system. That function has not traditionally and exclusively been performed by government.

Since the 1970s, when public access channels became a regular feature on cable systems, a variety of private and public actors have operated public access channels, including: private cable operators; private nonprofit organizations; municipalities; and other public and private community organizations such as churches, schools, and libraries. . . .

The history of public access channels in Manhattan further illustrates the point. In 1971, public access channels first started operating in Manhattan. . . . Those early Manhattan public access channels were operated in large part by private cable operators, with some help from private nonprofit organizations. . . . Those private cable operators continued to operate the public access channels until the early 1990s, when MNN (also a private entity) began to operate the public access channels.

In short, operating public access channels on a cable system is not a traditional, exclusive public function within the meaning of this Court's cases.

B

To avoid that conclusion, the producers widen the lens and contend that the relevant function here is not simply the operation of public access channels on a cable system, but rather is more generally the operation of a public forum for speech. And according to the producers, operation of a public forum for speech is a traditional, exclusive public function.

That analysis mistakenly ignores the threshold state-action question. When the government provides a forum for speech (known as a public forum), the government may be constrained by the First Amendment, meaning that the government ordinarily may not exclude speech or speakers from the forum on the basis of viewpoint, or sometimes even on the basis of content. See, *e.g.,*

---

[1] Relatedly, this Court has recognized that a private entity may, under certain circumstances, be deemed a state actor when the government has outsourced one of its constitutional obligations to a private entity. In West v. Atkins, for example, the State was constitutionally obligated to provide medical care to prison inmates. 487 U. S. 42, 56 (1988). That scenario is not present here because the government has no such obligation to operate public access channels.

Southeastern Promotions, Ltd. v. Conrad, 420 U. S. 546, 547, 555 (1975) (private theater leased to the city); Police Dept. of Chicago v. Mosley, 408 U. S. 92, 93, 96 (1972) (sidewalks); Hague v. Committee for Industrial Organization, 307 U. S. 496, 515–516 (1939) (streets and parks).

By contrast, when a private entity provides a forum for speech, the private entity is not ordinarily constrained by the First Amendment because the private entity is not a state actor. The private entity may thus exercise editorial discretion over the speech and speakers in the forum. This Court so ruled in its 1976 decision in Hudgens v. NLRB. There, the Court held that a shopping center owner is not a state actor subject to First Amendment requirements such as the public forum doctrine. 424 U. S., at 520–521; see also Lloyd Corp. v. Tanner, 407 U. S. 551, 569–570 (1972); Central Hardware Co. v. NLRB, 407 U. S. 539, 547 (1972); *Alliance for Community Media*, 56 F. 3d, at 121–123.

The *Hudgens* decision reflects a commonsense principle: Providing some kind of forum for speech is not an activity that only governmental entities have traditionally performed. Therefore, a private entity who provides a forum for speech is not transformed by that fact alone into a state actor. After all, private property owners and private lessees often open their property for speech. Grocery stores put up community bulletin boards. Comedy clubs host open mic nights. As [the dissenting judge below] explained, it "is not at all a near-exclusive function of the state to provide the forums for public expression, politics, information, or entertainment." . . .

In short, merely hosting speech by others is not a traditional, exclusive public function and does not alone transform private entities into state actors subject to First Amendment constraints.

If the rule were otherwise, all private property owners and private lessees who open their property for speech would be subject to First Amendment constraints and would lose the ability to exercise what they deem to be appropriate editorial discretion within that open forum. Private property owners and private lessees would face the unappetizing choice of allowing all comers or closing the platform altogether. "The Constitution by no means requires such an attenuated doctrine of dedication of private property to public use." *Hudgens*, 424 U. S., at 519 (internal quotation marks omitted). Benjamin Franklin did not have to operate his newspaper as "a stagecoach, with seats for everyone." F. Mott, American Journalism 55 (3d ed. 1962). That principle still holds true. As the Court said in *Hudgens*, to hold that private property owners providing a forum for speech are constrained by the First Amendment would be "to create a court-made law wholly disregarding the constitutional basis on which private ownership of property rests in this country." 424 U. S., at 517 (internal quotation marks omitted). The Constitution does not disable private property owners and private lessees from exercising editorial discretion over speech and speakers on their property.

The producers here are seeking in effect to circumvent this Court's case law, including *Hudgens*. But *Hudgens* is sound, and we therefore reaffirm our holding in that case.

C

Next, the producers retort that this case differs from *Hudgens* because New York City has designated MNN to operate the public access channels on Time Warner's cable system, and because New York State heavily regulates MNN with respect to the public access channels. Under this Court's cases, however, those facts do not establish that MNN is a state actor.

New York City's designation of MNN to operate the public access channels is analogous to a government license, a government contract, or a government-granted monopoly. But as the Court has long held, the fact that the government licenses, contracts with, or grants a monopoly to a private entity does not convert the private entity into a state actor—unless the private entity is performing a traditional, exclusive public function. See, *e.g., San Francisco Arts & Athletics*, 483 U. S., at 543–544 (exclusive-use rights and corporate charters); *Blum*, 457 U. S., at 1011 (licenses); *Rendell-Baker*, 457 U. S., at 840–841 (contracts); *Polk County*, 454 U. S., at 319, n. 9, and 320–322 (law licenses); *Jackson*, 419 U. S., at 351–352 (electric monopolies); Columbia Broadcasting System, Inc. v. Democratic National Committee, 412 U. S. 94, 120–121 (1973) (broadcast licenses); Moose Lodge No. 107 v. Irvis, 407 U. S. 163, 176–177 (1972) (liquor licenses); cf. Trustees of Dartmouth College v. Woodward, 4 Wheat. 518, 638–639 (1819) (corporate charters). The same principle applies if the government funds or subsidizes a private entity. . . .

Numerous private entities in America obtain government licenses, government contracts, or government-granted monopolies. If those facts sufficed to transform a private entity into a state actor, a large swath of private entities in America would suddenly be turned into state actors and be subject to a variety of constitutional constraints on their activities. As this Court's many state-action cases amply demonstrate, that is not the law. Here, therefore, the City's designation of MNN to operate the public access channels on Time Warner's cable system does not make MNN a state actor.

So, too, New York State's extensive regulation of MNN's operation of the public access channels does not make MNN a state actor. Under the State's regulations, air time on the public access channels must be free, and programming must be aired on a first-come, first-served basis. Those regulations restrict MNN's editorial discretion and in effect require MNN to operate almost like a common carrier. But under this Court's cases, those restrictions do not render MNN a state actor.

In Jackson v. Metropolitan Edison Co., the leading case on point, the Court stated that the "fact that a business is subject to state regulation does not by itself convert its action into that of the State." 419 U. S., at 350. In that case, the Court held that "a heavily regulated, privately owned utility, enjoying at least a partial monopoly in the providing of electrical service within its territory," was not a state actor. *Id.*, at 358. The Court explained that the "mere existence" of a "regulatory scheme"—even if "extensive and detailed"—did not render the utility a state actor. *Id.*, at 350, and n. 7. Nor did it matter whether the State had authorized the utility to provide electric service to the community, or whether the utility was the only entity providing electric service to much of that community.

This case closely parallels *Jackson*. Like the electric utility in *Jackson*, MNN is "a heavily regulated, privately owned" entity. *Id.*, at 358. As in *Jackson*, the regulations do not transform the regulated private entity into a state actor.

Put simply, being regulated by the State does not make one a state actor. . . . As the Court's cases have explained, the "being heavily regulated makes you a state actor" theory of state action is entirely circular and would significantly endanger individual liberty and private enterprise. The theory would be especially problematic in the speech context, because it could eviscerate certain private entities' rights to exercise editorial control over speech and speakers on their properties or platforms. Not surprisingly, . . . this Court has "never even hinted that regulatory control, and particularly direct regulatory control over a private entity's First Amendment speech rights," could justify subjecting the regulated private entity to the constraints of the First Amendment. . . .

In sum, we conclude that MNN is not subject to First Amendment constraints on how it exercises its editorial discretion with respect to the public access channels. To be sure, MNN is subject to state-law constraints on its editorial discretion (assuming those state laws do not violate a federal statute or the Constitution). If MNN violates those state laws, or violates any applicable contracts, MNN could perhaps face state-law sanctions or liability of some kind. We of course take no position on any potential state-law questions. We simply conclude that MNN, as a private actor, is not subject to First Amendment constraints on how it exercises editorial discretion over the speech and speakers on its public access channels.

III

Perhaps recognizing the problem with their argument that MNN is a state actor under ordinary state-action principles applicable to private entities and private property, the producers alternatively contend that the public access channels are actually the property of New York City, not the property of Time Warner or MNN. On this theory, the producers say (and the dissent agrees) that MNN is in essence simply managing government property on behalf of New York City.

The short answer to that argument is that the public access channels are not the property of New York City. Nothing in the record here suggests that a government (federal, state, or city) owns or leases either the cable system or the public access channels at issue here. Both Time Warner and MNN are private entities. Time Warner is the cable operator, and it owns its cable network, which contains the public access channels. MNN operates those public access channels with its own facilities and equipment. The City does not own or lease the public access channels, and the City does not possess a formal easement or other property interest in those channels. The franchise agreements between the City and Time Warner do not say that the City has any property interest in the public access channels. On the contrary, the franchise agreements expressly place the public access channels "under the jurisdiction" of MNN. App. 22. Moreover, the producers did not allege in their complaint that the City has a property interest in the channels. And the producers have not cited any basis in state law for such a conclusion. Put simply, the City does not have "any formal easement or other property interest in those channels." . . .

It does not matter that a provision in the franchise agreements between the City and Time Warner allowed the City to designate a private entity to operate the public access channels on Time Warner's cable system. Time Warner still owns the cable system. And MNN still operates the public access channels. To reiterate, nothing in the franchise agreements suggests that the City possesses any property interest in Time Warner's cable system, or in the public access channels on that system.

It is true that the City has allowed the cable operator, Time Warner, to lay cable along public rights-of-way in the City. But Time Warner's access to public rights-of-way does not alter the state-action analysis. For Time Warner, as for other cable operators, access to public rights-of-way is essential to lay cable and construct a physical cable infrastructure. . . . But the same is true for utility providers, such as the electric utility in *Jackson*. Put simply, a private entity's permission from government to use public rights-of-way does not render that private entity a state actor.

Having said all that, our point here should not be read too broadly. Under the laws in certain States, including New York, a local government may decide to itself operate the public access channels on a local cable system (as many local governments in New York State and around the country already do), or could take appropriate steps to obtain a property interest in the public access channels. Depending on the circumstances, the First Amendment might then constrain the local government's operation of the public access channels. We decide only the case before us in light of the record before us.

. . .

. . . We reverse in relevant part the judgment of the Second Circuit, and we remand the case for further proceedings consistent with this opinion.

■ JUSTICE SOTOMAYOR, with whom JUSTICE GINSBURG, JUSTICE BREYER and JUSTICE KAGAN join, dissenting.

The Court tells a very reasonable story about a case that is not before us. I write to address the one that is.

This is a case about an organization appointed by the government to administer a constitutional public forum. (It is not, as the Court suggests, about a private property owner that simply opened up its property to others.) New York City (the City) secured a property interest in public-access television channels when it granted a cable franchise to a cable company. State regulations require those public-access channels to be made open to the public on terms that render them a public forum. The City contracted out the administration of that forum to a private organization, petitioner Manhattan Community Access Corporation (MNN). By accepting that agency relationship, MNN stepped into the City's shoes and thus qualifies as a state actor, subject to the First Amendment like any other.

. . .

PART 4

CONSTITUTIONAL PROTECTION OF EXPRESSION AND CONSCIENCE

CHAPTER 13

GOVERNMENTAL CONTROL OF THE CONTENT OF EXPRESSION

3. SPEECH CONFLICTING WITH OTHER COMMUNITY VALUES: GOVERNMENT CONTROL OF THE CONTENT OF SPEECH

C. CONTROL OF "FIGHTING WORDS" AND OFFENSIVE SPEECH

Page 1336. Add the following before City of Houston, Texas v. Hill:

Matal v. Tam

582 U.S. ___, 137 S.Ct. 1744, 198 L.Ed.2d 366 (2017).

■ JUSTICE ALITO announced the judgment of the Court and delivered the opinion of the Court with respect to Parts I, II, and III-A, and an opinion with respect to Parts III-B, III-C, and IV, in which THE CHIEF JUSTICE, JUSTICE THOMAS, and JUSTICE BREYER join.

This case concerns a dance-rock band's application for federal trademark registration of the band's name, "The Slants." "Slants" is a derogatory term for persons of Asian descent, and members of the band are Asian-Americans. But the band members believe that by taking that slur as the name of their group, they will help to "reclaim" the term and drain its denigrating force.

The Patent and Trademark Office (PTO) denied the application based on a provision of federal law prohibiting the registration of trademarks that may "disparage . . . or bring . . . into contemp[t] or disrepute" any "persons, living or dead." 15 U. S. C. § 1052(a). We now hold that this provision violates the Free Speech Clause of the First Amendment. It offends a bedrock First Amendment principle: Speech may not be banned on the ground that it expresses ideas that offend.

I

A

"The principle underlying trademark protection is that distinctive marks—words, names, symbols, and the like—can help distinguish a particular artisan's goods from those of others." . . . A trademark "designate[s] the goods as the product of a particular trader" and "protect[s] his goodwill against the sale of another's product as his." . . . It helps consumers identify goods and services that they wish to purchase, as well as those they want to avoid. . . .

"[F]ederal law does not create trademarks." . . . Trademarks and their precursors have ancient origins, and trademarks were protected at common law and in equity at the time of the founding of our country. 3 J. McCarthy, Trademarks and Unfair Competition § 19:8 (4th ed. 2017) (hereinafter

McCarthy); 1 *id.*, §§ 5:1, 5:2, 5:3; Pattishall, The Constitutional Foundations of American Trademark Law, 78 Trademark Rep. 456, 457–458 (1988); Pattishall, Two Hundred Years of American Trademark Law, 68 Trademark Rep. 121, 121–123 (1978); . . . For most of the 19th century, trademark protection was the province of the States. . . . Eventually, Congress stepped in to provide a degree of national uniformity, passing the first federal legislation protecting trademarks in 1870. See Act of July 8, 1870, §§ 77–84, 16 Stat. 210–212. The foundation of current federal trademark law is the Lanham Act, enacted in 1946. See Act of July 5, 1946, ch. 540, 60 Stat. 427. By that time, trademark had expanded far beyond phrases that do no more than identify a good or service. Then, as now, trademarks often consisted of catchy phrases that convey a message.

Under the Lanham Act, trademarks that are "used in commerce" may be placed on the "principal register," that is, they may be federally registered. 15 U. S. C. § 1051(a)(1). And some marks "capable of distinguishing [an] applicant's goods or services and not registrable on the principal register . . . which are in lawful use in commerce by the owner thereof " may instead be placed on a different federal register: the supplemental register. § 1091(a). There are now more than two million marks that have active federal certificates of registration. PTO Performance and Accountability Report, Fiscal Year 2016, p. 192 (Table 15), https://www.uspto.gov/sites/default/files/documents/USPTOFY16PAR.pdf   (all Internet materials as last visited June 16, 2017). This system of federal registration helps to ensure that trademarks are fully protected and supports the free flow of commerce. "[N]ational protection of trademarks is desirable," we have explained, "because trademarks foster competition and the maintenance of quality by securing to the producer the benefits of good reputation." . . .

B

Without federal registration, a valid trademark may still be used in commerce. See 3 McCarthy § 19:8. And an unregistered trademark can be enforced against would-be infringers in several ways. Most important, even if a trademark is not federally registered, it may still be enforceable under § 43(a) of the Lanham Act, which creates a federal cause of action for trademark infringement. . . . Unregistered trademarks may also be entitled to protection under other federal statutes, such as the Anticybersquatting Consumer Protection Act, 15 U. S. C. § 1125(d). See 5 McCarthy § 25A:49, at 25A–198 ("[T]here is no requirement [in the Anticybersquatting Act] that the protected 'mark' be registered: unregistered common law marks are protected by the Act"). And an unregistered trademark can be enforced under state common law, or if it has been registered in a State, under that State's registration system. See 3 *id.*, § 19:3, at 19–23 (explaining that "[t]he federal system of registration and protection does not preempt parallel state law protection, either by state common law or state registration" and "[i]n the vast majority of situations, federal and state trademark law peacefully coexist"); *id.*, § 22:1(discussing state trademark registration systems).

Federal registration, however, "confers important legal rights and benefits on trademark owners who register their marks." . . . Registration on the principal register (1) "serves as 'constructive notice of the registrant's claim of ownership' of the mark," . . . ; (2) "is 'prima facie evidence of the validity of the registered mark and of the registration of the mark, of the owner's ownership of the mark, and of the owner's exclusive right to use the registered mark in commerce on or in connection with the goods or services specified in the certificate,' " . . .; and (3) can make a mark " 'incontestable' " once a mark has been registered for five years," . . . . Registration also enables the trademark holder "to stop the importation into the United States of articles bearing an infringing mark." 3 McCarthy § 19:9, at 19–38; see 15 U. S. C. § 1124.

C

The Lanham Act contains provisions that bar certain trademarks from the principal register. For example, a trademark cannot be registered if it is "merely descriptive or deceptively misdescriptive" of goods, § 1052(e)(1), or if it is so similar to an already registered trademark or trade name that it is "likely . . . to cause confusion, or to cause mistake, or to deceive," § 1052(d). At issue in this case is one such provision, which we will call "the disparagement clause." This provision prohibits the registration of a trademark "which may disparage . . . persons, living or dead, institutions, beliefs, or national symbols, or bring them into contempt, or disrepute." § 1052(a). This clause appeared in the original Lanham Act and has remained the same to this day. See § 2(a), 60 Stat. 428.

When deciding whether a trademark is disparaging, an examiner at the PTO generally applies a "two-part test." The examiner first considers "the likely meaning of the matter in question, taking into account not only dictionary definitions, but also the relationship of the matter to the other elements in the mark, the nature of the goods or services, and the manner in which the mark is used in the marketplace in connection with the goods or services." Trademark Manual of Examining Procedure § 1203.03(b)(i) (Apr. 2017), p. 1200–150, http:// tmep.uspto.gov. "If that meaning is found to refer to identifiable persons, institutions, beliefs or national symbols," the examiner moves to the second step, asking "whether that meaning may be disparaging to a substantial composite of the referenced group." *Ibid.* If the examiner finds that a "substantial composite, although not necessarily a majority, of the referenced group would find the proposed mark . . . to be disparaging in the context of contemporary attitudes," a prima facie case of disparagement is made out, and the burden shifts to the applicant to prove that the trademark is not disparaging. *Ibid.* What is more, the PTO has specified that "[t]he fact that an applicant may be a member of that group or has good intentions underlying its use of a term does not obviate the fact that a substantial composite of the referenced group would find the term objectionable." *Ibid.*

D

Simon Tam is the lead singer of "The Slants." . . . He chose this moniker in order to "reclaim" and "take ownership" of stereotypes about people of Asian ethnicity. . . . The group "draws inspiration for its lyrics from childhood slurs and mocking nursery rhymes" and has given its albums names such as "The Yellow Album" and "Slanted Eyes, Slanted Hearts." . . .

Tam sought federal registration of "THE SLANTS," on the principal register, App. 17, but an examining attorney at the PTO rejected the request, applying the PTO's two-part framework and finding that "there is . . . a substantial composite of persons who find the term in the applied-for mark offensive." . . . The examining attorney relied in part on the fact that "numerous dictionaries define 'slants' or 'slant-eyes' as a derogatory or offensive term." . . . The examining attorney also relied on a finding that "the band's name has been found offensive numerous times"—citing a performance that was canceled because of the band's moniker and the fact that "several bloggers and commenters to articles on the band have indicated that they find the term and the applied-for mark offensive." . . .

Tam contested the denial of registration before the examining attorney and before the PTO's Trademark Trial and Appeal Board (TTAB) but to no avail. Eventually, he took the case to federal court, where the en banc Federal Circuit ultimately found the disparagement clause facially unconstitutional under the First Amendment's Free Speech Clause. The majority found that the clause engages in viewpoint-based discrimination, that the clause regulates the expressive component of trademarks and consequently cannot be treated as commercial speech, and that the clause is subject to and cannot satisfy strict scrutiny. . . . The majority also rejected the Government's argument that registered trademarks constitute government speech, as well as the Government's contention that federal registration is a form of government subsidy. . . . And the majority opined that even if the disparagement clause were analyzed under this Court's commercial speech cases, the clause would fail the "intermediate scrutiny" that those cases prescribe. . . .

. . .

The Government filed a petition for certiorari, which we granted in order to decide whether the disparagement clause "is facially invalid under the Free Speech Clause of the First Amendment." . . .

II

Before reaching the question whether the disparagement clause violates the First Amendment, we consider Tam's argument that the clause does not reach marks that disparage racial or ethnic groups. The clause prohibits the registration of marks that disparage "persons," and Tam claims that the term "persons" "includes only natural and juristic persons," not "non-juristic entities such as racial and ethnic groups." . . .

. . .

Tam's argument is refuted by the plain terms of the disparagement clause. The clause applies to marks that disparage "persons." A mark that disparages a "substantial" percentage of the members of a racial or ethnic group, Trademark Manual § 1203.03(b)(i), at 1200–150, necessarily disparages many "persons," namely, members of that group. Tam's argument would fail even if the clause used the singular term "person," but Congress' use of the plural "persons" makes the point doubly clear.

. . .

III

Because the disparagement clause applies to marks that disparage the members of a racial or ethnic group, we must decide whether the clause violates the Free Speech Clause of the First Amendment. And at the outset, we must consider three arguments that would either eliminate any First Amendment protection or result in highly permissive rational-basis review. Specifically, the Government contends (1) that trademarks are government speech, not private speech, (2) that trademarks are a form of government subsidy, and (3) that the constitutionality of the disparagement clause should be tested under a new "government-program" doctrine. We address each of these arguments below.

A

The First Amendment prohibits Congress and other government entities and actors from "abridging the freedom of speech"; the First Amendment does not say that Congress and other government entities must abridge their own ability to speak freely. And our cases recognize that "[t]he Free Speech Clause . . . does not regulate government speech." . . .

As we have said, "it is not easy to imagine how government could function" if it were subject to the restrictions that the First Amendment imposes on private speech. . . . " '[T]he First Amendment forbids the government to regulate speech in ways that favor some viewpoints or ideas at the expense of others,' " . . . but imposing a requirement of viewpoint-neutrality on government speech would be paralyzing. When a government entity embarks on a course of action, it necessarily takes a particular viewpoint and rejects others. The Free Speech Clause does not require government to maintain viewpoint neutrality when its officers and employees speak about that venture.

Here is a simple example. During the Second World War, the Federal Government produced and distributed millions of posters to promote the war effort. There were posters urging enlistment, the purchase of war bonds, and the conservation of scarce resources. These posters expressed a viewpoint, but the First Amendment did not demand that the Government balance the message of these posters by producing and distributing posters encouraging Americans to refrain from engaging in these activities.

But while the government-speech doctrine is important—indeed, essential—it is a doctrine that is susceptible to dangerous misuse. If private speech could be passed off as government speech by simply affixing a government seal of approval, government could silence or muffle the expression of disfavored viewpoints. For this reason, we must exercise great caution before extending our government-speech precedents.

At issue here is the content of trademarks that are registered by the PTO, an arm of the Federal Government. The Federal Government does not dream up these marks, and it does not edit marks submitted for registration. Except as required by the statute involved here, 15 U. S. C. § 1052(a), an examiner may not reject a mark based on the viewpoint that it appears to express. Thus, unless that section is thought to apply, an examiner does not inquire whether any viewpoint conveyed by a mark is consistent with Government policy or whether any such viewpoint is consistent with that expressed by other marks already on the principal register. Instead, if the mark meets the Lanham Act's viewpoint-neutral requirements, registration is mandatory. . . . And if an examiner finds that a mark is eligible for placement on the principal register, that decision is not reviewed by any higher official unless the registration is challenged. See §§ 1062(a), 1071; 37 CFR § 41.31(a) (2016). Moreover, once a mark is registered, the PTO is not authorized to remove it from the register unless a party moves for cancellation, the registration expires, or the Federal Trade Commission initiates proceedings based on certain grounds. See 15 U. S. C. §§ 1058(a), 1059, 1064; 37 CFR §§ 2.111(b), 2.160.

In light of all this, it is far-fetched to suggest that the content of a registered mark is government speech. If the federal registration of a trademark makes the mark government speech, the Federal Government is babbling prodigiously and incoherently. It is saying many unseemly things. . . . It is expressing contradictory views. It is unashamedly endorsing a vast array of commercial products and services. And it is providing Delphic advice to the consuming public.

For example, if trademarks represent government speech, what does the Government have in mind when it advises Americans to "make.believe" (Sony), "Think different" (Apple), "Just do it" (Nike), or "Have it your way" (Burger King)? Was the Government warning about a coming disaster when it registered the mark "EndTime Ministries"?

The PTO has made it clear that registration does not constitute approval of a mark. See In re Old Glory Condom Corp., 26 USPQ 2d 1216, 1220, n. 3 (TTAB 1993) ("[I]ssuance of a trademark registration . . . is not a government imprimatur"). And it is unlikely that more than a tiny fraction of the public has any idea what federal registration of a trademark means. . . .

None of our government speech cases even remotely supports the idea that registered trademarks are government speech. In *Johanns* [v. *Livestock Marketing Assn.*, 544 U.S. 550 (2005)], we considered advertisements promoting the sale of beef products. A federal statute called for the creation of a program of paid advertising " 'to advance the image and desirability of beef and beef products.' " . . . Congress and the Secretary of Agriculture provided guidelines for the content of the ads, Department of Agriculture officials attended the meetings at which the content of specific ads was discussed, and the Secretary could edit or reject any proposed ad. . . . Noting that "[t]he message set out in the beef promotions [was] from beginning to end the message established by the Federal Government," we held that the ads were government speech. . . . The Government's involvement in the creation of these beef ads bears no resemblance to anything that occurs when a trademark is registered.

Our decision in [*Pleasant Grove* v.] *Summum*[, 555 U.S. 460 (2009)] is similarly far afield. A small city park contained 15 monuments. . . . Eleven had been donated by private groups, and one of these displayed the Ten Commandments. . . . A religious group claimed that the city, by accepting donated monuments, had created a limited public forum for private speech and was therefore obligated to place in the park a monument expressing the group's religious beliefs.

Holding that the monuments in the park represented government speech, we cited many factors. Governments have used monuments to speak to the public since ancient times; parks have traditionally been selective in accepting and displaying donated monuments; parks would be overrun if they were obligated to accept all monuments offered by private groups; "[p]ublic parks are often closely identified in the public mind with the government unit that owns the land"; and "[t]he monuments that are accepted . . . are meant to convey and have the effect of conveying a government message." . . .

Trademarks share none of these characteristics. Trademarks have not traditionally been used to convey a Government message. With the exception of the enforcement of 15 U. S. C. § 1052(a), the viewpoint expressed by a mark has not played a role in the decision whether to place it on the principal register. And there is no evidence that the public associates the contents of trademarks with the Federal Government.

This brings us to the case on which the Government relies most heavily, Walker [v. Texas Div., Sons of Confederate Veterans, Inc., 576 U.S. 200 (2015)] which likely marks the outer bounds of the government-speech doctrine. Holding that the messages on Texas specialty license plates are government speech, the *Walker* Court cited three factors distilled from *Summum*. . . . First, license plates have long been used by the States to convey state messages. . . . Second, license plates "are often closely identified in the public mind" with the State, since they are manufactured and owned by the State, generally designed by the State, and serve as a form of "government ID." . . . Third, Texas "maintain[ed] direct control over the messages conveyed on its specialty plates." . . . As explained above, none of these factors are present in this case.

In sum, the federal registration of trademarks is vastly different from the beef ads in *Johanns*, the monuments in *Summum*, and even the specialty license plates in *Walker*. Holding that the registration of a trademark converts the mark into government speech would constitute a huge and dangerous extension of the government-speech doctrine. For if the registration of trademarks constituted government speech, other systems of government registration could easily be characterized in the same way.

Perhaps the most worrisome implication of the Government's argument concerns the system of copyright registration. If federal registration makes a trademark government speech and thus eliminates all First Amendment protection, would the registration of the copyright for a book produce a similar transformation? . . .

The Government attempts to distinguish copyright on the ground that it is " 'the engine of free expression,' " Brief for Petitioner 47 . . . , but as this case illustrates, trademarks often have an expressive content. Companies spend huge amounts to create and publicize trademarks that convey a message. It is true that the necessary brevity of trademarks limits what they can say. But powerful messages can sometimes be conveyed in just a few words.

Trademarks are private, not government, speech.

B

We next address the Government's argument that this case is governed by cases in which this Court has upheld the constitutionality of government programs that subsidized speech expressing a particular viewpoint. These cases implicate a notoriously tricky question of constitutional law. "[W]e have held that the Government 'may not deny a benefit to a person on a basis that infringes his constitutionally protected . . . freedom of speech even if he has no entitlement to that benefit.' ". . . But at the same time, government is not required to subsidize activities that it does not wish to promote. . . . Determining which of these principles applies in a particular case "is not always self-evident," . . . but no difficult question is presented here.

Unlike the present case, the decisions on which the Government relies all involved cash subsidies or their equivalent. In Rust v. Sullivan, 500 U. S. 173 (1991), a federal law provided funds to private parties for family planning services. In National Endowment for Arts v. Finley, 524 U. S. 569 (1998), cash grants were awarded to artists. And federal funding for public libraries was at issue in United States v. American Library Assn., Inc., 539 U.S. 194 (2003). In other cases, we have regarded tax benefits as comparable to cash subsidies. See Regan v. Taxation With Representation of Wash., 461 U. S. 540 (1983); Cammarano v. United States, 358 U. S 498 (1959).

The federal registration of a trademark is nothing like the programs at issue in these cases. The PTO does not pay money to parties seeking registration of a mark. Quite the contrary is true: An applicant for registration must pay the PTO a filing fee of $225–$600. 37 CFR § 2.6(a)(1). . . . And to maintain federal registration, the holder of a mark must pay a fee of $300–$500 every 10 years. § 2.6(a)(5); see also 15 U. S. C. § 1059(a). The Federal Circuit concluded that these fees have fully supported the registration system for the past 27 years. . . .

The Government responds that registration provides valuable non-monetary benefits that "are directly traceable to the resources devoted by the federal government to examining, publishing, and issuing certificates of registration for those marks." . . . . But just about every government service requires the expenditure of government funds. This is true of services that benefit everyone, like police and fire protection, as well as services that are utilized by only some, *e.g.*, the adjudication of private lawsuits and the use of public parks and highways.

Trademark registration is not the only government registration scheme. For example, the Federal Government registers copyrights and patents. State governments and their subdivisions register the title to real property and security interests; they issue driver's licenses, motor vehicle registrations, and hunting, fishing, and boating licenses or permits.

Cases like *Rust* and *Finley* are not instructive in analyzing the constitutionality of restrictions on speech imposed in connection with such services.

C

Finally, the Government urges us to sustain the disparagement clause under a new doctrine that would apply to "government-program" cases. For the most part, this argument simply merges our government-speech cases and the previously discussed subsidy cases in an attempt to construct a broader doctrine that can be applied to the registration of trademarks. The only new element in this construct consists of two cases involving a public employer's collection of union dues from its employees. But those cases occupy a special area of First Amendment case law, and they are far removed from the registration of trademarks. In Davenport v. Washington Ed. Assn., 551 U. S. 177, 181–182 (2007), a Washington law permitted a public employer automatically to deduct from the wages of employees who chose not to join the union the portion of union dues used for activities related to collective bargaining. But unless these employees affirmatively consented, the law did not allow the employer to collect the portion of union dues that would be used in election activities. . . . A public employee union argued that this law unconstitutionally restricted its speech based on its content; that is, the law permitted the employer to assist union speech on matters relating to collective bargaining but made it harder for the union to collect money to support its election activities. . . . Upholding this law, we characterized it as imposing a "modest limitation" on an "extraordinary benefit," namely, taking money from the wages of non-union members and turning it over to the union free of charge. . . . Refusing to confer an even greater benefit, we held, did not upset the marketplace of ideas and did not abridge the union's free speech rights. . . .

Ysursa v. Pocatello Ed. Assn., 555 U. S. 353 (2009), is similar. There, we considered an Idaho law that allowed public employees to elect to have union dues deducted from their wages but did not allow such a deduction for money remitted to the union's political action committee. . . . We reasoned that "the government . . . [was] not required to assist others in funding the expression of particular ideas." . . .

Davenport and *Ysursa* are akin to our subsidy cases. Although the laws at issue in *Davenport* and *Ysursa* did not provide cash subsidies to the unions, they conferred a very valuable benefit—the right to negotiate a collective-bargaining agreement under which non-members would be obligated to pay an agency fee that the public employer would collect and turn over to the union free of charge. As in the cash subsidy cases, the laws conferred this benefit because it was thought that this arrangement served important government interests. See Abood v. Detroit Bd. of Ed., 431 U. S. 209, 224–226 (1977). But the challenged laws did not go further and provide convenient collection mechanisms for money to be used in political activities. In essence, the Washington and Idaho lawmakers chose to confer a substantial non-cash benefit for the purpose of furthering activities that they particularly desired to promote but not to provide a similar benefit for the purpose of furthering other activities. Thus, *Davenport* and *Ysursa* are no more relevant for present purposes than the subsidy cases previously discussed.

Potentially more analogous are cases in which a unit of government creates a limited public forum for private speech. . . . However, even in such cases, what we have termed "viewpoint discrimination" is forbidden. . . .

Our cases use the term "viewpoint" discrimination in a broad sense, . . . and in that sense, the disparagement clause discriminates on the bases of "viewpoint." To be sure, the clause evenhandedly prohibits disparagement of all groups. It applies equally to marks that damn Democrats and Republicans, capitalists and socialists, and those arrayed on both sides of every possible issue. It denies registration to any mark that is offensive to a substantial percentage of the members of any group. But in the sense relevant here, that is viewpoint discrimination: Giving offense is a viewpoint.

We have said time and again that "the public expression of ideas may not be prohibited merely because the ideas are themselves offensive to some of their hearers." Street v. New York, 394 U. S. 576, 592 (1969). See also Texas v. Johnson, 491 U. S. 397, 414 (1989) ("If there is a bedrock principle underlying the First Amendment, it is that the government may not prohibit the expression of an idea simply because society finds the idea itself offensive or disagreeable"); Hustler Magazine, Inc. v. Falwell, 485 U. S. 46, 55–56 (1988); Coates v. Cincinnati, 402 U. S. 611, 615 (1971); Bachellar v. Maryland, 397 U. S. 564, 567 (1970); Tinker v. Des Moines Independent Community School Dist., 393 U. S. 503, 509–514 (1969); Cox v. Louisiana, 379 U. S. 536, 551 (1965); Edwards v. South Carolina, 372 U. S. 229, 237–238 (1963); Terminiello v. Chicago, 337 U. S. 1, 4–5 (1949); Cantwell v. Connecticut, 310 U. S. 296, 311 (1940); Schneider v. State (Town of Irvington), 308 U. S. 147, 161 (1939); De Jonge v. Oregon, 299 U. S. 353, 365 (1937).

For this reason, the disparagement clause cannot be saved by analyzing it as a type of government program in which some content- and speaker-based restrictions are permitted.

IV

Having concluded that the disparagement clause cannot be sustained under our government-speech or subsidy cases or under the Government's proposed "government program" doctrine, we must confront a dispute between the parties on the question whether trademarks are commercial speech and are thus subject to the relaxed scrutiny outlined in Central Hudson Gas & Elec. Corp. v. Public Serv. Comm'n of N. Y., 447 U. S. 557 (1980). The Government and *amici* supporting its position argue that all trademarks are commercial speech. They note that the central purposes of trademarks are commercial and that federal law regulates trademarks to promote fair and orderly interstate commerce. Tam and his *amici*, on the other hand, contend that many, if not all, trademarks have an expressive component. In other words, these trademarks do not simply identify the source of a product or service but go on to say something more, either about the product or service or some broader issue. The trademark in this case illustrates this point. The name "The Slants" not only identifies the band but expresses a view about social issues.

We need not resolve this debate between the parties because the disparagement clause cannot withstand even *Central Hudson* review. Under *Central Hudson*, a restriction of speech must serve "a substantial interest," and it must be "narrowly drawn." . . . This means, among other things, that "[t]he regulatory technique may extend only as far as the interest it serves." . . . The disparagement clause fails this requirement.

It is claimed that the disparagement clause serves two interests. The first is phrased in a variety of ways in the briefs. Echoing language in one of the opinions below, the Government asserts an interest in preventing " 'underrepresented groups' " from being " 'bombarded with demeaning messages in commercial advertising.' " . . . . But no matter how the point is phrased, its unmistakable thrust is this: The Government has an interest in preventing speech expressing ideas that offend. And, as we have explained, that idea strikes at the heart of the First Amendment. Speech that demeans on the basis of race, ethnicity, gender, religion, age, disability, or any other similar ground is hateful; but the proudest boast of our free speech jurisprudence is that we protect the freedom to express "the thought that we hate." United States v. Schwimmer, 279 U. S. 644, 655 (1929) (Holmes, J., dissenting).

The second interest asserted is protecting the orderly flow of commerce. . . . Commerce, we are told, is disrupted by trademarks that "involv[e] disparagement of race, gender, ethnicity, national origin, religion, sexual orientation, and similar demographic classification." . . . Such trademarks are analogized to discriminatory conduct, which has been recognized to have an adverse effect on commerce. . . .

A simple answer to this argument is that the disparagement clause is not "narrowly drawn" to drive out trademarks that support invidious discrimination. The clause reaches any trademark that disparages *any person, group, or institution*. It applies to trademarks like the following: "Down with racists," "Down with sexists," "Down with homophobes." It is not an anti-discrimination clause; it is a happy-talk clause. In this way, it goes much further than is necessary to serve the interest asserted.

The clause is far too broad in other ways as well. The clause protects every person living or dead as well as every institution. Is it conceivable that commerce would be disrupted by a trademark saying: "James Buchanan was a disastrous president" or "Slavery is an evil institution"?

There is also a deeper problem with the argument that commercial speech may be cleansed of any expression likely to cause offense. The commercial market is well stocked with merchandise that disparages prominent figures and groups, and the line between commercial and non-commercial speech is not always clear, as this case illustrates. If affixing the commercial label permits the suppression of any speech that may lead to political or social "volatility," free speech would be endangered.

* * *

For these reasons, we hold that the disparagement clause violates the Free Speech Clause of the First Amendment. The judgment of the Federal Circuit is affirmed.

■ JUSTICE KENNEDY, with whom JUSTICE GINSBURG, JUSTICE SOTOMAYOR, and JUSTICE KAGAN join, concurring in part and concurring in the judgment.

. . .

As the Court is correct to hold, § 1052(a) constitutes viewpoint discrimination—a form of speech suppression so potent that it must be subject to rigorous constitutional scrutiny. The Government's action and the statute on which it is based cannot survive this scrutiny.

The Court is correct in its judgment, and I join Parts I, II, and III-A of its opinion. This separate writing explains in greater detail why the First Amendment's protections against viewpoint discrimination apply to the trademark here [and why] the viewpoint discrimination rationale renders unnecessary any extended treatment of other questions raised by the parties.

I

Those few categories of speech that the government can regulate or punish—for instance, fraud, defamation, or incitement—are well established within our constitutional tradition. . . . Aside from these and a few other narrow exceptions, it is a fundamental principle of the First Amendment that the government may not punish or suppress speech based on disapproval of the ideas or perspectives the speech conveys. . . .

The First Amendment guards against laws "targeted at specific subject matter," a form of speech suppression known as content based discrimination. . . . This category includes a subtype of laws that go further, aimed at the suppression of "particular views . . . on a subject." . . . . A law found to discriminate based on viewpoint is an "egregious form of content discrimination," which is "presumptively unconstitutional." . . .

At its most basic, the test for viewpoint discrimination is whether—within the relevant subject category—the government has singled out a subset of messages for disfavor based on the views expressed. . . . In the instant case, the disparagement clause the Government now seeks to implement and enforce identifies the relevant subject as "persons, living or dead, institutions, beliefs, or national symbols." 15 U. S. C. § 1052(a). Within that category, an applicant may register a positive or benign mark but not a derogatory one. The law thus reflects the Government's disapproval of a subset of messages it finds offensive. This is the essence of viewpoint discrimination.

The Government disputes this conclusion. It argues, to begin with, that the law is viewpoint neutral because it applies in equal measure to any trademark that demeans or offends. This misses the point. A subject that is first defined by content and then regulated or censored by mandating only one sort of comment is not viewpoint neutral. To prohibit all sides from criticizing their opponents makes a law more viewpoint based, not less so. . . . The logic of the Government's rule is that a law would be viewpoint neutral even if it provided that public officials could be praised but not condemned. The First Amendment's viewpoint neutrality principle protects more than the right to identify with a particular side. It protects the right to create and present arguments for particular positions in particular ways, as the speaker chooses. By mandating positivity, the law here might silence dissent and distort the marketplace of ideas.

The Government next suggests that the statute is viewpoint neutral because the disparagement clause applies to trademarks regardless of the applicant's personal views or reasons for using the mark. Instead, registration is denied based on the expected reaction of the applicant's audience. In this way, the argument goes, it cannot be said that Government is acting with hostility toward a particular point of view. For example, the Government does not dispute that respondent seeks to use his mark in a positive way. . . .

The Government may not insulate a law from charges of viewpoint discrimination by tying censorship to the reaction of the speaker's audience. The Court has suggested that viewpoint discrimination occurs when the government intends to suppress a speaker's beliefs, . . . but viewpoint discrimination need not take that form in every instance. The danger of viewpoint discrimination is that the government is attempting to remove certain ideas or perspectives from a broader debate. That danger is all the greater if the ideas or perspectives are ones a particular audience might think offensive, at least at first hearing. An initial reaction may prompt further reflection, leading to a more reasoned, more tolerant position. . . .

. . .

II

The parties dispute whether trademarks are commercial speech and whether trademark registration should be considered a federal subsidy. The former issue may turn on whether certain commercial concerns for the protection of trademarks might, as a general matter, be the basis for regulation. However that issue is resolved, the viewpoint based discrimination at issue here necessarily invokes heightened scrutiny.

"Commercial speech is no exception," the Court has explained, to the principle that the First Amendment "requires heightened scrutiny whenever the government creates a regulation of speech because of disagreement with the message it conveys." . . . Unlike content based discrimination, discrimination based on viewpoint, including a regulation that targets speech for its offensiveness, remains of serious concern in the commercial context. . . .

To the extent trademarks qualify as commercial speech, they are an example of why that term or category does not serve as a blanket exemption from the First Amendment's requirement of viewpoint neutrality. Justice Holmes' reference to the "free trade in ideas" and the "power of . . . thought to get itself accepted in the competition of the market," . . . was a metaphor. In the realm of trademarks, the metaphorical marketplace of ideas becomes a tangible, powerful reality. Here that real marketplace exists as a matter of state law and our common-law tradition, quite without regard to the Federal Government. . . . These marks make up part of the expression of everyday life, as with the names of entertainment groups, broadcast networks, designer clothing, newspapers, automobiles, candy bars, toys, and so on. . . . Nonprofit organizations—ranging from medical-research charities and other humanitarian causes to political advocacy groups—also have trademarks, which they use to compete in a real economic sense for funding and other resources as they seek to persuade others to join their cause. . . . To permit viewpoint discrimination in this context is to permit Government censorship.

This case does not present the question of how other provisions of the Lanham Act should be analyzed under the First Amendment. It is well settled, for instance, that to the extent a trademark is confusing or misleading the law can protect consumers and trademark owners. . . . This case also does not involve laws related to product labeling or otherwise designed to protect consumers. . . . These considerations, however, do not alter the speech principles that bar the viewpoint discrimination embodied in the statutory provision at issue here.

It is telling that the Court's precedents have recognized just one narrow situation in which viewpoint discrimination is permissible: where the government itself is speaking or recruiting others to communicate a message on its behalf. . . . The exception is necessary to allow the government to stake out positions and pursue policies. . . . But it is also narrow, to prevent the government from claiming that every government program is exempt from the First Amendment. These cases have identified a number of factors that, if present, suggest the government is speaking on its own behalf; but none are present here. . . .

. . .

* * *

A law that can be directed against speech found offensive to some portion of the public can be turned against minority and dissenting views to the detriment of all. The First Amendment does not entrust that power to the government's benevolence. Instead, our reliance must be on the substantial safeguards of free and open discussion in a democratic society.

For these reasons, I join the Court's opinion in part and concur in the judgment.

[Justice Thomas wrote separately, concurring in part and concurring in the judgment, to explain his failure to join Part II of Justice Alito's opinion (which involved a statutory interpretation argument Justice Thomas thought the Court should not address) and to reiterate his view that "when the government seeks to restrict truthful speech in order to suppress the ideas it conveys, strict scrutiny is appropriate, whether or not the speech in question may be characterized as 'commercial.' " . . .]

■ JUSTICE GORSUCH took no part in the consideration or decision of this case.

Iancu v. Brunetti, 588 U.S. ___, 139 S.Ct. 2294 (2019). Relying on the shared conclusion in Matal v. Tam, *supra*, that "the Lanham Act's bar on the registration of 'disparag[ing]' trademarks . . . violated the First Amendment because it discriminated on the basis of viewpoint[,]" in this case Justice Kagan wrote for a majority of the Court, holding that "a neighboring provision of the Act, prohibiting the registration of 'immoral[ ] or scandalous' trademarks . . . infringes the First Amendment for the same reason: It too disfavors certain ideas." The case involved an unsuccessful attempt by Brunetti, "an artist and entrepreneur who founded a clothing line that uses the trademark FUCT[,] . . . to register his mark with the U. S. Patent and Trademark Office (PTO)." The

PTO applied "the Lanham Act's prohibitions on registration [of] marks that '[c]onsist[ ] of or comprise[ ] immoral[ ] or scandalous matter[,]' . . . as a 'unitary provision,' rather than treating the two adjectives in it separately." Justice Kagan's opinion contained the following passages:

"To determine whether a mark fits in the category, the PTO asks whether a 'substantial composite of the general public' would find the mark 'shocking to the sense of truth, decency, or propriety'; 'giving offense to the conscience or moral feelings'; 'calling out for condemnation'; 'disgraceful'; 'offensive'; 'disreputable'; or 'vulgar.' . . .

"Both a PTO examining attorney and the PTO's Trademark Trial and Appeal Board decided that Brunetti's mark flunked that test. The attorney determined that FUCT was 'a total vulgar' and 'therefore[ ] unregistrable.' . . . On review, the Board stated that the mark was 'highly offensive' and 'vulgar,' and that it had 'decidedly negative sexual connotations.' . . . [T]he Board also considered evidence of how Brunetti used the mark. It found that Brunetti's website and products contained imagery, near the mark, of 'extreme nihilism' and 'antisocial' behavior. . . . In that context, the Board thought, the mark communicated 'misogyny, depravity,[and] violence.' . . . The Board concluded: 'Whether one considers [the mark] as a sexual term, or finds that [Brunetti] has used [the mark] in the context of extreme misogyny, nihilism or violence, we have no question but that [the term is] extremely offensive.'

"   . . .

"   . . . [I]n *Tam*, . . . [t]he eight-Justice Court divided evenly between two opinions and could not agree on the overall framework for deciding the case. (In particular, no majority emerged to resolve whether a Lanham Act bar is a condition on a government benefit or a simple restriction on speech.) But all the Justices agreed on two propositions. First, if a trademark registration bar is viewpoint-based, it is unconstitutional. . . . And second, the disparagement bar was viewpoint-based. . . .

"   . . .

"If the 'immoral or scandalous' bar similarly discriminates on the basis of viewpoint, it must also collide with our First Amendment doctrine. The Government does not argue otherwise. In briefs and oral argument, the Government offers a theory for upholding the bar if it is viewpoint-neutral (essentially, that the bar would then be a reasonable condition on a government benefit). . . . But the Government agrees that under *Tam* it may not 'deny registration based on the views expressed' by a mark. . . . So the key question becomes: Is the 'immoral or scandalous' criterion in the Lanham Act viewpoint-neutral or viewpoint-based?

"It is viewpoint-based. The meanings of 'immoral' and 'scandalous' are not mysterious, but resort to some dictionaries still helps to lay bare the problem. When is expressive material 'immoral'? According to a standard definition, when it is 'inconsistent with rectitude, purity, or good morals'; 'wicked'; or 'vicious.' Webster's New International Dictionary . . . . So the Lanham Act permits registration of marks that champion society's sense of rectitude and morality, but not marks that denigrate those concepts. And when is such material 'scandalous'? Says a typical definition, when it 'giv[es] offense to the conscience or moral feelings'; 'excite[s] reprobation'; or 'call[s] out condemnation.' Webster's . . . . So the Lanham Act allows registration of marks when their messages accord with, but not when their messages defy, society's sense of decency or propriety. Put the pair of overlapping terms together and the statute, on its face, distinguishes between two opposed sets of ideas: those aligned with conventional moral standards and those hostile to them; those inducing societal nods of approval and those provoking offense and condemnation. The statute favors the former, and disfavors the latter. 'Love rules'? 'Always be good'? Registration follows. 'Hate rules'? 'Always be cruel'? Not according to the Lanham Act's 'immoral or scandalous' bar.

"The facial viewpoint bias in the law results in viewpoint-discriminatory application. . . . [T]he PTO has refused to register marks communicating 'immoral' or 'scandalous' views about (among other things) drug use, religion, and terrorism. But all the while, it has approved registration of marks expressing more accepted views on the same topics. . . .

" . . .

". . . [T]he Government tells us to ignore how the Lanham Act's language, on its face, disfavors some ideas. In urging that course, the Government does not dispute that the statutory language—and words used to define it—have just that effect. . . . But no matter, says the Government, because the statute is 'susceptible of' a limiting construction that would remove this viewpoint bias. . . . The Government's idea, abstractly phrased, is to narrow the statutory bar to 'marks that are offensive [or] shocking to a substantial segment of the public because of their *mode* of expression, independent of any views that they may express.' . . . More concretely, the Government explains that this reinterpretation would mostly restrict the PTO to refusing marks that are 'vulgar'—meaning 'lewd,' 'sexually explicit or profane.'. . . Such a reconfigured bar, the Government says, would not turn on viewpoint, and so we could uphold it.

"But we cannot accept the Government's proposal, because the statute says something markedly different. . . . [E]ven assuming the Government's reading would eliminate First Amendment problems, we may adopt it only if we can see it in the statutory language. And we cannot. The 'immoral or scandalous' bar stretches far beyond the Government's proposed construction. The statute as written does not draw the line at lewd, sexually explicit, or profane marks. Nor does it refer only to marks whose 'mode of expression,' independent of viewpoint, is particularly offensive. . . . It covers the universe of immoral or scandalous—or (to use some PTO synonyms) offensive or disreputable—material. Whether or not lewd or profane. Whether the scandal and immorality comes from mode or instead from viewpoint. To cut the statute off where the Government urges is not to interpret the statute Congress enacted, but to fashion a new one.*

". . . [T]he Government gestures toward the idea that the provision is salvageable by virtue of its constitutionally permissible applications (in the Government's view, its applications to lewd, sexually explicit, or profane marks). . . . In other words, the Government invokes our First Amendment

---

* We reject the dissent's statutory surgery for the same reason. . . . Even if hived off from 'immoral' marks, the category of scandalous marks thus includes *both* marks that offend by the ideas they convey *and* marks that offend by their mode of expression. And its coverage of the former means that it discriminates based on viewpoint. We say nothing at all about a statute that covers only the latter—or, in the Government's more concrete description, a statute limited to lewd, sexually explicit, and profane marks. Nor do we say anything about how to evaluate viewpoint-neutral restrictions on trademark registration—because the 'scandalous' bar (whether or not attached to the 'immoral' bar) is not one.

overbreadth doctrine, and asks us to uphold the statute against facial attack because its unconstitutional applications are not 'substantial' relative to 'the statute's plainly legitimate sweep.' . . . But to begin with, this Court has never applied that kind of analysis to a viewpoint-discriminatory law. In *Tam*, for example, we did not pause to consider whether the disparagement clause might admit some permissible applications (say, to certain libelous speech) before striking it down. The Court's finding of viewpoint bias ended the matter. And similarly, it seems unlikely we would compare permissible and impermissible applications if Congress outright banned 'offensive' (or to use some other examples, 'divisive' or 'subversive') speech. Once we have found that a law 'aim[s] at the suppression of' views, why would it matter that Congress could have captured some of the same speech through a viewpoint-neutral statute? . . . But in any event, the 'immoral or scandalous' bar is substantially overbroad. There are a great many immoral and scandalous ideas in the world (even more than there are swearwords), and the Lanham Act covers them all. It therefore violates the First Amendment.

"We accordingly affirm the judgment . . . ."

A concurring opinion by Justice Alito emphasized this:

". . . Our decision does not prevent Congress from adopting a more carefully focused statute that precludes the registration of marks containing vulgar terms that play no real part in the expression of ideas. The particular mark in question in this case could be denied registration under such a statute. The term suggested by that mark is not needed to express any idea and, in fact, as commonly used today, generally signifies nothing except emotion and a severely limited vocabulary. The registration of such marks serves only to further coarsen our popular culture. But we are not legislators and cannot substitute a new statute for the one now in force."

Chief Justice Roberts concurred in part and dissented in part:

". . . I agree with the majority that the 'immoral' portion of the provision is not susceptible of a narrowing construction that would eliminate its viewpoint bias. As Justice Sotomayor explains, however, the 'scandalous' portion of the provision is susceptible of such a narrowing construction. Standing alone, the term 'scandalous' need not be understood to reach marks that offend because of the ideas they convey; it can be read more narrowly to bar only marks that offend because of their mode of expression—marks that are obscene, vulgar, or profane. That is how the PTO now understands the term, in light of our decision in Matal v. Tam, ... I agree with Justice Sotomayor that such a narrowing construction is appropriate in this context.

"I also agree that, regardless of how exactly the trademark registration system is best conceived under our precedents—a question we left open in *Tam*— refusing registration to obscene, vulgar, or profane marks does not offend the First Amendment. Whether such marks can be registered does not affect the extent to which their owners may use them in commerce to identify goods. No speech is being restricted; no one is being punished. The owners of such marks are merely denied certain additional benefits associated with federal trademark registration. The Government, meanwhile, has an interest in not associating itself with trademarks whose content is obscene, vulgar, or profane. The First Amendment protects the freedom of speech; it does not require the Government to give aid and comfort to those using obscene, vulgar, and profane modes of expression. . . .”

Justice Breyer also concurred in part and dissented in part. He did not think that the trademark statute “clearly fit within any of the outcome-determinative categories” such as commercial speech, government speech, public forum doctrine, or the often unclear distinction between viewpoint and content discrimination. Instead, he urged the Court, as he had before, to “focus on the interests the First Amendment protects and ask a more basic proportionality question: Does ‘the regulation at issue wor[k] harm to First Amendment interests that is disproportionate in light of the relevant regulatory objectives’? . . .” Using his proportionality analysis, Justice Breyer would have concluded “that the statute at issue here, as interpreted by Justice Sotomayor, does not violate the First Amendment.” He elaborated:

“How much harm to First Amendment interests does a bar on registering highly vulgar or obscene trademarks work? Not much. The statute leaves businesses free to use highly vulgar or obscene words on their products, and even to use such words directly next to other registered marks. Indeed, a business owner might even use a vulgar word as a trademark, provided that he or she is willing to forgo the benefits of registration. . . .

“Moreover, . . . trademark law, is a highly regulated [field] with a specialized mission . . . that . . ., by its very nature, requires the Government to impose limitations on speech. [It] forbids the registration of certain types of words—for example, those that will likely ‘cause confusion,’ or those that are ‘merely descriptive.’ 15 U. S. C. §§ 1052(d), (e). For that reason, an applicant who seeks to register a mark should not expect complete freedom to say what she wishes, but should instead expect linguistic regulation.

“. . . [B]y way of contrast, . . . [f]or one thing, when the Government registers a mark, it is necessarily ‘involv[ed] in promoting’ that mark. The Government has at least a reasonable interest in ensuring that it is not involved in promoting highly vulgar or obscene speech, and that it will not be associated with such speech.

“For another, scientific evidence suggests that certain highly vulgar words have a physiological and emotional impact that makes them different in kind from most other words. . . . [They] originate in a different part of our brains than most other words. . . . And these types of swear words tend to attract more attention and are harder to forget than other words. . . .

“These attention-grabbing words, though financially valuable to some businesses that seek to attract interest in their products, threaten to distract consumers and disrupt commerce. And they may lead to the creation of public spaces that many will find repellant, perhaps on occasion creating the risk of verbal altercations or even physical confrontations. (Just think about how you might react if you saw someone wearing a t-shirt or using a product emblazoned with an odious racial epithet.) The Government thus has an interest in seeking to disincentivize the use of such words in commerce by denying the benefit of trademark registration. . . .

“Finally, although some consumers may be attracted to products labeled with highly vulgar or obscene words, others may believe that such words should not be displayed in public spaces where goods are sold and where children are likely to be present. . . . [T]he Government may have an interest in protecting the sensibilities of children by barring the registration of such words. . . .

". . .

"I would conclude that the prohibition on registering 'scandalous' marks does not 'wor[k] harm to First Amendment interests that is disproportionate in light of the relevant regulatory objectives.' . . . I would therefore uphold this part of the statute. I agree with the Court, however, that the bar on registering 'immoral' marks violates the First Amendment. Because Justice Sotomayor reaches the same conclusions, using roughly similar reasoning, I join her opinion insofar as it is consistent with the views set forth here."

Finally, Justice Sotomayor, joined by Justice Breyer, also concurred in part and dissented in part, articulating her view this way:

". . . With the Lanham Act's scandalous-marks provision . . . struck down as unconstitutional viewpoint discrimination, the Government will have no statutory basis to refuse (and thus no choice but to begin) registering marks containing the most vulgar, profane, or obscene words and images imaginable.

". . . Rather than read the relevant text as the majority does, it is equally possible to read that provision's bar on the registration of scandalous marks to address only obscenity, vulgarity, and profanity. Such a narrowing construction would save that duly enacted legislative text by rendering it a reasonable, viewpoint-neutral restriction on speech that is permissible in the context of a beneficial governmental initiative like the trademark-registration system. I would apply that narrowing construction to the term 'scandalous' and accordingly reject petitioner Erik Brunetti's facial challenge.

". . .

". . . [A]s for the word 'immoral,' I agree with the majority that there is no tenable way to read it that would ameliorate the problem. . . .

"It is with regard to the word 'scandalous' that I part ways with the majority. . . .

"The word 'scandalous' on its own, then, is ambiguous: It can be read broadly (to cover both offensive ideas and offensive manners of expressing ideas), or it can be read narrowly (to cover only offensive modes of expression). . . .

". . .

". . . Congress used not only the word 'scandalous,' but also the words 'immoral' and 'disparage,' in the same block of statutory text—each as a separate feature that could render a mark unregistrable. . . .

"With marks that are offensive because they are disparaging and marks that are offensive because they are immoral already covered, what work did Congress intend for 'scandalous' to do? A logical answer is that Congress meant for 'scandalous' to target a third and distinct type of offensiveness: offensiveness in the mode of communication rather than the idea. The other two words cover marks that are offensive because of the ideas they express; the 'scandalous' clause covers marks that are offensive because of the mode of expression, apart from any particular message or idea.

". . .

". . . What would it mean for 'scandalous' in § 1052(a) to cover only offensive modes of expression? The most obvious ways—indeed, perhaps the only conceivable ways—in which a trademark can be expressed in a shocking or offensive manner are when the speaker employs obscenity, vulgarity, or profanity. . . . As for what constitutes 'scandalous' vulgarity or profanity, I do not offer a list, but I do interpret the term to allow the PTO to restrict (and potentially promulgate guidance to clarify) the small group of lewd words or 'swear' words that cause a visceral reaction, that are not commonly used around children, and that are prohibited in comparable settings. . . .

"A limiting construction . . . is both appropriate in this context and consistent with past precedent. . . . [M]ore caution is required . . . in the realm of criminal statutes, where considerations such as the prohibition against vagueness and the rule of lenity come into play[, but here] the question is only whether the Government must be forced to provide the ancillary benefit of trademark registration to pre-existing trademarks that use even the most extreme obscenity, vulgarity, or profanity. The stakes are far removed from a situation in which, say, Brunetti was facing a threat to his liberty, or even his right to use and enforce his trademark in commerce.

". . .

". . . Properly narrowed, 'scandalous' is a viewpoint-neutral form of content discrimination that is permissible in the kind of discretionary governmental program or limited forum typified by the trademark-registration system.

". . .

"A restriction on trademarks featuring obscenity, vulgarity, or profanity is . . . viewpoint neutral, though it is naturally content-based. . . . To treat a restriction on vulgarity, profanity, or obscenity as viewpoint discrimination would upend decades of precedent.

"Brunetti invokes Cohen v. California, 403 U. S. 15 (1971), to argue that the restriction at issue here is viewpoint discriminatory. . . .

". . .

"Yes, Brunetti has been, as Cohen was, subject to content discrimination, but that content discrimination is properly understood as viewpoint neutral. And whereas even viewpoint-neutral content discrimination is (in all but the most compelling cases, such as threats) impermissible in the context of a criminal prosecution like the one that Cohen faced, Brunetti is subject to such regulation only in the context of the federal trademark-registration system. . . .

". . .

". . . [T]he federal system of trademark registration . . . is, in essence, an opportunity to include one's trademark on a list and thereby secure the ancillary benefits that come with registration. Just as in the limited-forum and government-program cases, some speakers benefit, but no speakers are harmed. Brunetti, for example, can use, own, and enforce his mark regardless of whether it has been registered. Whether he may register his mark can therefore turn on reasonable, viewpoint-neutral content regulations.

"Prohibiting the registration of obscene, profane, or vulgar marks qualifies as reasonable, viewpoint-neutral, content-based regulation. Apart from any interest in regulating commerce itself, the Government has an interest in not promoting certain kinds of speech, whether because such speech could be perceived as suggesting governmental favoritism or simply because the Government does not wish to involve itself with that kind of speech. . . . The

Government has a reasonable interest in refraining from lending its ancillary support to marks that are obscene, vulgar, or profane. . . .

". . .

". . . I emphasize that Brunetti's challenge is a facial one. That means that he must show that 'a substantial number of [the scandalous-marks provision's] applications are unconstitutional, judged in relation to the [provision's] plainly legitimate sweep.'" United States v. Stevens, 559 U. S. 460, 473 (2010). With 'scandalous' narrowed to reach only obscene, profane, and vulgar content, the provision would not be overly broad. . . . Even so, hard cases would remain, and I would expect courts to take seriously as-applied challenges demonstrating a danger that the provision had been used to restrict speech based on the views expressed rather than the mode of expression. . . ."

D. REGULATION OF COMMERCIAL SPEECH

Page 1355. Add after Note, *Overbreadth and Commercial Speech*:

National Institute of Family and Life Advocates v. Becerra

585 U.S. ___, 138 S.Ct. 2361, 201 L.Ed.2d 835 (2018).

■ JUSTICE THOMAS delivered the opinion of the Court.

The California Reproductive Freedom, Accountability, Comprehensive Care, and Transparency Act (FACT Act) requires clinics that primarily serve pregnant women to provide certain notices. Cal. Health & Safety Code Ann. § 123470 *et seq.* (West 2018). Licensed clinics must notify women that California provides free or low-cost services, including abortions, and give them a phone number to call. Unlicensed clinics must notify women that California has not licensed the clinics to provide medical services. The question in this case is whether these notice requirements violate the First Amendment.

I

A

The California State Legislature enacted the FACT Act to regulate crisis pregnancy centers. Crisis pregnancy centers—according to a report commissioned by the California State Assembly . . .—are "pro-life (largely Christian belief-based) organizations that offer a limited range of free pregnancy options, counseling, and other services to individuals that visit a center." . . . "[U]nfortunately," the author of the FACT Act stated, "there are nearly 200 licensed and unlicensed" crisis pregnancy centers in California. . . . These centers "aim to discourage and prevent women from seeking abortions." . . . The author of the FACT Act observed that crisis pregnancy centers "are commonly affiliated with, or run by organizations whose stated goal" is to oppose abortion—including "the National Institute of Family and Life Advocates," one of the petitioners here. . . . To address this perceived problem, the FACT Act imposes two notice requirements on facilities that provide pregnancy-related services—one for licensed facilities and one for unlicensed facilities.

1

The first notice requirement applies to "licensed covered facilit[ies,]" [defined as] licensed primary care or specialty clinic[s] or [those that] qualify as an intermittent clinic. [The covered clinics] also must have the "primary purpose" of "providing family planning or pregnancy-related services" [a]nd . . . must satisfy at least two of the[se] six requirements:

"(1) The facility offers obstetric ultrasounds, obstetric sonograms, or prenatal care to pregnant women.

"(2) The facility provides, or offers counseling about, contraception or contraceptive methods.

"(3) The facility offers pregnancy testing or pregnancy diagnosis.

"(4) The facility advertises or solicits patrons with offers to provide prenatal sonography, pregnancy tests, or pregnancy options counseling.

"(5) The facility offers abortion services.

"(6) The facility has staff or volunteers who collect health information from clients." . . .

The FACT Act exempts . . . [c]linics operated by the United States or a federal agency . . ., [and] clinics that are "enrolled as a Medi-Cal provider" and participate in "the Family Planning, Access, Care, and Treatment Program" (Family PACT program)[, which requires] provid[ing] "the full scope of family planning . . . services specified for the program," . . . including sterilization and emergency contraceptive pills . . . .

If a clinic is a licensed covered facility, the FACT Act requires it to disseminate a government-drafted notice on site. . . . The notice states that "California has public programs that provide immediate free or low-cost access to comprehensive family planning services (including all FDA-approved methods of contraception), prenatal care, and abortion for eligible women. To determine whether you qualify, contact the county social services office at [insert the telephone number]." . . . This notice must be posted in the waiting room, printed and distributed to all clients, or provided digitally at check-in. . . . The notice must be in English and any additional languages identified by state law. . . . In some counties, that means the notice must be spelled out in 13 different languages. . . .

The stated purpose of the FACT Act . . . is to "ensure that California residents make their personal reproductive health care decisions knowing their rights and the health care services available to them." . . . The Legislature posited that "thousands of women remain unaware of the public programs available to provide them with contraception, health education and counseling, family planning, prenatal care, abortion, or delivery." . . . Citing the "time sensitive" nature of pregnancy-related decisions, . . . the Legislature concluded that requiring licensed facilities to inform patients themselves would be "[t]he most effective" way to convey this information . . . .

2

The second notice requirement . . . applies to "unlicensed covered facilit[ies," which are those without State licenses or licensed medical providers and which] have the "primary purpose" of "providing pregnancy-related services." . . . [They] also must satisfy at least two of the[se] four requirements:

"(1) The facility offers obstetric ultrasounds, obstetric sonograms, or prenatal care to pregnant women.

"(2) The facility offers pregnancy testing or pregnancy diagnosis.

"(3) The facility advertises or solicits patrons with offers to provide prenatal sonography, pregnancy tests, or pregnancy options counseling.

"(4) The facility has staff or volunteers who collect health information from clients." . . .

Clinics operated by the United States and licensed primary care clinics enrolled in Medi-Cal and Family PACT are excluded.

Unlicensed covered facilities must provide a government-drafted notice stating that "[t]his facility is not licensed as a medical facility by the State of California and has no licensed medical provider who provides or directly supervises the provision of services." . . . This notice must be provided on site and in all advertising materials. . . . Onsite, the notice must be posted "conspicuously" at the entrance of the facility and in at least one waiting area. . . . It must be "at least 8.5 inches by 11 inches and written in no less than 48-point type." . . . In advertisements, the notice must be in the same size or larger font than the surrounding text, or otherwise set off in a way that draws attention to it. . . . Like the licensed notice, the unlicensed notice must be in English and any additional languages specified by state law. . . . Its stated purpose is to ensure "that pregnant women in California know when they are getting medical care from licensed professionals." . . .

B

. . . [A] pregnancy center, an unlicensed pregnancy center, and an organization composed of crisis pregnancy centers [sued,] alleg[ing] that the [required] notices abridge the freedom of speech protected by the First Amendment. The District Court denied their motion for a preliminary injunction. [The Ninth Circuit affirmed,] conclud[ing] that the licensed notice survives the "lower level of scrutiny" that applies to regulations of "professional speech[,]" . . . [and] that the unlicensed notice satisfies any level of scrutiny.

We reverse with respect to both notice requirements.

II

A

. . .

The licensed notice is a content-based regulation of speech. By compelling individuals to speak a particular message, such notices "alte[r] the content of [their] speech." Riley v. National Federation of Blind of N. C., Inc., 487 U.S. 781, 795 (1988); . . . . Here, . . . licensed clinics must provide a government-drafted script about the availability of state-sponsored services, as well as contact information for how to obtain them. One of those services is abortion—the very practice that petitioners are devoted to opposing. By requiring petitioners to inform women how they can obtain state-subsidized abortions—at the same time petitioners try to dissuade women from choosing that option—the licensed notice plainly "alters the content" of petitioners' speech. . . .

B

Although the licensed notice is content based, the Ninth Circuit did not apply strict scrutiny because it concluded that the notice regulates "professional speech." . . . Some Courts of Appeals have recognized "professional speech" as a separate category of speech that is subject to different rules. . . . These courts define "professionals" as individuals who provide personalized services to clients and who are subject to "a generally applicable licensing and regulatory regime." . . . "Professional speech" is then defined as any speech by these individuals that is based on "[their] expert knowledge and judgment," . . . or that is "within the confines of [the] professional relationship," . . . . So defined, these courts except professional speech from the rule that content-based regulations of speech are subject to strict scrutiny. . . .

But this Court has not recognized "professional speech" as a separate category of speech. Speech is not unprotected merely because it is uttered by "professionals." This Court has "been reluctant to mark off new categories of speech for diminished constitutional protection." Denver Area Ed. Telecommunications Consortium, Inc. v. FCC, 518 U.S. 727, 804 (1996) (Kennedy, J., concurring in part, concurring in judgment in part, and dissenting in part). And it has been especially reluctant to "exemp[t] a category of speech from the normal prohibition on content-based restrictions." United States v. Alvarez, 567 U.S. 709, 722 (2012) (plurality opinion). This Court's precedents do not permit governments to impose content-based restrictions on speech without " 'persuasive evidence . . . of a long (if heretofore unrecognized) tradition' " to that effect. . . .

This Court's precedents do not recognize such a tradition for a category called "professional speech." This Court has afforded less protection for professional speech in two circumstances—neither of which turned on the fact that professionals were speaking. First, our precedents have applied more deferential review to some laws that require professionals to disclose factual, noncontroversial information in their "commercial speech." See, e.g., Zauderer v. Office of Disciplinary Counsel of Supreme Court of Ohio, 471 U.S. 626, 651 (1985); Milavetz, Gallop & Milavetz, P. A. v. United States, 559 U.S. 229, 250 (2010); Ohralik v. Ohio State Bar Assn., 436 U.S. 447, 455–456 (1978). Second, under our precedents, States may regulate professional conduct, even though that conduct incidentally involves speech. See, e.g., id., at 456; Planned Parenthood of Southeastern Pa. v. Casey, 505 U.S. 833, 884 (1992) (opinion of O'Connor, Kennedy, and Souter, JJ.). But neither line of precedents is implicated here.

1

This Court's precedents have applied a lower level of scrutiny to laws that compel disclosures in certain contexts. In Zauderer, for example, this Court upheld a rule requiring lawyers who advertised their services on a contingency-fee basis to disclose that clients might be required to pay some fees and costs. . . . Noting that the disclosure requirement governed only "commercial advertising" and required the disclosure of "purely factual and uncontroversial information about the terms under which . . . services will be available," the Court explained that such requirements should be upheld unless they are "unjustified or unduly burdensome." . . .

The *Zauderer* standard does not apply here. Most obviously, the licensed notice is not limited to "purely factual and uncontroversial information about the terms under which . . . services will be available." 471 U.S., at 651; see also Hurley v. Irish-American Gay, Lesbian and Bisexual Group of Boston, Inc., 515 U.S. 557, 573 (1995) (explaining that *Zauderer* does not apply outside of these circumstances). The notice in no way relates to the services that licensed clinics provide. Instead, it requires these clinics to disclose information about *state*-sponsored services—including abortion, anything but an "uncontroversial" topic. Accordingly, *Zauderer* has no application here.

2

In addition to disclosure requirements under *Zauderer*, this Court has upheld regulations of professional conduct that incidentally burden speech. "[T]he First Amendment does not prevent restrictions directed at commerce or conduct from imposing incidental burdens on speech," Sorrell v. IMS Health Inc., 564 U.S. 552, 567 (2011), and professionals are no exception to this rule, see *Ohralik* . . . .

In Planned Parenthood of Southeastern Pa. v. Casey, . . . this Court upheld a law requiring physicians to obtain informed consent before they could perform an abortion. 505 U.S., at 884 (joint opinion of O'Connor, Kennedy, and Souter, JJ.). Pennsylvania law required physicians to inform their patients of "the nature of the procedure, the health risks of the abortion and childbirth, and the 'probable gestational age of the unborn child.' " . . . The law also required physicians to inform patients of the availability of printed materials from the State, which provided information about the child and various forms of assistance.

The joint opinion in *Casey* rejected a free-speech challenge to this informed-consent requirement. . . . The joint opinion explained that the law regulated speech only "as part of the *practice* of medicine, subject to reasonable licensing and regulation by the State." . . .

The licensed notice at issue here is not an informed-consent requirement or any other regulation of professional conduct. The notice does not facilitate informed consent to a medical procedure. In fact, it is not tied to a procedure at all. It applies to all interactions between a covered facility and its clients, regardless of whether a medical procedure is ever sought, offered, or performed. If a covered facility does provide medical procedures, the notice provides no information about the risks or benefits of those procedures. Tellingly, many facilities that provide the exact same services as covered facilities—such as general practice clinics . . .—are not required to provide the licensed notice. The licensed notice regulates speech as speech.

3

Outside of the two contexts discussed above—disclosures under *Zauderer* and professional conduct—this Court's precedents have long protected the First Amendment rights of professionals. For example, this Court has applied strict scrutiny to content-based laws that regulate the noncommercial speech of lawyers, see . . . In re Primus, 436 U.S. 412, 432 (1978); professional fundraisers, see *Riley*, 487 U.S., at 798; and organizations that provided specialized advice about international law, see Holder v. Humanitarian Law Project, 561 U.S. 1, 27–28 (2010). And the Court emphasized that the lawyer's statements in *Zauderer* would have been "fully protected" if they were made in a context other than advertising. 471 U.S., at 637, n. 7. Moreover, this Court has stressed the danger of content-based regulations "in the fields of medicine and public health, where information can save lives." . . .

The dangers associated with content-based regulations of speech are also present in the context of professional speech. As with other kinds of speech, regulating the content of professionals' speech "pose[s] the inherent risk that the Government seeks not to advance a legitimate regulatory goal, but to suppress unpopular ideas or information." . . . Throughout history, governments have "manipulat[ed] the content of doctor-patient discourse" to increase state power and suppress minorities . . . .

Further, when the government polices the content of professional speech, it can fail to " 'preserve an uninhibited marketplace of ideas in which truth will ultimately prevail.' " McCullen v. Coakley, ...

"Professional speech" is also a difficult category to define with precision. . . . As defined by the courts of appeals, the professional-speech doctrine would cover a wide array of individuals—doctors, lawyers, nurses, physical therapists, truck drivers, bartenders, barbers, and many others. . . . All that is required to make something a "profession," according to these courts, is that it involves personalized services and requires a professional license from the State. But that gives the States unfettered power to reduce a group's First Amendment rights by simply imposing a licensing requirement. . . .

C

In sum, neither California nor the Ninth Circuit has identified a persuasive reason for treating professional speech as a unique category that is exempt from ordinary First Amendment principles. We do not foreclose the possibility that some such reason exists. We need not do so because the licensed notice cannot survive even intermediate scrutiny. California asserts a single interest to justify the licensed notice: providing low-income women with information about state-sponsored services. Assuming that this is a substantial state interest, the licensed notice is not sufficiently drawn to achieve it.

If California's goal is to educate low-income women about the services it provides, then the licensed notice is "wildly underinclusive." . . . The notice applies only to clinics that have a "primary purpose" of "providing family planning or pregnancy-related services" and that provide two of six categories of specific services. . . . Other clinics that have another primary purpose, or that provide only one category of those services, also serve low-income women and could educate them about the State's services. According to the legislative record, California has "nearly 1,000 community clinics"—including "federally designated community health centers, migrant health centers, rural health centers, and frontier health centers"—that "serv[e] more than 5.6 million patients . . . annually through over 17 million patient encounters." . . . But most of those clinics are excluded from the licensed notice requirement without explanation. Such "[u]nderinclusiveness raises serious doubts about whether the government is in fact pursuing the interest it invokes, rather than disfavoring a particular speaker or viewpoint." . . .

The FACT Act also excludes, without explanation, federal clinics and Family PACT providers from the licensed-notice requirement. California notes that those clinics can enroll women in California's programs themselves, but California's stated interest is informing women that these services exist in the first place. California has identified no evidence that the exempted clinics are more likely to provide this information than the covered clinics. In fact, the exempted clinics have long been able to enroll women in California's programs, but the FACT Act was premised on the notion that "thousands of women remain unaware of [them]." . . . If the goal is to maximize women's awareness of these programs, then it would seem that California would ensure that the places that can immediately enroll women also provide this information. . . .

Further, California could inform low-income women about its services "without burdening a speaker with unwanted speech." . . . Most obviously, it could inform the women itself with a public-information campaign. . . . California could even post the information on public property near crisis pregnancy centers. California argues that it has already tried an advertising campaign, and that many women who are eligible for publicly-funded healthcare have not enrolled. But California has identified no evidence to that effect. And regardless, a "tepid response" does not prove that an advertising campaign is not a sufficient alternative. United States v. Playboy Entertainment Group, Inc., 529 U.S. 803, 816 (2000). . . .

In short, petitioners are likely to succeed on the merits of their challenge to the licensed notice. Contrary to the suggestion in the dissent, we do not question the legality of health and safety warnings long considered permissible, or purely factual and uncontroversial disclosures about commercial products.

III

. . . The parties dispute whether the unlicensed notice is subject to deferential review under *Zauderer*. We need not decide [because e]ven under *Zauderer*, a disclosure requirement cannot be "unjustified or unduly burdensome." . . . Our precedents require disclosures to remedy a harm that is "potentially real not purely hypothetical," Ibanez v. Florida Dept. of Business and Professional Regulation, Bd. of Accountancy, 512 U.S. 136, 146 (1994), and to extend "no broader than reasonably necessary," . . . . Otherwise, they risk "chilling" protected speech." . . . Importantly, California has the burden to prove that the unlicensed notice is neither unjustified nor unduly burdensome. . . . It has not met its burden.

. . . California has not demonstrated any justification for the unlicensed notice that is more than "purely hypothetical." . . . The only justification that the California Legislature put forward was ensuring that "pregnant women in California know when they are getting medical care from licensed professionals." . . . At oral argument, however, California denied that the justification for the FACT Act was that women "go into [crisis pregnancy centers] and they don't realize what they are." . . . Indeed, California points to nothing suggesting that pregnant women do not already know that the covered facilities are staffed by unlicensed medical professionals. The services that trigger the unlicensed notice—such as having "volunteers who collect health information from clients," "advertis[ing] . . . pregnancy options counseling," and offering over-the-counter "pregnancy testing," . . .—do not require a medical license. And California already makes it a crime for individuals without a medical license to practice medicine. . . . At this preliminary stage of the litigation, we agree that petitioners are likely to prevail on the question whether California has proved a justification for the unlicensed notice.

Even if California had presented a nonhypothetical justification for the unlicensed notice, the FACT Act unduly burdens protected speech. The unlicensed notice imposes a government-scripted, speaker-based disclosure requirement that is wholly disconnected from California's informational interest. It requires covered facilities to post California's precise notice, no matter what the facilities say on site or in their advertisements. And it covers a curiously narrow subset of speakers. While the licensed notice applies to facilities that provide "family planning" services and "contraception or contraceptive methods," ... the California Legislature dropped these triggering conditions for the unlicensed notice. The unlicensed notice applies only to facilities that primarily provide "pregnancy-related" services. . . . Thus, a facility that advertises and provides pregnancy tests is covered by the unlicensed notice, but a facility across the street that advertises and provides nonprescription contraceptives is excluded—even though the latter is no less likely to make women think it is licensed. This Court's precedents are deeply skeptical of laws that "distinguis[h] among different speakers, allowing speech by some but not others." Citizens United v. Federal Election Comm'n, 558 U.S. 310, 340 (2010). Speaker-based laws run the risk that "the State has left unburdened those speakers whose messages are in accord with its own views." . . .

The application of the unlicensed notice to advertisements demonstrates just how burdensome it is. . . . As California conceded at oral argument, a billboard for an unlicensed facility that says "Choose Life" would have to surround that two-word statement with a 29-word statement from the government, in as many as 13 different languages. In this way, the unlicensed notice drowns out the facility's own message. . . .

For all these reasons, the unlicensed notice does not satisfy *Zauderer*, assuming that standard applies. California has offered no justification that the notice plausibly furthers. It targets speakers, not speech, and imposes an unduly burdensome disclosure requirement that will chill their protected speech. Taking all these circumstances together, we conclude that the unlicensed notice is unjustified and unduly burdensome under *Zauderer*. We express no view on the legality of a similar disclosure requirement that is better supported or less burdensome.

. . . We reverse . . . and remand . . . for further proceedings consistent with this opinion.

■ JUSTICE KENNEDY, with whom THE CHIEF JUSTICE, JUSTICE ALITO, and JUSTICE GORSUCH join, concurring.

I join the Court's opinion in all respects.

This separate writing seeks to underscore that the apparent viewpoint discrimination here is a matter of serious constitutional concern. The Court . . . is correct not to reach this question. It was not sufficiently developed, and the rationale for the Court's decision today suffices to resolve the case. And had the Court's analysis been confined to viewpoint discrimination, some legislators might have inferred that if the law were reenacted with a broader base and broader coverage it then would be upheld.

It does appear that viewpoint discrimination is inherent in the design and structure of this Act. This law is a paradigmatic example of the serious threat presented when government seeks to impose its own message in the place of individual speech, thought, and expression. For here the State requires primarily pro-life pregnancy centers to promote the State's own preferred message advertising abortions. This compels individuals to contradict their most deeply held beliefs, beliefs grounded in basic philosophical, ethical, or religious precepts, or all of these. And the history of the Act's passage and its underinclusive application suggest a real possibility that these individuals were targeted because of their beliefs.

The California Legislature included in its official history the congratulatory statement that the Act was part of California's legacy of "forward thinking." . . . But it is not forward thinking to force individuals to "be an instrument for fostering public adherence to an ideological point of view [they] fin[d] unacceptable." Wooley v. Maynard, 430 U.S. 705, 715 (1977). . . . Governments must not be allowed to force persons to express a message contrary to their deepest convictions. . . .

■ JUSTICE BREYER, with whom JUSTICE GINSBURG, JUSTICE SOTOMAYOR, and JUSTICE KAGAN join, dissenting.

> . . .

[The majority's] constitutional approach threatens to create serious problems. Because much, perhaps most, human behavior takes place through speech and because much, perhaps most, law regulates that speech in terms of its content, the majority's approach at the least threatens considerable litigation over the constitutional validity of much, perhaps most, government regulation. Virtually every disclosure law could be considered "content based," for virtually every disclosure law requires individuals "to speak a particular message." See Reed v. Town of Gilbert, 576 U.S. ___, ___ (2015) (Breyer, J., concurring in judgment) (slip op., at 3) (listing regulations that inevitably involve content discrimination, ranging from securities disclosures to signs at petting zoos). Thus, the majority's view, if taken literally, could radically change prior law, perhaps placing much securities law or consumer protection law at constitutional risk, depending on how broadly its exceptions are interpreted.

Many ordinary disclosure laws would fall outside the majority's exceptions for disclosures related to the professional's own services or conduct. These include numerous commonly found disclosure requirements relating to the medical profession. . . .

The majority . . . , perhaps recognizing this problem, . . . says that it does not "question the legality of health and safety warnings long considered permissible, or purely factual and uncontroversial disclosures about commercial products." But this generally phrased disclaimer would seem more likely to invite litigation than to provide needed limitation and clarification. The majority, for example, does not explain why the Act here, which is justified in part by health and safety considerations, does not fall within its "health" category. . . . [S]ee also Planned Parenthood of Southeastern Pa. v. Casey, 505 U.S. 833, 882–884 (1992) (joint opinion of O'Connor, Kennedy, and Souter, JJ.) (reasoning that disclosures related to fetal development and childbirth are related to the health of a woman seeking an abortion). Nor does the majority opinion offer any reasoned basis that might help apply its disclaimer for distinguishing lawful from unlawful disclosures. In the absence of a reasoned explanation of the disclaimer's meaning and rationale, the disclaimer is unlikely to withdraw the invitation to litigation that the majority's general broad "content-based" test issues. That test invites courts around the Nation to apply an unpredictable First Amendment to ordinary social and economic regulation, striking down disclosure laws that judges may disfavor, while upholding others, all without grounding their decisions in reasoned principle.

Notably, the majority says nothing about limiting its language to the kind of instance where the Court has traditionally found the First Amendment wary of content-based laws, namely, in cases of viewpoint discrimination. . . . But the mine run of disclosure requirements . . . simply alert the public about child seat belt laws, the location of stairways, and the process to have their garbage collected, among other things.

Precedent does not require a test such as the majority's. . . . Historically, the Court has been wary of claims that regulation of business activity, particularly health-related activity, violates the Constitution. . . .

The Court has taken this same respectful approach to economic and social legislation when a First Amendment claim like the claim present here is at issue. See, *e.g.,* Zauderer v. Office of Disciplinary Counsel of Supreme Court of Ohio, 471 U.S. 626, 651 (1985) (upholding reasonable disclosure requirements for attorneys); Milavetz, Gallop & Milavetz, P.A. v. United States, 559 U.S. 229, 252–253 (2010) (same); . . . .

Even during the *Lochner* era, when this Court struck down numerous economic regulations concerning industry, this Court was careful to defer to state legislative judgments concerning the medical profession. . . . In the name of the First Amendment, the majority today treads into territory where the pre-New Deal, as well as the post-New Deal, Court refused to go.

. . . [T]he majority pays . . . First Amendment goals a serious disservice through dilution. Using the First Amendment to strike down economic and social laws that legislatures long would have thought themselves free to enact will, for the American public, obscure, not clarify, the true value of protecting freedom of speech.

B

Still, what about this specific case? The disclosure at issue here concerns speech related to abortion. It involves health, differing moral values, and differing points of view. [R]ather than set forth broad, new, First Amendment principles, I believe that we should focus more directly upon precedent . . . [regarding] disclosure laws relating to reproductive health. Though those rules or holdings have changed over time, they should govern our disposition of this case.

. . .

[After reviewing earlier cases holding otherwise, and referring to the information requirement addressed in Planned Parenthood of Southeastern Pa. v. Casey, 505 U.S. 833 (1992), Justice Breyer observed that t]his time a joint opinion of the Court, in judging whether the State could impose these informational requirements, asked whether doing so imposed an "undue burden" upon women seeking an abortion [and] held that it did not. [And he observed that in] overruling the earlier cases, it wrote:

"To the extent *Akron I* and *Thornburgh* find a constitutional violation when the government requires, as it does here, the giving of truthful, nonmisleading information about the nature of the procedure, the attendant health risks and those of childbirth, and the 'probable gestational age' of the fetus, those cases go too far, are inconsistent with *Roe*'s acknowledgment of an important interest in potential life, and are overruled." . . .

The joint opinion . . . [also] concluded that the statute did not violate the First Amendment. It wrote:

> "All that is left of petitioners' argument is an asserted First Amendment right of a physician not to provide information about the risks of abortion, and childbirth, in a manner mandated by the State. To be sure, the physician's First Amendment rights not to speak are implicated, see Wooley v. Maynard, 430 U.S. 705 (1977), but only as part of the practice of medicine, subject to reasonable licensing and regulation by the State, cf. Whalen v. Roe, 429 U.S. 589, 603 (1977). We see no constitutional infirmity in the requirement that the physician provide the information mandated by the State here." *Casey*, 505 U.S., at 884.

Thus, the Court considered the State's statutory requirements, including the requirement that the doctor must inform his patient about where she could learn how to have the newborn child adopted (if carried to term) and how she could find related financial assistance. . . . To repeat the point, the Court then held that the State's requirements did *not* violate either the Constitution's protection of free speech or its protection of a woman's right to choose to have an abortion.

C

Taking *Casey* as controlling, the law's demand for evenhandedness requires a different answer than that perhaps suggested by *Akron* and *Thornburgh*. If a State can lawfully require a doctor to tell a woman seeking an abortion about adoption services, why should it not be able, as here, to require a medical counselor to tell a woman seeking prenatal care or other reproductive healthcare about childbirth and abortion services? As the question suggests, there is no convincing reason to distinguish between information about adoption and information about abortion in this context. . . .

1

The majority tries to distinguish *Casey* as concerning a regulation of professional conduct that only incidentally burdened speech. *Casey*, in its view, applies only when obtaining "informed consent" to a medical procedure is directly at issue.

This distinction, however, lacks moral, practical, and legal force. The individuals at issue here are all medical personnel engaging in activities that directly affect a woman's health—not significantly different from the doctors at issue in *Casey*. After all, the statute here applies only to "primary care clinics," which provide "services for the care and treatment of patients for whom the clinic accepts responsibility." . . . And the persons responsible for patients at those clinics are all persons "licensed, certified or registered to provide" pregnancy-related medical services. . . . The petitioners have not . . . provided any example of a covered clinic that is not operated by licensed doctors or what the statute specifies are equivalent professionals. . . .

The Act requires these medical professionals to disclose information about the possibility of abortion (including potential financial help) that is as likely helpful to granting "informed consent" as is information about the possibility of adoption and childbirth (including potential financial help). That is why I find it impossible to drive any meaningful legal wedge between the law, as interpreted in *Casey*, and the law as it should be applied in this case. If the law in *Casey* regulated speech "only 'as part of the *practice* of medicine,' " . . . so too here.

The majority contends that the disclosure here is unrelated to a "medical procedure," unlike that in *Casey*, and so the State has no reason to inform a woman about alternatives to childbirth (or, presumably, the health risks of childbirth). . . . Really? No one doubts that choosing an abortion is a medical procedure that involves certain health risks. . . . But the same is true of carrying a child to term and giving birth. . . . Indeed, nationwide "childbirth is 14 times more likely than abortion to result in" the woman's death. . . . Health considerations do not favor disclosure of alternatives and risks associated with the latter but not those associated with the former.

In any case, informed consent principles apply more broadly than only to discrete "medical procedures." Prescription drug labels warn patients of risks even though taking prescription drugs may not be considered a "medical procedure." 21 CFR § 201.56 (2017). In California, clinics that screen for breast cancer must post a sign in their offices notifying patients that, if they are diagnosed with breast cancer, their doctor must provide "a written summary of alternative efficacious methods of treatment," a notification that does not relate to the *screening* procedure at issue. . . . If even these disclosures fall outside the majority's cramped view of *Casey* and informed consent, it undoubtedly would invalidate the many other disclosures that are routine in the medical context as well.

The majority also finds it "[t]ellin[g]" that general practice clinics—*i.e.*, paid clinics—are not required to provide the licensed notice. But the lack-of-information problem that the statute seeks to ameliorate is a problem that the State explains is commonly found among low-income women. . . . That those with low income might lack the time to become fully informed and that this circumstance might prove disproportionately correlated with income is not intuitively surprising. Nor is it surprising that those with low income, whatever they choose in respect to pregnancy, might find information about financial assistance particularly useful. . . .

2

Separately, finding no First Amendment infirmity in the licensed notice is consistent with earlier Court rulings. [I]n *Zauderer* we . . . refused to apply heightened scrutiny, instead asking whether the disclosure requirements were "reasonably related to the State's interest in preventing deception of consumers." . . .

The majority concludes that *Zauderer* does not apply because the disclosure "in no way relates to the services that licensed clinics provide." But information about state resources for family planning, prenatal care, and abortion *is* related to the services that licensed clinics provide. These clinics provide counseling about contraception (which is a family-planning service), ultrasounds or pregnancy testing (which is prenatal care), or abortion. . . . The required disclosure is related to the clinic's services because it provides information about state resources for the very same services. A patient who knows that she can receive free prenatal care from the State may well prefer to forgo the prenatal care offered at one of the clinics here. And for those interested in family planning and abortion services, information about such alternatives is relevant information to patients offered prenatal care, just as *Casey* considered information about adoption to be relevant to the abortion decision.

Regardless, *Zauderer* is not so limited. *Zauderer* turned on the "material differences between disclosure requirements and outright prohibitions on speech." . . . A disclosure requirement does not prevent speakers "from conveying information to the public," but "only require[s] them to provide somewhat more information than they might otherwise be inclined to present." . . . Where a State's requirement to speak "purely factual and uncontroversial information" does not attempt "to 'prescribe what shall be orthodox in politics, nationalism, religion, or other matters of opinion or force citizens to confess by word or act their faith therein,'" it does not warrant heightened scrutiny. . . .

In *Zauderer*, the Court emphasized the reason that the First Amendment protects commercial speech at all: "the value to consumers of the information such speech provides." . . . For that reason, a professional's "constitutionally protected interest in *not* providing any particular factual information in his advertising is minimal." . . . But this rationale is not in any way tied to advertisements about a professional's own services. For instance, it applies equally to a law that requires doctors, when discharging a child under eight years of age, to "provide to and discuss with the parents . . . information on the current law requiring child passenger restraint systems, safety belts, and the transportation of children in rear seats." Cal. Veh. Code . . . . Even though child seat belt laws do not directly relate to the doctor's own services, telling parents about such laws does nothing to undermine the flow of factual information. Whether the context is advertising the professional's own services or other commercial speech, a doctor's First Amendment interest in not providing factual information to patients is the same: minimal, because his professional speech is protected precisely because of its informational value to patients. There is no reason to subject such laws to heightened scrutiny.

Accordingly, the majority's reliance on cases that prohibit rather than require speech is misplaced. I agree that "'in the fields of medicine and public heath, . . . information can save lives,'" but the licensed disclosure *serves* that informational interest by requiring clinics to notify patients of the availability of state resources for family planning services, prenatal care, and abortion, which—unlike the majority's examples of normative statements—is truthful and nonmisleading information. Abortion is a controversial topic and a source of normative debate, but the availability of state resources is not a normative statement or a fact of debatable truth. The disclosure . . . expresses no official preference for one choice over the other. Similarly, . . . the marketplace of ideas . . . is fostered, not hindered, by providing information to patients to enable them to make fully informed medical decisions in respect to their pregnancies.

Of course, one might take the majority's decision to mean that speech about abortion is special, that it involves in this case not only professional medical matters, but also views based on deeply held religious and moral beliefs about the nature of the practice. To that extent, arguably, the speech here is different from that at issue in *Zauderer*. But . . . the need for evenhandedness . . . should prove particularly weighty in a case involving abortion rights[,] because Americans hold strong, and differing, views about the matter. . . . [I]t is particularly important to interpret the First Amendment so that it applies evenhandedly as between those who disagree so strongly. For this reason too a Constitution that allows States to insist that medical providers tell women about the possibility of adoption should also allow States similarly to insist that medical providers tell women about the possibility of abortion.

D

It is particularly unfortunate that the majority . . . declines to reach . . . arguments that the Act discriminates on the basis of viewpoint. The petitioners argue that . . . the statute unnecessarily imposes a disproportionate burden upon facilities with pro-life views, the very facilities most likely to find the statute's references to abortion morally abhorrent. . . .

. . . [T]he majority . . . conclude[es] that the Act is underinclusive. But the key question is whether . . . exempt clinics are significantly more likely than are the pro-life clinics to tell or to have told their pregnant patients about the existence of these programs—in the absence of any statutory compulsion. If so, it may make sense—in terms of the statute's informational objective—to exempt them, namely if there is no need to cover them. . . . But, if there are not good reasons to exempt these clinics from coverage, *i.e.*, if, for example, they too frequently do not tell their patients about the availability of abortion services, the petitioners' claim of viewpoint discrimination becomes much stronger.

The petitioners, however, did not develop this point in the record below. . . . Given the absence of evidence in the record before the lower courts, the "viewpoint discrimination" claim could not justify the issuance of a preliminary injunction.

II

. . .

[With respect to the notice provision requiring facilities not licensed as medical facilities to say so,] the majority . . . applies a searching standard of review based on our precedents that deal with speech *restrictions*, not *disclosures*. . . . This approach is incompatible with *Zauderer*. . . .

There is no basis for finding the State's interest "hypothetical." The legislature heard that information-related delays in qualified healthcare negatively affect women seeking to terminate their pregnancies as well as women carrying their pregnancies to term, with delays in qualified prenatal care causing life-long health problems for infants. . . . Even without such testimony, it is "self-evident" that patients might think they are receiving qualified medical care when they enter facilities that collect health information, perform obstetric ultrasounds or sonograms, diagnose pregnancy, and provide counseling about pregnancy options or other prenatal care. . . . The State's conclusion to that effect is certainly reasonable.

The majority also suggests that the Act applies too broadly . . . . But the Court has long held that a law is not unreasonable merely because it is overinclusive. . . .

Relatedly, the majority suggests that the Act is suspect because it covers some speakers but not others. I agree that a law's exemptions can reveal viewpoint discrimination (although the majority does not reach this point). . . . Accordingly, where a law's exemptions "facilitate speech on only one side of the abortion debate," there is a "clear form of viewpoint discrimination." *McCullen*

. . . .

There is no cause for such concern here. The Act does not, on its face, distinguish between facilities that favor pro-life and those that favor pro-choice points of view. Nor is there any convincing evidence before us or in the courts below that discrimination was the purpose or the effect of the statute. Notably, California does not single out pregnancy-related facilities for this type of disclosure requirement. . . . And it is unremarkable that the State excluded the provision of family planning and contraceptive services as triggering conditions. After all, the State was seeking to ensure that "pregnant women in California know when they are getting medical care from licensed professionals," and pregnant women generally do not need contraceptive services.

Finally, . . . I agree that "unduly burdensome disclosure requirements might offend the First Amendment." *Zauderer*, ... But these and similar claims are claims that the statute could be applied unconstitutionally, not that it is unconstitutional on its face. . . . And it will be open to the petitioners to make these claims if and when the State threatens to enforce the statute in this way. But facial relief is inappropriate here . . . .

For instance, . . . I understand the Act [to] require disclosure in no more than two languages—English and Spanish—in the vast majority of California's 58 counties. The exception is Los Angeles County, where, given the large number of different-language speaking groups, expression in many languages may prove necessary to communicate the message to those whom that message will help. Whether the requirement of 13 different languages goes too far and is unnecessarily burdensome in light of the need to secure the statutory objectives is a matter that concerns Los Angeles County alone, and it is a proper subject for a Los Angeles-based as applied challenge in light of whatever facts a plaintiff finds relevant. At most, such facts might show a need for fewer languages, not invalidation of the statute.

. . .

Page 1376. Add at the end of the Section:

Barr v. American Association of Political Consultants, 591 U.S. ___, 140 S.Ct. 2335 (2020). The Telephone Consumer Protection Act enacted by Congress in 1991 (TCPA) prohibited almost all robocalls to cellphones; i.e., calls "using any automatic telephone dialing system or an artificial or prerecorded voice." § 227(b)(1)(A)(iii) In 2015, Congress amended that prohibition to permit robocalls to cellphones "made solely to collect a debt owed to or guaranteed by the United States." Political and nonprofit organizations wishing to make robocalls to cellphones to discuss candidates and issues, solicit donations, conduct polls, and get out the vote, sued for a declaratory judgment that the differential treatment violated their free speech rights. A 6–3 majority of the Court held that the content-based difference rendered the robocall restrictions unconstitutional, though no majority agreed on the rationale for that conclusion. A different 7–2 majority also held that the proper remedy was to invalidate the 2015 "government-debt exception" and solve the inequality defect by leaving the general prohibition in place. That left the plaintiffs with having won the battle for equal treatment, but having lost the war for freedom to place their desired robocalls to cellphones.

With respect to the free speech issue, Justice Kavanaugh, joined by Chief Justice Roberts and Justices Thomas and Alito, wrote in part:

". . . [T]he legality of a robocall turns on whether it is 'made solely to collect a debt owed to or guaranteed by the United States.' A robocall that says, 'Please pay your government debt' is legal. A robocall that says, 'Please donate to our political campaign' is illegal. That is about as content-based as it gets. Because the law favors speech made for collecting government debt over political and other speech, the law is a content-based restriction on speech.

"The Government advances three main arguments for deeming the statute content-neutral, but none is persuasive.

"*First*, the Government suggests that § 227(b)(1)(A)(iii) draws distinctions based on speakers (authorized debt collectors), not based on content. But that is not the law in front of us. This statute singles out calls 'made solely to collect a debt owed to or guaranteed by the United States,' not all calls from authorized debt collectors.

"In any event, 'the fact that a distinction is speaker based' does not 'automatically render the distinction content neutral.' Reed [v. Town of Gilbert], 576 U. S. [155,] at 170 [(2015)]; Sorrell v. IMS Health Inc., 564 U. S. 552, 563–564 (2011). Indeed, the Court has held that ' "laws favoring some speakers over others demand strict scrutiny when the legislature's speaker preference reflects a content preference." ' *Reed*, ...

"*Second*, the Government argues that the legality of a robocall under the statute depends simply on whether the caller is engaged in a particular economic activity, not on the content of speech. We disagree. The law here focuses on whether the caller is *speaking* about a particular topic. In *Sorrell*, this Court held that a law singling out pharmaceutical marketing for unfavorable treatment was content-based. . . . So too here.

"*Third*, according to the Government, if this statute is content-based because it singles out debt-collection speech, then so are statutes that *regulate* debt collection, like the Fair Debt Collection Practices Act. . . . That slippery-slope argument is unpersuasive in this case. As we explained in *Sorrell*, 'the First Amendment does not prevent restrictions directed at commerce or conduct from imposing incidental burdens on speech.' . . . . The law here, like the Vermont law in *Sorrell*, 'does not simply have an effect on speech, but is directed at certain content and is aimed at particular speakers.' . . . The Government's concern is understandable, but the courts have generally been able to distinguish impermissible content-based speech restrictions from traditional or ordinary economic regulation of commercial activity that imposes incidental burdens on speech. The issue before us concerns only robocalls to cell phones. Our decision today on that issue fits comfortably within existing First Amendment precedent. Our decision is not intended to expand existing First Amendment doctrine or to otherwise affect traditional or ordinary economic regulation of commercial activity.

". . . Under the Court's precedents, a 'law that is content based' is 'subject to strict scrutiny.' *Reed*, ... The Government concedes that it cannot satisfy strict scrutiny to justify the government-debt exception. We agree. The Government's stated justification for the government-debt exception is collecting government debt. Although collecting government debt is no doubt a worthy goal, the Government concedes that it has not sufficiently justified the differentiation between government-debt collection speech and other important categories of robocall speech, such as political speech, charitable fundraising, issue advocacy, commercial advertising, and the like."

Regarding the proper remedy for this free speech violation, Justice Kavanaugh (on this point without Justice Thomas joining) concluded that "the correct result in this case is to sever the 2015 government-debt exception and leave in place the longstanding robocall restriction." He elaborated:

". . . Plaintiffs want to be able to make political robocalls to cell phones, and they have not received *that* relief. But the First Amendment complaint at the heart of their suit was unequal treatment. Invalidating and severing the government-debt exception fully addresses that First Amendment injury."

Justice Sotomayor concurred in the judgment and wrote in part:

"I agree with much of [Justice Breyer's] partial dissent's explanation that strict scrutiny should not apply to all content-based distinctions. . . . In my view, however, the government-debt exception . . . still fails intermediate scrutiny because it is not 'narrowly tailored to serve a significant governmental interest.' . . . Even under intermediate scrutiny, the Government has not explained how a debt-collection robocall about a government-backed debt is any less intrusive or could be any less harassing than a debt-collection robocall about a privately backed debt. . . . The Government could have employed far less restrictive means to further its interest in collecting debt, such as 'secur[ing] consent from the debtors to make debt-collection calls' or 'plac[ing] the calls itself.' "

Justice Breyer, joined by Justices Ginsburg and Kagan, concurred in the judgment with respect to severability, but concluded that the government-debt exception does not violate the Constitution. His opinion included these elements:

"The problem with [the plurality's] approach, which reflexively applies strict scrutiny to all content-based speech distinctions, is that it is divorced from First Amendment values. This case primarily involves commercial regulation— namely, debt collection. And, in my view, there is no basis here to apply 'strict scrutiny' based on 'content-discrimination.'

"To appreciate why, it is important to understand at least one set of values that underlie the First Amendment and the related reasons why courts scrutinize some speech restrictions strictly. . . . For our government to remain a democratic republic, the people must be free to generate, debate, and discuss both general and specific ideas, hopes, and experiences. The people must then be able to transmit their resulting views and conclusions to their elected representatives, which they may do directly, or indirectly through the shaping of public opinion. The object of that transmission is to influence the public policy enacted by elected representatives. . . .

. . .

"From a democratic perspective, however, it is equally important that courts not use the First Amendment in a way that would threaten the workings of ordinary regulatory programs posing little threat to the free marketplace of ideas enacted as a result of that public discourse. As a general matter, the strictest scrutiny should not apply indiscriminately to the very 'political and social changes desired by the people'—that is, to those government programs which the 'unfettered interchange of ideas' has sought to achieve. . . . Otherwise, our democratic system would fail, not through the inability of the people to speak or to transmit their views to government, but because of an elected government's inability to translate those views into action.

. . .

". . . Regulation of debt collection does not fall on the first side of the democratic equation. It has next to nothing to do with the free marketplace of ideas or the transmission of the people's thoughts and will to the government. It has everything to do with the second side of the equation, that is, with government response to the public will through ordinary commercial regulation. . . .

"I recognize that the underlying cell phone robocall restriction primarily concerns a means of communication. And that fact . . . triggers some heightened scrutiny, reflected in an intermediate scrutiny standard. Strict scrutiny and its strong presumption of unconstitutionality, however, have no place here.

"The plurality claims that its approach . . . will not 'affect traditional or ordinary economic regulation of commercial activity.' But how is that so? . . . [M]uch regulatory activity turns upon speech content. . . . Consider, for example, the regulation of securities sales, drug labeling, food labeling, false advertising, workplace safety warnings, automobile airbag instructions, consumer electronic labels, tax forms, debt collection, and so on. All of those regulations necessarily involve content-based speech distinctions. What are the differences between regulatory programs themselves other than differences based on content? After all, the regulatory spheres in which the Securities and Exchange Commission or the Federal Trade Commission operate are defined by content. Put simply, treating all content-based distinctions on speech as presumptively unconstitutional is unworkable and would obstruct the ordinary workings of democratic governance.

. . .

"I would examine the validity of the regulation at issue here using a First Amendment standard that (unlike strict scrutiny) does not strongly presume that a regulation that affects speech is unconstitutional. However, given that the government-debt exception does directly impact a means of communication, the appropriate standard requires a closer look at the restriction than does a traditional 'rational basis' test. A proper inquiry should examine the seriousness of the speech-related harm, the importance of countervailing objectives, the likelihood that the restriction will achieve those objectives, and whether there are other, less restrictive ways of doing so. . . .

"Applying this Court's intermediate scrutiny analysis, I would begin by asking just what the First Amendment harm is here. . . . [T]he practical effect of the exception, taken together with the rest of the statute, is to put *non*-government debt collectors at a disadvantage. . . . While this is a speech-related harm, debt-collection speech is both commercial and highly regulated. . . . The speech-related harm at issue here—and any related effect on the marketplace of ideas—is modest.

". . . The purpose of the exception is to further the protection of the public fisc. That protection is an important governmental interest. . . .

"Finally, is the exception narrowly tailored? Its limited scope shows that it is. Congress has minimized any speech-related harm by tying the exception directly to the Government's interest in preserving the public fisc. . . ."

Lastly, Justice Gorsuch concurred in the judgment that plaintiffs had suffered a free speech violation, but, joined by Justice Thomas on this point, he dissented from the Court's conclusion that striking the government-debt exception and leaving the overall robocall ban intact was the correct remedy, rather than an injunction preventing enforcement of the robocall ban against the plaintiffs. His separate free speech analysis included the following:

". . . The government backs millions upon millions of loans—student loans, home mortgages, veterans' loans, farm loans, business loans. When it comes to student loans alone, the government guarantees more than $150 billion in private loans involving over 7 million individuals. And, to be clear, it's not just the government that's allowed to call about these loans. Private lenders and debt collectors are free to send in the robots too, so long as the debt at issue is ultimately guaranteed by the government.

. . .

"In my view, the TCPA's rule against cellphone robocalls is a content-based restriction that fails strict scrutiny. The statute is content-based because it allows speech on a subject the government favors (collecting its debts) while banning speech on other disfavored subjects (including political matters). Cf. (opinion of Breyer, J.) (mistakenly characterizing the content discrimination as 'not about' political activities). The statute fails strict scrutiny because the government offers no compelling justification for its prohibition against the plaintiffs' political speech. In fact, the government does not dispute that, if strict scrutiny applies, its law must fall.

". . . [I]f the government thinks consumer privacy interests are insufficient to overcome its interest in collecting debts, it's hard to see how the government might invoke consumer privacy interests to justify banning private political speech. Especially when consumers seem to find debt collection efforts particularly intrusive . . . . The nature and breadth of the law's exception calls into question the necessity of its rule.

. . .

". . . [I]f debt collection robocalls were less invasive of consumer privacy than other kinds of robocalls, or if they were inherently rare, an exception permitting debt collection calls might not undermine the government's claimed interest in banning other calls. But the government . . . has not even tried to suggest conditions like those are present here, and understandably so: The government-debt exception allows a seemingly *infinite* number of robocalls of the type consumers appear to find *most* invasive.

. . .

"In the end, I agree that 47 U. S. C. § 227(b)(1)(A)(iii) violates the First Amendment, though not for the reasons Justice Kavanaugh offers. . . ."

Matal v. Tam

582 U.S. ___, 137 S.Ct. 1744, 198 L.Ed.2d 366 (2017).

[The report of this case appears supra, at p. 163.]

CHAPTER 14

RESTRICTIONS ON TIME, PLACE, OR MANNER OF EXPRESSION

2. THE NON-TRADITIONAL FORUM: SPEECH ACTIVITIES IN PUBLIC PROPERTY OTHER THAN PARKS AND STREETS

Page 1422. Add after Lee v. International Society for Krishna Consciousness, Inc.:

Minnesota Voters Alliance v. Mansky, 585 U.S. ___, 138 S.Ct. 1876 (2018). The Court held that a Minnesota statute banning the wearing of a "political badge, political button, or other political insignia" inside a polling place on Election Day—in this case applied to the wearing of Tea Party shirts and "Please I.D. Me" buttons—"violates the Free Speech Clause of the First Amendment." Because the ban applied only to "the interior of a polling place" on Election Day, Chief Justice Roberts, in his opinion for the Court, stated that nonpublic forum analysis was appropriate, There being no claim of viewpoint discrimination, the question was therefore whether Minnesota's ban was " 'reasonable in light of the purpose served by the forum': voting."

The Court had upheld "a Tennessee law imposing a 100-foot campaign-free zone around polling place entrances" in Burson v. Freeman, 504 U.S. 191 (1992), and Chief Justice Roberts reaffirmed that a "State may reasonably take steps to ensure that partisan discord not follow the voter up to the voting booth, and distract from a sense of shared civic obligation at the moment it counts the most[—an] interest [that] may be thwarted by displays that do not raise significant concerns in other situations." Still, despite the objective being permissible, Minnesota failed to "draw a reasonable line" concerning what "political" items were prohibited and what were not, and "the unmoored use of the term 'political' in the Minnesota law, combined with haphazard interpretations the State has provided in official guidance and representations to this Court, cause Minnesota's restriction to fail even this forgiving test."

The Court determined that the "indeterminate scope of the political apparel provision" was not sufficiently clarified by the State's Election Day Policy, which was offered "as authoritative guidance regarding implementation of the statute." That guidance included as banned items " '[i]ssue oriented material designed to influence or impact voting,' [which] raises more questions than it answers." A "rule whose fair enforcement requires an election judge to maintain a mental index of the platforms and positions of every candidate and party on the ballot is not reasonable."

Another part of the Policy, which banned "any item 'promoting a group with recognizable political views,' . . . makes matters worse." It did not help that the "State construes the category as limited to groups with 'views' about 'the issues confronting voters in a given election[,]' " for "[a]ny number of associations, educational institutions, businesses, and religious organizations could have an opinion on an 'issue[ ] confronting voters in a given election.' " Nor did the State's suggestion that "the ban covers only apparel promoting groups whose political positions are sufficiently 'well-known[,]' " which "only increases the potential for erratic application."

Chief Justice Roberts further elaborated what would and would not suffice in these paragraphs:

"It is 'self-evident' that an indeterminate prohibition carries with it '[t]he opportunity for abuse, especially where [it] has received a virtually open-ended interpretation.' *Jews for Jesus*, 482 U. S., at 576; see Heffron v. International Soc. for Krishna Consciousness, Inc., 452 U. S. 640, 649 (1981) (warning of the 'more covert forms of discrimination that may result when arbitrary discretion is vested in some governmental authority'). . . . We do not doubt that the vast majority of election judges strive to enforce the statute in an evenhanded manner, nor that some degree of discretion in this setting is necessary. But that discretion must be guided by objective, workable standards. Without them, an election judge's own politics may shape his views on what counts as 'political.' And if voters experience or witness episodes of unfair or inconsistent enforcement of the ban, the State's interest in maintaining a polling place free of distraction and disruption would be undermined by the very measure intended to further it.

"That is not to say that Minnesota has set upon an impossible task. Other States have laws proscribing displays (including apparel) in more lucid terms. See, *e.g.*, Cal. Elec. Code Ann. § 319.5 (West Cum. Supp. 2018) (prohibiting 'the visible display . . . of information that advocates for or against any candidate or measure,' including the 'display of a candidate's name, likeness, or logo,' the 'display of a ballot measure's number, title, subject, or logo,' and '[b]uttons, hats,' or 'shirts' containing such information); Tex. Elec. Code Ann. § 61.010(a) . . . . We do not suggest that such provisions set the outer limit of what a State may proscribe, and do not pass on the constitutionality of laws that are not before us. But we do hold that if a State wishes to set its polling places apart as areas free of partisan discord, it must employ a more discernible approach than the one Minnesota has offered here.

". . . Minnesota has not supported its good intentions with a law capable of reasoned application."

A dissent by Justice Sotomayor, joined by Justice Breyer, contended that the Court should have "certif[ied] this case to the Minnesota Supreme Court for a definitive interpretation of the political apparel ban . . . , which likely would obviate the hypothetical line-drawing problems that form the basis of the Court's decision today." In her view, "[e]specially where there are undisputedly many constitutional applications of a state law that further weighty state interests, the Court should be wary of invalidating a law without giving the State's highest court an opportunity to pass upon it."

3. SPEECH ON PRIVATE PREMISES

Page 1447. Add at the end of the Section:

Packingham v. North Carolina, 582 U.S. ___, 137 S.Ct. 1730 (2017). A North Carolina law made it a felony for a registered sex offender "to gain access to a number of websites, including commonplace social media websites like Facebook and Twitter." A unanimous Court (with Justice Gorsuch not participating) held the law to be a violation of the First Amendment's Free Speech Clause, although three Justices concurred only in the judgment. Justice Kennedy's majority opinion observed that the statute "applies to about 20,000 people in North Carolina and the State has prosecuted over 1,000 people for violating it." As a 21-year-old college student, Packingham had sex with a 13-year-old girl and later pled guilty to a sex crime, which required him to register as a sex offender—a "status that can endure for 30 years or more." Eight years later, happy that a court had dismissed a traffic ticket, he posted a celebratory message on his Facebook profile, which led to his indictment for violating the statute. Though convicted, the Court noted that "[a]t no point during trial or sentencing did the State allege that petitioner contacted a minor—or committed any other illicit act—on the Internet." The Court of Appeals of North Carolina agreed with his First Amendment defense, but a divided North Carolina Supreme Court reversed, rejecting the constitutional claim. Justice Kennedy's opinion reversing that judgment included the following:

II

"A fundamental principle of the First Amendment is that all persons have access to places where they can speak and listen, and then, after reflection, speak and listen once more. The Court has sought to protect the right to speak in this spatial context. A basic rule, for example, is that a street or a park is a quintessential forum for the exercise of First Amendment rights. See Ward v. Rock Against Racism, 491 U. S. 781, 796 (1989). Even in the modern era, these places are still essential venues for public gatherings to celebrate some views, to protest others, or simply to learn and inquire. While in the past there may have been difficulty in identifying the most important places (in a spatial sense) for the exchange of views, today the answer is clear. It is cyberspace—the "vast democratic forums of the Internet" in general, Reno v. American Civil Liberties Union, 521 U. S. 844, 868 (1997), and social media in particular. Seven in ten American adults use at least one Internet social networking service. . . . One of the most popular of these sites is Facebook, the site used by petitioner leading to his conviction in this case. According to sources cited to the Court in this case, Facebook has 1.79 billion active users. . . . This is about three times the population of North America.

"Social media offers 'relatively unlimited, low-cost capacity for communication of all kinds.' . . . On Facebook, for example, users can debate religion and politics with their friends and neighbors or share vacation photos. On LinkedIn, users can look for work, advertise for employees, or review tips on entrepreneurship. And on Twitter, users can petition their elected representatives and otherwise engage with them in a direct manner. Indeed, Governors in all 50 States and almost every Member of Congress have set up accounts for this purpose. . . . In short, social media users employ these websites to engage in a wide array of protected First Amendment activity on topics 'as diverse as human thought.' Reno, ...

". . . While we now may be coming to the realization that the Cyber Age is a revolution of historic proportions, we cannot appreciate yet its full dimensions and vast potential to alter how we think, express ourselves, and define who we want to be. The forces and directions of the Internet are so new, so protean, and so far reaching that courts must be conscious that what they say today might be obsolete tomorrow.

"This case is one of the first this Court has taken to address the relationship between the First Amendment and the modern Internet. As a result, the Court must exercise extreme caution before suggesting that the First Amendment provides scant protection for access to vast networks in that medium.

III

"This background informs [our] analysis . . . . Even making the assumption that the statute is content neutral and thus subject to intermediate scrutiny, the provision cannot stand. In order to survive intermediate scrutiny, a law must be 'narrowly tailored to serve a significant governmental interest.' McCullen v. Coakley, ... In other words, the law must not 'burden substantially more speech than is necessary to further the government's legitimate interests.' "

[After reaffirming that "it is clear that a legislature 'may pass valid laws to protect children' and other victims of sexual assault 'from abuse[,]' " Justice Kennedy found it "necessary to make two assumptions to resolve this case. First, given the broad wording of the North Carolina statute at issue, it might well bar access not only to commonplace social media websites but also to websites as varied as Amazon.com, Washingtonpost.com, and Webmd.com."]

"Second, this opinion should not be interpreted as barring a State from enacting more specific laws than the one at issue. . . . Though the issue is not before the Court, it can be assumed that the First Amendment permits a State to enact specific, narrowly tailored laws that prohibit a sex offender from engaging in conduct that often presages a sexual crime, like contacting a minor or using a website to gather information about a minor. . . . Specific laws of that type must be the State's first resort to ward off the serious harm that sexual crimes inflict. (Of importance, the troubling fact that the law imposes severe restrictions on persons who already have served their sentence and are no longer subject to the supervision of the criminal justice system is also not an issue before the Court.)

"Even with these assumptions about the scope of the law and the State's interest, the statute here enacts a prohibition unprecedented in the scope of First Amendment speech it burdens. Social media allows users to gain access to information and communicate with one another about it on any subject that might come to mind. . . . By prohibiting sex offenders from using those websites, North Carolina with one broad stroke bars access to what for many are the principal sources for knowing current events, checking ads for employment, speaking and listening in the modern public square, and otherwise exploring the vast realms of human thought and knowledge. These websites can provide perhaps the most powerful mechanisms available to a private citizen to make his or her voice heard. . . .

"In sum, to foreclose access to social media altogether is to prevent the user from engaging in the legitimate exercise of First Amendment rights. It is unsettling to suggest that only a limited set of websites can be used even by persons who have completed their sentences. Even convicted criminals—and in some instances especially convicted criminals—might receive legitimate benefits from these means for access to the world of ideas, in particular if they seek to reform and to pursue lawful and rewarding lives."

As for the State's contention "that the law must be this broad to serve its preventative purpose of keeping convicted sex offenders away from vulnerable victims[,]" the State "has not . . . met its burden to show that this sweeping law is necessary or legitimate to serve that purpose." Justice Kennedy said that "no case or holding of this Court has approved of a statute as broad in its reach[,]" and he drew an analogy to "Board of Airport Comm'rs of Los Angeles v. Jews for Jesus, Inc., 482 U. S. 569 (1987), where the Court struck down an ordinance prohibiting any 'First Amendment activities' at Los Angeles International Airport because the ordinance covered all manner of protected, nondisruptive behavior including 'talking and reading, or the wearing of campaign buttons or symbolic clothing,' . . . . If a law prohibiting 'all protected expression' at a single airport is not constitutional . . ., it follows with even greater force that the State may not enact this complete bar to the exercise of First Amendment rights on websites integral to the fabric of our modern society and culture." He concluded the majority opinion this way:

"It is well established that, as a general rule, the Government 'may not suppress lawful speech as the means to suppress unlawful speech.' Ashcroft v. Free Speech Coalition, 535 U. S., at 255. That is what North Carolina has done here. Its law must be held invalid."

Justice Alito, joined by Chief Justice Roberts and Justice Thomas, concurred in the judgment "[b]ecause of the law's extraordinary breadth," but he objected to the majority's "undisciplined dicta." In particular, the "Court is unable to resist musings that seem to equate the entirety of the internet with public streets and parks. And this language is bound to be interpreted by some to mean that the States are largely powerless to restrict even the most dangerous sexual predators from visiting any internet sites, including, for example, teenage dating sites and sites designed to permit minors to discuss personal problems with their peers." His opinion emphasized the following:

"The State's interest in protecting children from recidivist sex offenders plainly applies to internet use. Several factors make the internet a powerful tool for the would-be child abuser. First, children often use the internet in a way that gives offenders easy access to their personal information—by, for example, communicating with strangers and allowing sites to disclose their location. Second, the internet provides previously unavailable ways of communicating with, stalking, and ultimately abusing children. An abuser can create a false profile that misrepresents the abuser's age and gender. The abuser can lure the minor into engaging in sexual conversations, sending explicit photos, or even meeting in person. And an abuser can use a child's location posts on the internet to determine the pattern of the child's day-to-day activities—and even the child's location at a given moment. . . .

"Because protecting children from abuse is a compelling state interest and sex offenders can (and do) use the internet to engage in such abuse, it is legitimate and entirely reasonable for States to try to stop abuse from occurring before it happens."

Nonetheless, the statute's "fatal problem . . . is that its wide sweep precludes access to a large number of websites that are most unlikely to facilitate the commission of a sex crime against a child." Taking as examples of the statute's coverage Amazon.com, Washingtonpost.com, and WebMD, Justice Alito concluded:

"As these examples illustrate, the North Carolina law has a very broad reach and covers websites that are ill suited for use in stalking or abusing children. The focus of the discussion on these sites—shopping, news, health—does not provide a convenient jumping off point for conversations that may lead to abuse. In addition, the social exchanges facilitated by these websites occur in the open, and this reduces the possibility of a child being secretly lured into an abusive situation. These websites also give sex offenders little opportunity to gather personal details about a child; the information that can be listed in a profile is limited, and the profiles are brief. What is more, none of these websites make it easy to determine a child's precise location at a given moment. For example, they do not permit photo streams (at most, a child could upload a single profile photograph), and they do not include up-to-the minute location services. Such websites would provide essentially no aid to a would-be child abuser.

"Placing this set of websites categorically off limits from registered sex offenders prohibits them from receiving or engaging in speech that the First Amendment protects and does not appreciably advance the State's goal of protecting children from recidivist sex offenders. I am therefore compelled to conclude that, while the law before us addresses a critical problem, it sweeps far too broadly to satisfy the demands of the Free Speech Clause.

II

"While I thus agree with the Court that the particular law at issue in this case violates the First Amendment, I am troubled by the Court's loose rhetoric. . . . [I]f the entirety of the internet or even just 'social media' sites are the 21st century equivalent of public streets and parks, then States may have little ability to restrict the sites that may be visited by even the most dangerous sex offenders. May a State preclude an adult previously convicted of molesting children from visiting a dating site for teenagers? Or a site where minors communicate with each other about personal problems? The Court should be more attentive to the implications of its rhetoric for, contrary to the Court's suggestion, there are important differences between cyberspace and the physical world.

"I will mention a few that are relevant to internet use by sex offenders. First, it is easier for parents to monitor the physical locations that their children visit and the individuals with whom they speak in person than it is to monitor their internet use. Second, if a sex offender is seen approaching children or loitering in a place frequented by children, this conduct may be observed by parents, teachers, or others. Third, the internet offers an unprecedented degree of anonymity and easily permits a would-be molester to assume a false identity."

5. GOVERNMENT SUBSIDIES TO SPEECH

Page 1498. Add after Walker v. Texas Division, Sons of Confederate Veterans:

Matal v. Tam

582 U.S. ___, 137 S.Ct. 1744, 198 L.Ed.2d 366 (2017).

[The report of this case appears supra, at p. 163.]

Page 1507. Add at end of Chapter 14:

Agency for International Development v. Alliance for Open Society International, Inc., 591 U.S. ___, 140 S.Ct. 2082 (2020). The victorious plaintiffs in the 2013 case just set forth above (AOSI I) sued again to prevent the Government from enforcing the Policy Requirement of the Leadership Act against their foreign affiliates, once again claiming a free speech violation. This time, however, in an opinion by Justice Kavanaugh for a 6–3 majority (Justice Kagan not participating), the Court rejected the free speech challenge. The majority relied on "two bedrock principles of American law"—first, that "it is long settled as a matter of American constitutional law that foreign citizens outside U. S. territory do not possess rights under the U. S. Constitution[,]" and second, that "it is long settled as a matter of American corporate law that separately incorporated organizations are separate legal units with distinct legal rights and obligations." Because "[p]laintiffs' foreign affiliates were incorporated in other countries and are legally separate from plaintiffs' American organizations[, . . . a]s foreign organizations operating abroad, plaintiffs' foreign affiliates possess no rights under the First Amendment." Two main arguments offered against the Court's position were rejected:

"*First*, plaintiffs theorize that the foreign affiliates' required statement of policy against prostitution and sex trafficking may be incorrectly attributed to the American organizations. Therefore, the theory goes, the American organizations themselves possess a First Amendment right against imposition of the Policy Requirement on their foreign affiliates."

Previous First Amendment cases "involving speech misattribution between formally distinct speakers[,]" such as *Hurley v. Irish-American Gay, Lesbian and Bisexual Group of Boston, Inc.*, . . . (1995), were inapposite, however, wrote Justice Kavanaugh, as they "arose because the State forced one speaker to host another speaker's speech[,]" whereas "[a]ny alleged misattribution in this case and any effect on the American organizations' message of neutrality toward prostitution stems from their choice to affiliate with foreign organizations, not from U. S. Government compulsion."

As for plaintiffs' second argument that AOSI I had essentially resolved their current claim in their favor, in AOSI I "the Court did not facially invalidate the Act's condition on funding" and "did not hold or suggest that the First Amendment requires the Government to exempt plaintiffs' foreign affiliates or other foreign organizations from the Policy Requirement."

Concurring, Justice Thomas wrote "separately to note my continued disagreement with *AOSI I* and to explain that the Policy Requirement does not violate the First Amendment for a far simpler reason: It does not compel anyone to say anything." Justice Breyer, joined by Justices Ginsburg and Sotomayor, on the other hand, dissented, writing in relevant part:

"The Court, in my view, asks the wrong question and gives the wrong answer. This case is not about the First Amendment rights of foreign organizations. It is about—and has always been about—the First Amendment rights of American organizations.

. . .

". . . Just as compelling a clearly identified *domestic* affiliate to espouse a government message distorts respondents' own protected speech, *AOSI I*, 570 U. S., at 219, so too does compelling a clearly identified *foreign* affiliate to espouse the same government message. Either way, federal funding conditioned on that affirmative avowal of belief comes at an unconstitutionally high "price of evident hypocrisy." . . .

"Properly understood, our speech-misattribution cases—in particular *Hurley v. Irish-American Gay, Lesbian and Bisexual Group of Boston, Inc.,* . . .— confirm that common-sense conclusion. Any other result would undermine First Amendment protections for the countless American speakers who address audiences overseas.

". . . [W]hen the Government demands as a condition of federal funding that their clearly identified affiliate 'espouse a specific belief as its own,' respondents may express a contrary view through some other corporate channel only on pain of appearing hypocritical. . . . Leveraging Congress' Article I spending power to distort respondents' protected speech in this way therefore violates *respondents'* First Amendment rights—whatever else might be said about the affiliate's own First Amendment rights (or asserted lack thereof). . . .

. . .

". . . Audiences everywhere attribute speech based on whom they perceive to be speaking, not on corporate paperwork they will never see. What mattered in *AOSI I* was thus how 'clearly identified' the affiliates were with respondents, not the fact that the affiliates were incorporated as separate legal entities. . . . And what matters now is once again how 'clearly identified' the affiliates are with respondents, not the fact that the affiliates were incorporated as *foreign* legal entities.

"[N]ot even the Government meaningfully disputes that respondents and their foreign affiliates are clearly identified with one another. Their appearances are the same. Their goals are the same. Their values are the same. *Their message* is the same. Leveraging Congress' spending power to demand speech from respondents' foreign affiliates distorts that shared message—and violates respondents' First Amendment rights. . . .

. . .

". . . The critical question here, as in *Hurley*, is simply whether the Government has demanded a profession of belief that will distort the speaker's message. *How* the Government causes that distortion makes no constitutional difference. And as explained, enforcing the Policy Requirement against respondents' clearly identified foreign affiliates would plainly distort *respondents'* message. . . .

. . .

"[I]t is difficult to accept the notion that the First Amendment permits the Government to suppress, compel, or otherwise distort any and all American speech transmitted abroad through a clearly identified foreign affiliate.

"The upshot is: (1) The messages at issue here belong to American speakers; (2) clearly identified foreign affiliates are a critical means of conveying those messages overseas; and (3) enforcing the Policy Requirement against those affiliates distorts respondents' own protected speech—and thus violates respondents' own First Amendment rights."

CHAPTER 15

PROTECTION OF PENUMBRAL FIRST AMENDMENT RIGHTS

2. COMPELLED AFFIRMATION OF BELIEF

Page 1525. Add after Rumsfeld v. Forum for Academic and Institutional Rights, Inc.:

National Institute of Family and Life Advocates v. Becerra

585 U.S. ___, 138 S.Ct. 2361, 201 L.Ed.2d 835 (2018).

[The report of this case appears supra, at p. 182.]

3. FREEDOM OF ASSOCIATION

D. COMPULSORY MEMBERSHIP AND FUNDING FOR ASSOCIATION SPEECH

Pages 1539–47. Replace Davenport v. Washington Education Association, Ysursa v. Pocatello Education Association, Knox v. Service Employees International Union and Harris v. Quinn with the following:

Janus v. American Federation of State, County and Municipal Employees, Council 31

585 U.S. ___, 138 S.Ct. 2448, 201 L.Ed.2d 924 (2018).

■ JUSTICE ALITO delivered the opinion of the Court.

Under Illinois law, public employees are forced to subsidize a union, even if they choose not to join and strongly object to the positions the union takes in collective bargaining and related activities. We conclude that this arrangement violates the free speech rights of nonmembers by compelling them to subsidize private speech on matters of substantial public concern.

We upheld a similar law in Abood v. Detroit Bd. of Ed., 431 U.S. 209 (1977), and we recognize the importance of following precedent unless there are strong reasons for not doing so. But there are very strong reasons in this case.

Fundamental free speech rights are at stake. *Abood* was poorly reasoned. It has led to practical problems and abuse. It is inconsistent with other First Amendment cases and has been undermined by more recent decisions.

Developments since *Abood* was handed down have shed new light on the issue of agency fees, and no reliance interests on the part of public-sector unions are sufficient to justify the perpetuation of the free speech violations that *Abood* has countenanced for the past 41 years. *Abood* is therefore overruled.

I

A

Under the Illinois Public Labor Relations Act (IPLRA), employees of the State and its political subdivisions are permitted to unionize. If a majority of the employees in a bargaining unit vote to be represented by a union, that union is designated as the exclusive representative of all the employees. Employees in the unit are not obligated to join the union selected by their co-workers, but whether they join or not, that union is deemed to be their sole permitted representative.

Once a union is so designated, it is vested with broad authority. Only the union may negotiate with the employer on matters relating to "pay, wages, hours[,] and other conditions of employment." . . . And this authority extends to the negotiation of what the IPLRA calls "policy matters," such as merit pay, the size of the work force, layoffs, privatization, promotion methods, and non-discrimination policies. . . .

Designating a union as the employees' exclusive representative substantially restricts the rights of individual employees. Among other things, this designation means that individual employees may not be represented by any agent other than the designated union; nor may individual employees negotiate directly with their employer. Protection of the employees' interests is placed in the hands of the union, and therefore the union is required by law to provide fair representation for all employees in the unit, members and nonmembers alike.

Employees who decline to join the union are not assessed full union dues but must instead pay what is generally called an "agency fee," which amounts to a percentage of the union dues. Under *Abood*, nonmembers may be charged for the portion of union dues attributable to activities that are "germane to [the union's] duties as collective-bargaining representative," . . . but nonmembers may not be required to fund the union's political and ideological projects. In labor-law parlance, the outlays in the first category are known as "chargeable" expenditures, while those in the latter are labeled "nonchargeable." . . .

Illinois law does not specify in detail which expenditures are chargeable and which are not. The IPLRA provides that an agency fee may compensate a union for the costs incurred in "the collective bargaining process, contract administration[,] and pursuing matters affecting wages, hours[,] and conditions of employment." . . . Excluded from the agency-fee calculation are union expenditures "related to the election or support of any candidate for political office." . . .

Applying this standard, a union categorizes its expenditures as chargeable or nonchargeable and thus determines a nonmember's "proportionate share," . . . this determination is then audited; the amount of the "proportionate share" is certified to the employer; and the employer automatically deducts that amount from the nonmembers' wages. Nonmembers need not be asked, and they are not required to consent before the fees are deducted.

After the amount of the agency fee is fixed each year, the union must send nonmembers what is known as a *Hudson* notice. See Teachers v. Hudson, 475 U.S. 292 (1986). This notice is supposed to provide nonmembers with "an adequate explanation of the basis for the [agency] fee." . . . If nonmembers "suspect that a union has improperly put certain expenses in the [chargeable] category," they may challenge that determination. . . .

As illustrated by the record in this case, unions charge nonmembers, not just for the cost of collective bargaining per se, but also for many other supposedly connected activities. See App. to Pet. for Cert. 28a–39a. Here, the nonmembers were told that they had to pay for "[l]obbying," "[s]ocial and recreational activities," "advertising," "[m]embership meetings and conventions," and "litigation," as well as other unspecified "[s]ervices" that "may ultimately inure to the benefit of the members of the local bargaining unit." . . . The total chargeable amount for nonmembers was 78.06% of full union dues.

B

Petitioner Mark Janus is employed by the Illinois Department of Healthcare and Family Services as a child support specialist. The employees in his unit are among the 35,000 public employees in Illinois who are represented by respondent American Federation of State, County, and Municipal Employees, Council 31 (Union). Janus refused to join the Union because he opposes "many of the public policy positions that [it] advocates," including the positions it takes in collective bargaining. Janus believes that the Union's "behavior in bargaining does not appreciate the current fiscal crises in Illinois and does not reflect his best interests or the interests of Illinois citizens." . . . Therefore, if he had the choice, he "would not pay any fees or otherwise subsidize [the Union]." . . . Under his unit's collective-bargaining agreement, however, he was required to pay an agency fee of $44.58 per month—which would amount to about $535 per year.

. . .

[The] amended complaint [Janus filed] claims that all "nonmember fee deductions are coerced political speech" and that "the First Amendment forbids coercing any money from the nonmembers." . . . Respondents moved to dismiss the amended complaint, correctly recognizing that the claim it asserted was foreclosed by *Abood*. The District Court granted the motion and the Court of Appeals for the Seventh Circuit affirmed. . . .

Janus then sought review in this Court, asking us to overrule *Abood* and hold that public-sector agency-fee arrangements are unconstitutional. We granted certiorari to consider this important question.

. . .

III

In *Abood*, the Court upheld the constitutionality of an agency-shop arrangement like the one now before us, but in more recent cases we have recognized that this holding is "something of an anomaly," Knox v. Service Employees, 567 U.S. 298, 311 (2012), and that *Abood*'s "analysis is questionable on several grounds," Harris v. Quinn, 573 U.S., at ___ (2014); see id. at ___ (discussing flaws in *Abood*'s reasoning). We have therefore refused to extend *Abood* to situations where it does not squarely control, see *Harris*, *supra*, at ___, while leaving for another day the question whether *Abood* should be overruled, *Harris*, *supra*, at ___, n. 19; see *Knox*, *supra*, at 310–311.

We now address that question. We first consider whether *Abood*'s holding is consistent with standard First Amendment principles.

A

The First Amendment, made applicable to the States by the Fourteenth Amendment, forbids abridgment of the freedom of speech. We have held time and again that freedom of speech "includes both the right to speak freely and the right to refrain from speaking at all." Wooley v. Maynard, 430 U.S. 705 (1977); see Riley v. National Federation of Blind of N. C., Inc., 487 U.S. 781, 796–797 (1988); Harper & Row, Publishers, Inc. v. Nation Enterprises, 471 U.S. 539, 559 (1985); Miami Herald Publishing Co. v. Tornillo, 418 U.S. 241, 256–257 (1974); accord, Pacific Gas & Elec. Co. v. Public Util. Comm'n of Cal., 475 U.S. 1, 9 (1986) (plurality opinion). The right to eschew association for expressive purposes is likewise protected. Roberts v. United States Jaycees, 468 U.S. 609, 623 (1984) ("Freedom of association . . . plainly presupposes a freedom not to associate"); see Pacific Gas & Elec., *supra*, at 12 ("[F]orced associations that burden protected speech are impermissible"). As Justice Jackson memorably put it: "If there is any fixed star in our constitutional constellation, it is that no official, high or petty, can prescribe what shall be orthodox in politics, nationalism, religion, or other matters of opinion or force citizens to confess by word or act their faith therein." West Virginia Bd. of Ed. v. Barnette, 319 U.S. 624, 642 (1943) (emphasis added).

Compelling individuals to mouth support for views they find objectionable violates that cardinal constitutional command, and in most contexts, any such effort would be universally condemned. Suppose, for example, that the State of Illinois required all residents to sign a document expressing support for a particular set of positions on controversial public issues—say, the platform of one of the major political parties. No one, we trust, would seriously argue that the First Amendment permits this.

Perhaps because such compulsion so plainly violates the Constitution, most of our free speech cases have involved restrictions on what can be said, rather than laws compelling speech. But measures compelling speech are at least as threatening.

Free speech serves many ends. It is essential to our democratic form of government, see, e.g., Garrison v. Louisiana, 379 U.S. 64, 74–75 (1964), and it furthers the search for truth, see, e.g., Thornhill v. Alabama, 310 U.S. 88, 95 (1940). Whenever the Federal Government or a State prevents individuals from saying what they think on important matters or compels them to voice ideas with which they disagree, it undermines these ends.

When speech is compelled, however, additional damage is done. In that situation, individuals are coerced into betraying their convictions. Forcing free and independent individuals to endorse ideas they find objectionable is always demeaning, and for this reason, one of our landmark free speech cases said that a law commanding "involuntary affirmation" of objected-to beliefs would require "even more immediate and urgent grounds" than a law demanding silence. *Barnette, supra*, at 633; see also *Riley, supra*, at 796–797 (rejecting "deferential test" for compelled speech claims).

Compelling a person to subsidize the speech of other private speakers raises similar First Amendment concerns. *Knox, supra*, at 309; United States v. United Foods, Inc., 533 U.S. 405, 410 (2001); *Abood, supra*, at 222, 234–235. As Jefferson famously put it, "to compel a man to furnish contributions of money for the propagation of opinions which he disbelieves and abhor[s] is sinful and tyrannical." A Bill for Establishing Religious Freedom, in 2 Papers of Thomas

Jefferson 545 (J. Boyd ed. 1950) (emphasis deleted and footnote omitted); see also *Hudson*, 475 U.S., at 305, n. 15. We have therefore recognized that a " 'significant impingement on First Amendment rights' " occurs when public employees are required to provide financial support for a union that "takes many positions during collective bargaining that have powerful political and civic consequences." *Knox, supra*, at 310–311 (quoting Ellis v. Railway Clerks, 466 U.S. 435, 455 (1984)).

Because the compelled subsidization of private speech seriously impinges on First Amendment rights, it cannot be casually allowed. Our free speech cases have identified "levels of scrutiny" to be applied in different contexts, and in three recent cases, we have considered the standard that should be used in judging the constitutionality of agency fees. See *Knox, supra*; *Harris, supra*; Friedrichs v. California Teachers Assn., 578 U.S. ___ (2016) (per curiam) (affirming decision below by equally divided Court).

In *Knox*, the first of these cases, we found it sufficient to hold that the conduct in question was unconstitutional under even the test used for the compulsory subsidization of commercial speech. Even though commercial speech has been thought to enjoy a lesser degree of protection, prior precedent in that area, specifically *United Foods, supra*, had applied what we characterized as "exacting" scrutiny, . . . a less demanding test than the "strict" scrutiny that might be thought to apply outside the commercial sphere. Under "exacting" scrutiny, we noted, a compelled subsidy must "serve a compelling state interest that cannot be achieved through means significantly less restrictive of associational freedoms."

In *Harris*, the second of these cases, we again found that an agency-fee requirement failed "exacting scrutiny." . . . But we questioned whether that test provides sufficient protection for free speech rights, since "it is apparent that the speech compelled" in agency-fee cases "is not commercial speech." . . .

Picking up that cue, petitioner in the present case contends that the Illinois law at issue should be subjected to "strict scrutiny." The dissent, on the other hand, proposes that we apply what amounts to rational-basis review, that is, that we ask only whether a government employer could reasonably believe that the exaction of agency fees serves its interests. See post, at ___ (KAGAN, J., dissenting) ("A government entity could reasonably conclude that such a clause was needed"). This form of minimal scrutiny is foreign to our free-speech jurisprudence, and we reject it here. At the same time, we again find it unnecessary to decide the issue of strict scrutiny because the Illinois scheme cannot survive under even the more permissive standard applied in *Knox* and *Harris*.

. . .

B

In *Abood*, the main defense of the agency-fee arrangement was that it served the State's interest in "labor peace." . . . By "labor peace," the *Abood* Court meant avoidance of the conflict and disruption that it envisioned would occur if the employees in a unit were represented by more than one union. In such a situation, the Court predicted, "inter-union rivalries" would foster "dissension within the work force," and the employer could face "conflicting demands from different unions." . . . Confusion would ensue if the employer entered into and attempted to "enforce two or more agreements specifying different terms and conditions of employment." And a settlement with one union would be "subject to attack from [a] rival labor organizatio[n]." . . .

We assume that "labor peace," in this sense of the term, is a compelling state interest, but *Abood* cited no evidence that the pandemonium it imagined would result if agency fees were not allowed, and it is now clear that *Abood*'s fears were unfounded. The *Abood* Court assumed that designation of a union as the exclusive representative of all the employees in a unit and the exaction of agency fees are inextricably linked, but that is simply not true. . . .

The federal employment experience is illustrative. Under federal law, a union chosen by majority vote is designated as the exclusive representative of all the employees, but federal law does not permit agency fees. See 5 U.S.C. §§ 7102, 7111(a), 7114(a). Nevertheless, nearly a million federal employees—about 27% of the federal work force—are union members. The situation in the Postal Service is similar. Although permitted to choose an exclusive representative, Postal Service employees are not required to pay an agency fee, 39 U.S.C. §§ 1203(a), 1209(c), and about 400,000 are union members. Likewise, millions of public employees in the 28 States that have laws generally prohibiting agency fees are represented by unions that serve as the exclusive representatives of all the employees. Whatever may have been the case 41 years ago when *Abood* was handed down, it is now undeniable that "labor peace" can readily be achieved "through means significantly less restrictive of associational freedoms" than the assessment of agency fees. . . .

C

In addition to the promotion of "labor peace," *Abood* cited "the risk of 'free riders' " as justification for agency fees. . . . Respondents and some of their amici endorse this reasoning, contending that agency fees are needed to prevent nonmembers from enjoying the benefits of union representation without shouldering the costs.

Petitioner strenuously objects to this free-rider label. He argues that he is not a free rider on a bus headed for a destination that he wishes to reach but is more like a person shanghaied for an unwanted voyage.

Whichever description fits the majority of public employees who would not subsidize a union if given the option, avoiding free riders is not a compelling interest. As we have noted, "free-rider arguments . . . are generally insufficient to overcome First Amendment objections." *Knox*, 567 U.S., at 311. To hold otherwise across the board would have startling consequences. Many private groups speak out with the objective of obtaining government action that will have the effect of benefiting nonmembers. May all those who are thought to benefit from such efforts be compelled to subsidize this speech?

Suppose that a particular group lobbies or speaks out on behalf of what it thinks are the needs of senior citizens or veterans or physicians, to take just a few examples. Could the government require that all seniors, veterans, or doctors pay for that service even if they object? It has never been thought that this is permissible. . . . In simple terms, the First Amendment does not permit the government to compel a person to pay for another party's speech just because the government thinks that the speech furthers the interests of the person who does not want to pay.

Those supporting agency fees contend that the situation here is different because unions are statutorily required to "represen[t] the interests of all public employees in the unit," whether or not they are union members. . . . Why might this matter?

We can think of two possible arguments. It might be argued that a State has a compelling interest in requiring the payment of agency fees because (1) unions would otherwise be unwilling to represent nonmembers or (2) it would be fundamentally unfair to require unions to provide fair representation for nonmembers if nonmembers were not required to pay. Neither of these arguments is sound.

First, it is simply not true that unions will refuse to serve as the exclusive representative of all employees in the unit if they are not given agency fees. As noted, unions represent millions of public employees in jurisdictions that do not permit agency fees. No union is ever compelled to seek that designation. On the contrary, designation as exclusive representative is avidly sought. Why is this so?

Even without agency fees, designation as the exclusive representative confers many benefits. As noted, that status gives the union a privileged place in negotiations over wages, benefits, and working conditions. . . . Not only is the union given the exclusive right to speak for all the employees in collective bargaining, but the employer is required by state law to listen to and to bargain in good faith with only that union. . . . Designation as exclusive representative thus "results in a tremendous increase in the power" of the union.

In addition, a union designated as exclusive representative is often granted special privileges, such as obtaining information about employees . . . and having dues and fees deducted directly from employee wages . . . . The collective-bargaining agreement in this case guarantees a long list of additional privileges.

These benefits greatly outweigh any extra burden imposed by the duty of providing fair representation for nonmembers. What this duty entails, in simple terms, is an obligation not to "act solely in the interests of [the union's] own members." . . .

What does this mean when it comes to the negotiation of a contract? The union may not negotiate a collective-bargaining agreement that discriminates against nonmembers, but the union's bargaining latitude would be little different if state law simply prohibited public employers from entering into agreements that discriminate in that way. And for that matter, it is questionable whether the Constitution would permit a public-sector employer to adopt a collective-bargaining agreement that discriminates against nonmembers. . . . It is noteworthy that neither respondents nor any of the 39 amicus briefs supporting them—nor the dissent—has explained why the duty of fair representation causes public-sector unions to incur significantly greater expenses than they would otherwise bear in negotiating collective-bargaining agreements.

What about the representation of nonmembers in grievance proceedings? Unions do not undertake this activity solely for the benefit of nonmembers— which is why Illinois law gives a public-sector union the right to send a representative to such proceedings even if the employee declines union representation. . . . Representation of nonmembers furthers the union's interest in keeping control of the administration of the collective-bargaining agreement, since the resolution of one employee's grievance can affect others. And when a union controls the grievance process, it may, as a practical matter, effectively subordinate "the interests of [an] individual employee . . . to the collective interests of all employees in the bargaining unit." . . .

In any event, whatever unwanted burden is imposed by the representation of nonmembers in disciplinary matters can be eliminated "through means significantly less restrictive of associational freedoms" than the imposition of agency fees. Individual nonmembers could be required to pay for that service or could be denied union representation altogether. Thus, agency fees cannot be sustained on the ground that unions would otherwise be unwilling to represent nonmembers.

Nor can such fees be justified on the ground that it would otherwise be unfair to require a union to bear the duty of fair representation. That duty is a necessary concomitant of the authority that a union seeks when it chooses to serve as the exclusive representative of all the employees in a unit. As explained, designating a union as the exclusive representative of nonmembers substantially restricts the nonmembers' rights. Protection of their interests is placed in the hands of the union, and if the union were free to disregard or even work against those interests, these employees would be wholly unprotected. That is why we said many years ago that serious "constitutional questions [would] arise" if the union were not subject to the duty to represent all employees fairly.

In sum, we do not see any reason to treat the free-rider interest any differently in the agency-fee context than in any other First Amendment context. We therefore hold that agency fees cannot be upheld on free-rider grounds.

IV

Implicitly acknowledging the weakness of *Abood*'s own reasoning, proponents of agency fees have come forward with alternative justifications for the decision, and we now address these arguments.

A

The most surprising of these new arguments is the Union respondent's originalist defense of *Abood*. According to this argument, *Abood* was correctly decided because the First Amendment was not originally understood to provide any protection for the free speech rights of public employees.

As an initial matter, we doubt that the Union—or its members—actually want us to hold that public employees have "*no* [free speech] rights." . . .

It is particularly discordant to find this argument in a brief that trumpets the importance of *stare decisis*. See Brief for Union Respondent 47–57. Taking away free speech protection for public employees would mean overturning decades of landmark precedent. Under the Union's theory, Pickering v. Board of Ed. of Township High School Dist. 205, Will Cty., 391 U.S. 563 (1968), and its progeny would fall. Yet *Pickering*, as we will discuss, is now the foundation for respondents' chief defense of *Abood*. And indeed, *Abood* itself would have to go if public employees have no free speech rights, since *Abood* holds that the First Amendment prohibits the exaction of agency fees for political or ideological purposes. Our political patronage cases would be doomed. See, e.g., Rutan v. Republican Party of Ill., 497 U.S. 62 (1990); Branti v. Finkel, 445 U.S. 507 (1980); Elrod v. Burns, 427 U.S. 347 (1976). Also imperiled would be older precedents like Wieman v. Updegraff, 344 U.S. 183 (1952) (loyalty oaths), Shelton v. Tucker, 364 U.S. 479 (1960) (disclosure of memberships and contributions), and Keyishian v. Board of Regents of Univ. of State of N. Y., 385 U.S. 589 (1967) (subversive speech). Respondents presumably want none of this, desiring instead that we apply the Constitution's supposed original meaning only when it suits them—to retain the part of *Abood* that they like. See Tr. of Oral Arg. 56–57. We will not engage in this halfway originalism.

Nor, in any event, does the First Amendment's original meaning support the Union's claim. The Union offers no persuasive founding-era evidence that public employees were understood to lack free speech protections. While it observes that restrictions on federal employees' activities have existed since the First Congress, most of its historical examples involved limitations on public officials' outside business dealings, not on their speech. The only early speech restrictions the Union identifies are an 1806 statute prohibiting military personnel from using "'contemptuous or disrespectful words against the President'" and other officials, and an 1801 directive limiting electioneering by top government employees. . . . But those examples at most show that the government was understood to have power to limit employee speech that threatened important governmental interests (such as maintaining military discipline and preventing corruption)—not that public employees' speech was entirely unprotected. Indeed, more recently this Court has upheld similar restrictions even while recognizing that government employees possess First Amendment rights. . . .

Ultimately, the Union relies, not on founding-era evidence, but on dictum from a 1983 opinion of this Court stating that, "[f]or most of th[e 20th] century, the unchallenged dogma was that a public employee had no right to object to conditions placed upon the terms of employment—including those which restricted the exercise of constitutional rights." Connick v. Myers, 461 U.S. 138, 143. Even on its own terms, this dictum about 20th-century views does not purport to describe how the First Amendment was understood in 1791. And a careful examination of the decisions by this Court that *Connick* cited to support its dictum reveals that none of them rested on the facile premise that public employees are unprotected by the First Amendment. Instead, they considered (much as we do today) whether particular speech restrictions were "necessary to protect" fundamental government interests. . . .

. . . We can safely say that, at the time of the adoption of the First Amendment, no one gave any thought to whether public-sector unions could charge nonmembers agency fees. Entities resembling labor unions did not exist at the founding, and public-sector unions did not emerge until the mid-20th century. The idea of public-sector unionization and agency fees would astound those who framed and ratified the Bill of Rights. Thus, the Union cannot point to any accepted founding-era practice that even remotely resembles the compulsory assessment of agency fees from public-sector employees. We do know, however, that prominent members of the founding generation condemned laws requiring public employees to affirm or support beliefs with which they disagreed. As noted, Jefferson denounced compelled support for such beliefs as "sinful and tyrannical," and others expressed similar views. . . .

. . .

B

The principal defense of *Abood* advanced by respondents and the dissent is based on our decision in *Pickering*, 391 U.S. 563, which held that a school district violated the First Amendment by firing a teacher for writing a letter critical of the school administration. Under *Pickering* and later cases in the same line, employee speech is largely unprotected if it is part of what the employee is paid to do, see Garcetti v. Ceballos, 547 U.S. 410, 421–422 (2006), or if it involved a matter of only private concern, see *Connick*. On the other hand, when a public employee speaks as a citizen on a matter of public concern, the employee's speech is protected unless " 'the interest of the state, as an employer, in promoting the efficiency of the public services it performs through its employees' outweighs 'the interests of the [employee], as a citizen, in commenting upon matters of public concern.' " *Pickering* was the centerpiece of the defense of *Abood* in *Harris*, see 573 U.S., at ___ (Kagan, J., dissenting), and we found the argument unpersuasive. . . . The intervening years have not improved its appeal.

As we pointed out in *Harris*, *Abood* was not based on *Pickering*. . . . And we have previously taken a dim view of similar attempts to recast problematic First Amendment decisions. . . . We see no good reason, at this late date, to try to shoehorn *Abood* into the *Pickering* framework.

Even if that were attempted, the shoe would be a painful fit for at least three reasons.

First, the *Pickering* framework was developed for use in a very different context—in cases that involve "one employee's speech and its impact on that employee's public responsibilities." . . . This case, by contrast, involves a blanket requirement that all employees subsidize speech with which they may not agree. While we have sometimes looked to *Pickering* in considering general rules that affect broad categories of employees, we have acknowledged that the standard *Pickering* analysis requires modification in that situation. A speech-restrictive law with "widespread impact," we have said, "gives rise to far more serious concerns than could any single supervisory decision." . . . Therefore, when such a law is at issue, the government must shoulder a correspondingly "heav[ier]" burden, and is entitled to considerably less deference in its assessment that a predicted harm justifies a particular impingement on First Amendment rights. . . . The end product of those adjustments is a test that more closely resembles exacting scrutiny than the traditional *Pickering* analysis.

The core collective-bargaining issue of wages and benefits illustrates this point. Suppose that a single employee complains that he or she should have received a 5% raise. This individual complaint would likely constitute a matter of only private concern and would therefore be unprotected under *Pickering*. But a public-sector union's demand for a 5% raise for the many thousands of employees it represents would be another matter entirely. Granting such a raise could have a serious impact on the budget of the government unit in question, and by the same token, denying a raise might have a significant effect on the performance of government services. When a large number of employees speak through their union, the category of speech that is of public concern is greatly enlarged, and the category of speech that is of only private concern is substantially shrunk. By disputing this, the dissent denies the obvious.

Second, the *Pickering* framework fits much less well where the government compels speech or speech subsidies in support of third parties. *Pickering* is based on the insight that the speech of a public-sector employee may interfere with the effective operation of a government office. When a public employer does not simply restrict potentially disruptive speech but commands that its employees mouth a message on its own behalf, the calculus is very different. Of course, if the speech in question is part of an employee's official duties, the employer may insist that the employee deliver any lawful message. Otherwise, however, it is not easy to imagine a situation in which a public employer has a legitimate need to demand that its employees recite words with which they disagree. And we have never applied *Pickering* in such a case.

. . .

Third, although both *Pickering* and *Abood* divided speech into two categories, the cases' categorization schemes do not line up. Superimposing the *Pickering* scheme on *Abood* would significantly change the *Abood* regime.

Let us first look at speech that is not germane to collective bargaining but instead concerns political or ideological issues. Under *Abood*, a public employer is flatly prohibited from permitting nonmembers to be charged for this speech, but under *Pickering*, the employees' free speech interests could be overcome if a court found that the employer's interests outweighed the employees'.

A similar problem arises with respect to speech that is germane to collective bargaining. The parties dispute how much of this speech is of public concern, but respondents concede that much of it falls squarely into that category. Under *Abood*, nonmembers may be required to pay for all this speech, but *Pickering* would permit that practice only if the employer's interests outweighed those of the employees. Thus, recasting *Abood* as an application of Pickering would substantially alter the *Abood* scheme.

For all these reasons, *Pickering* is a poor fit indeed.

. . .

VI

For the reasons given above, we conclude that public-sector agency-shop arrangements violate the First Amendment, and *Abood* erred in concluding otherwise. There remains the question whether *stare decisis* nonetheless counsels against overruling *Abood*. It does not.

"*Stare decisis* is the preferred course because it promotes the evenhanded, predictable, and consistent development of legal principles, fosters reliance on judicial decisions, and contributes to the actual and perceived integrity of the judicial process." . . . We will not overturn a past decision unless there are strong grounds for doing so. But as we have often recognized, *stare decisis* is " 'not an inexorable command.' " . . .

The doctrine "is at its weakest when we interpret the Constitution because our interpretation can be altered only by constitutional amendment or by overruling our prior decisions." . . . And *stare decisis* applies with perhaps least force of all to decisions that wrongly denied First Amendment rights: "This Court has not hesitated to overrule decisions offensive to the First Amendment (a fixed star in our constitutional constellation, if there is one)." . . .

Our cases identify factors that should be taken into account in deciding whether to overrule a past decision. Five of these are most important here: the quality of *Abood*'s reasoning, the workability of the rule it established, its consistency with other related decisions, developments since the decision was handed down, and reliance on the decision. After analyzing these factors, we conclude that *stare decisis* does not require us to retain *Abood*.

A

. . .

Abood went wrong at the start when it concluded that two prior decisions, Railway Employes v. Hanson, 351 U.S. 225 (1956), and Machinists v. Street, 367 U.S. 740 (1961), "appear[ed] to require validation of the agency-shop agreement before [the Court]." . . . Properly understood, those decisions did no such thing. Both cases involved Congress's "bare authorization" of private-sector union shops under the Railway Labor Act.[24] *Abood* failed to appreciate that a very different First Amendment question arises when a State requires its employees to pay agency fees.

Moreover, neither *Hanson* nor *Street* gave careful consideration to the First Amendment. . . . *Abood* nevertheless took the view that *Hanson* and *Street* "all but decided" the important free speech issue that was before the Court. . . .

Abood's unwarranted reliance on *Hanson* and *Street* appears to have contributed to another mistake: *Abood* judged the constitutionality of public-sector agency fees under a deferential standard that finds no support in our free speech cases. . . .

. . .

In sum . . . *Abood* was not well reasoned.

B

Another relevant consideration in the *stare decisis* calculus is the workability of the precedent in question, and that factor also weighs against *Abood*.

1

Abood's line between chargeable and nonchargeable union expenditures has proved to be impossible to draw with precision. . . .

In *Knox*, for example, we confronted a union's claim that the costs of lobbying the legislature and the electorate about a ballot measure were chargeable expenses. . . . The Court rejected this claim out of hand, 567 U.S., at 320–321, but the dissent refused to do so, id., at 336 (opinion of Breyer, J.). And in the present case, nonmembers are required to pay for unspecified "[l]obbying" expenses and for "[s]ervices" that "may ultimately inure to the benefit of the members of the local bargaining unit." App. to Pet. for Cert. 31a–32a. That formulation is broad enough to encompass just about anything that the union might choose to do.

Respondents agree that *Abood*'s chargeable-nonchargeable line suffers from "a vagueness problem," that it sometimes "allows what it shouldn't allow," and that "a firm[er] line c[ould] be drawn." Tr. of Oral Arg. 47–48. They therefore

---

[24] No First Amendment issue could have properly arisen in those cases unless Congress's enactment of a provision allowing, but not requiring, private parties to enter into union-shop arrangements was sufficient to establish governmental action. That proposition was debatable when Abood was decided, and is even more questionable today. See American Mfrs. Mut. Ins. Co. v. Sullivan, 526 U.S. 40, 53 (1999); Jackson v. Metropolitan Edison Co., 419 U.S. 345, 357 (1974). Compare, e.g., White v. Communications Workers of Am., AFL-CIO, Local 1300, 370 F.3d 346, 350 (C.A.3 2004) (no state action), and Kolinske v. Lubbers, 712 F.2d 471, 477–478 (C.A.D.C.1983) (same), with Beck v. Communications Workers of Am., 776 F.2d 1187, 1207 (C.A.4 1985) (state action), and Linscott v. Millers Falls Co., 440 F.2d 14, 16, and n. 2 (C.A.1 1971) (same). We reserved decision on this question in Communications Workers v. Beck, 487 U.S. 735, 761 (1988), and do not resolve it here.

argue that we should "consider revisiting" this part of *Abood*. Tr. of Oral Arg. 66; see Brief for Union Respondent 46–47; Brief for State Respondents 30. This concession only underscores the reality that *Abood* has proved unworkable: Not even the parties defending agency fees support the line that it has taken this Court over 40 years to draw.

. . .

C

Developments since *Abood*, both factual and legal, have also "eroded" the decision's "underpinnings" and left it an outlier among our First Amendment cases.

1

Abood pinned its result on the "unsupported empirical assumption" that "the principle of exclusive representation in the public sector is dependent on a union or agency shop." But, as already noted, experience has shown otherwise.

It is also significant that the Court decided *Abood* against a very different legal and economic backdrop. Public-sector unionism was a relatively new phenomenon in 1977. . . . Since then, public-sector union membership has come to surpass private-sector union membership, even though there are nearly four times as many total private-sector employees as public-sector employees.

This ascendance of public-sector unions has been marked by a parallel increase in public spending. In 1970, total state and local government expenditures amounted to $646 per capita in nominal terms, or about $4,000 per capita in 2014 dollars. See Dept. of Commerce, Statistical Abstract of the United States: 1972, p. 419 . . . . By 2014, that figure had ballooned to approximately $10,238 per capita. ProQuest, Statistical Abstract of the United States: 2018, pp. 17, Table 14, 300, Table 469. Not all that increase can be attributed to public-sector unions, of course, but the mounting costs of public-employee wages, benefits, and pensions undoubtedly played a substantial role. We are told, for example, that Illinois' pension funds are underfunded by $129 billion as a result of generous public-employee retirement packages. . . . Unsustainable collective-bargaining agreements have also been blamed for multiple municipal bankruptcies. See Brief for State of Michigan et al. as Amici Curiae 10–19. These developments, and the political debate over public spending and debt they have spurred, have given collective-bargaining issues a political valence that *Abood* did not fully appreciate.

Abood is also an "anomaly" in our First Amendment jurisprudence, as we recognized in *Harris* and *Knox* . . .

. . .

D

In some cases, reliance provides a strong reason for adhering to established law, and this is the factor that is stressed most strongly by respondents, their amici, and the dissent. They contend that collective-bargaining agreements now in effect were negotiated with agency fees in mind and that unions may have given up other benefits in exchange for provisions granting them such fees. In this case, however, reliance does not carry decisive weight.

For one thing, it would be unconscionable to permit free speech rights to be abridged in perpetuity in order to preserve contract provisions that will expire on their own in a few years' time. "The fact that [public-sector unions] may view [agency fees] as an entitlement does not establish the sort of reliance interest that could outweigh the countervailing interest that [nonmembers] share in having their constitutional rights fully protected." Arizona v. Gant, 556 U.S. 332, 349 (2009).

For another, *Abood* does not provide "a clear or easily applicable standard, so arguments for reliance based on its clarity are misplaced." South Dakota v. Wayfair, Inc., 585 U.S. ___, ___ (2018).

. . .

We recognize that the loss of payments from nonmembers may cause unions to experience unpleasant transition costs in the short term, and may require unions to make adjustments in order to attract and retain members. But we must weigh these disadvantages against the considerable windfall that unions have received under *Abood* for the past 41 years. It is hard to estimate how many billions of dollars have been taken from nonmembers and transferred to public-sector unions in violation of the First Amendment. Those unconstitutional exactions cannot be allowed to continue indefinitely.

. . .

VII

For these reasons, States and public-sector unions may no longer extract agency fees from nonconsenting employees. Under Illinois law, if a public-sector collective-bargaining agreement includes an agency-fee provision and the union certifies to the employer the amount of the fee, that amount is automatically deducted from the nonmember's wages. . . . No form of employee consent is required.

This procedure violates the First Amendment and cannot continue. Neither an agency fee nor any other payment to the union may be deducted from a nonmember's wages, nor may any other attempt be made to collect such a payment, unless the employee affirmatively consents to pay. By agreeing to pay, nonmembers are waiving their First Amendment rights, and such a waiver cannot be presumed. Rather, to be effective, the waiver must be freely given and shown by "clear and compelling" evidence. Unless employees clearly and affirmatively consent before any money is taken from them, this standard cannot be met.

Abood was wrongly decided and is now overruled. The judgment of the United States Court of Appeals for the Seventh Circuit is reversed, and the case is remanded for further proceedings consistent with this opinion.

. . .

■ JUSTICE SOTOMAYOR, dissenting.

I join Justice Kagan's dissent in full. Although I joined the majority in Sorrell v. IMS Health Inc., 564 U.S. 552 (2011), I disagree with the way that this Court has since interpreted and applied that opinion. . . . Having seen the troubling development in First Amendment jurisprudence over the years, both in this Court and in lower courts, I agree fully with Justice Kagan that *Sorrell*— in the way it has been read by this Court—has allowed courts to "wiel[d] the First Amendment in . . . an aggressive way" just as the majority does today. . . .

■ JUSTICE KAGAN, with whom JUSTICE GINSBURG, JUSTICE BREYER, and JUSTICE SOTOMAYOR join, dissenting.

For over 40 years, [*Abood*] struck a stable balance between public employees' First Amendment rights and government entities' interests in running their workforces as they thought proper. Under that decision, a government entity could require public employees to pay a fair share of the cost that a union incurs when negotiating on their behalf over terms of employment. But no part of that fair-share payment could go to any of the union's political or ideological activities.

That holding fit comfortably with this Court's general framework for evaluating claims that a condition of public employment violates the First Amendment. The Court's decisions have long made plain that government entities have substantial latitude to regulate their employees' speech—especially about terms of employment—in the interest of operating their workplaces effectively. *Abood* allowed governments to do just that. While protecting public employees' expression about non-workplace matters, the decision enabled a government to advance important managerial interests—by ensuring the presence of an exclusive employee representative to bargain with. Far from an "anomaly," the *Abood* regime was a paradigmatic example of how the government can regulate speech in its capacity as an employer.

Not any longer. Today, the Court succeeds in its 6-year campaign to reverse *Abood*. See Friedrichs v. California Teachers Assn., 578 U.S. ___ (2016) (per curiam); Harris v. Quinn, 573 U.S. ___ (2014); Knox v. Service Employees, 567 U.S. 298 (2012). Its decision will have large-scale consequences. Public employee unions will lose a secure source of financial support. State and local governments that thought fair-share provisions furthered their interests will need to find new ways of managing their workforces. Across the country, the relationships of public employees and employers will alter in both predictable and wholly unexpected ways.

Rarely if ever has the Court overruled a decision—let alone one of this import—with so little regard for the usual principles of *stare decisis*. There are no special justifications for reversing *Abood*. It has proved workable. No recent developments have eroded its underpinnings. And it is deeply entrenched, in both the law and the real world. More than 20 States have statutory schemes built on the decision. Those laws underpin thousands of ongoing contracts involving millions of employees. Reliance interests do not come any stronger than those surrounding *Abood*. And likewise, judicial disruption does not get any greater than what the Court does today. I respectfully dissent.

I

I begin with *Abood*, the 41-year-old precedent the majority overrules. That case involved a union that had been certified as the exclusive representative of Detroit's public school teachers. The union's collective-bargaining agreement with the city included an "agency shop" clause, which required teachers who had not joined the union to pay it "a service charge equal to the regular dues required of [u]nion members." . . . A group of non-union members sued over that clause, arguing that it violated the First Amendment.

In considering their challenge, the Court canvassed the purposes of the "agency shop" clause. It was rooted, the Court understood, in the "principle of exclusive union representation"—a "central element" in "industrial relations" since the New Deal. Significant benefits, the Court explained, could derive from the "designation of a single [union] representative" for all similarly situated employees in a workplace. . . . In particular, such arrangements: "avoid[ ] the confusion that would result from attempting to enforce two or more agreements specifying different terms and conditions of employment"; "prevent[ ] inter-union rivalries from creating dissension within the work force"; "free[ ] the employer from the possibility of facing conflicting demands from different unions"; and "permit[ ] the employer and a single union to reach agreements and settlements that are not subject to attack from rival labor organizations." . . . As proof, the Court pointed to the example of exclusive-representation arrangements in the private-employment sphere: There, Congress had long thought that such schemes would promote "peaceful labor relations" and "labor stability." . . . A public employer like Detroit, the Court believed, could reasonably make the same calculation.

But for an exclusive-bargaining arrangement to work, such an employer often thought, the union needed adequate funding. . . . "The tasks of negotiating and administering a collective-bargaining agreement and representing the interests of employees in settling disputes and processing grievances are continuing and difficult ones." . . . Those activities, the Court noted, require the "expenditure of much time and money"—for example, payment for the "services of lawyers, expert negotiators, economists, and a research staff." . . . And there is no way to confine the union's services to union members alone (and thus to trim costs) because unions must by law fairly represent all employees in a given bargaining unit—union members and non-members alike. . . .

But the Court acknowledged as well the "First Amendment interests" of dissenting employees. . . . It recognized that some workers might oppose positions the union takes in collective bargaining, or even "unionism itself." . . . And still more, it understood that unions often advance "political and ideological" views outside the collective-bargaining context—as when they "contribute to political candidates." . . . Employees might well object to the use of their money to support such "ideological causes." . . .

So the Court struck a balance, which has governed this area ever since. On the one hand, employees could be required to pay fees to support the union in "collective bargaining, contract administration, and grievance adjustment." . . . There, the Court held, the "important government interests" in having a stably funded bargaining partner justify "the impingement upon" public employees' expression. . . . But on the other hand, employees could not be compelled to fund the union's political and ideological activities. Outside the collective-bargaining sphere, the Court determined, an employee's First Amendment rights defeated any conflicting government interest.

II

Unlike the majority, I see nothing "questionable" about *Abood*'s analysis. . . .

A

Abood's reasoning about governmental interests has three connected parts. First, exclusive representation arrangements benefit some government entities because they can facilitate stable labor relations. . . . Second, the government may be unable to avail itself of those benefits unless the single union has a secure source of funding. . . . And third, agency fees are often needed to ensure such stable funding. That is because without those fees, employees have every incentive to free ride on the union dues paid by others.

The majority does not take issue with the first point. . . . The majority claims that the second point never appears in *Abood*, but is willing to assume it for the sake of argument. So the majority stakes everything on the third point— the conclusion that maintaining an effective system of exclusive representation often entails agency fees.

But basic economic theory shows why a government would think that agency fees are necessary for exclusive representation to work. What ties the two together, as *Abood* recognized, is the likelihood of free-riding when fees are absent. Remember that once a union achieves exclusive-representation status, the law compels it to fairly represent all workers in the bargaining unit, whether or not they join or contribute to the union. Because of that legal duty, the union cannot give special advantages to its own members. And that in turn creates a collective action problem of nightmarish proportions. Everyone—not just those who oppose the union, but also those who back it—has an economic incentive to withhold dues; only altruism or loyalty—as against financial self-interest—can explain why an employee would pay the union for its services. . . .

The majority's initial response to this reasoning is simply to dismiss it. "[F]ree rider arguments,". . . the majority pronounces, "are generally insufficient to overcome First Amendment objections." . . . "To hold otherwise," it continues, "would have startling consequences" because "[m]any private groups speak out" in ways that will "benefit[ ] nonmembers." . . . But that disregards the defining characteristic of this free-rider argument—that unions, unlike those many other private groups, must serve members and non-members alike. Groups advocating for "senior citizens or veterans" (to use the majority's examples) have no legal duty to provide benefits to all those individuals: They can spur people to pay dues by conferring all kinds of special advantages on their dues-paying members. Unions are—by law—in a different position, as this Court has long recognized. . . . That special feature was what justified *Abood*: "Where the state imposes upon the union a duty to deliver services, it may permit the union to demand reimbursement for them." . . .

The majority's fallback argument purports to respond to the distinctive position of unions, but still misses *Abood*'s economic insight. Here, the majority delivers a four-page exegesis on why unions will seek to serve as an exclusive bargaining representative even "if they are not given agency fees." . . . The gist of the account is that "designation as the exclusive representative confers many benefits,". . . which outweigh the costs of providing services to non-members. But that response avoids the key question, which is whether unions without agency fees will be able to (not whether they will want to) carry on as an effective exclusive representative. And as to that question, the majority again fails to reckon with how economically rational actors behave—in public as well as private workplaces. Without a fair-share agreement, the class of union non-members spirals upward. Employees (including those who love the union) realize that they can get the same benefits even if they let their memberships expire. And as more and more stop paying dues, those left must take up the financial slack (and anyway, begin to feel like suckers)—so they too quit the union. And when the vicious cycle finally ends, chances are that the union will lack the resources to effectively perform the responsibilities of an exclusive representative—or, in the worst case, to perform them at all. The result is to frustrate the interests of every government entity that thinks a strong exclusive-representation scheme will promote stable labor relations.

Of course, not all public employers will share that view. Some would rather not bargain with an exclusive representative. Others would prefer that representative to be poorly funded—to serve more as a front than an effectual bargaining partner. But as reflected in the number of fair-share statutes and contracts across the Nation, many government entities think that effective exclusive representation makes for good labor relations—and recognize, just as *Abood* did, that representation of that kind often depends on agency fees. . . .

B

1

In many cases over many decades, this Court has addressed how the First Amendment applies when the government, acting not as sovereign but as employer, limits its workers' speech. Those decisions have granted substantial latitude to the government, in recognition of its significant interests in managing its workforce so as to best serve the public. *Abood* fit neatly with that caselaw, in both reasoning and result. Indeed, its reversal today creates a significant anomaly—an exception, applying to union fees alone, from the usual rules governing public employees' speech.

. . .

In striking the proper balance between employee speech rights and managerial interests, the Court has long applied a test originating in [*Pickering*]. . . .

Abood coheres with that framework. The point here is not, as the majority suggests, that *Abood* is an overt, one-to-one "application of *Pickering*." It is not. *Abood* related to a municipality's labor policy, and so the Court looked to prior cases about unions, not to *Pickering*'s analysis of an employee's dismissal. (And truth be told, *Pickering* was not at that time much to look at: What the Court now thinks of as the two-step *Pickering* test, as the majority's own citations show, really emerged from *Garcetti* and *Connick*—two cases post-dating *Abood*). But *Abood* and *Pickering* raised variants of the same basic issue: the extent of the government's authority to make employment decisions affecting expression. And in both, the Court struck the same basic balance, enabling the government to curb speech when—but only when—the regulation was designed to protect its managerial interests. . . .

. . .

Abood thus dovetailed with the Court's usual attitude in First Amendment cases toward the regulation of public employees' speech. That attitude is one of respect—even solicitude—for the government's prerogatives as an employer. So long as the government is acting as an employer—rather than exploiting the employment relationship for other ends—it has a wide berth, comparable to that of a private employer. And when the regulated expression concerns the terms and conditions of employment—the very stuff of the employment relationship—the government really cannot lose. There, managerial interests are obvious and strong. And so government employees are . . . just employees, even though they work for the government. Except that today the government does lose, in a first for the law. Now, the government can constitutionally adopt all policies regulating core workplace speech in pursuit of managerial goals—save this single one.

. . .

2

The majority claims it is not making a special and unjustified exception. It offers two main reasons for declining to apply here our usual deferential approach, as exemplified in *Pickering*, to the regulation of public employee speech. First, the majority says, this case involves a "blanket" policy rather than an individualized employment decision, so *Pickering* is a "painful fit." Second, the majority asserts, the regulation here involves compelling rather than restricting speech, so the pain gets sharper still. . . .

First, this Court has applied the same basic approach whether a public employee challenges a general policy or an individualized decision. . . .

Second, the majority's distinction between compelling and restricting speech also lacks force. The majority posits that compelling speech always works a greater injury, and so always requires a greater justification. . . . But the only case the majority cites for that reading of our precedent is possibly (thankfully) the most exceptional in our First Amendment annals: It involved the state forcing children to swear an oath contrary to their religious beliefs. . . . Regulations challenged as compelling expression do not usually look anything like that—and for that reason, the standard First Amendment rule is that the "difference between compelled speech and compelled silence" is "without constitutional significance." . . . And if anything, the First Amendment scales tip the opposite way when (as here) the government is not compelling actual speech, but instead compelling a subsidy that others will use for expression. See Brief for Eugene Volokh et al. as *Amici Curiae* 4–5 (offering many examples to show that the First Amendment "simply do[es] not guarantee that one's hard-earned dollars will never be spent on speech one disapproves of"). So when a government mandates a speech subsidy from a public employee—here, we might think of it as levying a tax to support collective bargaining—it should get at least as much deference as when it restricts the employee's speech. As this case shows, the former may advance a managerial interest as well as the latter—in which case the government's "freer hand" in dealing with its employees should apply with equal (if not greater) force.

. . .

III

But the worse part of today's opinion is where the majority subverts all known principles of *stare decisis*. The majority makes plain, in the first 33 pages of its decision, that it believes *Abood* was wrong. But even if that were true (which it is not), it is not enough. "Respecting *stare decisis* means sticking to some wrong decisions." Kimble v. Marvel Entertainment, LLC, 576 U.S. ___ (2015). Any departure from settled precedent (so the Court has often stated) demands a "special justification—over and above the belief that the precedent was wrongly decided." Id., at ___ . . .; see, e.g., Arizona v. Rumsey, 467 U.S. 203, 212 (1984). And the majority does not have anything close. To the contrary: all that is "special" in this case—especially the massive reliance interests at stake— demands retaining *Abood*, beyond even the normal precedent.

Consider first why these principles about precedent are so important. *Stare decisis*—"the idea that today's Court should stand by yesterday's decisions"—is "a foundation stone of the rule of law." . . . It "promotes the evenhanded, predictable, and consistent development" of legal doctrine. . . . It fosters respect for and reliance on judicial decisions. And it "contributes to the actual and perceived integrity of the judicial process," by ensuring that decisions are "founded in the law rather than in the proclivities of individuals." . . .

And *Abood* is not just any precedent: It is embedded in the law (not to mention . . . in the world) in a way not many decisions are. Over four decades, this Court has cited *Abood* favorably many times, and has affirmed and applied its central distinction between the costs of collective bargaining (which the government can charge to all employees) and those of political activities (which it cannot). . . .

Ignoring our repeated validation of *Abood*, the majority claims it has become "an outlier among our First Amendment cases." . . . That claim fails most spectacularly for reasons already discussed: *Abood* coheres with the *Pickering* approach to reviewing regulation of public employees' speech. . . . Dicta in . . . recent decisions indeed began the assault on *Abood* that has culminated today. But neither actually addressed the extent to which a public employer may regulate its own employees' speech. Relying on them is bootstrapping—and mocking *stare decisis*. Don't like a decision? Just throw some gratuitous criticisms into a couple of opinions and a few years later point to them as "special justifications."

The majority is likewise wrong to invoke "workability" as a reason for overruling *Abood*. Does *Abood* require drawing a line? Yes, between a union's collective-bargaining activities and its political activities. Is that line perfectly and pristinely "precis[e]," as the majority demands? . . . Well, not quite that—but as exercises of constitutional linedrawing go, *Abood* stands well above average. In the 40 years since *Abood*, this Court has had to resolve only a handful of cases raising questions about the distinction. To my knowledge, the circuit courts are not divided on any classification issue; neither are they issuing distress signals of the kind that sometimes prompt the Court to reverse a decision. And that tranquility is unsurprising: There may be some gray areas (there always are), but in the mine run of cases, everyone knows the difference between politicking and collective bargaining. The majority cites some disagreement in two of the classification cases this Court decided—as if non-unanimity among Justices were something startling. . . . As I wrote in *Harris* a few Terms ago: "If the kind of hand-wringing about blurry lines that the majority offers were enough to justify breaking with precedent, we might have to discard whole volumes of the United States Reports. . . .

And in any event, one *stare decisis* factor—reliance—dominates all others here and demands keeping *Abood*. *Stare decisis*, this Court has held, "has added force when the legislature, in the public sphere, and citizens, in the private realm, have acted in reliance on a previous decision." . . . That is because overruling a decision would then "require an extensive legislative response" or "dislodge settled rights and expectations." . . . Both will happen here: The Court today wreaks havoc on entrenched legislative and contractual arrangements.

Over 20 States have by now enacted statutes authorizing fair-share provisions. To be precise, 22 States, the District of Columbia, and Puerto Rico—plus another two States for police and firefighter unions. Many of those States have multiple statutory provisions, with variations for different categories of public employees. See, e.g., Brief for State of California as Amicus Curiae 24–25. Every one of them will now need to come up with new ways—elaborated in new statutes—to structure relations between government employers and their workers. The majority responds . . . that this is of no proper concern to the Court. But in fact, we have weighed heavily against "abandon[ing] our settled jurisprudence" that "[s]tate legislatures have relied upon" it and would have to "reexamine [and amend] their statutes" if it were overruled. . . .

     . . .

The majority asserts that no one should care much because the canceled agreements are "of rather short duration" . . . and would "expire on their own in a few years' time." . . . But to begin with, that response ignores the substantial time and effort that state legislatures will have to devote to revamping their statutory schemes. And anyway, it misunderstands the nature of contract negotiations when the parties have a continuing relationship. The parties, in renewing an old collective-bargaining agreement, don't start on an empty page. Instead, various "long-settled" terms—like fair-share provisions—are taken as a given. So the majority's ruling does more than advance by a few years a future renegotiation (though even that would be significant). In most cases, it commands new bargaining over how to replace a term that the parties never expected to change. And not just new bargaining; given the interests at stake, complicated and possibly contentious bargaining as well.

The majority, though, offers another reason for not worrying about reliance: . . . Here, the majority proudly lays claim to its 6-year crusade to ban agency fees [and the notice that provided to public-sector unions.] . . .

But that argument reflects a radically wrong understanding of how *stare decisis* operates. Justice Scalia once confronted a similar argument for "disregard[ing] reliance interests" and showed how antithetical it was to rule-of-law principles. Quill Corp. v. North Dakota, 504 U.S. 298, 320 (1992) (concurring opinion). He noted first what we always tell lower courts: "If a precedent of this Court has direct application in a case, yet appears to rest on reasons rejected in some other line of decisions, [they] should follow the case which directly controls, leaving to this Court the prerogative of overruling its own decisions." . . . That instruction, Justice Scalia explained, was "incompatible" with an expectation that "private parties anticipate our overrulings." 504 U.S., at 320. He concluded: "[R]eliance upon a square, unabandoned holding of the Supreme Court is always justifiable reliance." . . . *Abood*'s holding was square. It was unabandoned before today. It was, in other words, the law—however much some were working overtime to make it not. Parties, both unions and governments, were thus justified in relying on it. And they did rely, to an extent rare among our decisions. To dismiss the overthrowing of their settled expectations as entailing no more than some "adjustments" and "unpleasant transition costs," . . . is to trivialize *stare decisis*.

IV

There is no sugarcoating today's opinion. The majority overthrows a decision entrenched in this Nation's law—and in its economic life—for over 40 years. As a result, it prevents the American people, acting through their state and local officials, from making important choices about workplace governance.

And it does so by weaponizing the First Amendment, in a way that unleashes judges, now and in the future, to intervene in economic and regulatory policy.

. . . The majority has overruled *Abood* for no exceptional or special reason, but because it never liked the decision. It has overruled *Abood* because it wanted to.

Because, that is, it wanted to pick the winning side in what should be—and until now, has been—an energetic policy debate. Some state and local governments (and the constituents they serve) think that stable unions promote healthy labor relations and thereby improve the provision of services to the public. Other state and local governments (and their constituents) think, to the contrary, that strong unions impose excessive costs and impair those services. Americans have debated the pros and cons for many decades—in large part, by deciding whether to use fair-share arrangements. Yesterday, 22 States were on one side, 28 on the other (ignoring a couple of in-betweeners). Today, that healthy—that democratic—debate ends. The majority has adjudged who should prevail. Indeed, the majority is bursting with pride over what it has accomplished: Now those 22 States, it crows, "can follow the model of the federal government and 28 other States." . . .

And maybe most alarming, the majority has chosen the winners by turning the First Amendment into a sword, and using it against workaday economic and regulatory policy. Today is not the first time the Court has wielded the First Amendment in such an aggressive way. See, e.g., National Institute of Family and Life Advocates v. Becerra, ___ U.S. ___ (2018) (invalidating a law requiring medical and counseling facilities to provide relevant information to users); Sorrell v. IMS Health Inc., 564 U.S. 552 (2011) (striking down a law that restricted pharmacies from selling various data). And it threatens not to be the last. Speech is everywhere—a part of every human activity (employment, health care, securities trading, you name it). For that reason, almost all economic and regulatory policy affects or touches speech. So the majority's road runs long. And at every stop are black-robed rulers overriding citizens' choices. The First Amendment was meant for better things. It was meant not to undermine but to protect democratic governance—including over the role of public-sector unions.

CHAPTER 17

RELIGION AND THE CONSTITUTION

1. THE ESTABLISHMENT CLAUSE

A. INTRODUCTION

Page 1697. Add after Note, *Denominational Preferences*:

Trump v. Hawaii

585 U.S. ___, 138 S.Ct. 2392, 201 L.Ed.2d 775 (2018).

■ CHIEF JUSTICE ROBERTS delivered the opinion of the Court.

Under the Immigration and Nationality Act, foreign nationals seeking entry into the United States undergo a vetting process to ensure that they satisfy the numerous requirements for admission. The Act also vests the President with authority to restrict the entry of aliens whenever he finds that their entry "would be detrimental to the interests of the United States." 8 U.S.C. § 1182(f). Relying on that delegation, the President concluded that it was necessary to impose entry restrictions on nationals of countries that do not share adequate information for an informed entry determination, or that otherwise present national security risks. Presidential Proclamation No. 9645, 82 Fed. Reg. 45161 (2017) (Proclamation). The plaintiffs . . . challenged the application of those entry restrictions to certain aliens abroad. We now decide whether the President had authority under the Act to issue the Proclamation, and whether the entry policy violates the Establishment Clause of the First Amendment.

I

A

Shortly after taking office, President Trump signed [Executive Order 13769 (EO-1),] direct[ing] the Secretary of Homeland Security to conduct a review to examine the adequacy of information provided by foreign governments about their nationals seeking to enter the United States . . . [and] suspend[ing] for 90 days the entry of foreign nationals from seven countries—Iran, Iraq, Libya, Somalia, Sudan, Syria, and Yemen—that had been previously identified by Congress or prior administrations as posing heightened terrorism risks. . . .

[The order was stayed by lower courts, and] the President revoked EO-1, replacing it with Executive Order No. 13780 [EO-2], which again directed a worldwide review. Citing investigative burdens on agencies and the need to diminish the risk that dangerous individuals would enter without adequate vetting, EO-2 also temporarily restricted [for 90 days] the entry (with case-by-case waivers) of foreign nationals from six of the countries covered by EO-1: Iran, Libya, Somalia, Sudan, Syria, and Yemen. The order explained that those countries had been selected because each "is a state sponsor of terrorism, has been significantly compromised by terrorist organizations, or contains active conflict zones." . . .

. . . District Courts for . . . Maryland and Hawaii entered nationwide preliminary injunctions barring enforcement of the entry suspension, [which] the respective Courts of Appeals upheld . . . . This Court . . . stayed the injunctions—allowing the entry suspension to go into effect—with respect to foreign nationals who lacked a "credible claim of a bona fide relationship" with a person or entity in the United States. Trump v. IRAP, 582 U.S. ___, ___ (2017) (*per curiam*) . . . . The temporary restrictions in EO-2 expired before this Court took any action, and we vacated the lower court decisions as moot. . . .

On September 24, 2017, after completion of the worldwide review, the President issued the Proclamation before us—Proclamation No. 9645, Enhancing Vetting Capabilities and Processes for Detecting Attempted Entry Into the United States by Terrorists or Other Public-Safety Threats. 82 Fed. Reg. 45161. The Proclamation (as its title indicates) sought to improve vetting procedures by identifying ongoing deficiencies in the information needed to assess whether nationals of particular countries present "public safety threats." § 1(a). To further that purpose, the Proclamation placed entry restrictions on the nationals of eight foreign states whose systems for managing and sharing information about their nationals the President deemed inadequate.

The Proclamation described how foreign states were selected for inclusion based on the review undertaken pursuant to EO-2. As part of that review, the Department of Homeland Security (DHS), in consultation with the State Department and several intelligence agencies, developed a "baseline" for the information required from foreign governments to confirm the identity of individuals seeking entry into the United States, and to determine whether those individuals pose a security threat. § 1(c). The baseline included three components. The first, "identity-management information," focused on whether a foreign government ensures the integrity of travel documents by issuing electronic passports, reporting lost or stolen passports, and making available additional identity-related information. Second, the agencies considered the extent to which the country discloses information on criminal history and suspected terrorist links, provides travel document exemplars, and facilitates the U.S. Government's receipt of information about airline passengers and crews traveling to the United States. Finally, the agencies weighed various indicators of national security risk, including whether the foreign state is a known or potential terrorist safe haven and whether it regularly declines to receive returning nationals following final orders of removal from the United States. *Ibid.*

DHS collected and evaluated data regarding all foreign governments. § 1(d). It identified 16 countries as having deficient information-sharing practices and presenting national security concerns, and another 31 countries as "at risk" of similarly failing to meet the baseline. § 1(e). The State Department then undertook diplomatic efforts over a 50-day period to encourage all foreign governments to improve their practices. § 1(f). As a result of that effort, numerous countries provided DHS with travel document exemplars and agreed to share information on known or suspected terrorists. *Ibid.*

Following the 50-day period, the Acting Secretary of Homeland Security concluded that eight countries—Chad, Iran, Iraq, Libya, North Korea, Syria, Venezuela, and Yemen—remained deficient in terms of their risk profile and willingness to provide requested information. The Acting Secretary recommended that the President impose entry restrictions on certain nationals from all of those countries except Iraq. . . . She also concluded that although Somalia generally satisfied the information-sharing component of the baseline standards, its "identity-management deficiencies" and "significant terrorist presence" presented special circumstances justifying additional limitations. She therefore recommended entry limitations for certain nationals of that country. . . . As for Iraq, the Acting Secretary found that entry limitations on its nationals were not warranted given the close cooperative relationship between the U.S. and Iraqi Governments and Iraq's commitment to combating ISIS. . . .

After consulting with multiple Cabinet members and other officials, the President adopted the Acting Secretary's recommendations and issued the Proclamation. Invoking his authority under 8 U.S.C. § 1182(f) and 1185(a), the President determined that certain entry restrictions were necessary to "prevent the entry of those foreign nationals about whom the United States Government lacks sufficient information"; "elicit improved identity-management and information-sharing protocols and practices from foreign governments"; and otherwise "advance [the] foreign policy, national security, and counterterrorism objectives" of the United States. Proclamation § 1(h). The President explained that these restrictions would be the "most likely to encourage cooperation" while "protect[ing] the United States until such time as improvements occur." *Ibid.*

The Proclamation imposed a range of restrictions that vary based on the "distinct circumstances" in each of the eight countries. . . . For countries that do not cooperate with the United States in identifying security risks (Iran, North Korea, and Syria), the Proclamation suspends entry of all nationals, except for Iranians seeking nonimmigrant student and exchange-visitor visas. . . . For countries that have information-sharing deficiencies but are nonetheless "valuable counterterrorism partner[s]" (Chad, Libya, and Yemen), it restricts entry of nationals seeking immigrant visas and nonimmigrant business or tourist visas. . . . Because Somalia generally satisfies the baseline standards but was found to present special risk factors, the Proclamation suspends entry of nationals seeking immigrant visas and requires additional scrutiny of nationals seeking nonimmigrant visas. . . . And for Venezuela, which refuses to cooperate in information sharing but for which alternative means are available to identify its nationals, the Proclamation limits entry only of certain government officials and their family members on nonimmigrant business or tourist visas. . . .

The Proclamation exempts lawful permanent residents and foreign nationals who have been granted asylum. § 3(b). It also provides for case-by-case waivers when a foreign national demonstrates undue hardship, and that his entry is in the national interest and would not pose a threat to public safety. § 3(c)(i); see also § 3(c)(iv) (listing examples of when a waiver might be appropriate, such as if the foreign national seeks to reside with a close family member, obtain urgent medical care, or pursue significant business obligations). The Proclamation further directs DHS to assess on a continuing basis whether entry restrictions should be modified or continued, and to report to the President every 180 days. § 4. Upon completion of the first such review period, the President, on the recommendation of the Secretary of Homeland Security, determined that Chad had sufficiently improved its practices, and he accordingly lifted restrictions on its nationals. Presidential Proclamation No. 9723 . . . (2018).

B

[The State of Hawaii, which operates its University, which in turn "recruits students and faculty from the designated countries," three individual "U.S. citizens or lawful permanent residents who have relatives from Iran, Syria, and Yemen applying for immigrant or nonimmigrant visas," and the Muslim Association of Hawaii, which "operates a mosque in Hawaii," "challenged the Proclamation—except as applied to North Korea and Venezuela" for contravening the Immigration and Nationality Act (INA), and for "violat[ing] the Establishment Clause of the First Amendment, because it was motivated not by concerns pertaining to national security but by animus toward Islam."]

The District Court granted a nationwide preliminary injunction barring enforcement of the entry restrictions [based on violations of the INA. After an intervening stay from the Supreme Court, the Ninth Circuit affirmed the District Court ruling, but "did not reach plaintiffs' Establishment Clause claim."]

. . .

III

. . .

By its plain language, § 1182(f) [which the Court also wrote "exudes deference to the President in every clause"] grants the President broad discretion to suspend the entry of aliens into the United States. The President lawfully exercised that discretion based on his findings—following a worldwide, multiagency review—that entry of the covered aliens would be detrimental to the national interest. And plaintiffs' attempts to identify a conflict with other provisions in the INA, and their appeal to the statute's purposes and legislative history, fail to overcome the clear statutory language.

. . .

We may assume that § 1182(f) does not allow the President to expressly override particular provisions of the INA. But plaintiffs have not identified any conflict between the statute and the Proclamation that would implicitly bar the President from addressing deficiencies in the Nation's vetting system.

. . .

The Proclamation is squarely within the scope of Presidential authority under the INA. Indeed, neither dissent even attempts any serious argument to the contrary, despite the fact that plaintiffs' primary contention below and in their briefing before this Court was that the Proclamation violated the statute.

IV

A

We now turn to plaintiffs' claim that the Proclamation was issued for the unconstitutional purpose of excluding Muslims. . . .

. . .

. . . [T]he individual plaintiffs have Article III standing to challenge the exclusion of their relatives under the Establishment Clause.

B

. . . Our cases recognize that "[t]he clearest command of the Establishment Clause is that one religious denomination cannot be officially preferred over another." Larson v. Valente, 456 U.S. 228, 244 (1982). Plaintiffs believe that the

Proclamation violates this prohibition by singling out Muslims for disfavored treatment. The entry suspension, they contend, operates as a "religious gerrymander," in part because most of the countries covered by the Proclamation have Muslim-majority populations. And in their view, deviations from the information-sharing baseline criteria suggest that the results of the multi-agency review were "foreordained." Relying on Establishment Clause precedents concerning laws and policies applied domestically, plaintiffs allege that the primary purpose of the Proclamation was religious animus and that the President's stated concerns about vetting protocols and national security were but pretexts for discriminating against Muslims. . . .

At the heart of plaintiffs' case is a series of statements by the President and his advisers casting doubt on the official objective of the Proclamation. For example, while a candidate on the campaign trail, the President published a "Statement on Preventing Muslim Immigration" that called for a "total and complete shutdown of Muslims entering the United States until our country's representatives can figure out what is going on." . . . That statement remained on his campaign website until May 2017. . . . Then-candidate Trump also stated that "Islam hates us" and asserted that the United States was "having problems with Muslims coming into the country." . . . Shortly after being elected, when asked whether violence in Europe had affected his plans to "ban Muslim immigration," the President replied, "You know my plans. All along, I've been proven to be right." . . .

One week after his inauguration, the President issued EO-1. In a television interview, one of the President's campaign advisers explained that when the President "first announced it, he said, 'Muslim ban.' He called me up. He said, 'Put a commission together. Show me the right way to do it legally.' " . . . The adviser said he assembled a group of Members of Congress and lawyers that "focused on, instead of religion, danger. . . . [The order] is based on places where there [is] substantial evidence that people are sending terrorists into our country." . . .

Plaintiffs also note that after issuing EO-2 to replace EO-1, the President expressed regret that his prior order had been "watered down" and called for a "much tougher version" of his "Travel Ban." Shortly before the release of the Proclamation, he stated that the "travel ban . . . should be far larger, tougher, and more specific," but "stupidly that would not be politically correct." . . . More recently, on November 29, 2017, the President retweeted links to three anti-Muslim propaganda videos. In response to questions about those videos, the President's deputy press secretary denied that the President thinks Muslims are a threat to the United States, explaining that "the President has been talking about these security issues for years now, from the campaign trail to the White House" and "has addressed these issues with the travel order that he issued earlier this year and the companion proclamation." . . .

The President of the United States possesses an extraordinary power to speak to his fellow citizens and on their behalf. Our Presidents have frequently used that power to espouse the principles of religious freedom and tolerance on which this Nation was founded. In 1790 George Washington reassured the Hebrew Congregation of Newport, Rhode Island that "happily the Government of the United States . . . gives to bigotry no sanction, to persecution no assistance [and] requires only that they who live under its protection should demean themselves as good citizens." . . . President Eisenhower, at the opening of the

Islamic Center of Washington, similarly pledged to a Muslim audience that "America would fight with her whole strength for your right to have here your own church," declaring that "[t]his concept is indeed a part of America." . . . And just days after the attacks of September 11, 2001, President George W. Bush returned to the same Islamic Center to implore his fellow Americans—Muslims and non-Muslims alike—to remember during their time of grief that "[t]he face of terror is not the true faith of Islam," and that America is "a great country because we share the same values of respect and dignity and human worth." . . . Yet it cannot be denied that the Federal Government and the Presidents who have carried its laws into effect have—from the Nation's earliest days—performed unevenly in living up to those inspiring words.

Plaintiffs argue that this President's words strike at fundamental standards of respect and tolerance, in violation of our constitutional tradition. But the issue before us is not whether to denounce the statements. It is instead the significance of those statements in reviewing a Presidential directive, neutral on its face, addressing a matter within the core of executive responsibility. In doing so, we must consider not only the statements of a particular President, but also the authority of the Presidency itself.

The case before us differs in numerous respects from the conventional Establishment Clause claim. Unlike the typical suit involving religious displays or school prayer, plaintiffs seek to invalidate a national security directive regulating the entry of aliens abroad. Their claim accordingly raises a number of delicate issues regarding the scope of the constitutional right and the manner of proof. The Proclamation, moreover, is facially neutral toward religion. Plaintiffs therefore ask the Court to probe the sincerity of the stated justifications for the policy by reference to extrinsic statements—many of which were made before the President took the oath of office. These various aspects of plaintiffs' challenge inform our standard of review.

C

For more than a century, this Court has recognized that the admission and exclusion of foreign nationals is a "fundamental sovereign attribute exercised by the Government's political departments largely immune from judicial control." Fiallo v. Bell, 430 U.S. 787, 792 (1977) . . . . Because decisions in these matters may implicate "relations with foreign powers," or involve "classifications defined in the light of changing political and economic circumstances," such judgments "are frequently of a character more appropriate to either the Legislature or the Executive." Mathews v. Diaz, 426 U.S. 67, 81 (1976).

Nonetheless, although foreign nationals seeking admission have no constitutional right to entry, this Court has engaged in a circumscribed judicial inquiry when the denial of a visa allegedly burdens the constitutional rights of a U.S. citizen. In Kleindienst v. Mandel, the Attorney General denied admission to a Belgian journalist and self-described "revolutionary Marxist," . . . who had been invited to speak at a conference at Stanford University. . . . The professors who wished to hear Mandel speak challenged that decision under the First Amendment, and we acknowledged that their constitutional "right to receive information" was implicated. . . . But we limited our review to whether the Executive gave a "facially legitimate and bona fide" reason for its action. . . . Given the authority of the political branches over admission, we held that "when the Executive exercises this [delegated] power negatively on the basis of a facially legitimate and bona fide reason, the courts will neither look behind the exercise of that discretion, nor test it by balancing its justification" against the asserted constitutional interests of U.S. citizens. . . .

The principal dissent suggests that *Mandel* has no bearing on this case (opinion of Sotomayor, J.) . . ., but our opinions have reaffirmed and applied its deferential standard of review across different contexts and constitutional claims. . . .

Mandel's narrow standard of review "has particular force" in admission and immigration cases that overlap with "the area of national security." *Din*, 576 U.S., at ___ (Kennedy, J., concurring in judgment) . . . For one, "[j]udicial inquiry into the national-security realm raises concerns for the separation of powers" by intruding on the President's constitutional responsibilities in the area of foreign affairs. Ziglar v. Abbasi, 582 U.S. ___, ___ (2017) . . . . For another, "when it comes to collecting evidence and drawing inferences" on questions of national security, "the lack of competence on the part of the courts is marked." *Humanitarian Law Project*, 561 U.S., at 34.

The upshot of our cases in this context is clear: "Any rule of constitutional law that would inhibit the flexibility" of the President "to respond to changing world conditions should be adopted only with the greatest caution," and our inquiry into matters of entry and national security is highly constrained. *Mathews*, ... We need not define the precise contours of that inquiry in this case. A conventional application of *Mandel*, asking only whether the policy is facially legitimate and bona fide, would put an end to our review. But the Government has suggested that it may be appropriate here for the inquiry to extend beyond the facial neutrality of the order. . . . For our purposes today, we assume that we may look behind the face of the Proclamation to the extent of applying rational basis review. That standard of review considers whether the entry policy is plausibly related to the Government's stated objective to protect the country and improve vetting processes. See Railroad Retirement Bd. v. Fritz, 449 U.S. 166, 179 (1980). As a result, we may consider plaintiffs' extrinsic evidence, but will uphold the policy so long as it can reasonably be understood to result from a justification independent of unconstitutional grounds.[5]

D

Given the standard of review, it should come as no surprise that the Court hardly ever strikes down a policy as illegitimate under rational basis scrutiny. On the few occasions where we have done so, a common thread has been that the laws at issue lack any purpose other than a "bare . . . desire to harm a politically unpopular group." Department of Agriculture v. Moreno, 413 U.S. 528, 534 (1973)[; . . .] Cleburne v. Cleburne Living Center, Inc.[; . . .] Romer v. Evans . . . .

The Proclamation does not fit this pattern. It cannot be said that it is impossible to "discern a relationship to legitimate state interests" or that the policy is "inexplicable by anything but animus." . . . [B]ecause there is persuasive evidence that the entry suspension has a legitimate grounding in national

---

[5] The dissent finds "perplexing" the application of rational basis review in this context. But what is far more problematic is the dissent's assumption that courts should review immigration policies, diplomatic sanctions, and military actions under the *de novo* "reasonable observer" inquiry applicable to cases involving holiday displays and graduation ceremonies. . . . [A] circumscribed inquiry applies to any constitutional claim concerning the entry of foreign nationals. . . . The dissent can cite no authority for its proposition that the more free-ranging inquiry it proposes is appropriate in the national security and foreign affairs context.

security concerns, quite apart from any religious hostility, we must accept that independent justification.

The Proclamation is expressly premised on legitimate purposes: preventing entry of nationals who cannot be adequately vetted and inducing other nations to improve their practices. The text says nothing about religion. Plaintiffs and the dissent nonetheless emphasize that five of the seven nations currently included in the Proclamation have Muslim-majority populations. Yet that fact alone does not support an inference of religious hostility, given that the policy covers just 8% of the world's Muslim population and is limited to countries that were previously designated by Congress or prior administrations as posing national security risks. . . .

The Proclamation, moreover, reflects the results of a worldwide review process undertaken by multiple Cabinet officials and their agencies. Plaintiffs . . . point[ ] to deviations from the review's baseline criteria resulting in the inclusion of Somalia and omission of Iraq. But . . . Somalia . . . "stands apart . . . in the degree to which [it] lacks command and control of its territory." Proclamation § 2(h)(i). As for Iraq, the Secretary of Homeland Security determined that entry restrictions were not warranted in light of the close cooperative relationship between the U.S. and Iraqi Governments and the country's key role in combating terrorism in the region. § 1(g). It is, in any event, difficult to see how exempting one of the largest predominantly Muslim countries in the region from coverage under the Proclamation can be cited as evidence of animus toward Muslims.

> . . .

More fundamentally, plaintiffs and the dissent challenge the entry suspension based on their perception of its effectiveness and wisdom. They suggest that the policy is overbroad and does little to serve national security interests. But we cannot substitute our own assessment for the Executive's predictive judgments on such matters . . . .

Three additional features of the entry policy support the Government's claim of a legitimate national security interest. First, since the President introduced entry restrictions in January 2017, three Muslim-majority countries—Iraq, Sudan, and Chad—have been removed from the list of covered countries. . . .

Second, for those countries that remain subject to entry restrictions, the Proclamation includes significant exceptions for various categories of foreign nationals. . . . The[ ] carveouts for nonimmigrant visas are substantial: Over the last three fiscal years—before the Proclamation was in effect—the majority of visas issued to nationals from the covered countries were nonimmigrant visas. . . . The Proclamation also exempts permanent residents and individuals who have been granted asylum. . . .

Third, the Proclamation creates a waiver program open to all covered foreign nationals seeking entry as immigrants or nonimmigrants. . . .[7]

Finally, the dissent invokes Korematsu v. United States, 323 U.S. 214 (1944). . . . *Korematsu* has nothing to do with this case. The forcible relocation of

---

[7]   . . . Justice Breyer suggests that not enough individuals are receiving waivers or exemptions. Yet even if such an inquiry were appropriate under rational basis review, the evidence he cites provides "but a piece of the picture" and does not affect our analysis.

U. S. citizens to concentration camps, solely and explicitly on the basis of race, is objectively unlawful and outside the scope of Presidential authority. But it is wholly inapt to liken that morally repugnant order to a facially neutral policy denying certain foreign nationals the privilege of admission. The entry suspension is an act that is well within executive authority and could have been taken by any other President—the only question is evaluating the actions of this particular President in promulgating an otherwise valid Proclamation.

The dissent's reference to *Korematsu*, however, affords this Court the opportunity to make express what is already obvious: *Korematsu* was gravely wrong the day it was decided, has been overruled in the court of history, and—to be clear—"has no place in law under the Constitution." 323 U.S., at 248 (Jackson, J., dissenting).

* * *

Under these circumstances, the Government has set forth a sufficient national security justification to survive rational basis review. We express no view on the soundness of the policy. We simply hold today that plaintiffs have not demonstrated a likelihood of success on the merits of their constitutional claim.

V

. . . [W]e reverse the grant of the preliminary injunction as an abuse of discretion. . . . The case now returns to the lower courts for such further proceedings as may be appropriate. . . .

. . .

■ JUSTICE KENNEDY, concurring.

I join the Court's opinion in full.

There may be some common ground between the opinions in this case, in that the Court does acknowledge that in some instances, governmental action may be subject to judicial review to determine whether or not it is "inexplicable by anything but animus," Romer v. Evans, 517 U.S. 620, 632 (1996), which in this case would be animosity to a religion. Whether judicial proceedings may properly continue in this case, in light of the substantial deference that is and must be accorded to the Executive in the conduct of foreign affairs, and in light of today's decision, is a matter to be addressed in the first instance on remand. And even if further proceedings are permitted, it would be necessary to determine that any discovery and other preliminary matters would not themselves intrude on the foreign affairs power of the Executive.

. . . There are numerous instances in which the statements and actions of Government officials are not subject to judicial scrutiny or intervention. That does not mean those officials are free to disregard the Constitution and the rights it proclaims and protects. . . . [T]he very fact that an official may have broad discretion, discretion free from judicial scrutiny, makes it all the more imperative for him or her to adhere to the Constitution and to its meaning and its promise.

The First Amendment prohibits the establishment of religion and promises the free exercise of religion. . . . It is an urgent necessity that officials adhere to these constitutional guarantees and mandates in all their actions, even in the sphere of foreign affairs. . . .

■ THOMAS, J., concurring.

I join the Court's opinion, which highlights just a few of the many problems with the plaintiffs' claims. There are several more. Section 1182(f) does not set forth any judicially enforceable limits that constrain the President. . . . Nor could it, since the President has *inherent* authority to exclude aliens from the country. . . . Further, the Establishment Clause does not create an individual right to be free from all laws that a "reasonable observer" views as religious or antireligious. See Town of Greece v. Galloway, 572 U.S. ___, ___ (2014) (Thomas, J., concurring in part and concurring in judgment) . . . . The plaintiffs cannot raise any other First Amendment claim, since the alleged religious discrimination in this case was directed at aliens abroad. . . . And, even on its own terms, the plaintiffs' proffered evidence of anti-Muslim discrimination is unpersuasive.

Merits aside, I write separately to address the ["universal" or "nationwide" injunction the District Court imposed] . . . that barred the Government from enforcing the President's Proclamation against anyone, not just the plaintiffs. . . .

I am skeptical that district courts have the authority to enter universal injunctions. . . .

. . .

■ JUSTICE BREYER, with whom JUSTICE KAGAN joins, dissenting.

. . . Members of the Court principally disagree . . . about whether or the extent to which religious animus played a significant role in the Proclamation's promulgation or content.

In my view, the Proclamation's elaborate system of exemptions and waivers can and should help us answer this question. . . .

On the one hand, if the Government is applying the exemption and waiver provisions as written, then its argument for the Proclamation's lawfulness is strengthened. For one thing, the Proclamation then resembles more closely the two important Presidential precedents on point, President Carter's Iran order and President Reagan's Cuba proclamation, both of which contained similar categories of persons authorized to obtain case-by-case exemptions. . . . For another thing, the Proclamation then follows more closely the basic statutory scheme, which provides for strict case-by-case scrutiny of applications. It would deviate from that system, not across the board, but where circumstances may require that deviation.

Further, since the case-by-case exemptions and waivers apply without regard to the individual's religion, application of that system would help make clear that the Proclamation does not deny visas to numerous Muslim individuals (from those countries) who do not pose a security threat. And that fact would help to rebut the First Amendment claim that the Proclamation rests upon anti-Muslim bias rather than security need. Finally, of course, the very fact that Muslims from those countries would enter the United States (under Proclamation-provided exemptions and waivers) would help to show the same thing.

On the other hand, if the Government is *not* applying the system of exemptions and waivers that the Proclamation contains, then its argument for the Proclamation's lawfulness becomes significantly weaker. . . .

. . .

. . . [I]f the Government is not applying the Proclamation's exemption and waiver system, the claim that the Proclamation is a "Muslim ban," rather than a "security-based" ban, becomes much stronger. How could the Government successfully claim that the Proclamation rests on security needs if it is excluding Muslims who satisfy the Proclamation's own terms? At the same time, denying visas to Muslims who meet the Proclamation's own security terms would support the view that the Government excludes them for reasons based upon their religion.

Unfortunately there is evidence that supports the second possibility, *i.e.*, that the Government is not applying the Proclamation as written. The Proclamation provides that the Secretary of State and the Secretary of Homeland Security "shall coordinate to adopt guidance" for consular officers to follow when deciding whether to grant a waiver. . . . Yet, to my knowledge, no guidance has issued . . . for consular officers as to how they are to exercise their discretion. . . .

An examination of publicly available statistics also provides cause for concern. The State Department reported that during the Proclamation's first month, two waivers were approved out of 6,555 eligible applicants. . . . [T]he Government claims that number increased from 2 to 430 during the first four months of implementation. . . . That number, . . . however, when compared with the number of pre-Proclamation visitors, accounts for a miniscule percentage of those likely eligible for visas, in such categories as persons requiring medical treatment, academic visitors, students, family members, and others belonging to groups that, when considered as a group (rather than case by case), would not seem to pose security threats.

Amici have suggested that there are numerous applicants who could meet the waiver criteria[, such as 2100 scholars.] . . . [Separately, t]he Pars Equality Center identified 1,000 individuals—including parents and children of U.S. citizens—who sought and were denied entry under the Proclamation['s close family member waiver opportunity], hundreds of whom seem to meet the waiver criteria. . . .

Other data suggest the same. The Proclamation does not apply to asylum seekers or refugees. . . . Yet few refugees have been admitted since the Proclamation took effect. While more than 15,000 Syrian refugees arrived in the United States in 2016, only 13 have arrived since January 2018. . . . Similarly few refugees have been admitted since January from Iran (3), Libya (1), Yemen (0), and Somalia (122).

. . .

. . . [O]nly 258 student visas were issued to applicants from Iran (189), Libya (29), Yemen (40), and Somalia (0) in the first three months of 2018. . . . This is less than a quarter of the volume needed to be on track for 2016 student visa levels. And only 40 nonimmigrant visas have been issued to Somali nationals, a decrease of 65 percent from 2016. . . . While this is but a piece of the picture, it does not provide grounds for confidence.

. . .

[I]n a pending case in the Eastern District of New York, a consular official has filed a sworn affidavit asserting that he and other officials do not, in fact, have discretion to grant waivers. . . .

Declarations, anecdotal evidence, facts, and numbers taken from *amicus* briefs are not judicial factfindings. The Government has not had an opportunity to respond, and a court has not had an opportunity to decide. But, given the importance of the decision in this case, the need for assurance that the Proclamation does not rest upon a "Muslim ban," and the assistance in deciding the issue that answers to the "exemption and waiver" questions may provide, I would send this case back to the District Court for further proceedings. And, I would leave the injunction in effect while the matter is litigated. Regardless, the Court's decision today leaves the District Court free to explore these issues on remand.

If this Court must decide the question without this further litigation, I would, on balance, find the evidence of antireligious bias, including statements on a website taken down only after the President issued the two executive orders preceding the Proclamation, along with the other statements also set forth in Justice Sotomayor's opinion, a sufficient basis to set the Proclamation aside. And for these reasons, I respectfully dissent.

■ JUSTICE SOTOMAYOR, with whom JUSTICE GINSBURG joins, dissenting.

. . . The Court's decision today . . . leaves undisturbed a policy first advertised openly and unequivocally as a "total and complete shutdown of Muslims entering the United States" because the policy now masquerades behind a façade of national-security concerns. But this repackaging does little to cleanse Presidential Proclamation No. 9645 of the appearance of discrimination that the President's words have created. Based on the evidence in the record, a reasonable observer would conclude that the Proclamation was motivated by anti-Muslim animus. That alone suffices to show that plaintiffs are likely to succeed on the merits of their Establishment Clause claim. . . .

I

. . . Whatever the merits of plaintiffs' complex statutory claims, the Proclamation . . . runs afoul of the Establishment Clause's guarantee of religious neutrality.

A

. . . The "clearest command" of the Establishment Clause is that the Government cannot favor or disfavor one religion over another. . . . Consistent with that clear command, this Court has long acknowledged that governmental actions that favor one religion "inevitabl[y]" foster "the hatred, disrespect and even contempt of those who [hold] contrary beliefs." Engel v. Vitale, 370 U.S. 421, 431 (1962). That is so, this Court has held, because such acts send messages to members of minority faiths " 'that they are outsiders, not full members of the political community.' " Santa Fe Independent School Dist. v. Doe, 530 U.S. 290, 309 (2000). To guard against this serious harm, the Framers mandated a strict "principle of denominational neutrality." *Larson*, ...

"When the government acts with the ostensible and predominant purpose" of disfavoring a particular religion, "it violates that central Establishment Clause value of official religious neutrality, there being no neutrality when the government's ostensible object is to take sides." McCreary County v. American Civil Liberties Union of Ky., 545 U.S. 844, 860 (2005). To determine whether plaintiffs have proved an Establishment Clause violation, the Court asks whether a reasonable observer would view the government action as enacted for the purpose of disfavoring a religion. See *id.*, at 862, 866; accord, Town of Greece v. Galloway, 572 U.S. ___, ___ (2014) (plurality opinion) . . . .

In answering that question, this Court has generally considered the text of the government policy, its operation, and any available evidence regarding "the historical background of the decision under challenge, the specific series of events leading to the enactment or official policy in question, and the legislative or administrative history, including contemporaneous statements made by" the decisionmaker. . . . At the same time, however, courts must take care not to engage in "any judicial psychoanalysis of a drafter's heart of hearts." . . .

B

1

. . . The full record paints a . . . harrowing picture, from which a reasonable observer would readily conclude that the Proclamation was motivated by hostility and animus toward the Muslim faith.

. . . [President Trump's campaign] statement, which remained on his campaign website until May 2017 (several months into his Presidency), read in full:

> "Donald J. Trump is calling for a total and complete shutdown of Muslims entering the United States until our country's representatives can figure out what is going on. According to Pew Research, among others, there is great hatred towards Americans by large segments of the Muslim population. Most recently, a poll from the Center for Security Policy released data showing '25% of those polled agreed that violence against Americans here in the United States is justified as a part of the global jihad' and 51% of those polled 'agreed that Muslims in America should have the choice of being governed according to Shariah.' Shariah authorizes such atrocities as murder against nonbelievers who won't convert, beheadings and more unthinkable acts that pose great harm to Americans, especially women.

> "Mr. Trum[p] stated, 'Without looking at the various polling data, it is obvious to anybody the hatred is beyond comprehension. Where this hatred comes from and why we will have to determine. Until we are able to determine and understand this problem and the dangerous threat it poses, our country cannot be the victims of the horrendous attacks by people that believe only in Jihad, and have no sense of reason or respect of human life. If I win the election for President, we are going to Make America Great Again.'—Donald J. Trump." . . .

On December 8, 2015, Trump justified his proposal during a television interview by noting that President Franklin D. Roosevelt "did the same thing" with respect to the internment of Japanese Americans during World War II. . . . In January 2016, during a Republican primary debate, Trump was asked whether he wanted to "rethink [his] position" on "banning Muslims from entering the country." . . . He answered, "No." . . . A month later, at a rally in South Carolina, Trump told an apocryphal story about United States General John J. Pershing killing a large group of Muslim insurgents in the Philippines with bullets dipped in pigs' blood in the early 1900's. . . . In March 2016, he expressed his belief that "Islam hates us. . . . [W]e can't allow people coming into this country who have this hatred of the United States . . . [a]nd of people that are not Muslim." . . . That same month, Trump asserted that "[w]e're having problems with the Muslims, and we're having problems with Muslims coming into the country." . . . He therefore called for surveillance of mosques in the United States, blaming terrorist attacks on Muslims' lack of "assimilation" and their commitment to "sharia law." . . . A day later, he opined that Muslims "do not respect us at all" and "don't respect a lot of the things that are happening throughout not only our country, but they don't respect other things." . . .

As Trump's presidential campaign progressed, he began to describe his policy proposal in slightly different terms. . . . Asked in July 2016 whether he was "pull[ing] back from" his pledged Muslim ban, Trump responded, "I actually don't think it's a rollback. In fact, you could say it's an expansion." . . . He then explained that he used different terminology because "[p]eople were so upset when [he] used the word Muslim." . . .

. . .

[The day he signed EO-1,] President Trump explained to the media that, under EO-1, Christians would be given priority for entry as refugees into the United States. In particular, he bemoaned the fact that in the past, "[i]f you were a Muslim [refugee from Syria] you could come in, but if you were a Christian, it was almost impossible." . . . Considering that past policy "very unfair," President Trump explained that EO-1 was designed "to help" the Christians in Syria. . . . The following day, one of President Trump's key advisers candidly drew the connection between EO-1 and the "Muslim ban" that the President had pledged to implement if elected. . . . According to that adviser, "[W]hen [Donald Trump] first announced it, he said, 'Muslim ban.' He called me up. He said, 'Put a commission together. Show me the right way to do it legally.' " . . .

. . .

While litigation over EO-2 was ongoing, President Trump repeatedly made statements alluding to a desire to keep Muslims out of the country. . . . During a rally in April 2017, President Trump recited the lyrics to a song called "The Snake," a song about a woman who nurses a sick snake back to health but then is attacked by the snake, as a warning about Syrian refugees entering the country. . . . And in June 2017, the President stated on Twitter that the Justice Department had submitted a "watered down, politically correct version" of the "original Travel Ban" "to S[upreme] C[ourt]." . . . . The President went on to tweet: "People, the lawyers and the courts can call it whatever they want, but I am calling it what we need and what it is, a TRAVEL BAN!" . . . He added: "That's right, we need a TRAVEL BAN for certain DANGEROUS countries, not some politically correct term that won't help us protect our people!" . . . Then, on August 17, 2017, President Trump issued yet another tweet about Islam, once more referencing the story about General Pershing's massacre of Muslims in the Philippines: "Study what General Pershing . . . did to terrorists when caught. There was no more Radical Islamic Terror for 35 years!" . . .

In September 2017, President Trump tweeted that "[t]he travel ban into the United States should be far larger, tougher and more specific—but stupidly, that would not be politically correct!" . . . Later that month, on September 24, 2017, President Trump issued Presidential Proclamation No. 9645 . . . . On November 29, 2017, President Trump "retweeted" three anti-Muslim videos, entitled "Muslim Destroys a Statue of Virgin Mary!", "Islamist mob pushes teenage boy off roof and beats him to death!", and "Muslim migrant beats up Dutch boy on crutches!" . . .

<h3 align="center">2</h3>

As the majority correctly notes, "the issue before us is not whether to denounce" these offensive statements. Rather, the dispositive and narrow question here is whether a reasonable observer, presented with all "openly available data," the text and "historical context" of the Proclamation, and the "specific sequence of events" leading to it, would conclude that the primary purpose of the Proclamation is to disfavor Islam and its adherents by excluding them from the country. See *McCreary*, ... The answer is unquestionably yes.

. . .

. . . Given President Trump's failure to correct the reasonable perception of his apparent hostility toward the Islamic faith, it is unsurprising that the President's lawyers have, at every step in the lower courts, failed in their attempts to launder the Proclamation of its discriminatory taint. . . . Notably, the Court recently found less pervasive official expressions of hostility and the failure to disavow them to be constitutionally significant. Cf. Masterpiece Cakeshop, Ltd. v. Colorado Civil Rights Comm'n, 584 U.S. ___, ___ (2018) . . . . It should find the same here.

Ultimately, what began as a policy explicitly "calling for a total and complete shutdown of Muslims entering the United States" has since morphed into a "Proclamation" putatively based on national-security concerns. But this new window dressing cannot conceal an unassailable fact: the words of the President and his advisers create the strong perception that the Proclamation is contaminated by impermissible discriminatory animus against Islam and its followers.

<h3 align="center">II</h3>

. . . [T]he Government urges this Court to . . . defer to the President on issues related to immigration and national security. The majority accepts that invitation and incorrectly applies a watered-down legal standard in an effort to short circuit plaintiffs' Establishment Clause claim.

. . . The extent to which *Mandel* and *Din* apply at all to this case is unsettled, and there is good reason to think they do not.[5] Indeed, even the Government agreed at oral argument that where the Court confronts a situation involving "all kinds of denigrating comments about" a particular religion and a subsequent policy that is designed with the purpose of disfavoring that religion but that

---

[5] *Mandel* and *Din* are readily distinguishable from this case for a number of reasons. First, *Mandel* and *Din* each involved a constitutional challenge to an Executive Branch decision to exclude a single foreign national under a specific statutory ground of inadmissibility. . . . Here, by contrast, President Trump . . . promulgated an executive order affecting millions of individuals on a categorical basis. Second, *Mandel* and *Din* did not purport to establish the framework for adjudicating cases (like this one) involving claims that the Executive Branch violated the Establishment Clause by acting pursuant to an unconstitutional purpose. Applying *Mandel*'s narrow standard of review to such a claim would run contrary to this Court's repeated admonition that "[f]acial neutrality is not determinative" in the Establishment Clause context. . . . Likewise, the majority's passing invocation of Fiallo v. Bell, 430 U.S. 787 (1977), is misplaced. *Fiallo*, unlike this case, addressed a constitutional challenge to a statute enacted by Congress, not an order of the President. . . . Finally, even assuming that *Mandel* and *Din* apply here, they would not preclude us from looking behind the face of the Proclamation because plaintiffs have made "an affirmative showing of bad faith," *Din*, . . . by the President who, among other things, instructed his subordinates to find a "lega[l]" way to enact a Muslim ban . . . .

"dot[s] all the i's and . . . cross[es] all the t's," *Mandel* would not "pu[t] an end to judicial review of that set of facts." . . .

. . . [T]he Court, without explanation or precedential support, limits its review of the Proclamation to rational-basis scrutiny. . . . That approach is perplexing, given that in other Establishment Clause cases, including those involving claims of religious animus or discrimination, this Court has applied a more stringent standard of review. . . . As explained above, the Proclamation is plainly unconstitutional under that heightened standard.

But even under rational-basis review, the Proclamation must fall . . . because the Proclamation is " 'divorced from any factual context from which we could discern a relationship to legitimate state interests,' and 'its sheer breadth [is] so discontinuous with the reasons offered for it' " that the policy is " 'inexplicable by anything but animus.' " . . . The President's statements, which the majority utterly fails to address in its legal analysis, strongly support the conclusion that the Proclamation was issued to express hostility toward Muslims and exclude them from the country. Given the overwhelming record evidence of anti-Muslim animus, it simply cannot be said that the Proclamation has a legitimate basis. . . .

. . . [E]ven a cursory review of the Government's asserted national-security rationale reveals that the Proclamation is nothing more than a " 'religious gerrymander.' " *Lukumi* . . . .

. . . [T]he Proclamation, just like its predecessors, overwhelmingly targets Muslim-majority nations. . . . [T]he inclusion of North Korea and Venezuela, and the removal of other countries, simply reflect subtle efforts to start "talking territory instead of Muslim," . . . precisely so the Executive Branch could evade criticism or legal consequences for the Proclamation's otherwise clear targeting of Muslims. The Proclamation's effect on North Korea and Venezuela, for example, is insubstantial, if not entirely symbolic. A prior sanctions order already restricts entry of North Korean nationals, . . . and the Proclamation targets only a handful of Venezuelan government officials and their immediate family members . . . . As such, the President's inclusion of North Korea and Venezuela does little to mitigate the anti-Muslim animus that permeates the Proclamation.

. . .

. . . [T]he worldwide review does little to break the clear connection between the Proclamation and the President's anti-Muslim statements. . . .

[T]he majority empowers the President to hide behind an administrative review process that the Government refuses to disclose to the public. . . . Furthermore, evidence of which we can take judicial notice indicates that the multiagency review process could not have been very thorough. . . . [T]he September 2017 report the Government produced after its review process was a mere 17 pages. . . . That the Government's analysis of the vetting practices of hundreds of countries boiled down to such a short document raises serious questions about the legitimacy of the President's proclaimed national-security rationale.

Beyond that, Congress has already addressed the national-security concerns supposedly undergirding the Proclamation through an "extensive and complex" framework governing "immigration and alien status." . . .

. . .

Put simply, Congress has already erected a statutory scheme that fulfills the putative national-security interests the Government now puts forth to justify the Proclamation. Tellingly, the Government remains wholly unable to articulate any credible national-security interest that would go unaddressed by the current statutory scheme absent the Proclamation. . . .

For many of these reasons, several former national-security officials from both political parties . . . have advised that the Proclamation and its predecessor orders "do not advance the national-security or foreign policy interests of the United States, and in fact do serious harm to those interests." . . . .

. . . In addition, the Proclamation permits certain nationals from the countries named in the Proclamation to obtain nonimmigrant visas, which undermines the Government's assertion that it does not already have the capacity and sufficient information to vet these individuals adequately. . . .

Equally unavailing is the majority's reliance on the Proclamation's waiver program[, as] there is reason to suspect that the Proclamation's waiver program is nothing more than a sham. . . . The remote possibility of obtaining a waiver pursuant to an ad hoc, discretionary, and seemingly arbitrary process scarcely demonstrates that the Proclamation is rooted in a genuine concern for national security. See (Breyer, J., dissenting) (outlining evidence suggesting "that the Government is not applying the Proclamation as written," that "waivers are not being processed in an ordinary way," and that consular and other officials "do not, in fact, have discretion to grant waivers").

In sum, none of the features of the Proclamation highlighted by the majority supports the Government's claim that the Proclamation is genuinely and primarily rooted in a legitimate national-security interest. What the unrebutted evidence actually shows is that a reasonable observer would conclude, quite easily, that the primary purpose and function of the Proclamation is to disfavor Islam by banning Muslims from entering our country.

III

As the foregoing analysis makes clear, plaintiffs are likely to succeed on the merits of their Establishment Clause claim. . . .

. . .

IV

The First Amendment stands as a bulwark against official religious prejudice and embodies our Nation's deep commitment to religious plurality and tolerance. . . . Instead of vindicating those principles, today's decision tosses them aside. . . .

. . .

Today's holding is all the more troubling given the stark parallels between the reasoning of this case and that of Korematsu v. United States, 323 U.S. 214 (1944). . . . As here, the Government invoked an ill-defined national-security threat to justify an exclusionary policy of sweeping proportion. . . . As here, the exclusion order was rooted in dangerous stereotypes about, *inter alia*, a particular group's supposed inability to assimilate and desire to harm the United States. . . . As here, the Government was unwilling to reveal its own intelligence agencies' views of the alleged security concerns to the very citizens it purported to protect. . . . And as here, there was strong evidence that impermissible hostility and animus motivated the Government's policy.

> . . .

In the intervening years since *Korematsu*, our Nation has done much to leave its sordid legacy behind. . . . Today, the Court takes the important step of finally overruling *Korematsu*, denouncing it as "gravely wrong the day it was decided." . . . This formal repudiation of a shameful precedent is laudable and long overdue. But it does not make the majority's decision here acceptable or right. By blindly accepting the Government's misguided invitation to sanction a discriminatory policy motivated by animosity toward a disfavored group, all in the name of a superficial claim of national security, the Court redeploys the same dangerous logic underlying *Korematsu* and merely replaces one "gravely wrong" decision with another.

. . . [W]ith profound regret, I dissent.

B. GOVERNMENT RELIGIOUS EXERCISES, CEREMONIES, DISPLAYS, AND PRACTICES

2. RELIGIOUS SPEECH AND DISPLAYS ON PUBLIC PROPERTY

Pages 1720–27. Delete Van Orden v. Perry.

Page 1738. Add after Town of Greece v. Galloway:

American Legion v. American Humanist Assn.
588 U.S. ___, 139 S.Ct. 2067, 204 L.Ed.2d 452 (2019).

■ JUSTICE ALITO announced the judgment of the Court and delivered the opinion of the Court with respect to Parts I, II-B, II-C, III, and IV, and an opinion with respect to Parts II-A and II-D, in which THE CHIEF JUSTICE, JUSTICE BREYER, and JUSTICE KAVANAUGH join.

Since 1925, the Bladensburg Peace Cross (Cross) has stood as a tribute to 49 area soldiers who gave their lives in the First World War. Eighty-nine years after the dedication of the Cross, respondents filed this lawsuit, claiming that they are offended by the sight of the memorial on public land and that its presence there and the expenditure of public funds to maintain it violate the Establishment Clause of the First Amendment. To remedy this violation, they asked a federal court to order the relocation or demolition of the Cross or at least the removal of its arms. The . . . Fourth Circuit agreed that the memorial is unconstitutional and remanded for a determination of the proper remedy. We now reverse.

Although the cross has long been a preeminent Christian symbol, its use in the Bladensburg memorial has a special significance. After the First World War, the picture of row after row of plain white crosses marking the overseas graves of soldiers who had lost their lives in that horrible conflict was emblazoned on the minds of Americans at home, and the adoption of the cross as the Bladensburg memorial must be viewed in that historical context. For nearly a century, the Bladensburg Cross has expressed the community's grief at the loss of the young men who perished, its thanks for their sacrifice, and its dedication to the ideals for which they fought. It has become a prominent community landmark, and its removal or radical alteration at this date would be seen by many not as a neutral act but as the manifestation of "a hostility toward religion that has no place in our Establishment Clause traditions." Van Orden v. Perry, 545 U. S. 677, 704 (2005) (Breyer, J., concurring in judgment). And . . . there is no evidence of discriminatory intent in the selection of the design of the memorial or the decision of a Maryland commission to maintain it. The Religion Clauses of the Constitution aim to foster a society in which people of all beliefs can live together harmoniously, and the presence of the Bladensburg Cross on the land where it has stood for so many years is fully consistent with that aim.

I

A

The cross came into widespread use as a symbol of Christianity by the fourth century, and it retains that meaning today. But there are many contexts in which the symbol has also taken on a secular meaning. . . .

A cross appears as part of many registered trademarks held by businesses and secular organizations, including Blue Cross Blue Shield . . . . Many of these marks relate to health care, and it is likely that the association of the cross with healing had a religious origin. But the current use of these marks is indisputably secular.

The familiar symbol of the Red Cross . . . shows how the meaning of a symbol that was originally religious can be transformed. The International Committee of the Red Cross (ICRC) . . . selected this symbol for an essentially secular reason [from the Swiss flag to associate it with Switzerland's neutrality], and the current secular message of the symbol is shown by its use today in nations with only tiny Christian populations. But the cross was originally chosen for the Swiss flag for religious reasons. So an image that began as an expression of faith was transformed.

The image used in the Bladensburg memorial—a plain Latin cross—also took on new meaning after World War I. "During and immediately after the war, the army marked soldiers' graves with temporary wooden crosses or Stars of David"—a departure from the prior practice of marking graves in American military cemeteries with uniform rectangular slabs. . . . The vast majority of these grave markers consisted of crosses, and thus when Americans saw photographs of these cemeteries, what struck them were rows and rows of plain white crosses. As a result, the image of a simple white cross "developed into a 'central symbol' " of the conflict. . . .

After the 1918 armistice, the War Department announced plans to replace the wooden crosses and Stars of David with uniform marble slabs like those previously used in American military cemeteries. . . . But the public outcry against that proposal was swift and fierce. Many organizations, including the American War Mothers, a nonsectarian group founded in 1917, urged the Department to retain the design of the temporary markers. . . . When the American Battle Monuments Commission took over the project of designing the headstones, it responded to this public sentiment by opting to replace the wooden crosses and Stars of David with marble versions of those symbols. . . . A Member of Congress likewise introduced a resolution noting that "these wooden symbols have, during and since the World War, been regarded as emblematic of the great sacrifices which that war entailed, have been so treated by poets and artists and have become peculiarly and inseparably associated in the thought of surviving relatives and comrades and of the Nation with these World War graves." . . . This national debate and its outcome confirmed the cross's widespread resonance as a symbol of sacrifice in the war.

B

Recognition of the cross's symbolism extended to local communities across the country. In late 1918, residents of Prince George's County, Maryland, formed a committee for the purpose of erecting a memorial for the county's fallen soldiers. . . . Among the committee's members were the mothers of 10 deceased soldiers. . . . The committee decided that the memorial should be a cross . . . . Although we do not know precisely why the committee chose the cross, it is unsurprising that the committee—and many others commemorating World War I—adopted a symbol so widely associated with that wrenching event.

. . .

The Cross was to stand at the terminus of another World War I memorial— the National Defense Highway, which connects Washington to Annapolis. The community gathered for a joint groundbreaking ceremony for both memorials on September 28, 1919 . . . . By 1922, . . . the committee had run out of funds . . . . The local post of the American Legion took over the project, and the monument was finished in 1925.

The completed monument is a 32-foot tall Latin cross that sits on a large pedestal. The American Legion's emblem is displayed at its center, and the words "Valor," "Endurance," "Courage," and "Devotion" are inscribed at its base, one on each of the four faces. The pedestal also features a 9- by 2.5-foot bronze plaque explaining that the monument is "Dedicated to the heroes of Prince George's County, Maryland who lost their lives in the Great War for the liberty of the world." . . . The plaque lists the names of 49 local men, both Black and White, who died in the war. It identifies the dates of American involvement, and quotes President Woodrow Wilson's request for a declaration of war . . . .

At the dedication ceremony, a local Catholic priest offered an invocation. . . . [A Congressman] delivered the keynote address, honoring the " 'men of Prince George's County' " who " 'fought for the sacred right of all to live in peace and security.' " . . . He encouraged the community to look to the " 'token of this cross, symbolic of Calvary,' " to " 'keep fresh the memory of our boys who died for a righteous cause.' " . . . . The ceremony closed with a benediction offered by a Baptist pastor.

Since its dedication, the Cross has served as the site of patriotic events honoring veterans, including gatherings on Veterans Day, Memorial Day, and Independence Day. Like the dedication itself, these events have typically included an invocation, a keynote speaker, and a benediction. . . . Over the years, memorials honoring the veterans of other conflicts have been added to the surrounding area, which is now known as Veterans Memorial Park. These include a World War II Honor Scroll; a Pearl Harbor memorial; a Korea-Vietnam veterans memorial; a September 11 garden; a War of 1812 memorial; and two recently added 38-foot-tall markers depicting British and American soldiers in the Battle of Bladensburg. . . . Because the Cross is located on a traffic island with limited space, the closest of these other monuments is about 200 feet away in a park across the road.

As the area around the Cross developed, the monument came to be at the center of a busy intersection. In 1961, the Maryland-National Capital Park and

Planning Commission (Commission) acquired the Cross and the land on which it sits in order to preserve the monument and address traffic-safety concerns. . . . The American Legion reserved the right to continue using the memorial to host a variety of ceremonies, including events in memory of departed veterans. . . . Over the next five decades, the Commission spent approximately $117,000 to maintain and preserve the monument. In 2008, it budgeted an additional $100,000 for renovations and repairs to the Cross.

C

In 2012, nearly 90 years after the Cross was dedicated and more than 50 years after the Commission acquired it, the American Humanist Association (AHA) [complained to] the Commission . . . that the Cross's presence on public land and the Commission's maintenance of the memorial violate the Establishment Clause of the First Amendment. The AHA, along with three residents of Washington, D. C., and Maryland, also sued the Commission in . . . District Court . . ., making the same claim. The AHA sought declaratory and injunctive relief requiring "removal or demolition of the Cross, or removal of the arms from the Cross to form a non-religious slab or obelisk." . . . The American Legion intervened to defend the Cross.

The District Court granted summary judgment for the Commission and the American Legion. The Cross, the District Court held, satisfies both the three-pronged test announced in Lemon v. Kurtzman, 403 U. S. 602 (1971), and the analysis applied by Justice Breyer in upholding the Ten Commandments monument at issue in Van Orden v. Perry, 545 U. S. 677. Under the *Lemon* test, a court must ask whether a challenged government action (1) has a secular purpose; (2) has a "principal or primary effect" that "neither advances nor inhibits religion"; and (3) does not foster "an excessive government entanglement with religion," . . . . Applying that test, the District Court determined that the Commission had secular purposes for acquiring and maintaining the Cross— namely, to commemorate World War I and to ensure traffic safety. The court also found that a reasonable observer aware of the Cross's history, setting, and secular elements "would not view the Monument as having the effect of impermissibly endorsing religion." . . . Nor, according to the court, did the Commission's maintenance of the memorial create the kind of "continued and repeated government involvement with religion" that would constitute an excessive entanglement. . . . Finally, in light of the factors that informed its analysis of *Lemon*'s "effects" prong, the court concluded that the Cross is constitutional under Justice Breyer's approach in *Van Orden*. . . .

A divided . . . Fourth Circuit reversed.

. . .

II

A

. . . *Lemon* ambitiously attempted to distill from the Court's existing case law a test that would bring order and predictability to Establishment Clause decisionmaking. That test . . . called on courts to examine the purposes and effects of a challenged government action, as well as any entanglement with religion that it might entail. . . . The Court later elaborated that the "effect[s]" of a challenged action should be assessed by asking whether a "reasonable observer" would conclude that the action constituted an "endorsement" of religion. County of Allegheny v. American Civil Liberties Union, Greater

Pittsburgh Chapter, 492 U. S. 573, 592 (1989); *id.,* at 630 (O'Connor, J., concurring in part and concurring in judgment).

If the *Lemon* Court thought that its test would provide a framework for all future Establishment Clause decisions, its expectation has not been met. In many cases, this Court has either expressly declined to apply the test or has simply ignored it. [Listing cases, including] Town of Greece v. Galloway, 572 U. S. 565 (2014); Trump v. Hawaii, 585 U. S. ___ (2018).

. . . As Establishment Clause cases involving a great array of laws and practices came to the Court, it became more and more apparent that the *Lemon* test could not resolve them. It could not "explain the Establishment Clause's tolerance, for example, of the prayers that open legislative meetings, . . . certain references to, and invocations of, the Deity in the public words of public officials; the public references to God on coins, decrees, and buildings; or the attention paid to the religious objectives of certain holidays, including Thanksgiving." *Van Orden,* . . . (opinion of Breyer, J.). The test has been harshly criticized by Members of this Court, lamented by lower court judges, and questioned by a diverse roster of scholars.

For at least four reasons, the *Lemon* test presents particularly daunting problems in cases, including the one now before us, that involve the use, for ceremonial, celebratory, or commemorative purposes, of words or symbols with religious associations. Together, these considerations counsel against efforts to evaluate such cases under *Lemon* and toward application of a presumption of constitutionality for longstanding monuments, symbols, and practices.

B

First, these cases often concern monuments, symbols, or practices that were first established long ago, and in such cases, identifying their original purpose or purposes may be especially difficult. . . .

. . .

Second, as time goes by, the purposes associated with an established monument, symbol, or practice often multiply. Take the example of Ten Commandments monuments, the subject we addressed in *Van Orden,* . . . and McCreary County v. American Civil Liberties Union of Ky., 545 U. S. 844 (2005). For believing Jews and Christians, the Ten Commandments are the word of God handed down to Moses on Mount Sinai, but the image of the Ten Commandments has also been used to convey other meanings. They have historical significance as one of the foundations of our legal system, and for largely that reason, they are depicted in the marble frieze in our courtroom and in other prominent public buildings in our Nation's capital. . . . In *Van Orden* and *McCreary*, no Member of the Court thought that these depictions are unconstitutional. . . .

. . . [T]he litigation in *Van Orden* and *McCreary* showed that secular motivations played a part in the proliferation of Ten Commandments monuments in the 1950s[, for example] . . . as a way of combating juvenile delinquency . . . [or] in shaping civic morality. . . .

The existence of multiple purposes is not exclusive to longstanding monuments, symbols, or practices, but this phenomenon is more likely to occur in such cases. Even if the original purpose of a monument was infused with religion, the passage of time may obscure that sentiment. As our society becomes more and more religiously diverse, a community may preserve such monuments, symbols, and practices for the sake of their historical significance or their place in a common cultural heritage. . . .

Third, just as the purpose for maintaining a monument, symbol, or practice may evolve, "[t]he 'message' conveyed . . . may change over time." . . .

With sufficient time, religiously expressive monuments, symbols, and practices can become embedded features of a community's landscape and identity. The community may come to value them without necessarily embracing their religious roots. . . .

[C]onsider the many cities and towns across the United States that bear religious names. Religion undoubtedly motivated those who named Bethlehem, Pennsylvania; Las Cruces, New Mexico; Providence, Rhode Island; Corpus Christi, Texas; Nephi, Utah, and the countless other places in our country with names that are rooted in religion. Yet few would argue that this history requires that these names be erased from the map. . . . Familiarity itself can become a reason for preservation.

Fourth, when time's passage imbues a religiously expressive monument, symbol, or practice with this kind of familiarity and historical significance, removing it may no longer appear neutral, especially to the local community for which it has taken on particular meaning. A government that roams the land, tearing down monuments with religious symbolism and scrubbing away any reference to the divine will strike many as aggressively hostile to religion. . . . [T]he image of monuments being taken down will be evocative, disturbing, and divisive. Cf. *Van Orden*, 545 U. S., at 704 (opinion of Breyer, J.) ("[D]isputes concerning the removal of longstanding depictions of the Ten Commandments from public buildings across the Nation . . . could thereby create the very kind of religiously based divisiveness that the Establishment Clause seeks to avoid").

These four considerations show that retaining established, religiously expressive monuments, symbols, and practices is quite different from erecting or adopting new ones. The passage of time gives rise to a strong presumption of constitutionality.

C

The role of the cross in World War I memorials is illustrative of each of the four preceding considerations. . . . [T]he cross had become a symbol closely linked to the war. . . . In the wake of the war, the United States adopted the cross as part of its military honors, establishing the Distinguished Service Cross and the Navy Cross in 1918 and 1919, respectively. . . . The solemn image of endless rows of white crosses became inextricably linked with and symbolic of the ultimate price paid by 116,000 soldiers. And this relationship between the cross and the war undoubtedly influenced the design of the many war memorials that sprang up across the Nation.

This is not to say that the cross's association with the war was the sole or dominant motivation for the inclusion of the symbol in every World War I memorial that features it. But today, it is all but impossible to tell whether that was so. The passage of time means that testimony from those actually involved in the decisionmaking process is generally unavailable, and attempting to uncover their motivations invites rampant speculation. And no matter what the original purposes for the erection of a monument, a community may wish to preserve it for very different reasons, such as the historic preservation and traffic-safety concerns the Commission has pressed here.

In addition, the passage of time may have altered the area surrounding a monument in ways that change its meaning and provide new reasons for its preservation. Such changes are relevant here, since the Bladensburg Cross now sits at a busy traffic intersection, and numerous additional monuments are located nearby.

. . .

Similar reasoning applies to other memorials and monuments honoring important figures in our Nation's history. When faith was important to the person whose life is commemorated, it is natural to include a symbolic reference to faith in the design of the memorial. For example, many memorials for Dr. Martin Luther King, Jr., make reference to his faith. . . . In Atlanta, the Ebenezer Baptist Church sits on the grounds of the Martin Luther King, Jr. National Historical Park. National Statuary Hall in the Capitol honors a variety of religious figures . . . . These monuments honor men and women who have played an important role in the history of our country, and where religious symbols are included in the monuments, their presence acknowledges the centrality of faith to those whose lives are commemorated.

Finally, as World War I monuments have endured through the years and become a familiar part of the physical and cultural landscape, requiring their removal would not be viewed by many as a neutral act. And an alteration like . . . amputating the arms of the Cross . . . would be seen by many as profoundly disrespectful. . . . [A] campaign to obliterate items with religious associations may evidence hostility to religion even if those religious associations are no longer in the forefront.

[F]ew would say that the State of California is attempting to convey a religious message by retaining the names given to many of the State's cities by their original Spanish settlers—San Diego, Los Angeles, Santa Barbara, San Jose, San Francisco, etc. But it would be something else entirely if the State undertook to change all those names. Much the same is true about monuments to soldiers who sacrificed their lives for this country more than a century ago.

D

While the *Lemon* Court ambitiously attempted to find a grand unified theory of the Establishment Clause, in later cases, we have taken a more modest approach that focuses on the particular issue at hand and looks to history for guidance. Our cases involving prayer before a legislative session are an example.

In Marsh v. Chambers, 463 U. S. 783 (1983), the Court upheld the Nebraska Legislature's practice of beginning each session with a prayer by an official chaplain, and in so holding, the Court conspicuously ignored *Lemon* and did not respond to Justice Brennan's argument in dissent that the legislature's practice could not satisfy the *Lemon* test. . . . Instead, the Court found it highly persuasive that Congress for more than 200 years had opened its sessions with a prayer and that many state legislatures had followed suit. . . . We took a similar approach more recently in *Town of Greece*, ...

We reached these results even though it was clear, as stressed by the *Marsh* dissent, that prayer is by definition religious. . . .

. . . The First Congress . . . chose to begin its sessions with a prayer. This practice was designed to solemnize congressional meetings, unifying those in attendance as they pursued a common goal of good governance.

To achieve that purpose, legislative prayer needed to be inclusive rather than divisive, and that required a determined effort even in a society that was much more religiously homogeneous than ours today. . . .

Over time, the members of the clergy invited to offer prayers at the opening of a session grew more and more diverse. . . .

In *Town of Greece,* which concerned prayer before a town council meeting, there was disagreement about the inclusiveness of the town's practice. . . . But there was no disagreement that the Establishment Clause permits a nondiscriminatory practice of prayer at the beginning of a town council session. . . . [W]hat mattered was that the town's practice "fi[t] within the tradition long followed in Congress and the state legislatures." . . .

The practice begun by the First Congress stands out as an example of respect and tolerance for differing views, an honest endeavor to achieve inclusivity and nondiscrimination, and a recognition of the important role that religion plays in the lives of many Americans. Where categories of monuments, symbols, and practices with a longstanding history follow in that tradition, they are likewise constitutional.

III

Applying these principles, we conclude that the Bladensburg Cross does not violate the Establishment Clause.

. . . [T]he Bladensburg Cross carries special significance in commemorating World War I. . . . That the cross originated as a Christian symbol and retains that meaning in many contexts does not change the fact that the symbol took on an added secular meaning when used in World War I memorials.

Not only did the Bladensburg Cross begin with this meaning, but with the passage of time, it has acquired historical importance. It reminds the people of Bladensburg and surrounding areas of the deeds of their predecessors and of the sacrifices they made in a war fought in the name of democracy. As long as it is retained in its original place and form, it speaks as well of the community that erected the monument nearly a century ago and has maintained it ever since. The memorial represents what the relatives, friends, and neighbors of the fallen soldiers felt at the time and how they chose to express their sentiments. And the monument has acquired additional layers of historical meaning in subsequent years. The Cross now stands among memorials to veterans of later wars. It has become part of the community.

The monument would not serve that role if its design had deliberately disrespected area soldiers who perished in World War I. More than 3,500 Jewish soldiers gave their lives for the United States in that conflict, and some have wondered whether the names of any Jewish soldiers from the area were deliberately left off the list on the memorial or whether the names of any Jewish soldiers were included on the Cross against the wishes of their families. There is no evidence that either thing was done, and we do know that one of the local American Legion leaders responsible for the Cross's construction was a Jewish veteran. . . .

. . .

Finally, it is surely relevant that the monument commemorates the death of particular individuals. It is natural and appropriate for those seeking to honor the deceased to invoke the symbols that signify what death meant for those who are memorialized. . . .

IV

The cross is undoubtedly a Christian symbol, but that fact should not blind us to everything else that the Bladensburg Cross has come to represent. For some, that monument is a symbolic resting place for ancestors who never returned home. For others, it is a place for the community to gather and honor all veterans and their sacrifices for our Nation. For others still, it is a historical landmark. For many of these people, destroying or defacing the Cross that has stood undisturbed for nearly a century would not be neutral and would not further the ideals of respect and tolerance embodied in the First Amendment. For all these reasons, the Cross does not offend the Constitution.

. . .

■ JUSTICE BREYER, with whom JUSTICE KAGAN joins, concurring.

I have long maintained that there is no single formula for resolving Establishment Clause challenges. See Van Orden v. Perry, 545 U. S. 677, 698 (2005) (opinion concurring in judgment). The Court must instead consider each case in light of the basic purposes that the Religion Clauses were meant to serve: assuring religious liberty and tolerance for all, avoiding religiously based social conflict, and maintaining that separation of church and state that allows each to flourish in its "separate spher[e]." . . .

I agree with the Court that allowing the State of Maryland to display and maintain the Peace Cross poses no threat to those ends. The Court's opinion eloquently explains why that is so: The Latin cross is uniquely associated with the fallen soldiers of World War I; the organizers of the Peace Cross acted with the undeniably secular motive of commemorating local soldiers; no evidence suggests that they sought to disparage or exclude any religious group; the secular values inscribed on the Cross and its place among other memorials strengthen its message of patriotism and commemoration; and, finally, the Cross has stood on the same land for 94 years, generating no controversy in the community until this lawsuit was filed. Nothing in the record suggests that the lack of public outcry "was due to a climate of intimidation." Van Orden, 545 U. S., at 702 (Breyer, J., concurring in judgment). In light of all these circumstances, the Peace Cross cannot reasonably be understood as "a government effort to favor a particular religious sect" or to "promote religion over nonreligion." Ibid. And, as the Court explains, ordering its removal or alteration at this late date would signal "a hostility toward religion that has no place in our Establishment Clause traditions." Id., at 704.

The case would be different, in my view, if there were evidence that the organizers had "deliberately disrespected" members of minority faiths or if the Cross had been erected only recently, rather than in the aftermath of World War I. See . . . Van Orden, 545 U. S., at 703 (opinion of Breyer, J.) (explaining that, in light of the greater religious diversity today, "a more contemporary state effort" to put up a religious display is "likely to prove divisive in a way that [a] longstanding, pre-existing monument [would] not"). But those are not the circumstances presented to us here, and I see no reason to order this cross torn down simply because other crosses would raise constitutional concerns.

Nor do I understand the Court's opinion today to adopt a "history and tradition test" that would permit any newly constructed religious memorial on public land. See . . . (Kavanaugh, J., concurring); cf. . . . (Gorsuch, J., concurring in judgment). The Court appropriately "looks to history for guidance," but it upholds the constitutionality of the Peace Cross only after considering its particular historical context and its long-held place in the community. A newer memorial, erected under different circumstances, would not necessarily be permissible under this approach. . . .

. . .

■ JUSTICE KAVANAUGH, concurring.

I join the Court's eloquent and persuasive opinion in full. I write separately to emphasize two points.

I

Consistent with the Court's case law, the Court today applies a history and tradition test in examining and upholding the constitutionality of the Bladensburg Cross. See Marsh v. Chambers, 463 U. S. 783, 787–792, 795 (1983); Van Orden v. Perry, 545 U. S. 677, 686–690 (2005) (plurality opinion); Town of Greece v. Galloway, 572 U. S. 565, 575–578 (2014).

As this case again demonstrates, this Court no longer applies the old test articulated in Lemon v. Kurtzman . . . . If *Lemon* guided this Court's understanding of the Establishment Clause, then many of the Court's Establishment Clause cases over the last 48 years would have been decided differently . . . .

. . .

. . . [E]ach category of Establishment Clause cases has its own principles based on history, tradition, and precedent. And the cases together lead to an overarching set of principles: If the challenged government practice is not coercive *and* if it (i) is rooted in history and tradition; or (ii) treats religious people, organizations, speech, or activity equally to comparable secular people, organizations, speech, or activity; or (iii) represents a permissible legislative accommodation or exemption from a generally applicable law, then there ordinarily is no Establishment Clause violation.

The practice of displaying religious memorials, particularly religious war memorials, on public land is not coercive and is rooted in history and tradition. The Bladensburg Cross does not violate the Establishment Clause. . . .

II

. . . I have deep respect for the plaintiffs' sincere objections to seeing the cross on public land. I have great respect for the Jewish war veterans who in an *amicus* brief say that the cross on public land sends a message of exclusion. I recognize their sense of distress and alienation. Moreover, I fully understand the deeply religious nature of the cross. It would demean both believers and nonbelievers to say that the cross is not religious, or not all that religious. A case like this is difficult because it represents a clash of genuine and important interests. Applying our precedents, we uphold the constitutionality of the cross. In doing so, it is appropriate to also restate this bedrock constitutional principle: All citizens are equally American, no matter what religion they are, or if they have no religion at all.

The conclusion that the cross does not violate the Establishment Clause does not necessarily mean that those who object to it have no other recourse. . . .

The Maryland Legislature could enact new laws requiring removal of the cross or transfer of the land. . . . The Maryland Constitution . . . may speak to this question. And if not, the people of Maryland can amend the State Constitution.

. . .

■ JUSTICE KAGAN, concurring in part.

I fully agree with the Court's reasons for allowing the Bladensburg Peace Cross to remain as it is, and so join Parts I, II-B, II-C, III, and IV of its opinion, as well as Justice Breyer's concurrence. Although I agree that rigid application of the *Lemon* test does not solve every Establishment Clause problem, I think that test's focus on purposes and effects is crucial in evaluating government action in this sphere—as this very suit shows. I therefore do not join Part II-A. I do not join Part II-D out of perhaps an excess of caution. Although I too "look[ ] to history for guidance," I prefer at least for now to do so case-by-case, rather than to sign on to any broader statements about history's role in Establishment Clause analysis. But I find much to admire in this section of the opinion— particularly, its emphasis on whether longstanding monuments, symbols, and practices reflect "respect and tolerance for differing views, an honest endeavor to achieve inclusivity and nondiscrimination, and a recognition of the important role that religion plays in the lives of many Americans." Here, as elsewhere, the opinion shows sensitivity to and respect for this Nation's pluralism, and the values of neutrality and inclusion that the First Amendment demands.

■ JUSTICE THOMAS, concurring in the judgment.

The Establishment Clause states that "Congress shall make no law respecting an establishment of religion." . . . The text and history of this Clause suggest that it should not be incorporated against the States. Even if the Clause expresses an individual right enforceable against the States, it is limited by its text to "law[s]" enacted by a legislature, so it is unclear whether the Bladensburg Cross would implicate any incorporated right. And even if it did, this religious display does not involve the type of actual legal coercion that was a hallmark of historical establishments of religion. Therefore, the Cross is clearly constitutional.

. . .

As to the long-discredited test set forth in Lemon v. Kurtzman, 403 U. S. 602, 612–613 (1971), and reiterated in County of Allegheny v. American Civil Liberties Union, Greater Pittsburgh Chapter, 492 U. S. 573, 592–594 (1989), the plurality rightly rejects its relevance to claims, like this one, involving "religious references or imagery in public monuments, symbols, mottos, displays, and ceremonies." I agree with that aspect of its opinion. I would take the logical next step and overrule the *Lemon* test in all contexts. . . .

Regrettably, I cannot join the Court's opinion because it does not adequately clarify the appropriate standard for Establishment Clause cases. Therefore, I concur only in the judgment.

■ JUSTICE GORSUCH, with whom JUSTICE THOMAS joins, concurring in the judgment.

. . . Today, the Court explains that the plaintiffs are not entitled to demand the destruction of longstanding monuments, and I find much of its opinion compelling. In my judgment, however, it follows from the Court's analysis that suits like this one should be dismissed for lack of standing. Accordingly, while I concur in the judgment to reverse and remand . . ., I would do so with additional instructions to dismiss the case.

*

The Association claims that its members "regularly" come into "unwelcome direct contact" with a World War I memorial cross in Bladensburg, Maryland "while driving in the area." . . . And this, the Association suggests, is enough to allow it to insist on a federal judicial decree ordering the memorial's removal. . . . [T]he Association assures us . . . its members are offended enough—and with sufficient frequency—that they may sue.

This "offended observer" theory of standing has no basis in law. . . .

. . .

Offended observer standing cannot be squared with this Court's longstanding teachings about the limits of Article III. . . .

. . . Lower courts invented offended observer standing for Establishment Clause cases in the 1970s in response to this Court's decision in Lemon v. Kurtzman . . . . [They] reasoned that, if the Establishment Clause forbids anything a reasonable observer would view as an endorsement of religion, then such an observer must be able to sue. . . .

As today's plurality rightly indicates in Part II-A, however, *Lemon* was a misadventure. . . .

In place of *Lemon*, Part II-D of the plurality opinion relies on a more modest, historically sensitive approach, recognizing that "the Establishment Clause must be interpreted by reference to historical practices and understandings." . . .

I agree . . . that the monument before us is constitutional in light of the nation's traditions. But then the plurality continues on to suggest that "longstanding monuments, symbols, and practices" are "presumpt[ively]" constitutional. And about that, it's hard not to wonder: How old must a monument, symbol, or practice be to qualify for this new presumption? It seems 94 years is enough, but what about the Star of David monument erected in South Carolina in 2001 to commemorate victims of the Holocaust, or the cross that marines in California placed in 2004 to honor their comrades who fell during the War on Terror? And where exactly in the Constitution does this presumption come from? The plurality does not say, nor does it even explain what work its presumption does. To the contrary, the plurality proceeds to analyze the "presumptively" constitutional memorial in this case for its consistency with " 'historical practices and understandings' " under *Marsh* and *Town of Greece*— exactly the same approach that the plurality, quoting *Town of Greece*, recognizes " 'must be' " used *whenever* we interpret the Establishment Clause. . . . Though the plurality does not say so in as many words, the message for our lower court colleagues seems unmistakable: Whether a monument, symbol, or practice is old or new, apply *Town of Greece*, not *Lemon*. Indeed, some of our colleagues recognize this implication and blanch at its prospect. See (Breyer, J., concurring); (Kagan, J., concurring in part) (declining to join Parts II-A & II-D); (Ginsburg, J., dissenting). But if that's the real message of the plurality's opinion, it seems to me exactly right—because what matters when it comes to assessing a monument, symbol, or practice isn't its age but its compliance with ageless principles. The Constitution's meaning is fixed, . . . and a practice consistent with our nation's traditions is just as permissible whether undertaken today or 94 years ago.

*

With *Lemon* now shelved, little excuse will remain for the anomaly of offended observer standing . . . .

Abandoning offended observer standing will mean only a return to the usual demands of Article III, requiring a real controversy with real impact on real persons to make a federal case out of it. Along the way, this will bring with it the welcome side effect of rescuing the federal judiciary from the sordid business of having to pass aesthetic judgment, one by one, on every public display in this country for its perceived capacity to give offense. It's a business that has consumed volumes of the federal reports, invited erratic results, frustrated generations of judges, and fomented "the very kind of religiously based divisiveness that the Establishment Clause seeks to avoid." Van Orden v. Perry, 545 U. S. 677, 704 (2005) (Breyer, J., concurring in judgment). . . .

. . .

■ JUSTICE GINSBURG, with whom JUSTICE SOTOMAYOR joins, dissenting.

. . .

. . . Today the Court erodes [its] neutrality commitment, diminishing precedent designed to preserve individual liberty and civic harmony in favor of a "presumption of constitutionality for longstanding monuments, symbols, and practices."

. . .

By maintaining the Peace Cross on a public highway, the Commission elevates Christianity over other faiths, and religion over nonreligion. Memorializing the service of American soldiers is an "admirable and unquestionably secular" objective. Van Orden v. Perry, 545 U. S. 677, 715 (2005) (Stevens, J., dissenting). But the Commission does not serve that objective by displaying a symbol that bears "a starkly sectarian message." Salazar v. Buono, 559 U. S. 700, 736 (2010) (Stevens, J., dissenting).

. . .

In cases challenging the government's display of a religious symbol, the Court has tested fidelity to the principle of neutrality by asking whether the display has the "effect of 'endorsing' religion." *County of Allegheny* . . . . The display fails this requirement if it objectively "convey[s] a message that religion or a particular religious belief is favored or preferred." . . . .[3] . . .

As I see it, when a cross is displayed on public property, the government may be presumed to endorse its religious content. The venue is surely associated with the State; the symbol and its meaning are just as surely associated exclusively with Christianity. . . . To non-Christians, nearly 30% of the population of the United States, . . . the State's choice to display the cross on public buildings or spaces conveys a message of exclusion: It tells them they "are outsiders, not full members of the political community," *County of Allegheny*, 492 U. S., at 625 (O'Connor, J., concurring in part and concurring in judgment) . . . .

---

[3]   Justice Gorsuch's "no standing" opinion is startling in view of the many religious-display cases this Court has resolved on the merits. . . .

A presumption of endorsement, of course, may be overcome. . . . A display does not run afoul of the neutrality principle if its "setting . . . plausibly indicates" that the government has not sought "either to adopt [a] religious message or to urge its acceptance by others." *Van Orden*, 545 U. S., at 737 (Souter, J., dissenting). The "typical museum setting," for example, "though not neutralizing the religious content of a religious painting, negates any message of endorsement of that content." Lynch v. Donnelly, 465 U. S. 668, 692 (1984) (O'Connor, J., concurring). Similarly, when a public school history teacher discusses the Protestant Reformation, the setting makes clear that the teacher's purpose is to educate, not to proselytize. The Peace Cross, however, is not of that genre.

II

A

"For nearly two millennia," the Latin cross has been the "defining symbol" of Christianity, . . . evoking the foundational claims of that faith. . . .

An exclusively Christian symbol, the Latin cross is not emblematic of any other faith. . . . The principal symbol of Christianity around the world should not loom over public thoroughfares, suggesting official recognition of that religion's paramountcy.

B

The Commission urges in defense of its monument that the Latin cross "is not merely a reaffirmation of Christian beliefs"; rather, "when used in the context of a war memorial," the cross becomes "a universal symbol of the sacrifices of those who fought and died." . . .

The Commission's "[a]ttempts to secularize what is unquestionably a sacred [symbol] defy credibility and disserve people of faith." *Van Orden*, 545 U. S., at 717 (Stevens, J., dissenting). See, *e.g.,* Brief for *Amici* Christian and Jewish Organizations 7 ("For Christians who think seriously about the events and message that the cross represents, [the Commission's] claims are deeply offensive."). . . .

. . .

The cross affirms that, thanks to the soldier's embrace of Christianity, he will be rewarded with eternal life. . . . Scarcely "a universal symbol of sacrifice," the cross is "the symbol of one particular sacrifice." *Buono*, 559 U. S., at 748, n. 8 (Stevens, J., dissenting).

Every Court of Appeals to confront the question has held that "[m]aking a . . . Latin cross a war memorial does not make the cross secular," it "makes the war memorial sectarian." . . .

The Peace Cross is no exception. That was evident from the start. At the dedication ceremony, the keynote speaker analogized the sacrifice of the honored soldiers to that of Jesus Christ, calling the Peace Cross "symbolic of Calvary," . . . where Jesus was crucified. Local reporters variously described the monument as "[a] mammoth cross, a likeness of the Cross of Calvary, as described in the Bible," . . .; "a monster [C]alvary cross," . . . and "a huge sacrifice cross," . . . . The character of the monument has not changed with the passage of time.

C

The Commission nonetheless urges that the Latin cross is a "well-established" secular symbol commemorating, in particular, "military valor and sacrifice [in] World War I." . . . Calling up images of United States cemeteries overseas showing row upon row of cross-shaped gravemarkers, . . . the Commission overlooks this reality: The cross was never perceived as an appropriate headstone or memorial for Jewish soldiers and others who did not adhere to Christianity.

1

. . .

When the War Department began preparing designs for permanent headstones in 1919, "no topic managed to stir more controversy than the use of religious symbolism." . . . Everyone involved in the dispute, however, saw the Latin cross as a Christian symbol, not as a universal or secular one. . . .

. . .

Throughout the headstone debate, no one doubted that the Latin cross and the Star of David were sectarian gravemarkers, and therefore appropriate only for soldiers who adhered to those faiths. . . .

. . .

2

Reiterating its argument that the Latin cross is a "universal symbol" of World War I sacrifice, the Commission states that "40 World War I monuments . . . built in the United States . . . bear the shape of a cross." . . . This figure includes memorials that merely "incorporat[e]" a cross. . . . Moreover, the 40 monuments compose only 4% of the "948 outdoor sculptures commemorating the First World War." . . . The Court lists just seven free-standing cross memorials, less than 1% of the total number of monuments to World War I in the United States . . . . Cross memorials, in short, are outliers. The overwhelming majority of World War I memorials contain no Latin cross.

In fact, the "most popular and enduring memorial of the [post-World War I] decade" was "[t]he mass-produced *Spirit of the American Doughboy* statue." . . . The Peace Cross, as Plaintiffs' expert historian observed, was an "aberration . . . even in the era [in which] it was built and dedicated." . . .

Like cities and towns across the country, the United States military comprehended the importance of "pay[ing] equal respect to all members of the Armed Forces who perished in the service of our country," *Buono*, 559 U. S., at 759 (Stevens, J., dissenting), and therefore avoided incorporating the Latin cross into memorials. The construction of the Tomb of the Unknown Soldier is illustrative. When a proposal to place a cross on the Tomb was advanced, the Jewish Welfare Board objected; no cross appears on the Tomb. . . .

D

. . .

Recognizing that a Latin cross does not belong on a public highway or building does not mean the monument must be "torn down." . . . In some instances, the violation may be cured by relocating the monument to private land or by transferring ownership of the land and monument to a private party.

* * *

. . . The Establishment Clause, which preserves the integrity of both church and state, guarantees that "however . . . individuals worship, they will count as full and equal American citizens." *Town of Greece*, 572 U. S., at 615 (Kagan, J., dissenting). "If the aim of the Establishment Clause is genuinely to uncouple government from church," the Clause does "not permit . . . a display of th[e] character" of Bladensburg's Peace Cross. . . .

2.   THE FREE EXERCISE OF RELIGION

Page 1804. Add after Church of the Lukumi Babalu Aye, Inc. v. City of Hialeah:

Our Lady of Guadalupe School v. Morrissey-Berru, 591 U.S. ___, 140 S.Ct. 2049 (2020). Two lay teachers at Catholic elementary schools in the diocese of Los Angeles brought suits claiming that their employers fired them in violation of generally applicable laws prohibiting employment discrimination, one on the basis of age, and the other on the basis of disability. The Court held, however, that their claims were barred by the "ministerial exception" first embraced by the Court in Hosanna-Tabor Evangelical Lutheran Church and School v. Equal Employment Opportunity Commission, 565 U.S. 171 (2012). *Hosanna-Tabor* held that both the Free Exercise Clause *and* the Establishment Clause "preclude[ ] application of such legislation to claims concerning the employment relationship between a religious institution and its ministers." Chief Justice Roberts wrote the Court's unanimous opinion in that case, saying in support of the ministerial exception:

". . . Requiring a church to accept or retain an unwanted minister, or punishing a church for failing to do so, intrudes upon more than a mere employment decision. Such action interferes with the internal governance of the church, depriving the church of control over the selection of those who will personify its beliefs. By imposing an unwanted minister, the state infringes the Free Exercise Clause, which protects a religious group's right to shape its own faith and mission through its appointments. According the state the power to determine which individuals will minister to the faithful also violates the Establishment Clause, which prohibits government involvement in such ecclesiastical decisions."

The Chief Justice rejected the contention that Employment Division, Department of Human Resources v. Smith "precludes recognition of a ministerial exception." Although the anti-discrimination law in *Hosanna-Tabor* also "is a valid and neutral law of general applicability[,] a church's selection of its ministers is unlike an individual's ingestion of peyote. *Smith* involved government regulation of only outward physical acts. The present case, in contrast, concerns government interference with an internal church decision that affects the faith and mission of the church itself. . . . The contention that *Smith* forecloses recognition of a ministerial exception rooted in the Religion Clauses has no merit."

Deciding that the ministerial exception applied in *Hosanna-Tabor*, Chief Justice Roberts eschewed "a rigid formula for deciding when an employee qualifies as a minister[,]" but concluded that it applied to the teacher there, "given all the circumstances of her employment." Those circumstances included that she and the Church held her out as a commissioned minister, that she had received a significant degree of religious training, that her "job duties reflected a role in conveying the Church's message and carrying out its mission[,]" that, among other activities, she "taught her students religion four days a week, and led them in prayer three times a day[,]" and that, in general, "[a]s a source of religious instruction, [she] performed an important role in transmitting the Lutheran faith to the next generation."

The current case raised the issue of the scope of the ministerial exception. Justice Alito's majority opinion again found the ministerial exception applicable, "[a]lthough these teachers were not given the title of 'minister' and have less religious training . . . ." According to Justice Alito, "[i]n determining whether a particular position falls within the *Hosanna-Tabor* exception, a variety of factors may be important." The title "minister" might be important, but it is not necessary. Similarly, "the academic requirements of a position may show that the church in question regards the position as having an important responsibility in elucidating or teaching the tenets of the faith[,]" but these circumstances "are not inflexible requirements and may have far less significance in some cases." Rather:

"What matters, at bottom, is what an employee does. And implicit in our decision in *Hosanna-Tabor* was a recognition that educating young people in their faith, inculcating its teachings, and training them to live their faith are responsibilities that lie at the very core of the mission of a private religious school."

As applied to the two teachers in this case,

". . . There is abundant record evidence that they both performed vital religious duties. Educating and forming students in the Catholic faith lay at the core of the mission of the schools where they taught, and their employment agreements and faculty handbooks specified in no uncertain terms that they were expected to help the schools carry out this mission and that their work would be evaluated to ensure that they were fulfilling that responsibility. As elementary school teachers responsible for providing instruction in all subjects, including religion, they were the members of the school staff who were entrusted most directly with the responsibility of educating their students in the faith. And not only were they obligated to provide instruction about the Catholic faith, but they were also expected to guide their students, by word and deed, toward the goal of living their lives in accordance with the faith. They prayed with their students, attended Mass with the students, and prepared the children for their participation in other religious activities. . . . Their titles did not include the term 'minister,' and they had less formal religious training, but their core responsibilities as teachers of religion were essentially the same. And both their schools expressly saw them as playing a vital part in carrying out the mission of the church, and the schools' definition and explanation of their roles is important. In a country with the religious diversity of the United States, judges cannot be expected to have a complete understanding and appreciation of the role played by every person who performs a particular role in every religious tradition. A religious institution's explanation of the role of such employees in the life of the religion in question is important."

Finally, Justice Alito rejected the suggestion "that an employee can never come within the *Hosanna-Tabor* exception unless the employee is a 'practicing' member of the religion with which the employer is associated." To do so "would create a host of problems[,"] including that it "would risk judicial entanglement in religious issues."

Justice Thomas, joined by Justice Gorsuch, concurred in the Court's opinion, but wrote separately to reiterate his view in *Hosanna-Tabor* "that the Religion Clauses require civil courts to defer to religious organizations' good-faith claims that a certain employee's position is 'ministerial.'" Justice Sotomayor, joined by Justice Ginsburg, dissented, writing in part:

"*Hosanna-Tabor*'s well-rounded approach ensured that a church could not categorically disregard generally applicable antidiscrimination laws for nonreligious reasons. By analyzing objective and easily discernable markers like titles, training, and public-facing conduct, *Hosanna-Tabor* charted a way to separate leaders who 'personify' a church's 'beliefs' or who 'minister to the faithful' from individuals who may simply relay religious tenets.... This balanced First Amendment concerns of state-church entanglement while avoiding an overbroad carve-out from employment protections."

In this case, "the Court's apparent deference ... threatens to make nearly anyone whom the schools might hire 'ministers' unprotected from discrimination in the hiring process." In her view, "neither school had shown that the ministerial exception barred the teachers' claims for disability and age discrimination." Because "neither school publicly represented that either teacher was a Catholic spiritual leader or 'minister'"; "neither teacher had a 'significant degree of religious training' or underwent a 'formal process of commissioning'"; "neither ... held herself out as having a leadership role in the faith community[, or] claimed any benefits (tax, governmental, ceremonial, or administrative) available only to spiritual leaders"; and "both were like any public school teacher in California, subject to the same statewide curriculum guidelines" in that they spend the vast majority of their time teaching "subjects like reading, writing, spelling, grammar, vocabulary, math, science, social studies, and geography[,"] their "almost exclusively secular duties [make] it especially improper to deprive them of all legal protection when their employers have not offered any religious reason for the alleged discrimination." In short, "teaching religion in school alone cannot dictate ministerial status."

Justice Sotomayor's conclusion included the following:

"Pause ... on the Court's conclusion: Even if the teachers were not Catholic, and even if they were forbidden to participate in the church's sacramental worship, they would nonetheless be 'ministers' of the Catholic faith simply because of their supervisory role over students in a religious school. That stretches the law and logic past their breaking points....

"The Court's conclusion portends grave consequences.... As the Government ... explained, ... 'thousands of Catholic teachers' may lose employment law protections because of today's outcome.... And that says nothing of the rights of countless coaches, camp counselors, nurses, social-service workers, in-house lawyers, media-relations personnel, and many others who work for religious institutions. All these employees could be subject to discrimination for reasons completely irrelevant to their employers' religious tenets."

Masterpiece Cakeshop, Ltd. v. Colorado Civil Rights Commission

584 U.S. ___, 138 S.Ct. 1719, 201 L.Ed.2d 35 (2018).

■ JUSTICE KENNEDY delivered the opinion of the Court.

[In 2012, when same-sex marriage was not yet legal in Colorado, two gay men, who planned to wed in Massachusetts and later hold a reception in Denver, were rebuffed by a Colorado baker, Phillips, when they asked him to create a wedding cake for their celebration. Phillips cited his religious opposition to same-sex marriage as the reason, although he offered to make their birthday cakes and shower cakes and to sell them brownies or cookies.] The couple filed a charge with the Colorado Civil Rights Commission alleging discrimination on the basis of sexual orientation in violation of the Colorado Anti-Discrimination Act[—a charge the Commission upheld and whose enforcement the state courts affirmed.]

The case presents difficult questions as to the proper reconciliation of at least two principles. The first is the authority of a State and its governmental entities to protect the rights and dignity of gay persons who are, or wish to be, married but who face discrimination when they seek goods or services. The second is the right of all persons to exercise fundamental freedoms under the First Amendment[—here "both the freedom of speech and the free exercise of religion."]

. . . The free speech aspect of this case is difficult, for few persons who have seen a beautiful wedding cake might have thought of its creation as an exercise of protected speech. This is an instructive example, however, of the proposition that the application of constitutional freedoms in new contexts can deepen our understanding of their meaning.

One of the difficulties in this case is that the parties disagree as to the extent of the baker's refusal to provide service. If a baker refused to design a special cake with words or images celebrating the marriage—for instance, a cake showing words with religious meaning—that might be different from a refusal to sell any cake at all. In defining whether a baker's creation can be protected, these details might make a difference.

The same difficulties arise in determining whether a baker has a valid free exercise claim. A baker's refusal to attend the wedding to ensure that the cake is cut the right way, or a refusal to put certain religious words or decorations on the cake, or even a refusal to sell a cake that has been baked for the public generally but includes certain religious words or symbols on it are just three examples of possibilities that seem all but endless.

Whatever the confluence of speech and free exercise principles might be in some cases, the Colorado Civil Rights Commission's consideration of this case was inconsistent with the State's obligation of religious neutrality. The reason and motive for the baker's refusal were based on his sincere religious beliefs and convictions. The Court's precedents make clear that the baker, in his capacity as the owner of a business serving the public, might have his right to the free exercise of religion limited by generally applicable laws. Still, the delicate question of when the free exercise of his religion must yield to an otherwise valid exercise of state power needed to be determined in an adjudication in which religious hostility on the part of the State itself would not be a factor in the balance the State sought to reach. That requirement, however, was not met here. When the Colorado Civil Rights Commission considered this case, it did not do so with the religious neutrality that the Constitution requires.

. . . [W]hatever the outcome of some future controversy involving facts similar to these, the Commission's actions here violated the Free Exercise Clause . . . .

I

. . .

[The Colorado Anti-Discrimination Act (CADA), amended in 2007 and 2008 to add sexual orientation to the list of prohibited discrimination in places of public accommodation (defined broadly to include any place of business that sells goods or services to the public), uses an administrative system to resolve discrimination claims. Complaints are investigated by the Colorado Civil Rights Division, which refers the matter to the Commission if probable cause that CADA has been violated is found.] The Commission, in turn, decides whether to initiate a formal hearing before a state Administrative Law Judge (ALJ), who will hear evidence and argument before issuing a written decision. . . . The decision of the ALJ may be appealed to the full Commission, a seven-member appointed body. The Commission holds a public hearing and deliberative session before voting on the case. If the Commission determines that the evidence proves a CADA violation, it may impose [certain] remedial measures [that do not include assessing money damages or fines.]

. . .

[In this case, the Civil Rights Division investigator] found that "on multiple occasions," Phillips "turned away potential customers on the basis of their sexual orientation, stating that he could not create a cake for a same-sex wedding ceremony or reception" because his religious beliefs prohibited it and because the potential customers "were doing something illegal" at that time. . . . The investigation found that Phillips had declined to sell custom wedding cakes to about six other same-sex couples on this basis. . . . [T]he Division found probable cause that Phillips violated CADA and referred the case to the . . . Commission.

The Commission . . . sent the case to a[n] ALJ[, . . . who] determined that Phillips' actions constituted prohibited discrimination on the basis of sexual orientation, not simply opposition to same-sex marriage as Phillips contended. . . .

[The ALJ rejected Phillips' free speech and free exercise arguments. With respect to the latter, c]iting this Court's precedent in Employment Div., Dept. of Human Resources of Ore. v. Smith, 494 U.S. 872 (1990), the ALJ determined that CADA is a "valid and neutral law of general applicability" and therefore that applying it to Phillips in this case did not violate the Free Exercise Clause. . . .

The Commission affirmed the ALJ's decision[, issued a cease and desist order, and ordered staff training and quarterly compliance reports. On appeal, the Colorado Court of Appeals affirmed the Commission's legal determinations and remedial order, and the Colorado Supreme Court declined review.]

II

A

Our society has come to the recognition that gay persons and gay couples cannot be treated as social outcasts or as inferior in dignity and worth. . . . The exercise of their freedom on terms equal to others must be given great weight and respect by the courts. At the same time, the religious and philosophical objections to gay marriage are protected views and in some instances protected forms of expression. . . . Nevertheless, . . . it is a general rule that such objections do not allow business owners and other actors in the economy and in society to deny protected persons equal access to goods and services under a neutral and generally applicable public accommodations law. See Newman v. Piggy Park Enterprises, Inc., 390 U.S. 400, 402, n. 5 (1968) (*per curiam*); see also Hurley v. Irish-American Gay, Lesbian and Bisexual Group of Boston, Inc., 515 U.S. 557, 572 (1995) . . . .

. . . [I]t can be assumed that a member of the clergy who objects to gay marriage on moral and religious grounds could not be compelled to perform the ceremony without denial of his or her right to the free exercise of religion. . . . Yet if that exception were not confined, then a long list of persons who provide goods and services for marriages and weddings might refuse to do so for gay persons, thus resulting in a community-wide stigma inconsistent with the history and dynamics of civil rights laws that ensure equal access to goods, services, and public accommodations.

It is unexceptional that Colorado law can protect gay persons, just as it can protect other classes of individuals, in acquiring whatever products and services they choose on the same terms and conditions as are offered to other members of the public. . . . Petitioners conceded, moreover, that if a baker refused to sell any goods or any cakes for gay weddings, that would be a different matter . . . .

Phillips claims, however, that a narrower issue is presented. He argues that he had to use his artistic skills to make an expressive statement, a wedding endorsement in his own voice and of his own creation[, which] . . . he could not express in a way consistent with his religious beliefs.

Phillips' dilemma was particularly understandable given [that at the time] . . . Colorado did not recognize the validity of gay marriages performed in its own State. . . . [Thus,] there is some force to the argument that the baker was not unreasonable in deeming it lawful to decline to take an action that he understood to be an expression of support for their validity when that expression was contrary to his sincerely held religious beliefs, . . . even one planned to take place in another State.

At the time, state law also afforded storekeepers some latitude to decline to create specific messages the storekeeper considered offensive. Indeed, while enforcement proceedings against Phillips were ongoing, the Colorado Civil Rights Division itself endorsed this proposition in cases involving other bakers' creation of cakes, concluding on at least three occasions that a baker acted lawfully in declining to create cakes with decorations that demeaned gay persons or gay marriages. [The *Jack* cases.]

. . . [A]ny decision in favor of the baker would have to be sufficiently constrained, lest all purveyors of goods and services who object to gay marriages for moral and religious reasons in effect be allowed to put up signs saying "no goods or services will be sold if they will be used for gay marriages," something that would impose a serious stigma on gay persons. But, nonetheless, Phillips was entitled to the neutral and respectful consideration of his claims in all the circumstances of the case.

B

The neutral and respectful consideration . . . was compromised here, however. The . . . Commission's treatment of his case has some elements of a clear and impermissible hostility toward the sincere religious beliefs that motivated his objection.

That hostility surfaced at the Commission's formal, public hearings . . . . At several points during its meeting, commissioners endorsed the view that religious beliefs cannot legitimately be carried into the public sphere or commercial domain, implying that religious beliefs and persons are less than fully welcome in Colorado's business community. One commissioner suggested that Phillips can believe "what he wants to believe," but cannot act on his religious beliefs "if he decides to do business in the state." . . . A few moments later, the commissioner restated the same position: "[I]f a businessman wants to do business in the state and he's got an issue with the—the law's impacting his personal belief system, he needs to look at being able to compromise." . . . Standing alone, these statements . . . might mean simply that a business cannot refuse to provide services based on sexual orientation, regardless of the proprietor's personal views. On the other hand, they might be seen as inappropriate and dismissive comments showing lack of due consideration for Phillips' free exercise rights and the dilemma he faced. In view of the comments that followed, the latter seems the more likely.

[At a later Commission hearing,] another commissioner . . . said far more to disparage Phillips' beliefs. The commissioner stated:

> "I would also like to reiterate what we said in the hearing or the last meeting. Freedom of religion and religion has been used to justify all kinds of discrimination throughout history, whether it be slavery, whether it be the holocaust, whether it be—I mean, we—we can list hundreds of situations where freedom of religion has been used to justify discrimination. And to me it is one of the most despicable pieces of rhetoric that people can use to—to use their religion to hurt others."
>
> . . .

To describe a man's faith as "one of the most despicable pieces of rhetoric that people can use" is to disparage his religion in at least two distinct ways: by describing it as despicable, and also by characterizing it as merely rhetorical—something insubstantial and even insincere. The commissioner even went so far as to compare Phillips' invocation of his sincerely held religious beliefs to defenses of slavery and the Holocaust. This sentiment is inappropriate for a Commission charged with the solemn responsibility of fair and neutral enforcement of Colorado's antidiscrimination law—a law that protects discrimination on the basis of religion as well as sexual orientation.

The record shows no objection to these comments from other commissioners. And the later state-court ruling reviewing the Commission's decision did not mention those comments, much less express concern with their content. Nor were the comments by the commissioners disavowed in the briefs filed in this Court. For these reasons, the Court cannot avoid the conclusion that these statements cast doubt on the fairness and impartiality of the Commission's adjudication of Phillips' case. Members of the Court have disagreed on the question whether statements made by lawmakers may properly be taken into account in determining whether a law intentionally discriminates on the basis of religion. See Church of Lukumi Babalu Aye, Inc. v. Hialeah, 508 U.S. 520, 540–542 (1993); *id.*, at 558 (Scalia, J., concurring in part and concurring in judgment). In this case, however, the remarks were made in a very different context—by an adjudicatory body deciding a particular case.

Another indication of hostility is the difference in treatment between Phillips' case and the cases of other bakers who objected to a requested cake on the basis of conscience and prevailed before the Commission.

. . .

. . . The Commission ruled against Phillips in part on the theory that any message the requested wedding cake would carry would be attributed to the customer, not to the baker. Yet the Division did not address this point in any of the [*Jack*] cases with respect to the cakes depicting anti-gay marriage symbolism. Additionally, the Division found no violation of CADA in the other cases in part because each bakery was willing to sell other products, including those depicting Christian themes, to the prospective customers. But the Commission dismissed Phillips' willingness to sell "birthday cakes, shower cakes, [and] cookies and brownies," . . . to gay and lesbian customers as irrelevant. The treatment of the other cases and Phillips' case could reasonably be interpreted as being inconsistent as to the question of whether speech is involved, quite apart from whether the cases should ultimately be distinguished. In short, the Commission's consideration of Phillips' religious objection did not accord with its treatment of these other objections.

[T]he Colorado Court of Appeals . . . relegated its complete analysis of the [claimed disparate treatment] issue to a footnote[, finding no impermissible discrimination] ". . . against a Christian patron on the basis of his creed" . . . because "the Division found that the bakeries . . . refuse[d] the patron's request . . . because of the offensive nature of the requested message." . . .

A principled rationale for the difference in treatment of these two instances cannot be based on the government's own assessment of offensiveness. . . . [I]t is . . . the role of the State or its officials to prescribe what shall be offensive. . . . The Colorado court's attempt to account for the difference in treatment elevates one view of what is offensive over another and itself sends a signal of official disapproval of Phillips' religious beliefs. The court's footnote does not, therefore, answer the baker's concern that the State's practice was to disfavor the religious basis of his objection.

C

. . .

In *Church of Lukumi Babalu Aye, supra,* the Court made clear that the government . . . cannot impose regulations that are hostile to the religious beliefs of affected citizens and cannot act in a manner that passes judgment upon or presupposes the illegitimacy of religious beliefs and practices. The Free Exercise Clause bars even "subtle departures from neutrality" on matters of religion. . . . Here, that means the Commission was obliged under the Free Exercise Clause to proceed in a manner neutral toward and tolerant of Phillips' religious beliefs. . . .

. . . It hardly requires restating that government has no role in deciding or even suggesting whether the religious ground for Phillips' conscience-based objection is legitimate or illegitimate. On these facts, the Court must draw the inference that Phillips' religious objection was not considered with the neutrality that the Free Exercise Clause requires.

. . . [T]he State's interest could have been weighed against Phillips' sincere religious objections in a way consistent with the requisite religious neutrality that must be strictly observed. The official expressions of hostility to religion in some of the commissioners' comments—comments that were not disavowed at the Commission or by the State at any point in the proceedings that led to affirmance of the order—were inconsistent with what the Free Exercise Clause requires. The Commission's disparate consideration of Phillips' case compared to the cases of the other bakers suggests the same. For these reasons, the order must be set aside.

III

. . .

The outcome of cases like this in other circumstances must await further elaboration in the courts, all in the context of recognizing that these disputes must be resolved with tolerance, without undue disrespect to sincere religious beliefs, and without subjecting gay persons to indignities when they seek goods and services in an open market.

The judgment . . . is reversed.

■ JUSTICE KAGAN, with whom JUSTICE BREYER joins, concurring.

. . . I write separately to elaborate on one of the bases for the Court's holding.

. . . The Court partly relies on the "disparate consideration of Phillips' case compared to the cases of [three] other bakers" who "objected to a requested cake on the basis of conscience." . . . As the Court states, a "principled rationale for the difference in treatment" cannot be "based on the government's own assessment of offensiveness." . . .

. . .

What makes the state agencies' consideration yet more disquieting is that a proper basis for distinguishing the cases was available—in fact, was obvious. . . . CADA . . . makes it unlawful for a place of public accommodation to deny "the full and equal enjoyment" of goods and services to individuals based on certain characteristics, including sexual orientation and creed. . . . The three bakers in the Jack cases did not violate that law. Jack requested them to make a cake (one denigrating gay people and same-sex marriage) that they would not have made for any customer. In refusing that request, the bakers did not single out Jack because of his religion, but instead treated him in the same way they would have treated anyone else—just as CADA requires. By contrast, the same-sex couple in this case requested a wedding cake that Phillips would have made for an opposite-sex couple. In refusing that request, Phillips contravened CADA's demand that customers receive "the full and equal enjoyment" of public accommodations irrespective of their sexual orientation. . . . The different outcomes in the Jack cases and the Phillips case could thus have been justified by a plain reading and neutral application of Colorado law—untainted by any bias against a religious belief.*

... Colorado can treat a baker who discriminates based on sexual orientation differently from a baker who does not discriminate on that or any other prohibited ground. But only, as the Court rightly says, if the State's decisions are not infected by religious hostility or bias. . . .

■ JUSTICE GORSUCH, with whom JUSTICE ALITO joins, concurring.

. . .

... [T]wo of our colleagues have written separately to suggest that the Commission acted neutrally toward his faith when it treated him differently from the other bakers—or that it could have easily done so consistent with the First Amendment. (Ginsburg, J., dissenting); (Kagan, J., concurring). But, respectfully, I do not see how we might rescue the Commission from its error.

. . .

The facts show that the two cases share all legally salient features. In both cases, the effect on the customer was the same: bakers refused service to persons who bore a statutorily protected trait (religious faith or sexual orientation). But in both cases the bakers refused service intending only to honor a personal conviction. To be sure, the bakers *knew* their conduct promised the effect of leaving a customer in a protected class unserved. But there's no indication the bakers actually *intended* to refuse service *because of* a customer's protected characteristic. We know this because all of the bakers explained without contradiction that they would not sell the requested cakes to anyone, while they would sell other cakes to members of the protected class (as well as to anyone else). So, for example, the bakers in the first case would have refused to sell a cake denigrating same-sex marriage to an atheist customer, just as the baker in the second case would have refused to sell a cake celebrating same-sex marriage to a heterosexual customer. And the bakers in the first case were generally happy to sell to persons of faith, just as the baker in the second case was generally happy to sell to gay persons. In both cases, it was the kind of cake, not the kind of customer, that mattered to the bakers.

. . .

... In Mr. Jack's case, the Commission chose to distinguish carefully between intended and knowingly accepted effects. Even though the bakers knowingly denied service to someone in a protected class, the Commission found no violation because the bakers only intended to distance themselves from "the

---

*   Justice Gorsuch disagrees. In his view, the Jack cases and the Phillips case must be treated the same because the bakers in all those cases "would not sell the requested cakes to anyone." That description perfectly fits the Jack cases—and explains why the bakers there did not engage in unlawful discrimination. But it is a surprising characterization of the Phillips case, given that Phillips routinely sells wedding cakes to opposite-sex couples. Justice Gorsuch can make the claim only because he does not think a "wedding cake" is the relevant product. As [he] sees it, the product that Phillips refused to sell here—and would refuse to sell to anyone— was a "cake celebrating same-sex marriage." But that is wrong. The cake requested was not a special "cake celebrating same-sex marriage." It was simply a wedding cake—one that (like other standard wedding cakes) is suitable for use at same-sex and opposite-sex weddings alike. . . . A vendor can choose the products he sells, but not the customers he serves—no matter the reason. Phillips sells wedding cakes. As to that product, he unlawfully discriminates: He sells it to opposite-sex but not to same-sex couples. And on that basis—which has nothing to do with Phillips' religious beliefs—Colorado could have distinguished Phillips from the bakers in the Jack cases, who did not engage in any prohibited discrimination.

offensive nature of the requested message." . . . Yet, in Mr. Phillips's case, the Commission . . . concluded instead that an "intent to disfavor" a protected class of persons should be "readily . . . presumed" from the knowing failure to serve someone who belongs to that class.

. . . In the end, the Commission's decisions simply reduce to this: it *presumed* that Mr. Phillips harbored an intent to discriminate against a protected class in light of the foreseeable effects of his conduct, but it declined to presume the same intent in Mr. Jack's case even though the effects of the bakers' conduct were just as foreseeable. Underscoring the double standard, a state appellate court said that "no such showing" of actual "animus"—or intent to discriminate against persons in a protected class—was even required in Mr. Phillips's case. . . .

The Commission cannot have it both ways. The Commission cannot slide up and down the *mens rea* scale, picking a mental state standard to suit its tastes depending on its sympathies. . . . [I]t can't . . . apply a more generous legal test to secular objections than religious ones. See *Church of Lukumi Babalu Aye,* 508 U.S., at 543–544. That is anything but the neutral treatment of religion.

. . . [A]s the Court explains, it appears the Commission wished to condemn Mr. Phillips for expressing just the kind of "irrational" or "offensive . . . message" that the bakers in the first case refused to endorse. . . . In this country, the place of secular officials isn't to sit in judgment of religious beliefs, but only to protect their free exercise. . . . It is in protecting unpopular religious beliefs that we prove this country's commitment to serving as a refuge for religious freedom. . . .

. . . It is no answer . . . to observe that Mr. Jack requested a cake with text on it while Mr. Craig and Mr. Mullins sought a cake celebrating their wedding without discussing its decoration . . . See . . . (Ginsburg, J., dissenting). It is no answer either simply to slide up a level of generality to redescribe Mr. Phillips's case as involving only a wedding cake like any other, so the fact that Mr. Phillips would make one for some means he must make them for all. See . . . (Kagan, J., concurring). These arguments . . . fail to afford Mr. Phillips's faith neutral respect.

. . . To suggest that cakes with words convey a message but cakes without words do not—all in order to excuse the bakers in Mr. Jack's case while penalizing Mr. Phillips—is irrational. . . . Words or not and whatever the exact design, it celebrates a wedding, and if the wedding cake is made for a same-sex couple it celebrates a same-sex wedding. . . . It is precisely . . . approval that Mr. Phillips intended to withhold in keeping with his religious faith. The Commission denied Mr. Phillips that choice, even as it afforded the bakers in Mr. Jack's case the choice to refuse to advance a message they deemed offensive to their secular commitments. That is not neutral.

. . .

The second suggestion fares no better. Suggesting that this case is only about "wedding cakes"—and not a wedding cake celebrating a same-sex wedding—actually points up the problem. . . . We are told . . . to apply a sort of Goldilocks rule: describing the cake by its ingredients is *too general*; understanding it as celebrating a same-sex wedding is *too specific*; but regarding it as a generic wedding cake is *just right*. The problem is, the Commission didn't play with the level of generality in Mr. Jack's case in this way. It didn't declare, for example, that because the cakes Mr. Jack requested were just cakes about weddings generally, and all such cakes were the same, the bakers had to produce them. Instead, the Commission accepted the bakers' view that the specific cakes Mr. Jack requested conveyed a message offensive to their convictions and allowed them to refuse service. Having done that there, it must do the same here.

. . . Neither the Commission nor this Court may apply a more specific level of generality in Mr. Jack's case (a cake that conveys a message regarding same-sex marriage) while applying a higher level of generality in Mr. Phillips's case (a cake that conveys no message regarding same-sex marriage). Of course, under *Smith* a vendor cannot escape a public accommodations law just because his religion frowns on it. But for any law to comply with the First Amendment and *Smith*, it must be applied in a manner that treats religion with neutral respect. That means the government must apply the *same* level of generality across cases—and that did not happen here.

There is another problem with sliding up the generality scale: it risks denying constitutional protection to religious beliefs that draw distinctions more specific than the government's preferred level of description. To some, all wedding cakes may appear indistinguishable. But *to Mr. Phillips* that is not the case—his faith teaches him otherwise. And his religious beliefs are entitled to no less respectful treatment than the bakers' secular beliefs in Mr. Jack's case. . . . It is no more appropriate for the United States Supreme Court to tell Mr. Phillips that a wedding cake is just like any other—without regard to the religious significance his faith may attach to it—than it would be for the Court to suggest that for all persons sacramental bread is *just* bread or a kippah is *just* a cap.

. . .

■ JUSTICE THOMAS, with whom JUSTICE GORSUCH joins, concurring in part and concurring in the judgment.

I agree that the . . . Commission . . . violated Jack Phillips' right to freely exercise his religion. As Justice Gorsuch explains, the Commission treated Phillips' case differently from a similar case involving three other bakers, for reasons that can only be explained by hostility toward Phillips' religion. . . . Although the Commissioners' comments are certainly disturbing, the discriminatory application of Colorado's public-accommodations law is enough on its own to violate Phillips' rights. To the extent the Court agrees, I join its opinion.

. . . I write separately to address his free-speech claim.

. . . [T]he Court of Appeals concluded that Phillips' conduct was not expressive and was not protected speech. It reasoned that an outside observer would think that Phillips was merely complying with Colorado's public-accommodations law, not expressing a message, and that Phillips could post a disclaimer to that effect. This reasoning flouts bedrock principles of our free-speech jurisprudence and would justify virtually any law that compels individuals to speak. It should not pass without comment.

. . .

. . . Colorado is punishing [Phillips] because he refuses to create custom wedding cakes that express approval of same-sex marriage. In cases like this one, our precedents demand " 'the most exacting scrutiny.' "

. . .

■ JUSTICE GINSBURG, with whom JUSTICE SOTOMAYOR joins, dissenting.

. . .

. . . The different outcomes the Court features do not evidence hostility to religion of the kind we have previously held to signal a free-exercise violation, nor do the comments by one or two members of one of the four decisionmaking entities considering this case justify reversing the judgment below.

I

. . . Jack['s] visit[s to] three Colorado bakeries . . . followed a similar pattern. He requested two cakes

> "made to resemble an open Bible. He also requested that each cake be decorated with Biblical verses. [He] requested that one of the cakes include an image of two groomsmen, holding hands, with a red 'X' over the image. On one cake, he requested [on] one side[,] . . . 'God hates sin. Psalm 45:7' and on the opposite side of the cake 'Homosexuality is a detestable sin. Leviticus 18:2.' On the second cake, [the one] with the image of the two groomsmen covered by a red 'X' [Jack] requested [these words]: 'God loves sinners' and on the other side 'While we were yet sinners Christ died for us. Romans 5:8.' " . . .

In contrast to Jack, Craig and Mullins simply requested a wedding cake: They mentioned no message or anything else distinguishing the cake they wanted to buy from any other wedding cake Phillips would have sold.

One bakery told Jack it would make cakes in the shape of Bibles, but would not decorate them with the requested messages; the owner told Jack her bakery "does not discriminate" and "accept[s] all humans." . . . The second bakery owner told Jack he "had done open Bibles and books many times and that they look amazing," but declined to make the specific cakes Jack described because the baker regarded the messages as "hateful." . . . The third bakery, according to Jack, said it would bake the cakes, but would not include the requested message.

. . . The Division found no probable cause to support Jack's claims of unequal treatment and denial of goods or services based on his Christian religious beliefs. . . . In this regard, the Division observed that the bakeries regularly produced cakes and other baked goods with Christian symbols and had denied other customer requests for designs demeaning people whose dignity the Colorado Antidiscrimination Act (CADA) protects. . . .

The Court concludes that "the Commission's consideration of Phillips' religious objection did not accord with its treatment of [the other bakers'] objections." . . . But the cases the Court aligns are hardly comparable. The bakers would have refused to make a cake with Jack's requested message for any customer, regardless of his or her religion. And the bakers visited by Jack would have sold him any baked goods they would have sold anyone else. The bakeries' refusal to make Jack cakes of a kind they would not make for any customer scarcely resembles Phillips' refusal to serve Craig and Mullins: Phillips would *not* sell to Craig and Mullins, for no reason other than their sexual orientation, a cake of the kind he regularly sold to others. When a couple contacts a bakery for a wedding cake, the product they are seeking is a cake celebrating *their* wedding—not a cake celebrating heterosexual weddings or same-sex weddings— and that is the service Craig and Mullins were denied. . . . Jack . . . suffered no service refusal on the basis of his religion or any other protected characteristic.

He was treated as any other customer would have been treated—no better, no worse.[3]

The fact that Phillips might sell other cakes and cookies to gay and lesbian customers was irrelevant . . . . What matters is that Phillips would not provide a good or service to a same-sex couple that he would provide to a heterosexual couple. In contrast, the other bakeries' sale of other goods to Christian customers was relevant: It shows that there were no goods the bakeries would sell to a non-Christian customer that they would refuse to sell to a Christian customer.

Nor was the Colorado Court of Appeals' "difference in treatment of these two instances . . . based on the government's own assessment of offensiveness." Phillips declined to make a cake he found offensive where the offensiveness of the product was determined solely by the identity of the customer requesting it. The three other bakeries declined to make cakes where their objection to the product was due to the demeaning message the requested product would literally display. . . .[5] . . .

II

Statements made at the Commission's public hearings on Phillips' case provide no firmer support for the Court's holding today. Whatever one may think of the statements in historical context, I see no reason why the comments of one or two Commissioners should be taken to overcome Phillips' refusal to sell a wedding cake to Craig and Mullins. The proceedings involved several layers of independent decisionmaking, of which the Commission was but one. . . . What prejudice infected the determinations of the adjudicators in the case before and after the Commission? The Court does not say. Phillips' case is thus far removed from the only precedent upon which the Court relies, Church of Lukumi Babalu Aye, Inc. v. Hialeah, 508 U.S. 520 (1993), where the government action that violated a principle of religious neutrality implicated a sole decisionmaking body, the city council . . . .

. . .

---

[3]   Justice Gorsuch argues that the situations "share all legally salient features." But what critically differentiates them is the role the customer's "statutorily protected trait" played in the denial of service. Change Craig and Mullins' sexual orientation (or sex), and Phillips would have provided the cake. Change Jack's religion, and the bakers would have been no more willing to comply with his request. The bakers' objections to Jack's cakes had nothing to do with "religious opposition to same-sex weddings." (Gorsuch, J., concurring). Instead, the bakers simply refused to make cakes bearing statements demeaning to people protected by CADA. . . . Phillips did, therefore, discriminate *because of* sexual orientation; the other bakers did not discriminate *because of* religious belief; and the Commission properly found discrimination in one case but not the other. . . .

[5]   . . . [W]hile Jack requested cakes with particular text inscribed, Craig and Mullins were refused the sale of any wedding cake at all. They were turned away before any specific cake design could be discussed. . . . The Division and the Court of Appeals could rationally and lawfully distinguish between a case involving disparaging text and images and a case involving a wedding cake of unspecified design. The distinction is not between a cake with text and one without, see (Gorsuch, J., concurring); it is between a cake with a particular design and one whose form was never even discussed.

Page 1804. Replace Locke v. Davey with the following:

Espinoza v. Montana Department of Revenue

591 U.S. ___, 140 S.Ct. 2246 (2020).

■ CHIEF JUSTICE ROBERTS delivered the opinion of the Court.

The Montana Legislature[, seeking "to provide parental and student choice in education",] established a program [in 2015] to provide tuition assistance to parents who send their children to private schools. The program grants a tax credit to [any taxpayer] who donates to certain organizations that in turn award scholarships to selected students attending such schools. When petitioners sought to use the scholarships at a religious school, the Montana Supreme Court struck down the program. The Court relied on the "no-aid" provision of the State Constitution, which prohibits any aid to a school controlled by a "church, sect, or denomination." The question presented is whether the Free Exercise Clause of the United States Constitution barred that application of the no-aid provision.

I

A

. . .

A family whose child is awarded a scholarship under the program may use it at any "qualified education provider"—that is, any private school that meets certain accreditation, testing, and safety requirements. . . . Virtually every private school in Montana qualifies. Upon receiving a scholarship, the family designates its school of choice, and the scholarship organization sends the scholarship funds directly to the school. . . . Neither the scholarship organization nor its donors can restrict awards to particular types of schools.

The Montana Legislature allotted $3 million annually to fund the tax credits . . . . The program is slated to expire in 2023. . . .

The Montana Legislature also directed that the program be administered in accordance with Article X, section 6, of the Montana Constitution, which contains a "no-aid" provision barring government aid to sectarian schools. . . .

Shortly after the scholarship program was created, the Montana Department of Revenue promulgated "Rule 1," over the objection of the Montana Attorney General. That administrative rule prohibited families from using scholarships at religious schools. . . . The Department explained that the Rule was needed to reconcile the scholarship program with the no-aid provision of the Montana Constitution.

The Montana Attorney General disagreed. In a letter to the Department, he advised that the Montana Constitution did not require excluding religious schools from the program, and if it did, it would "very likely" violate the United States Constitution by discriminating against the schools and their students. . . .

B

This suit was brought by three mothers whose children attend . . . a [pre-K through 12th grade] private Christian school that meets the statutory criteria for "qualified education providers." [P]etitioners chose the school in large part because it "teaches the same Christian values that [they] teach at home." . . . Rule 1 blocked petitioners from using scholarship funds for [their] tuition[, and their suit in state court] claimed that Rule 1 conflicted with the statute that created the scholarship program and could not be justified on the ground that it was compelled by the Montana Constitution's no-aid provision. Petitioners further alleged that the Rule discriminated on the basis of their religious views and the religious nature of the school they had chosen for their children.

The trial court enjoined Rule 1, holding that . . . [it] was not required by the no-aid provision, because that provision prohibits only "appropriations" that aid religious schools, "not tax credits." . . .

. . .

[. . .T]he Montana Supreme Court reversed[, . . .] first . . . holding that the program aided religious schools in violation of the no-aid provision of the Montana Constitution. In the Court's view, the no-aid provision "broadly and strictly prohibits aid to sectarian schools." . . . The scholarship program provided such aid by using tax credits to "subsidize tuition payments" at private schools that are "religiously affiliated" or "controlled in whole or in part by churches." . . . In that way, the scholarship program flouted the State Constitution's "guarantee to all Montanans that their government will not use state funds to aid religious schools." . . .

The Montana Supreme Court went on to hold that the violation of the no-aid provision required invalidating the entire scholarship program. The Court explained that the program provided "no mechanism" for preventing aid from flowing to religious schools, and therefore the scholarship program could not "under *any* circumstance" be construed as consistent with the no-aid provision. . . . As a result, the tax credit is no longer available to support scholarships at either religious or secular private schools.

The Montana Supreme Court acknowledged that "an overly-broad" application of the no-aid provision "could implicate free exercise concerns" and that "there may be a case" where "prohibiting the aid would violate the Free Exercise Clause." . . . But . . . "this is not one of those cases." . . .

Finally, the Court agreed with petitioners that the Department had exceeded its authority in promulgating Rule 1. The Court explained that the statute creating the scholarship program had broadly defined qualifying schools to include all private schools, including religious ones, and the Department lacked authority to "transform" that definition with an administrative rule. . . .

. . .

II

A

The Religion Clauses of the First Amendment provide that "Congress shall make no law respecting an establishment of religion, or prohibiting the free exercise thereof." We have recognized a " 'play in the joints' between what the Establishment Clause permits and the Free Exercise Clause compels." Trinity Lutheran Church of Columbia, Inc. v. Comer, 582 U. S. ___, ___ (2017) (slip op., at 6) (quoting Locke v. Davey, 540 U. S. 712, 718 (2004)). Here, the parties do not dispute that the scholarship program is permissible under the Establishment Clause. Nor could they. We have repeatedly held that the Establishment Clause is not offended when religious observers and organizations benefit from neutral government programs. See, e.g., Locke, 540 U. S., at 719; Rosenberger v. Rector and Visitors of Univ. of Va., 515 U. S. 819, 839 (1995). See also Trinity Lutheran,

582 U. S., at ___ (slip op., at 6) (noting the parties' agreement that the Establishment Clause was not violated by including churches in a playground resurfacing program). Any Establishment Clause objection to the scholarship program here is particularly unavailing because the government support makes its way to religious schools only as a result of Montanans independently choosing to spend their scholarships at such schools. See Locke, 540 U. S., at 719; Zelman v. Simmons-Harris, 536 U. S. 639, 649–653 (2002). The Montana Supreme Court, however, held as a matter of state law that even such indirect government support qualified as "aid" prohibited under the Montana Constitution.

. . . [W]e accept the Montana Supreme Court's interpretation of state law—including its determination that the scholarship program provided impermissible "aid" within the meaning of the Montana Constitution—and we assess whether excluding religious schools and affected families from that program was consistent with the Federal Constitution.[2]

The Free Exercise Clause, which applies to the States under the Fourteenth Amendment, "protects religious observers against unequal treatment" and against "laws that impose special disabilities on the basis of religious status." *Trinity Lutheran*, ... Those "basic principle[s]" have long guided this Court. *Trinity Lutheran*, . . . See, e.g., Everson v. Board of Ed. of Ewing, 330 U. S. 1, 16 (1947) (a State "cannot exclude individual Catholics, Lutherans, Mohammedans, Baptists, Jews, Methodists, Non-believers, Presbyterians, or the members of any other faith, because of their faith, or lack of it, from receiving the benefits of public welfare legislation"); Lyng v. Northwest Indian Cemetery Protective Assn., 485 U. S. 439, 449 (1988) (the Free Exercise Clause protects against laws that "penalize religious activity by denying any person an equal share of the rights, benefits, and privileges enjoyed by other citizens").

Most recently, *Trinity Lutheran* distilled these and other decisions to the same effect into the "unremarkable" conclusion that disqualifying otherwise eligible recipients from a public benefit "solely because of their religious character" imposes "a penalty on the free exercise of religion that triggers the most exacting scrutiny." . . . In *Trinity Lutheran*, Missouri provided grants to help nonprofit organizations pay for playground resurfacing, but a state policy disqualified any organization "owned or controlled by a church, sect, or other religious entity." . . . Because of that policy, an otherwise eligible church-owned preschool was denied a grant to resurface its playground. Missouri's policy discriminated against the Church "simply because of what it is—a church," and so the policy was subject to the "strictest scrutiny," which it failed. . . . We acknowledged that the State had not "criminalized" the way in which the Church worshipped or "told the Church that it cannot subscribe to a certain view of the Gospel." . . . But the State's discriminatory policy was "odious to our Constitution all the same."

Here too Montana's no-aid provision bars religious schools from public benefits solely because of the religious character of the schools. The provision also bars parents who wish to send their children to a religious school from those same benefits, again solely because of the religious character of the school. This is apparent from the plain text. The provision bars aid to any school "controlled

---

[2] Justice Sotomayor argues that the Montana Supreme Court "expressly declined to reach any federal issue." Not so. [T]he Montana Supreme Court recognized that certain applications of the no-aid provision could "violate the Free Exercise Clause." . . . But the Court expressly concluded that "this is not one of those cases."

in whole or in part by any church, sect, or denomination." Mont. Const., Art. X, § 6(1). The provision's title—"Aid prohibited to sectarian schools"—confirms that the provision singles out schools based on their religious character. . . . And the Montana Supreme Court explained that the provision forbids aid to any school that is "sectarian," "religiously affiliated," or "controlled in whole or in part by churches." . . . The provision plainly excludes schools from government aid solely because of religious status. See *Trinity Lutheran*, ...

The Department counters that *Trinity Lutheran* does not govern here because the no-aid provision applies not because of the religious character of the recipients, but because of how the funds would be used—for "religious education." . . . In *Trinity Lutheran*, a majority of the Court concluded that the Missouri policy violated the Free Exercise Clause because it discriminated on the basis of religious status. A plurality declined to address discrimination with respect to "religious uses of funding or other forms of discrimination." . . . The plurality saw no need to consider such concerns because Missouri had expressly discriminated "based on religious identity," . . . which was enough to invalidate the state policy without addressing how government funds were used.

This case also turns expressly on religious status and not religious use. The Montana Supreme Court applied the no-aid provision solely by reference to religious status. The Court repeatedly explained that the no-aid provision bars aid to "schools controlled in whole or in part by churches," "sectarian schools," and "religiously affiliated schools." . . . Applying this provision to the scholarship program, the Montana Supreme Court noted that most of the private schools that would benefit from the program were "religiously affiliated" and "controlled by churches," and the Court ultimately concluded that the scholarship program ran afoul of the Montana Constitution by aiding "schools controlled by churches." . . . The Montana Constitution discriminates based on religious status just like the Missouri policy in *Trinity Lutheran*, which excluded organizations "owned or controlled by a church, sect, or other religious entity."

The Department points to some language in the decision below indicating that the no-aid provision has the goal or effect of ensuring that government aid does not end up being used for "sectarian education" or "religious education." . . . The Department also contrasts what it characterizes as the "completely non-religious" benefit of playground resurfacing in *Trinity Lutheran* with the unrestricted tuition aid at issue here. . . . General school aid, the Department stresses, could be used for religious ends by some recipients, particularly schools that believe faith should "permeate[ ]" everything they do. . . .

Regardless, those considerations were not the Montana Supreme Court's basis for applying the no-aid provision to exclude religious schools; that hinged solely on religious status. Status-based discrimination remains status based even if one of its goals or effects is preventing religious organizations from putting aid to religious uses.

Undeterred by *Trinity Lutheran*, the Montana Supreme Court applied the no-aid provision to hold that religious schools could not benefit from the scholarship program. . . . So applied, the provision "impose[s] special disabilities on the basis of religious status" and "condition[s] the availability of benefits upon a recipient's willingness to surrender [its] religiously impelled status." *Trinity Lutheran*, . . . (quoting Church of Lukumi Babalu Aye, Inc. v. Hialeah, 508 U. S. 520, 533 (1993), and McDaniel v. Paty, 435 U. S. 618, 626 (1978) (plurality opinion) . . . .) To be eligible for government aid under the Montana Constitution, a school must divorce itself from any religious control or affiliation. Placing such a condition on benefits or privileges "inevitably deters or discourages the exercise of First Amendment rights." *Trinity Lutheran* . . . . The Free Exercise Clause protects against even "indirect coercion," and a State "punishe[s] the free exercise of religion" by disqualifying the religious from government aid as Montana did here. *Trinity Lutheran* . . . . Such status-based discrimination is subject to "the strictest scrutiny." . . .

None of this is meant to suggest that we agree with the Department . . . that some lesser degree of scrutiny applies to discrimination against religious uses of government aid. . . . Some Members of the Court, moreover, have questioned whether there is a meaningful distinction between discrimination based on use or conduct and that based on status. See *Trinity Lutheran*, . . . (Gorsuch, J., joined by Thomas, J., concurring in part) . . . . We acknowledge the point but need not examine it here. It is enough in this case to conclude that strict scrutiny applies under *Trinity Lutheran* because Montana's no-aid provision discriminates based on religious status.

B

Seeking to avoid *Trinity Lutheran*, the Department contends that this case is instead governed by Locke v. Davey, 540 U. S. 712 (2004). . . . *Locke* also involved a scholarship program. The State of Washington provided scholarships paid out of the State's general fund to help students pursuing postsecondary education. The scholarships could be used at accredited religious and non-religious schools alike, but Washington prohibited students from using the scholarships to pursue devotional theology degrees, which prepared students for a calling as clergy. This prohibition prevented Davey from using his scholarship to obtain a degree that would have enabled him to become a pastor. We held that Washington had not violated the Free Exercise Clause.

Locke differs from this case in two critical ways. First, Locke explained that Washington had "merely chosen not to fund a distinct category of instruction": the "essentially religious endeavor" of training a minister "to lead a congregation." . . . Thus, Davey "was denied a scholarship because of what he proposed to do—use the funds to prepare for the ministry." *Trinity Lutheran*, ... Apart from that narrow restriction, Washington's program allowed scholarships to be used at "pervasively religious schools" that incorporated religious instruction throughout their classes. . . . By contrast, Montana's Constitution does not zero in on any particular "essentially religious" course of instruction at a religious school. Rather, . . . the no-aid provision bars all aid to a religious school "simply because of what it is," putting the school to a choice between being religious or receiving government benefits. *Trinity Lutheran*, ... At the same time, the provision puts families to a choice between sending their children to a religious school or receiving such benefits.

Second, *Locke* invoked a "historic and substantial" state interest in not funding the training of clergy, . . . explaining that "opposition to . . . funding 'to support church leaders' lay at the historic core of the Religion Clauses," *Trinity Lutheran*, . . . (quoting *Locke*, . . .). As evidence of that tradition, the Court in *Locke* emphasized that the propriety of state-supported clergy was a central subject of founding-era debates, and that most state constitutions from that era prohibited the expenditure of tax dollars to support the clergy. . . .

But no comparable "historic and substantial" tradition supports Montana's decision to disqualify religious schools from government aid. In the founding era and the early 19th century, governments provided financial support to private schools, including denominational ones. . . . Local governments provided grants to private schools, including religious ones, for the education of the poor. . . . Even States with bans on government-supported clergy, such as New Jersey, Pennsylvania, and Georgia, provided various forms of aid to religious schools. . . . Early federal aid (often land grants) went to religious schools. . . . Congress provided support to denominational schools in the District of Columbia until 1848, . . . and Congress paid churches to run schools for American Indians through the end of the 19th century . . . . After the Civil War, Congress spent large sums on education for emancipated freedmen, often by supporting denominational schools in the South through the Freedmen's Bureau. . . .[3]

The Department argues that a tradition *against* state support for religious schools arose in the second half of the 19th century, as more than 30 States—including Montana—adopted no-aid provisions. . . . Such a development, of course, cannot by itself establish an early American tradition. Justice Sotomayor questions our reliance on aid provided during the same era by the Freedmen's Bureau, but we see no inconsistency in recognizing that such evidence may reinforce an early practice but cannot create one. In addition, many of the no-aid provisions belong to a more checkered tradition shared with the Blaine Amendment of the 1870s. That proposal—which Congress nearly passed—would have added to the Federal Constitution a provision similar to the state no-aid provisions, prohibiting States from aiding "sectarian" schools. . . . "[I]t was an open secret that 'sectarian' was code for 'Catholic.' " . . . The Blaine Amendment was "born of bigotry" and "arose at a time of pervasive hostility to the Catholic Church and to Catholics in general"; many of its state counterparts have a similarly "shameful pedigree." . . . The no-aid provisions of the 19th century hardly evince a tradition that should inform our understanding of the Free Exercise Clause.

The Department argues that several States have rejected referendums to overturn or limit their no-aid provisions, and that Montana even re-adopted its own in the 1970s, for reasons unrelated to anti-Catholic bigotry. . . . But, on the other side of the ledger, many States today—including those with no-aid provisions—provide support to religious schools through vouchers, scholarships, tax credits, and other measures. . . . According to petitioners, 20 of 37 States with no-aid provisions allow religious options in publicly funded scholarship programs, and almost all allow religious options in tax credit programs.

---

[3] Justice Breyer sees "no meaningful difference" between concerns animating bans on support for clergy and bans on support for religious schools. But evidently early American governments did. Justice Breyer contests particular examples but acknowledges that some bans on clergy support did not bar certain "sponsorship" of religious schools. And, central to the issue here, he certainly does not identify a consistent early tradition, of the sort invoked in *Locke*, against support for religious schools. Virginia's opposition to establishing university theology professorships and chartering theological seminaries . . . Justice Breyer also invokes Madison's objections to the Virginia Assessment Bill, but Madison objected in part because the Bill provided special support to certain churches and clergy, thereby "violat[ing] equality by subjecting some to peculiar burdens." Memorial and Remonstrance Against Religious Assessments, Art. 4, reprinted in Everson, 330 U. S., at 66 (appendix to dissenting opinion of Rutledge, J.) . . . .It is far from clear that the same objections extend to programs that provide equal support to all private primary and secondary schools. If anything, excluding religious schools from such programs would appear to impose the "peculiar burdens" feared by Madison.

All to say, we agree with the Department that the historical record is "complex." . . . And it is true that governments over time have taken a variety of approaches to religious schools. But it is clear that there is no "historic and substantial" tradition against aiding such schools comparable to the tradition against state-supported clergy invoked by *Locke*.

C

Two dissenters would chart new courses. Justice Sotomayor would grant the government "some room" to "single . . . out" religious entities "for exclusion," based on what she views as "the interests embodied in the Religion Clauses." Justice Breyer, building on his solo opinion in *Trinity Lutheran*, would adopt a "flexible, context-specific approach" that "may well vary" from case to case. . . . As best we can tell, courts applying this approach would contemplate the particular benefit and restriction at issue and discern their relationship to religion and society, taking into account "context and consequences measured in light of [the] purposes" of the Religion Clauses. . . . What is clear is that Justice Breyer would afford much freer rein to judges than our current regime, arguing that "there is 'no test-related substitute for the exercise of legal judgment.' " . . .

The simplest response is that these dissents follow from prior separate writings, not from the Court's decision in *Trinity Lutheran* or the decades of precedent on which it relied. These precedents have "repeatedly confirmed" the straightforward rule that we apply today: When otherwise eligible recipients are disqualified from a public benefit "solely because of their religious character," we must apply strict scrutiny. *Trinity Lutheran* . . . .

. . .

D

Because the Montana Supreme Court applied the no-aid provision to discriminate against schools and parents based on the religious character of the school, the "strictest scrutiny" is required. . . .

The Montana Supreme Court asserted that the no-aid provision serves Montana's interest in separating church and State "more fiercely" than the Federal Constitution. . . . But "that interest cannot qualify as compelling" in the face of the infringement of free exercise here. *Trinity Lutheran* . . . . A State's interest "in achieving greater separation of church and State than is already ensured under the Establishment Clause . . . is limited by the Free Exercise Clause." . . .

The Department, for its part, asserts that the no-aid provision actually *promotes* . . . the religious liberty of taxpayers by ensuring that their taxes are not directed to religious organizations, and it safeguards the freedom of religious organizations by keeping the government out of their operations. . . . An infringement of First Amendment rights, however, cannot be justified by a State's alternative view that the infringement advances religious liberty. . . .

Furthermore, we do not see how the no-aid provision promotes religious freedom. As noted, this Court has repeatedly upheld government programs that spend taxpayer funds on equal aid to religious observers and organizations, particularly when the link between government and religion is attenuated by private choices. A school, concerned about government involvement with its religious activities, might reasonably decide for itself not to participate in a government program. But we doubt that the school's liberty is enhanced by eliminating any option to participate in the first place.

The Department's argument is especially unconvincing because the infringement of religious liberty here broadly affects both religious schools and adherents. Montana's no-aid provision imposes a categorical ban—"broadly and strictly" prohibiting "any type of aid" to religious schools. . . . This prohibition is far more sweeping than the policy in *Trinity Lutheran*, which barred churches from one narrow program for playground resurfacing—causing "in all likelihood" only "a few extra scraped knees." . . .

And the prohibition before us today burdens not only religious schools but also the families whose children attend or hope to attend them. . . . [T]he no-aid provision penalizes [the constitutionally protected] decision [by parents to send their children to religious schools] by cutting families off from otherwise available benefits if they choose a religious private school rather than a secular one, and for no other reason.

The Department also suggests that the no-aid provision advances Montana's interests in public education . . . by ensuring that government support is not diverted to private schools. . . . . But, under that framing, the no-aid provision is fatally underinclusive because its "proffered objectives are not pursued with respect to analogous nonreligious conduct." *Lukumi*, ... On the Department's view, an interest in public education is undermined by diverting government support to *any* private school, yet the no-aid provision bars aid only to *religious* ones. . . .

A State need not subsidize private education. But once a State decides to do so, it cannot disqualify some private schools solely because they are religious.

III

The Department argues that . . . there is no free exercise violation here because the Montana Supreme Court ultimately eliminated the scholarship program altogether. According[ly,] . . . religious schools and adherents cannot complain that they are excluded from any generally available benefit.

Two dissenters agree. Justice Ginsburg reports that the State of Montana simply chose to "put all private school parents in the same boat" by invalidating the scholarship program, and Justice Sotomayor describes the decision below as resting on state law grounds having nothing to do with the federal Free Exercise Clause.

The descriptions are not accurate. The Montana Legislature created the scholarship program; the Legislature never chose to end it . . . . The program was eliminated by . . . the Montana Supreme Court[, which] invalidated the program pursuant to a state law provision that expressly discriminates on the basis of religious status. The Court applied that provision to hold that religious schools were barred from participating in the program. Then, seeing no other "mechanism" to make absolutely sure that religious schools received no aid, the court chose to invalidate the entire program. . . .

The final step in this line of reasoning eliminated the program, to the detriment of religious and non-religious schools alike. But the Court's error of federal law occurred at the beginning. When the Court was called upon to apply a state law no-aid provision to exclude religious schools from the program, it was obligated by the Federal Constitution to reject the invitation. . . . Because the elimination of the program flowed directly from the Montana Supreme Court's failure to follow the dictates of federal law, it cannot be defended as a neutral policy decision, or as resting on adequate and independent state law grounds.[4]

. . . Given the conflict between the Free Exercise Clause and the application of the no-aid provision here, the Montana Supreme Court should have "disregard[ed]" the no-aid provision and decided this case "conformably to the [C]onstitution" of the United States. *Marbury v. Madison*, ... [E]xclusion [of religious schools and the families whose children who attend them] from the scholarship program here is "odious to our Constitution" and "cannot stand." *Trinity Lutheran*, ...

■ JUSTICE THOMAS, with whom JUSTICE GORSUCH joins, concurring.

. . . I write separately to explain how this Court's interpretation of the Establishment Clause continues to hamper free exercise rights. Until we correct course on that interpretation, individuals will continue to face needless obstacles in their attempts to vindicate their religious freedom.

. . . Under the modern, but erroneous, view of the Establishment Clause, the government must treat all religions equally and treat religion equally to nonreligion. . . . This "equality principle," the theory goes, prohibits the government from expressing any preference for religion—or even permitting any signs of religion in the governmental realm. Thus, when a plaintiff brings a free exercise claim, the government may defend its law, as Montana did here, on the ground that the law's restrictions are *required* to prevent it from "establishing" religion.

This understanding of the Establishment Clause is unmoored from the original meaning of the First Amendment. . . .

. . .

Thus, the modern view, which presumes that States must remain both completely separate from and virtually silent on matters of religion to comply with the Establishment Clause, is fundamentally incorrect. Properly understood, the Establishment Clause does not prohibit States from favoring religion. . . .

I have previously made these points in Establishment Clause cases to show that the Clause likely has no application to the States or, if it is capable of incorporation, that the Court employs a far broader test than the Clause's original meaning. . . . But the Court's wayward approach to the Establishment Clause also impacts its free exercise jurisprudence. Specifically, its overly expansive understanding of the former Clause has led to a correspondingly cramped interpretation of the latter.

. . .

. . . The Court's distorted view of the Establishment Clause . . . removes the entire subject of religion from the realm of permissible governmental activity, instead mandating strict separation.

---

[4]   Justice Sotomayor worries that, in light of our decision, the Montana Supreme Court must "order the State to recreate" a scholarship program that "no longer exists." But it was the Montana Supreme Court that eliminated the program, in the decision below, which remains under review. Our reversal of that decision simply restores the status quo established by the Montana Legislature before the Court's error of federal law. We do not consider any alterations the Legislature may choose to make in the future.

. . . [O]perat[ing] as a type of content-based restriction on the government[, this interpretation] communicates a message that religion is dangerous and in need of policing, which in turn has the effect of tilting society in favor of devaluing religion.

Historical evidence suggests that many advocates for this separationist view were originally motivated by hostility toward certain disfavored religions. . . . And this Court's adoption of a separationist interpretation has itself sometimes bordered on religious hostility. . . .

. . . So long as this hostility remains, fostered by our distorted understanding of the Establishment Clause, free exercise rights will continue to suffer.

. . . The Free Exercise Clause . . . rests on the lowest rung of the Court's ladder of rights, and precariously so at that. Returning the Establishment Clause to its proper scope will not completely rectify the Court's disparate treatment of constitutional rights, but it will go a long way toward allowing free exercise of religion to flourish as the Framers intended. . . .

■ JUSTICE ALITO, concurring.

. . .

. . . Montana's ["no-aid"] provision was modeled on the failed Blaine Amendment to the Constitution of the United States. Named after House Speaker James Blaine, the Congressman who introduced it in 1875, the amendment was prompted by virulent prejudice against immigrants, particularly Catholic immigrants. . . .

The Blaine Amendment was narrowly defeated, passing in the House but falling just short of the two-thirds majority needed in the Senate to refer the amendment to the States. . . . Afterwards, most States adopted provisions like Montana's to achieve the same objective at the state level, often as a condition of entering the Union. Thirty-eight States still have these "little Blaine Amendments" today. . . .

. . .

. . . Montana's no-aid provision retains the bigoted code language used throughout state Blaine Amendments.

. . .

Backers of the Blaine Amendment either held nativist views or capitalized on them. When Blaine introduced the amendment, The Nation reported that it was "a Constitutional amendment directed against the Catholics . . . ." . . .

Montana's no-aid provision was the result of this same prejudice. When Congress allowed Montana into the Union in 1889, it still included prominent supporters of the failed Blaine Amendment. . . . The Act enabling Montana to become a State required "[t]hat provision shall be made for the establishment and maintenance of systems of public schools . . . free from sectarian control." . . . Montana thereafter adopted its constitutional rule against public funding for any school "controlled" by a "sect." Mont. Const., Art. XI, § 8 (1889). There appears to have been no doubt which schools that meant. As petitioners show, Montana's religious schools—and its private schools in general—were predominantly Catholic, . . . and anti-Catholicism was alive in Montana too. . . .

. . .

Respondents and one dissent argue that Montana's no-aid provision was cleansed of its bigoted past because it was readopted for non-bigoted reasons in Montana's 1972 constitutional convention. . . . They emphasize that the convention included Catholics . . . . [I]t emphatically does not matter whether Montana readopted the no-aid provision for benign reasons. . . . And here, it is not so clear that the animus was scrubbed.

Delegates at Montana's constitutional convention in 1972 acknowledged that the no-aid provision was "a badge of bigotry," with one Catholic delegate recalling "being let out of school in the fourth grade to erase three 'Ks' on the front doors of the Catholic church in Billings." Nevertheless the convention proposed, and the State adopted, a provision with the *same* material language, prohibiting public aid "for any *sectarian* purpose or to aid any . . . school . . . controlled in whole or in part by any church, *sect*, or denomination." Mont. Const., Art. X, § 6(1) (1972) (emphasis added). A leading definition of "sect" at the time, as during the Blaine era, was "a dissenting religious body; *esp: one that is heretical in the eyes of other members within the same communion.*" Webster's Third New International Dictionary 2052 (1971) (emphasis added).

. . . [W]hereas the no-aid provision had originally been foisted on Montana, the State readopted it voluntarily—"sectarian" references included. Whether or not the State did so for any reason that could be called legitimate, the convention delegates recognized that the provision would "continue to mean and do whatever it does now," . . . and the discrimination in this case shows that the provision continues to have its originally intended effect. . . .

. . . [M]any parents of many different faiths still believe that their local schools inculcate a worldview that is antithetical to what they teach at home. Many have turned to religious schools, at considerable expense, or have undertaken the burden of homeschooling. The tax-credit program adopted by the Montana Legislature but overturned by the Montana Supreme Court provided necessary aid for parents who pay taxes to support the public schools but who disagree with the teaching there. The program helped parents of modest means do what more affluent parents can do: send their children to a school of their choice. The argument that the decision below treats everyone the same is reminiscent of Anatole France's sardonic remark that " '[t]he law, in its majestic equality, forbids the rich as well as the poor to sleep under bridges, to beg in the streets, and to steal bread.' " . . .

■ JUSTICE GORSUCH, concurring.

. . .

. . . I . . . join [the Court's] opinion in full. I write separately only to address an additional point.

The Court characterizes the Montana Constitution as discriminating against parents and schools based on "religious status and not religious use." No doubt, the Court proceeds as it does to underscore how the outcome of this case follows from Trinity Lutheran Church of Columbia, Inc. v. Comer, 582 U. S. ___ (2017), where the Court struck down a similar public benefits restriction that, it held, discriminated on the basis of religious status. No doubt, too, discrimination on the basis of religious status raises grave constitutional questions for the reasons the Court describes. But I was not sure about characterizing the State's discrimination in *Trinity Lutheran* as focused only on religious status, and I am even less sure about characterizing the State's discrimination here that way.

In the first place, discussion of religious activity, uses, and conduct—not just status—pervades this record. The Montana Constitution forbids the use of public funds "for any sectarian purpose," including to "aid" sectarian schools. Art. X, § 6(1). Tracking this directive, the State Supreme Court reasoned that the legislature's tax credit program could be used to "subsidiz[e] the sectarian school's educational program" and thereby "strengthen . . . religious education." . . . Meanwhile, Ms. Espinoza admits that she would like to use scholarship funds to enable her daughters to be taught in school the "same Christian values" they are taught at home. . . . Finally, . . . Montana has represented that its Constitution focuses on preventing the use of tax credits to subsidize religious activity.

. . . [A]ny jurisprudence grounded on a status-use distinction seems destined to yield more questions than answers. Does Montana seek to prevent religious parents and schools from participating in a public benefits program (status)? Or does the State aim to bar public benefits from being employed to support religious education (use)? Maybe it's possible to describe what happened here as status-based discrimination. But it seems equally, and maybe more, natural to say that the State's discrimination focused on what religious parents and schools *do*—teach religion. . . .

Most importantly, though, it is not as if the First Amendment cares. The Constitution forbids laws that prohibit the free exercise of religion. That guarantee protects not just the right to *be* a religious person, holding beliefs inwardly and secretly; it also protects the right to *act* on those beliefs outwardly and publicly. . . . So whether the Montana Constitution is better described as discriminating against religious status or use makes no difference . . . .

Our cases have long recognized the importance of protecting religious actions, not just religious status. . . .

   . . .

Consistently, too, we have recognized the First Amendment's protection for religious conduct in public benefits cases. When the government chooses to offer scholarships, unemployment benefits, or other affirmative assistance to its citizens, those benefits necessarily affect the "baseline against which burdens on religion are measured." Locke v. Davey, 540 U. S. 712, 726 (2004) (Scalia, J., dissenting) (citing Everson v. Board of Ed. of Ewing, 330 U. S. 1, 16 (1947)). . . . [T]he government "penalize[s] religious activity" whenever it denies to religious persons an "equal share of the rights, benefits, and privileges enjoyed by other citizens." Lyng v. Northwest Indian Cemetery Protective Assn., 485 U. S. 439, 449 (1988). What benefits the government decides to give, whether meager or munificent, it must give without discrimination against religious conduct.

   . . .

The First Amendment protects religious uses and actions for good reason. What point is it to tell a person that he is free to be Muslim but he may be subject to discrimination for doing what his religion commands, attending Friday prayers, living his daily life in harmony with the teaching of his faith, and educating his children in its ways? . . . The right to *be* religious without the right to *do* religious things would hardly amount to a right at all.

   . . .

Montana's Supreme Court . . . [e]ffectively . . . told the state legislature and parents of Montana like Ms. Espinoza: You can have school choice, but if anyone dares to choose to send a child to an accredited religious school, the program will be shuttered. That condition on a public benefit discriminates against the free exercise of religion. Calling it discrimination on the basis of religious status or religious activity makes no difference: It is unconstitutional all the same.

■ JUSTICE GINSBURG, with whom JUSTICE KAGAN joins, dissenting.

. . . Importantly, the parents . . . disclaim any challenge to the no-aid provision on its face. They instead argue—and this Court's majority accepts—that the provision is unconstitutional as applied because the First Amendment prohibits discrimination in tuition-benefit programs based on a school's religious status. Because the state court's decision does not so discriminate, I would reject petitioners' free exercise claim.

. . .

. . . Recall that the Montana court remedied the state constitutional violation by striking the scholarship program in its entirety. Under that decree, secular and sectarian schools alike are ineligible for benefits, so the decision cannot be said to entail differential treatment based on petitioners' religion. Put somewhat differently, petitioners argue that the Free Exercise Clause requires a State to treat institutions and people neutrally when doling out a benefit—and neutrally is how Montana treats them in the wake of the state court's decision.

Accordingly, the Montana Supreme Court's decision does not place a burden on petitioners' religious exercise. Petitioners may still send their children to a religious school. And the Montana Supreme Court's decision does not pressure them to do otherwise. Unlike the law in *Trinity Lutheran*, the decision below puts petitioners to no "choice": Neither giving up their faith, nor declining to send their children to sectarian schools, would affect their entitlement to scholarship funding. . . . There simply are no scholarship funds to be had.

True, petitioners expected to be eligible for scholarships under the legislature's program, and to use those scholarships at a religious school. And true, the Montana court's decision disappointed those expectations along with those of parents who send their children to secular private schools. But, as Justice Sotomayor observes, this Court has consistently refused to treat neutral government action as unconstitutional solely because it fails to benefit religious exercise. . . .

. . . [T]he Court decides a question that, in my view, this case does not present . . . .

. . . Declining to rewrite the statute to exclude [religious] schools, the state court struck the program in full. . . . In doing so, the court never made religious schools ineligible for an otherwise available benefit, and it never decided that the Free Exercise Clause would allow that outcome.[1]

---

[1]   In its opinion, Montana's highest court stated without explanation that this case is not one in which application of the no-aid provision violates the Free Exercise Clause. . . . When the court made that statement, it had already invalidated the entire scholarship program. . . . Accordingly, the court's statement cannot be understood to have approved of excluding religious schools from an otherwise available scholarship. Instead, the statement is most fairly read to convey that the Free Exercise Clause allows a State to decline to fund any private schools, an outcome that avoids state aid to religious schools.

. . . The no-aid provision can be implemented in two ways. A State may distinguish within a benefit program between secular and sectarian schools, or it may decline to fund all private schools. The Court agrees that the First Amendment permits the latter course. Because that is the path the Montana Supreme Court took in this case, there was no reason for this Court to address the alternative.

. . .

. . . [T]he Court writes: "A State need not subsidize private education. But once a State decides to do so, it cannot disqualify some private schools solely because they are religious." Because Montana's Supreme Court did not make such a decision—its judgment put all private school parents in the same boat—this Court had no occasion to address the matter. On that sole ground, and reaching no other issue, I dissent from the Court's judgment.

■ JUSTICE BREYER, with whom JUSTICE KAGAN joins as to Part I, dissenting.

. . .

. . . [T]he Court has said [that] there must be constitutional room, or " 'play in the joints,' " between "what the Establishment Clause permits and the Free Exercise Clause compels." Trinity Lutheran Church of Columbia, Inc. v. Comer, 582 U. S. ___, ___ (2017) (slip op., at 6) (quoting Locke v. Davey, 540 U. S. 712, 718 (2004)). Whether a particular state program falls within that space depends upon the nature of the aid at issue, considered in light of the Clauses' objectives.

The majority barely acknowledges the play-in-the-joints doctrine here. It holds that the Free Exercise Clause forbids a State to draw any distinction between secular and religious uses of government aid to private schools that is not required by the Establishment Clause. The majority's approach and its conclusion . . . risk the kind of entanglement and conflict that the Religion Clauses are intended to prevent. I consequently dissent.

I

. . .

. . . I shall assume, for purposes of this opinion, that petitioners' free exercise claim survived the Montana Supreme Court's wholesale invalidation of the tax credit program.

We all recognize that the First Amendment prohibits discrimination against religion. At the same time, our history and federal constitutional precedent reflect a deep concern that state funding for religious teaching, by stirring fears of preference or in other ways, might fuel religious discord and division and thereby threaten religious freedom itself. . . .

. . .

It may be that, under our precedents, the Establishment Clause does not *forbid* Montana to subsidize the education of petitioners' children. But, the question here is whether the Free Exercise Clause *requires* it to do so. The majority believes that the answer to that question is "yes." It writes that "once a State decides" to support nonpublic education, "it cannot disqualify some private schools solely because they are religious." I shall explain why I disagree.

As the majority acknowledges, two cases are particularly relevant: Trinity Lutheran Church of Columbia, Inc. v. Comer, 582 U. S. ___, and Locke v. Davey, 540 U. S. 712. . . .

... [I]n *Locke*[,] ... the Court assumed that the Establishment Clause *permitted* the State to support students seeking such degrees. 540 U. S., at 719. But the Court concluded that the Free Exercise Clause did not *require* it to do so.

The Court observed that the State's decision not to fund devotional degrees did not penalize religious exercise or require anyone to choose between their faith and a "government benefit." ... Rather, the State had "merely chosen not to fund a distinct category of instruction" that was "essentially religious." ... Although Washington's Constitution drew "a more stringent line than that drawn by the United States Constitution," the Court found that the State's position was consistent with the widely shared view, dating to the founding of the Republic, that taxpayer-supported religious indoctrination poses a threat to individual liberty.... Given this "historic and substantial state interest," the Court concluded, it would be inappropriate to subject Washington's law to a "presumption of unconstitutionality." ... And, without such a presumption, the claim that the exclusion of devotional studies violated the Free Exercise Clause "must fail," for "[i]f any room exists between the two Religion Clauses, it must be here." ...

The majority finds that the school-playground case, *Trinity Lutheran*, and not the religious-studies case, *Locke*, controls here. I disagree.... Like the State of Washington in *Locke*, Montana has chosen not to fund (at a distance) "an essentially religious endeavor"—an education designed to " 'induce religious faith.' " *Locke* .... That kind of program simply cannot be likened to Missouri's decision to exclude a church school from applying for a grant to resurface its playground.

. . .

It is true that Montana's no-aid provision broadly bars state aid to schools based on their religious affiliation. But this case does not involve a claim of status-based discrimination. The schools do not apply or compete for scholarships, they are not parties to this litigation, and no one here purports to represent their interests. We are instead faced with a suit by *parents* who assert that their free exercise rights are violated by the application of the no-aid provision to prevent them from using taxpayer-supported scholarships to attend the schools of their choosing. In other words, the problem, as in *Locke*, is what petitioners " 'propos[e] to do—use the funds to' " obtain a religious education.

Even if the schools' status were relevant, I do not see what bearing the majority's distinction could have here. There is no dispute that religious schools seek generally to inspire religious faith and values in their students. How else could petitioners claim that barring them from using state aid to attend these schools violates their free exercise rights? Thus, the question in this case—unlike in *Trinity Lutheran*—boils down to what the schools would do with state support. And the upshot is that here, as in *Locke*, we confront a State's decision not to fund the inculcation of religious truths.

The majority next contends that there is no " 'historic and substantial' tradition against aiding" religious schools "comparable to the tradition against state-supported clergy invoked by *Locke*." But the majority ignores the reasons for the founding era bans that we relied upon in *Locke*.

. . .

That is not to deny that the history of state support for denominational schools is " 'complex.' " But founding era attitudes toward compelled support of clergy were no less complex. . . .

This diversity of opinion made no difference in *Locke* and it makes no difference here. For our purposes it is enough to say that, among those who gave shape to the young Republic were people, including Madison and Jefferson, who perceived a grave threat to individual liberty and communal harmony in tax support for the teaching of religious truths. These "historic and substantial" concerns have consistently guided the Court's application of the Religion Clauses since. *Locke* . . . . The Court's special attention to these views should come as no surprise, for the risks the Founders saw have only become more apparent over time. In the years since the Civil War, the number of religions practiced in our country has grown to scores. And that has made it more difficult to avoid suspicions of favoritism—or worse—when government becomes entangled with religion.

Nor can I see how it could make a difference that the Establishment Clause might permit the State to subsidize religious education through a program like Montana's. . . . The majority points to cases in which we have upheld programs where, as here, state funds make their way to religious schools by means of private choices. . . . As the Court acknowledged in *Trinity Lutheran*, however, that does not answer the question whether providing such aid is *required*. . . .

. . . Private choice cannot help the taxpayer who does not want to finance the propagation of religious beliefs, whether his own or someone else's. It will not help religious minorities too few in number to support a school that teaches their beliefs. And it will not satisfy those whose religious beliefs preclude them from participating in a government-sponsored program. . . .

. . .

If, for 250 years, we have drawn a line at forcing taxpayers to pay the salaries of those who teach their faith from the pulpit, I do not see how we can today require Montana to adopt a different view respecting those who teach it in the classroom.

II

. . .

. . . I think the majority is wrong to replace the flexible, context-specific approach of our precedents with a test of "strict" or "rigorous" scrutiny. And it is wrong to imply that courts should use that same heightened scrutiny whenever a government benefit is at issue.

. . .

The Court . . . in *Locke* . . . considered the same precedents the majority today cites in support of its presumption of unconstitutionality. But it found that applying the presumption set forth in those cases to Washington's decision not to fund devotional degrees would "extend" them "well beyond not only their facts but their reasoning." . . . In my view, that analysis applies equally to this case.

Montana's law does not punish religious exercise. . . . . It does not deny anyone, because of their faith, the right to participate in political affairs of the community. . . . And it does not require students to choose between their religious beliefs and receiving secular government aid such as unemployment benefits. . . . The State has simply chosen not to fund programs that, in significant part, typically involve the teaching and practice of religious devotion. . . .

. . .

I agree with the majority that it is preferable in some areas of the law to develop generally applicable tests. The problem, as our precedents show, is that the interaction of the Establishment and Free Exercise Clauses makes it particularly difficult to design a test that vindicates the Clauses' competing interests in all—or even most—cases. That is why, far from embracing mechanical formulas, our precedents repeatedly and frankly acknowledge the need for precisely the kind of " 'judgment-by-judgment analysis' " the majority rejects. . . .

. . . [R]igid, bright-line rules like the one the Court adopts today too often work against the underlying purposes of the Religion Clauses. And a test that fails to advance the Clauses' purposes is, in my view, far worse than no test at all.

. . .

It is not easy to discern "the boundaries of the neutral area between" the two Religion Clauses "within which the legislature may legitimately act." . . . And it is more difficult still in cases, such as this one, where the Constitution's policy in favor of free exercise, on one hand, and against state sponsorship, on the other, are in conflict. . . . Here, those purposes, along with the examples set by our decisions in *Locke* and *Trinity Lutheran*, lead me to believe that Montana's differential treatment of religious schools is constitutional. "If any room exists between the two Religion Clauses, it must be here." *Locke*, ... For these reasons, I respectfully dissent from the Court's contrary conclusion.

■ JUSTICE SOTOMAYOR, dissenting.

. . . The Montana Supreme Court invalidated the program on state-law grounds, thereby foreclosing the as-applied challenge petitioners raise here. . . . The Court nevertheless reframes the case and appears to ask whether a longstanding Montana constitutional provision is facially invalid under the Free Exercise Clause, even though petitioners disavowed bringing such a claim. But by resolving a constitutional question not presented, the Court fails to heed Article III principles older than the Religion Clause it expounds. . . .

Not only is the Court wrong to decide this case at all, it decides it wrongly. . . . Because this decision further "slights both our precedents and our history" and "weakens this country's longstanding commitment to a separation of church and state beneficial to both," . . . I respectfully dissent.

The Montana Supreme Court . . . declined to resolve federal constitutional issues. . . . The court also remedied the only potential harm of discriminatory treatment by striking down the program altogether. After the state court's decision, neither secular nor sectarian schools receive the program's tax benefits.

Petitioners' free exercise claim is not cognizable. The Free Exercise Clause . . . protects against "indirect coercion or penalties on the free exercise of religion." Lyng v. Northwest Indian Cemetery Protective Assn., 485 U. S. 439, 450 (1988). Accordingly, this Court's cases have required not only differential treatment, but also a resulting burden on religious exercise, *Lyng*, ...

Neither differential treatment nor coercion exists here . . . . Because no secondary school (secular or sectarian) is eligible for benefits, the state court's ruling neither treats petitioners differently based on religion nor burdens their religious exercise. . . .

Notably, petitioners did not allege that the no-aid provision itself caused their harm or that invalidating the entire tax-credit scheme would create independent constitutional concerns. . . .

. . .

[T]he decision below neither upheld a program that "disqualif[ies] some private schools solely because they are religious," nor otherwise decided the case on federal grounds. The Court's opinion thus turns on a counterfactual hypothetical it is powerless (and unwise) to decide.

Even on its own terms, the Court's answer to its hypothetical question is incorrect. . . .

The Court's analysis of Montana's defunct tax program reprises the error in *Trinity Lutheran*. Contra the Court's current approach, our free exercise precedents had long granted the government "some room to recognize the unique status of religious entities and to single them out on that basis for exclusion from otherwise generally applicable laws." . . .

Until *Trinity Lutheran*, the right to exercise one's religion did not include a right to have the State pay for that religious practice. . . . That is because a contrary rule risks reading the Establishment Clause out of the Constitution. . . . The relevant question had always been not whether a State singles out religious entities, but why it did so.

Here, a State may refuse to extend certain aid programs to religious entities when doing so avoids "historic and substantial" antiestablishment concerns. *Locke*, ... Properly understood, this case is no different from *Locke* because petitioners seek to procure what the plaintiffs in *Locke* could not: taxpayer funds to support religious schooling. . . .

The Court maintains that this case differs from *Locke* because no pertinent " 'historic and substantial' " tradition supports Montana's decision. But the Court's historical analysis is incomplete at best. For one thing, the Court discounts anything beyond the 1850s as failing to "establish an early American tradition," while itself relying on examples from around that time. For another, although the States may have had "rich diversity of experience" at the founding, "the story relevant here is one of consistency." *Trinity Lutheran*, . . . (Sotomayor, J., dissenting) . . . . The common thread was that "those who lived under the laws and practices that formed religious establishments made a considered decision that civil government should not fund ministers and their houses of worship." . . .

The Court further suggests that by abstaining from funding religious activity, the State is " 'suppress[ing]' " and "penaliz[ing]" religious activity. But a State's decision not to fund religious activity does not "disfavor religion; rather, it represents a valid choice to remain secular in the face of serious establishment and free exercise concerns." *Trinity Lutheran*, . . . (Sotomayor, J., dissenting) . . . .

Finally, it is no answer to say that this case involves "discrimination." A "decision to treat entities differently based on distinctions that the Religion Clauses make relevant does not amount to discrimination." *Trinity Lutheran*, . . . (Sotomayor, J., dissenting) . . . .

. . .

South Bay United Pentecostal Church v. Newsom, 590 U.S. ___, 140 S.Ct. 1613 (2020). The Court, 5–4, denied without opinion the Church's application to enjoin an Executive Order issued by California Governor Newsom during a pandemic that was designed to limit the spread of the deadly coronavirus, COVID-19, by imposing restrictions on the size of public gatherings, including a limit on attendance at places of worship to 25% of building capacity or a maximum of 100 attendees, whichever was lower. The Church contended that the Order violated its rights under the Free Exercise Clause because it did not impose a 25% cap on certain secular businesses. In response to the dissenters, Chief Justice Roberts issued an opinion concurring in the denial of the application for injunctive relief, which said in part:

"Although California's guidelines place restrictions on places of worship, those restrictions appear consistent with the Free Exercise Clause of the First Amendment. Similar or more severe restrictions apply to comparable secular gatherings, including lectures, concerts, movie showings, spectator sports, and theatrical performances, where large groups of people gather in close proximity for extended periods of time. And the Order exempts or treats more leniently only dissimilar activities, such as operating grocery stores, banks, and laundromats, in which people neither congregate in large groups nor remain in close proximity for extended periods.

". . . Our Constitution principally entrusts '[t]he safety and the health of the people' to the politically accountable officials of the States 'to guard and protect.' . . . When those officials 'undertake[ ] to act in areas fraught with medical and scientific uncertainties,' their latitude 'must be especially broad.' . . . Where those broad limits are not exceeded, they should not be subject to second-guessing by an "unelected federal judiciary," which lacks the background, competence, and expertise to assess public health and is not accountable to the people. . . .

"That is especially true where, as here, a party seeks emergency relief in an interlocutory posture, while local officials are actively shaping their response to changing facts on the ground. The notion that it is 'indisputably clear' that the Government's limitations are unconstitutional seems quite improbable."

Justice Kavanaugh dissented, joined by Justices Thomas and Gorsuch. In his view, the Order discriminated against religious worship services in violation of the Free Exercise Clause, because what he perceived as "comparable secular businesses are not subject to a 25% occupancy cap, including factories, offices, supermarkets, restaurants, retail stores, pharmacies, shopping malls, pet grooming shops, bookstores, florists, hair salons, and cannabis dispensaries." Although "California undoubtedly has a compelling interest in combating the spread of COVID-19 and protecting the health of its citizens[,]" it failed to demonstrate "a compelling justification for distinguishing between (i) religious worship services and (ii) the litany of other secular businesses that are not subject to an occupancy cap"—especially given that "the Church is willing to abide by the State's rules that apply to comparable secular businesses, including the rules regarding social distancing and hygiene."

"California has ample options . . . without discriminating against religion. The State could 'insist that the congregants adhere to social-distancing and other health requirements and leave it at that—just as the Governor has done for comparable secular activities.' . . . Or alternatively, the State could impose reasonable occupancy caps across the board. But . . . the State may not take a looser approach with, say, supermarkets, restaurants, factories, and offices while imposing stricter requirements on places of worship.

. . .

"In sum, California's 25% occupancy cap on religious worship services indisputably discriminates against religion, and such discrimination violates the First Amendment. . . ."

Page 1813. Add after Burwell v. Hobby Lobby Stores, Inc.:

Little Sisters of the Poor Saints Peter and Paul Home v. Pennsylvania, 591 U.S. ___, 140 S.Ct. 2367 (2020). In 2017, during the new Trump Administration, the Departments of Health and Human Services, Labor, and the Treasury promulgated two new rules that modified the contraceptive mandate addressed in *Hobby Lobby*. As described in Justice Thomas' majority opinion rejecting statutory challenges to these rules, the first "significantly broadened the definition of an exempt religious employer to encompass an employer that 'objects . . . based on its sincerely held religious beliefs,' 'to its establishing, maintaining, providing, offering, or arranging [for] coverage or payments for some or all contraceptive services.' 82 Fed. Reg. 47812 (2017). Among other things, this definition included for-profit and publicly traded entities." In support of this rule, "the Departments announced for the first time that RFRA compelled the creation of, or at least provided the discretion to create, the religious exemption." As for the "second [rule, it] created a similar 'moral exemption' for employers—including nonprofits and for-profits with no publicly traded components—with 'sincerely held moral' objections to providing some or all forms of contraceptive coverage."

Pennsylvania and New Jersey successfully challenged the rules in the lower federal courts as unauthorized by either the ACA or RFRA, but the Supreme Court reversed. The majority first said that "[i]n light of our holding that the ACA provided a basis for both exemptions, we need not reach" the Departments' contention "that RFRA independently compelled the Departments' [approach] or that it at least authorized it." Justice Thomas then continued:

". . . We do, however, address respondents' argument that the Departments could not even consider RFRA as they formulated the religious exemption from the contraceptive mandate. Particularly in the context of these cases, it was appropriate for the Departments to consider RFRA.

. . .

". . . [After] *Hobby Lobby* . . . the potential for conflict between the contraceptive mandate and RFRA is well settled. . . .

"[O]ur decisions all but instructed the Departments to consider RFRA going forward. For instance, . . . in *Hobby Lobby* . . . we made it abundantly clear that, under RFRA, the Departments must accept the sincerely held complicity-based objections of religious entities.

. . .

". . . If the Departments did not look to RFRA's requirements or discuss RFRA at all when formulating their solution, they would certainly be susceptible to claims that the rules were arbitrary and capricious for failing to consider an important aspect of the problem. Thus, respondents' argument that the

Departments erred by looking to RFRA as a guide when framing the religious exemption is without merit."

A concurring opinion by Justice Alito, joined by Justice Gorsuch, would have gone further and held that "RFRA compels an exemption for the Little Sisters and any other employer with a similar objection to what has been called the accommodation to the contraceptive mandate." (The "accommodation" was contained in a 2013 regulation providing that a covered employer could comply with the mandate if it certified its religious objection to its insurer, which would then provide contraceptive coverage to the objecting entity's employees directly.) He wrote in part:

". . . Applying RFRA to the contraceptive mandate . . . presents three questions. First, would the mandate substantially burden an employer's exercise of religion? Second, if the mandate would impose such a burden, would it nevertheless serve a 'compelling interest'? And third, if it serves such an interest, would it represent 'the least restrictive means of furthering' that interest?"

He concluded, first, that "the contraceptive mandate imposes a substantial burden on any employer who, like the Little Sisters, has a sincere religious objection to the use of a listed contraceptive and a sincere religious belief that compliance with the mandate (through the accommodation or otherwise) makes it complicit in the provision to the employer's workers of a contraceptive to which the employer has a religious objection." As for the second question:

"In *Hobby Lobby*, the Government asserted and we assumed for the sake of argument that the Government had a compelling interest in 'ensuring that all women have access to all FDA-approved contraceptives without cost sharing.' . . . Now, the Government concedes that it lacks a compelling interest in providing such access, . . . and this time, the Government is correct.

. . .

". . . We can answer the compelling interest question simply by asking whether *Congress* has treated the provision of free contraceptives to all women as a compelling interest.

". . . The ACA—which fails to ensure that millions of women have access to free contraceptives—unmistakably shows that Congress, at least to date, has not regarded this interest as compelling.

"First, the ACA does not provide contraceptive coverage for women who do not work outside the home. . . .

"Second, if Congress thought that there was a compelling need to provide cost-free contraceptives for all working women, why didn't Congress mandate that coverage in the ACA itself? . . .

"Third, the . . . ACA "exempts a great many employers from most of its coverage requirements." *Hobby Lobby*, ...

"Fourth, the Court's recognition in today's decision that the ACA authorizes the creation of exemptions that go beyond anything required by the Constitution provides further evidence that Congress did not regard the provision of cost-free contraceptives to all women as a compelling interest."

Nor, for reasons largely canvassed in *Hobby Lobby*, would the more limited prior accommodation have satisfied the required "least-restrictive means standard" for burdening the Little Sisters' exercise of religion. So, "[i]n sum, the

Departments were right to conclude that applying the accommodation to sincere religious objectors violates RFRA." The consequence, wrote Justice Alito, is this:

". . . Once it is recognized that the prior accommodation violated RFRA in some of its applications, it was incumbent on the Departments to eliminate those violations, and they had discretion in crafting what they regarded as the best solution.

"The solution they devised cures the problem, and it is not clear that any narrower exemption would have been sufficient with respect to parties with religious objections to the accommodation. . . .

. . .

"I would hold not only that it was appropriate for the Departments to consider RFRA, but also that the Departments were required by RFRA to create the religious exemption (or something very close to it)."

Justice Kagan, joined by Justice Breyer, concurred only in the Court's judgment of statutory authorization for the rules. Justice Ginsburg, joined by Justice Sotomayor, dissented, concluding ultimately that the "blanket exemption for religious and moral objectors to contraception . . . is inconsistent with the text of, and Congress' intent for, both the ACA and RFRA." In particular, she would have held "the religious exemption neither required nor permitted by RFRA." She agreed with Pennsylvania and New Jersey that the "exemption is not authorized by RFRA . . . because the self-certification accommodation it replaced was sufficient to alleviate any substantial burden on religious exercise." She elaborated in part:

"For years, religious organizations have challenged the self-certification accommodation as insufficiently protective of their religious rights. . . . While I do not doubt the sincerity of these organizations' opposition to that accommodation, *Hobby Lobby*, . . . (Ginsburg. J., dissenting), I agree . . . that the accommodation does not substantially burden objectors' religious exercise.

. . .

". . . Counsel for the Little Sisters . . . conceded that religious 'employers could [not] object at all' to a 'government obligation' to provide contraceptive coverage 'imposed directly on the insurers.' . . .[24]

"But that is precisely what the self-certification accommodation does. . . . Under the self-certification accommodation, . . . the objecting employer is absolved of any obligation to provide the contraceptive coverage to which it objects; that obligation is transferred to the insurer."

---

[24] Justice Alito ignores the distinction between (1) a request for an accommodation with regard to one's own conduct, and (2) an attempt to require others to conform their conduct to one's own religious beliefs. This distinction is fatal to Justice Alito's argument that the self-certification accommodation violates RFRA.